Hello! 365 Italian Recipes

(Italian Recipes - Volume 1)

Best Italian Cookbook Ever For Beginners

Mr. Walls

Mr. World

Copyright: Published in the United States by Mr. World/ © MR. WORLD

Published on January, 16 2020

All rights reserved. No part of this publication may be reproduced, stored in retrieval system, copied in any form or by any means, electronic, mechanical, photocopying, recording or otherwise transmitted without written permission from the publisher. Please do not participate in or encourage piracy of this material in any way. You must not circulate this book in any format. MR. WORLD does not control or direct users' actions and is not responsible for the information or content shared, harm and/or actions of the book readers.

In accordance with the U.S. Copyright Act of 1976, the scanning, uploading and electronic sharing of any part of this book without the permission of the publisher constitute unlawful piracy and theft of the author's intellectual property. If you would like to use material from the book (other than just simply for reviewing the book), prior permission must be obtained by contacting the author at mrworld@mrandmscooking.com

Thank you for your support of the author's rights

.

Content

- CONTENT 3
- INTRODUCTION 8
- LIST OF ABBREVIATIONS 9
- CHAPTER 1: ITALIAN AMERICAN RECIPES 10
    1. "antipasto" Pasta With Sausage, Artichoke Hearts, And Sun-dried Tomatoes 10
    2. Ba's Best Eggplant Parmesan 10
    3. Baked Polenta With Tomato Sauce And Ricotta 12
    4. Baked Rigatoni Alla Norma 12
    5. Baked Stuffed Shells (conchiglie Ripiene Al Forno) 13
    6. Barbecue Chicken Meatballs 14
    7. Black Cod With Fennel Chowder And Smoked Oyster Panzanella 15
    8. Breakfast Risotto 15
    9. Broccoli Sautéed In Wine And Garlic (broccoli Al Frascati) 16
    10. Bruschetta With Fava Beans, Greens, And Blood Oranges 16
    11. Caramelized-onion And Gorgonzola Grilled Pizza 17
    12. Carrot Pizza With Fontina And Red Onion   18
    13. Castellane Pasta With Sausage, Peppers, Cherry Tomatoes, And Marjoram 19
    14. Chicken Scarpariella 19
    15. Classic Marinara Sauce 20
    16. Eggplant Marinara Flatbread 21
    17. Eggplant Parmesan Rolls With Swiss Chard And Fresh Mint 21
    18. Eggplant, Tomato, And Fontina Pizza . 22
    19. Farfalle With Chicken, Tomatoes, Caramelized Onions, And Goat Cheese 23
    20. Fastest Chicken Parm 24
    21. Four-cheese Manicotti 24
    22. Fresh Tomato Sauce 25
    23. Fried Egg And Sausage Ciabatta Breakfast Pizzas 26
    24. Garlic-and-herb-braised Squid 26
    25. Grilled Eggplant With Caponata Salsa . 27
    26. Hoagies 28
    27. Homemade Pappardelle With Bolognese Sauce   28
    28. Inside-out Eggplant Parmigiana 29
    29. Italian Deli Sandwiches With Marjoram-caper Dressing 30
    30. Italian Sausage With Grilled Broccolini, Kale, And Lemon 30
    31. Italian Spoon Biscuits With Tomato Sauce And Cheese 31
    32. Lasagna With Turkey Sausage Bolognese   32
    33. Lasagne Bolognese With Spinach 32
    34. Leaving-home Penne Rigate With Broccoli 34
    35. Lemon Pepper Acini Di Pepe 34
    36. Limoncello Champagne Cocktails With Mint   34
    37. Limoncello Gelato 35
    38. Linguine With Herb Broth And Clams . 35
    39. Linguine With Pesto Trapanese 36
    40. Linguine With Rustic "meatballs" 37
    41. Meatballs With Parsley And Parmesan . 37
    42. Microwave Lasagna With Spinach, Mushrooms, And Three Cheeses 38
    43. Minted Green Salad 39
    44. Mixed-berry Tiramisù With Lime Curd 39
    45. Mueller's Classic Lasagna 40
    46. My Hero 41
    47. New Chicken Parmesan 41
    48. Orecchiette With Salsa Cruda And Ricotta 42
    49. Our Favorite Lasagna With Sausage, Spinach, And Three Cheeses 42
    50. Our Favorite Spaghetti And Meatballs . 43
    51. Pan-fried Hawaiian Pizza 44
    52. Pan-seared Steak Pizzaiola 45
    53. Pancetta And Taleggio Lasagna With Treviso 45
    54. Pappardelle With Chicken And Mushroom Ragù 46
    55. Parmesan Toasts 47
    56. Pasta Shells With Prosciutto, Ricotta And Mushrooms 47

57. Pasta Tonnato Nests................................48
58. Pasta With 10-minute Pesto 48
59. Pasta With 15-minute Ham, Pea, And Cream Sauce 49
60. Pasticciata Bolognese—lasagna With Spinach Noodles And Bolognese Sauce.............50
61. Penne With Meat Sauce 51
62. Pickled Fig, Robiola, & Pistachio Oil Crostini 51
63. Pizza Bianca With Rosemary And Sea Salt 52
64. Pizza Dough..52
65. Pizza Margherita.....................................52
66. Polenta Cacio E Pepe 53
67. Pressure-cooker Mini Meatballs With Radiatori 54
68. Presto Pesto Pizza....................................54
69. Prosciutto And Fig Panini 55
70. Quick Tomato Sauce 56
71. Ramp And Sausage Risotto 56
72. Rigatoni With Eggplant And Pine Nut Crunch 57
73. Salmon Panzanella With Green Beans . 58
74. Sausage Meatball Sandwiches................58
75. Shaved Raw Brussels Sprouts With Castelrosso 59
76. Shrimp And Pancetta On Polenta.........59
77. Smoked Trout Crostini With Grilled Fennel And Red Onion..60
78. Spaghetti Pie..60
79. Spaghetti With Cremini Mushrooms, Lemon, And Thyme...61
80. Spaghetti With Mussels (spaghetti Con Le Cozze) 62
81. Spaghetti With No-cook Tomato Sauce And Hazelnuts 62
82. Spaghetti With Red Clam Sauce 63
83. Spicy Cheese Pizza Bread 63
84. Spinach, Pesto, And Fontina Lasagna .. 64
85. Springtime Pasta Primavera....................65
86. Sunday Sauce With Braciole, Meatballs, And Sausage 66
87. Sunday Stash Marinara Sauce.................67
88. The Duckor Deluxe Wood-fired Pizza.68
89. Tomato Sauce 68
90. Tomato, Mozzarella & Thai Basil Crostini 69

91. Tortellini With Italian Sausage, Fennel, And Mushroom..69
92. Trenton Tomato Pie Pizza......................70
93. Turkey Meatball Garlic Bread Heroes ..70
94. Turkey Tonnato 72
95. Veal And Roasted Vegetable Lasagne Anderson 73
96. Veal Cutlets With Mushrooms And Tomatoes...74
97. Zeppole..74
98. Zucchini Blossom And Chicken Saltimbocca 75

CHAPTER 2: ITALIAN BREAKFAST RECIPES.. 75

99. Arugula & Mushroom Breakfast Pizza.75
100. Best-of-show Tomato Quiche................76
101. Blt Brunch Pie 76
102. Breakfast Pizza Skillet.............................77
103. Calico Pepper Frittata............................77
104. Caramelized Mushroom And Onion Frittata 78
105. Cheesy Vegetable Frittata.......................78
106. Chicken 'n' Ham Frittata 79
107. Christmas Morning Frittata 79
108. Colorful Frittata......................................80
109. Country Oven Omelet...........................80
110. Eggs Florentine.......................................81
111. Flavorful Frittata.....................................81
112. Florentine Egg Bake...............................82
113. Florentine Frittata For Two...................82
114. Fresh Vegetable Frittata 83
115. Garden Cheddar Frittata 83
116. Garlic Zucchini Frittata 84
117. Ham And Egg Breakfast Casseroles 85
118. Hashbrown And Sausage Breakfast Pizza 85
119. Hearty Potato Frittata 86
120. Impossible Garden Pie 86
121. Individual Italian Frittatas 87
122. Italian Apricot-pancetta Strata 87
123. Italian Baked Eggs & Sausage 88
124. Italian Breakfast Casseroles 89
125. Italian Brunch Bake................................89
126. Italian Brunch Torte...............................90
127. Italian Cloud Eggs 91
128. Italian Egg Bake......................................91

129. Italian Eggs Benedict With Pesto Hollandaise 91
130. Italian Frittata 92
131. Italian Mini Frittatas 93
132. Italian Omelet 93
133. Italian Pizza Omelet 94
134. Italian Sausage Biscuit Bake 94
135. Italian Sausage Casserole 95
136. Italian Sausage Egg Bake 95
137. Italian Spinach Sausage Pie 96
138. Italian Tomato Onion Quiche 96
139. Mascarpone-mushroom Frittata Stack .. 97
140. Mini Frittatas 97
141. Mini Italian Frittatas 98
142. Mini Sausage Quiches 99
143. Mushroom Sausage Omelets 99
144. Pasta Frittata 100
145. Pear-pecan Sausage Quiche 100
146. Pepperoni Cheese Bake 101
147. Pepperoni Frittata 101
148. Pesto Chicken Strata 102
149. Petite Sausage Quiches 102
150. Pizza Omelet 103
151. Poached Eggs With Tarragon Asparagus 103
152. Potato & Bacon Frittata 104
153. Potato Sausage Frittata 104
154. Prosciutto-pesto Breakfast Strata 105
155. Quiche Italiano 105
156. Ratatouille Frittata 106
157. Ratatouille Quiche 106
158. Ricotta & Cheddar Zucchini Frittata .. 107
159. Rock 'n' River Breakfast Quiche 107
160. Sausage & Mushroom Pizza Frittata ... 108
161. Sausage 'n' Spinach Eggs 108
162. Savory Italian Sausage Strata 109
163. Savory Salami Strata 109
164. Savory Tomato Pie 110
165. Scrambled Egg Pockets 110
166. Scrambled Egg Spinach Casserole 111
167. Six-veggie Bake 112
168. Spinach Bacon Brunch Pizza 112
169. Spinach Brunch Pizza 113
170. Spinach Omelet Brunch Roll 113
171. Spinach-sausage Egg Bake 114
172. Spiral Omelet Supreme 114
173. Tiramisu Crepes 115
174. Tomato Asparagus Frittata 115
175. Tomato Onion Quiche 116
176. Vegetarian Egg Strata 117
177. Zippy Strata 117
178. Zucchini Crepes 118

CHAPTER 3: ITALIAN BRUNCH RECIPES 118

179. Artichoke Quiche 119
180. Breakfast Bread Bowls 119
181. Breakfast Pepperoni Pizza 119
182. Brunch Lasagna 120
183. Brunch Risotto 120
184. Christmas Breakfast Casserole 121
185. Egg And Tomato Scramble 122
186. Egg 'n' Pepperoni Bundles 122
187. Frittata Florentine 123
188. Full Garden Frittata 123
189. Italian Garden Frittata 124
190. Italian Sausage Strata 124
191. Mini Spinach Frittatas 125
192. Mozzarella Vegetable Strata 125
193. Parmesan Ham Frittata 126
194. Pepper And Fresh Herb Frittata 126
195. Quick Anise Fruit Bowl 127
196. Sausage And Hashbrown Breakfast Pizza 127
197. Sausage Mushroom Quiche 128
198. Super-stuffed Omelet 128
199. Tomato Herb Frittata 129
200. Too-yummy-to-share Scramble 129
201. Triple-cheese Florentine Frittata 130
202. Veggie Breakfast Pizza 130
203. Veggie Sausage Strata 131
204. Wine 'n' Cheese Strata 132

CHAPTER 4: ITALIAN DINNER RECIPES 132

205. Angel Hair Pasta With Sausage & Spinach 132
206. Bacon Bolognese 133
207. Baked Ziti With Fresh Tomatoes 133
208. Beef & Bacon Gnocchi Skillet 134
209. Best Lasagna 134
210. Cabbage Goulash 135
211. Caprese Chicken With Bacon 136
212. Cheese & Prosciutto-stuffed Chicken 136

213. Cheese-stuffed Shells 137
214. Chicken & Spinach Mostaccioli 138
215. Chicken And Tomato Scampi 138
216. Chicken Parmesan With Mushrooms . 139
217. Chicken With Red Pepper Sauce And Spinach 139
218. Citrus Garlic Shrimp 140
219. Crab-stuffed Flounder With Herbed Aioli 140
220. Creamy Chicken Tetrazzini Casserole 141
221. Creamy Pesto Shrimp Linguine 141
222. Double-duty Chicken With Olives & Artichokes 142
223. Eggplant & Zucchini Rollatini 143
224. Fast Italian Stew 143
225. Favorite Chicken Marsala 144
226. Fettuccine With Black Bean Sauce 145
227. Fettuccine With Porter Beer Meat Ragu 145
228. French Bread Pizza 146
229. Garlic Shrimp Spaghetti 146
230. Garlic Tilapia With Mushroom Risotto 147
231. Golden Burger Spirals 147
232. Ham & Sun-dried Tomato Alfredo 148
233. Hawaiian Pizza 148
234. Healthy Shrimp Piccata Pasta 148
235. Hearty Lasagna 149
236. Homemade Spaghetti And Meatballs . 150
237. Italian Baked Chicken Breasts 150
238. Italian Cabbage And Rice 151
239. Italian Meatball Mix 151
240. Italian Sausage Lasagna Rolls 152
241. Italian Sausage Skillet 152
242. Lasagna With White Sauce 153
243. Make Once, Eat Twice Lasagna 154
244. Meatless Spaghetti 154
245. No-bake Mushroom Lasagna 155
246. Pasta Arrabbiata (angry Pasta) 155
247. Pasta With Sausage And Tomatoes 156
248. Penne & Sausage Casseroles 156
249. Penne With Tomatoes & White Beans 157
250. Penne With Veggies And Black Beans 157
251. Pepperoni Pasta 158
252. Personal Pizzas 158
253. Pesto-olive Chicken 159
254. Pizza Pancakes 159
255. Pizza With Wheat Crust 160
256. Pork With Gorgonzola Sauce 160
257. Potato Pizza Casserole 161
258. Puffed Pan Pizza 161
259. Reynolds Italian Meatballs 162
260. Rich Italian Beef Roll Ups 162
261. Romano Basil Turkey Breast 163
262. Saucy Chicken & Tortellini 163
263. Saucy Garlic Chicken For Two 164
264. Saucy Stuffed Zucchini 164
265. Sausage, Artichoke & Sun-dried Tomato Ragu 165
266. Sauteed Scallops & Shrimp Pasta 166
267. Savory Spaghetti Sauce 166
268. Seafood-stuffed Shells 167
269. Shrimp And Pasta Supper 167
270. Simple Chicken Parmesan 168
271. Simple Italian Pork Chops 169
272. Simply Great Chicken 169
273. Skillet-roasted Lemon Chicken With Potatoes 169
274. Slow Cooker Sweet Sour Meatballs 170
275. Slow-cooked Chicken Cacciatore 170
276. Smoked Turkey Sausage Pizza 171
277. Spaghetti Sauce 171
278. Spicy Sausage Linguine 172
279. Spicy Shrimp & Peppers With Pasta .. 172
280. Spinach Pasta Sauce 173
281. Spinach-stuffed Chicken Parmesan 174
282. Spooky Pizza 174
283. Super Spaghetti Sauce 175
284. Swiss Chicken Rolls 175
285. Tomato Zucchini Stew 176
286. Tortellini With Salmon-ricotta Sauce . 176
287. Turkey Pasta Toss 177
288. Turkey Penne With Lemon Cream Sauce 177
289. Turkey Spaghetti Sauce 178
290. Tuscan Chicken And Beans 178
291. Where's The Squash Lasagna 179
292. White Lasagna 179
293. Ziti Supper For Two 180
294. Zucchini And Corn-stuffed Chicken . 181
295. Zucchini Pesto With Shrimp And Farfalle 181

CHAPTER 5: ITALIAN VEGETARIAN RECIPES 182

296. Artichoke Crostini 182
297. Artichoke-red Pepper Tossed Salad 182
298. Arugula Salad With Shaved Parmesan 183
299. Asparagus Linguine 183
300. Asparagus With Fresh Basil Sauce 184
301. Baked Ziti With Cheese 184
302. Balsamic Arugula Salad 185
303. Basil Tomato Bread 185
304. Broccoli Fettuccine Alfredo 185
305. Broccoli N Tomato Pasta 186
306. Bruschetta Polenta 186
307. Cannellini Spinach Pasta Salad 187
308. Cheese & Pumpkin-filled Manicotti 187
309. Colorful Grilled Veggies 188
310. Cool Cucumber Pasta 188
311. Corn Relish Salad 189
312. Cranberry Ricotta Gnocchi With Brown Butter Sauce 189
313. Crispy Eggplant Bruschetta 190
314. Cucumber-dill Pasta Salad 190
315. Dill Vinaigrette 191
316. Four-cheese Spinach Pizza 191
317. Garlic Parmesan Orzo 192
318. Gnocchi Alfredo 192
319. Green Beans Provencale 192
320. Herbed Cheesecake 193
321. Herbed Pasta Sauce 194
322. Herbed Tomatoes 194
323. Honey-garlic Angel Hair 194
324. Italian Cheese Twists 195
325. Italian Herb Salad Dressing 195
326. Italian Side Salad 196
327. Linguine With Artichoke-tomato Sauce 196
328. Makeover Penne With Vodka Cream Sauce 197
329. Meatless Spinach Lasagna 197
330. Mini Italian Herb Bread 198
331. Mushroom Bread 198
332. One-pan Tuscan Ravioli 199
333. Onion Tomato Soup 199
334. Oregano Garlic Bread 200
335. Parmesan Cloverleaf Rolls 200
336. Parmesan Fondue 200
337. Parmesan Herbed Noodles 201
338. Pasta Salad With Poppy Seed Dressing 201
339. Pasta With Marinara Sauce 202
340. Pinwheel Pizza Snacks 202
341. Quick Fettuccini Alfredo 203
342. Quick Italian Salad Dressing 203
343. Ranch Garlic Bread 204
344. Roasted Parmesan Potato Wedges 204
345. Roasted Red Pepper Sauce 204
346. Roasted Vegetable Lasagna 205
347. Rosemary Butternut Squash Lasagna . 206
348. Rosemary Olive Focaccia 206
349. Sicilian Salad 207
350. Spinach And Artichoke Pizza 207
351. Spinach Cheese Swirls 208
352. Squash Provencal 208
353. Three-cheese Garlic Bread 209
354. Tomato Basil Bruschetta 209
355. Tomato N Cheese Pasta 210
356. Tomato-mushroom Bow Tie Pasta 210
357. Triple Tomato Flatbread 211
358. Vegetable & Cheese Focaccia 211
359. Vegetarian Cabbage Rolls 212
360. Vegetarian Pasta 213
361. Viva Panzanella 213
362. Warm Goat Cheese In Marinara 214
363. Warm Pesto Dip 214
364. Warm Tuscan Bean Salad 215
365. White Bean Crostini 215

INDEX 216

CONCLUSION 227

Introduction

***

TASTE THE FLAVORS OF THE WORLD IN YOUR OWN KITCHEN

Hi all,

Welcome to MrandMsCooking.com—a website created by a community of cooking enthusiasts with the goal of providing books for novice cooks featuring the best recipes, at the most affordable prices, and valuable gifts.

Before we go to the recipes in the book "Hello! 365 Italian Recipes", I have some interesting things to share with you.

With the many great ingredients from around the world in today's markets, this is a great time to start experimenting with them in the kitchen. Healthy food choices are highly available along with a variety of flavors to please everyone's taste buds. This is all thanks to globalization.

As much as I wanted to capture all the variety of dishes around the world, it is impossible, so, I will share a fair amount in this series.

The World Cuisines series presents a vast array of the most delicious dishes from around the world and allows much freedom in the kitchen. The choice is yours.

Authentic cooking techniques and ingredients have been included in most of the recipes to recreate the dish as similar to the local fare of the country where it originated. The ingredients needed for these recipes are easy to find and available almost anywhere. In case any ingredient would not be on stock in grocery stores, don't worry, I have included an easy-to-find alternative here. From your kitchen and eventually to your dining table, let this series surprise you by bringing some of the world's famous dishes to your table.

I can guarantee you all recipes are healthy and easy to make as I have personally tested each recipe in my kitchen. You are lucky because no ingredient is hard to find. This series is all about balance, moderation and variety.

Not only will you be able to cook a dish from another country, you will develop a better sense of taste, reap more health benefits and have a deeper understanding of your own culture. It's now easier to enjoy the different flavors of the world with the help of this series and ingredients from your local market. Happy eating!

For more recipes for international cuisines, check out the following:

- African Recipes
- Asian Recipes
- European Recipes
- …

You have reached the end of the article. Thank you for your support and for choosing "Hello! 365 Italian Recipes". Let this series be an inspiration when preparing food from around the world in your kitchen.

Hope you'll enjoy the different flavors of the world!

List of Abbreviations

COOKing LIST OF ABBREVIATIONS	
tbsp(s).	tablespoon(s)
tsp(s).	teaspoon(s)
c.	cup(s)
oz.	ounce(s)
lb(s).	pound(s)

Chapter 1: Italian American Recipes

***

1. "antipasto" Pasta With Sausage, Artichoke Hearts, And Sun-dried Tomatoes

"Easy-to-make, fast, and Italian antipasto platters-inspired pasta dish that is made with basic ingredients that you can find in your pantry. It features pasta with olive oil and tomato paste sauce, dry-cured sausage, sun-dried tomatoes, artichoke hearts plus pepperoncini and roasted pine nuts on top."
Serving: 4 servings | Prep: 25m

Ingredients

- 1 lb. spaghetti or other long pasta
- Kosher salt
- 1/4 cup pine nuts (about 1.5 oz.)
- 2 tbsps. extra-virgin olive oil
- 4 oz. dry-cured sausage, quartered lengthwise, thinly sliced
- 2 tbsps. tomato paste
- 24 oz. marinated artichoke hearts, drained, cut into 1/2"-thick wedges if large
- 3/4 cup thinly sliced drained oil-packed sun-dried tomatoes (about 2 oz.)
- Freshly ground black pepper
- 1/4 cup thinly sliced peperoncini

Direction

- In a big pot with boiling salted water, cook pasta until al dente while mixing from time to time; drain. Set aside a cup of the pasta cooking liquid. Put the pasta back in the pot.
- On medium heat, toast pine nuts in a small and dry pan for 3-5mins until pale brown; mixing sometimes. Move to a small bowl.
- In the meantime, on medium-high heat, heat oil in a medium pan. Cook and stir tomato paste and sausage in hot oil for a minute. Mix in sun-dried tomatoes and artichokes; cook and stir for 2mins until completely heated. Take off heat.
- Put 3/4 cup pasta cooking liquid and the sausage mixture in the pasta pot; sprinkle a quarter tsp. pepper. Mix to coat. If needed to loosen the mixture, pour in the remaining quarter cup of the pasta cooking liquid.
- Split the pasta between plates; sprinkle pepper to season. Add pepperoncini on top.

Nutrition Information

- Calories: 827
- Total Carbohydrate: 102 g
- Cholesterol: 20 mg
- Total Fat: 40 g
- Fiber: 11 g
- Protein: 26 g
- Sodium: 974 mg
- Saturated Fat: 4 g

2. Ba's Best Eggplant Parmesan

"To get the cheesy ooze, cut this eggplant parmesan while it's still hot. Let it sit for at least half an hour at room temperature to firm before serving."
Serving: Serves 12

Ingredients

- 1/4 cup olive oil
- 1 head of garlic, cloves crushed
- 1 large red onion, chopped
- 3 oil-packed anchovy fillets (optional)
- 1/2 tsp. crushed red pepper flakes
- 1 tbsp. tomato paste
- 1/4 cup dry white wine
- 2 (28-oz.) cans whole peeled tomatoes
- 1/4 cup torn basil leaves

- 1/2 tsp. dried oregano
- Kosher salt
- 4 lbs. Italian eggplants (about 4 medium), peeled, sliced lengthwise 1/2–3/4 inch thick
- Kosher salt
- 3 cups panko (Japanese breadcrumbs)
- 1 1/2 tsp. dried oregano
- 1 tsp. freshly ground black pepper
- 1 1/2 cups finely grated Parmesan, divided
- 1 1/2 cups all-purpose flour
- 5 large eggs, beaten to blend
- 1 1/3 cups olive oil
- 1/2 cup finely chopped basil and parsley, plus basil leaves for serving
- 6 oz. low-moisture mozzarella, grated (about 1 1/3 cups)
- 8 oz. fresh mozzarella, thinly sliced

Direction

- Prepare the Marinara. Preheat the oven to 350 degrees F. On medium heat, heat oil in a big heavy ovenproof pot; cook and stir garlic for 4mins until golden. Put in onion, red pepper flakes, and anchovies if using; cook and stir for 5mins until the onion is translucent. Mix in tomato paste; cook and stir for 2mins until a bit darkened. Pour in wine then boil; cook for a minute until nearly totally evaporated. Crumble the tomatoes with your hands then mix tomatoes including their juices in together with oregano and basil to blend. Pour in 1 1/2 cup water in 1 tomato can and another; swirl to rinse then pour the liquid in the pot. Sprinkle salt. Move the pot in the oven; roast for 2 to 2 1/2hrs until the tomatoes are brown on the sides and top of the pot and the sauce is thick. Mix halfway through.
- Cool the sauce slightly; process in a food processor or push through big food mill holes until mostly smooth. Season with salt to taste.
- Sprinkle salt lightly all over the eggplant slices to season; arrange in one layer on a couple of paper towel layers in a rimmed baking sheet. Place another paper towel layer then more eggplant slices; repeat as necessary. Put a final paper towel layer then another rimmed baking sheet on top; place a heavy pot to weigh down. Let it sit for 45-60mins until the eggplants release the extra liquid. This will make the eggplant creamier when baked.
- In the meantime, finely ground 3/4 cup Parmesan, panko, pepper, and oregano in a food processor; move to a shallow bowl.
- Preheat the oven to 350 degrees F. In a separate shallow bowl, put flour. Put eggs in another shallow bowl. Roll the slices of eggplant one at a time in flour; submerge in egg then let the extra drip down. Dredge in breadcrumbs while packing all over then shake the extra crumbs off. Arrange on wire racks.
- On medium-high heat, heat 2-3 cup oil in a big cast iron pan. Cook as much slices that can fit comfortably in the pan for 5mins until deep golden, flip once. Drain the oil on paper towels, pressing instantly with additional paper to absorb oil. Repeat with the rest of the slices in batches. Pour the remaining 2/3 cup oil then wipe the pan as necessary. Sprinkle salt to taste.
- In a medium bowl, combine the remaining 3/4 cup Parmesan, low-moisture mozzarella, and chopped herbs. In a 13-in by 9-in baking pan, spread a cup of sauce then top with eggplant slices. Trim the eggplant as needed. Spread a cup of sauce all over then top with 1/3 cheese mixture. Repeat with the rest of the slices, cheese mixture, and sauce; use foil to cover. Bake for 45-60mins on a rimmed baking sheet until the eggplant turns custardy.
- Take it out of the oven then top with fresh mozzarella. Turn the heat to 425 degrees F; bake for another 15-20mins without cover until there are brown spots and the cheese is bubbling. Let it sit for half an hour. Add basil leaves on top before cutting.
- You can make the Marinara two days in advance; cover then refrigerate.
- The eggplant parmesan can be prepared two days in advance; cool. Use foil to cover then refrigerate. Reheat in a 350 degrees F oven until the edges are gently bubbling. Remove the cover halfway through.

Nutrition Information

- Calories: 612
- Total Carbohydrate: 40 g
- Cholesterol: 110 mg
- Total Fat: 42 g
- Fiber: 7 g
- Protein: 20 g
- Sodium: 1002 mg
- Saturated Fat: 11 g

3. Baked Polenta With Tomato Sauce And Ricotta

"If you're looking for a comfort food this simple polenta dish with tomato sauce and ricotta is for you."
Serving: 4 servings

Ingredients

- 4 tomatoes
- 1 medium yellow onion, skin on
- 1 small bulb garlic
- 2 tbsps. extra-virgin olive oil
- Salt
- 1 cup polenta
- 1 tbsp. extra-virgin olive oil
- 4 tbsps. chopped fresh basil
- 1/2 cup ricotta cheese
- Salt and freshly ground black pepper
- 1/4 cup grated Parmesan cheese
- 4 tbsps. chopped basil

Direction

- Make the tomato sauce: Preheat the oven to 425 degrees F. In a baking pan, put garlic, yellow onion, and tomatoes; bake for 45 mins or until the tomato skins are peeling off and the garlic is soft. Take the pan out of the oven then cool to room temperature. Peel off the tomatoes skin then place in a saucepan. Squeeze out the garlic from the bulb then put into the tomatoes. Peel off the onion skin then coarsely chop; add into the pot of tomatoes.
- Pour olive oil over the tomatoes; use a handheld immersion blender to puree until smooth. If the liquid is not enough, pour in up to 1/3 cup of water. Sprinkle salt to season. Warm the tomato sauce just before using.
- Make the polenta. Preheat oven to 400 degrees F. Simmer three cups of water in a medium saucepan; add polenta in a stream then mix until there are no lumps. Put on the lid to cover then keep cooking for 20 mins on low heat, mix every 3 mins. Be careful while mixing the polenta because it tends to spit out very hot cornmeal pieces. Take off the heat then mix in basil and olive oil. Put in ricotta cheese by dropping in tsp.-sized portions. Evenly spread in the polenta into an 8-in square baking pan then scatter Parmesan cheese on top; let it stand for an hour or until the polenta is firm. Bake polenta for 15 mins in the oven or until thoroughly heated. Equally slice the polenta into eight portions.
- In order to serve, in four shallow bowls, put half a cup of warm tomato sauce then add two polenta pieces on top. Garnish with sprinkled chopped basil.

Nutrition Information

- Calories: 367
- Total Carbohydrate: 43 g
- Cholesterol: 21 mg
- Total Fat: 17 g
- Fiber: 4 g
- Protein: 11 g
- Sodium: 589 mg
- Saturated Fat: 5 g

4. Baked Rigatoni Alla Norma

Serving: Makes 6 to 8 servings | Prep: 45m

Ingredients

- 2 lbs. eggplant, cut into 1-inch cubes
- 1 cup olive oil
- 1 medium onion, chopped

- 2 1/2 cups marinara sauce (homemade or use 24 to 26 oz. bottled sauce)
- 1 lb. dried rigatoni
- 1 lb. cold mozzarella (preferably salted fresh), cut into 1/2-inch cubes

Direction

- In a colander, toss 2tsp salt and eggplant; drain for half an hour. Rinse the eggplant then squeeze the excess moisture out; pat dry.
- Place the rack in the center of the oven then preheat to 350 degrees F.
- On medium-high heat, heat oil in a big heavy pot until shimmering. In three batches, fry eggplant for 5mins on each batch while mixing from time to time until brown. Use a slotted spoon to move eggplants on paper towels; drain.
- Remove all but 2tbsp oil from the pan; sauté a quarter tsp. each of pepper and salt plus onion for 8mins until golden. Mix in eggplant and sauce; let it simmer for 5mins.
- In the meantime, in a pasta pot with boiling salted water, cook rigatoni until al dente; drain. Use 2btsp salt for 6-qt water. In a pot, mix 1/2 of the mozzarella, sauce, and pasta; move to a 3-qt baking dish then top with the remaining mozzarella. Bake for 45mins until there are golden spots and the cheese is melted. Let it sit for 5mins. Serve.

Nutrition Information

- Calories: 925
- Total Carbohydrate: 77 g
- Cholesterol: 62 mg
- Total Fat: 56 g
- Fiber: 9 g
- Protein: 30 g
- Sodium: 944 mg
- Saturated Fat: 15 g

5. Baked Stuffed Shells (Conchiglie Ripiene Al Forno)

"These stuffed shells are really pretty to look at especially when served in separate dishes with sauce and cheese on top."

Serving: 6 servings (about 5 stuffed shells for each serving)

Ingredients

- 1 1/2 lbs. fresh ricotta or packaged whole-milk ricotta
- 1 (35-oz.) can peeled Italian plum tomatoes (preferably San Marzano)
- Salt
- 1 lb. fresh mozzarella cheese
- 1 cup freshly grated Parmigiano-Reggiano cheese
- 1/3 cup chopped fresh Italian parsley
- Freshly ground white pepper
- 1 large egg
- 1/4 cup extra-virgin olive oil
- 6 cloves garlic, crushed
- 1/2 tsp. crushed hot red pepper
- 10 fresh basil leaves
- 1 lb. jumbo pasta shells

Direction

- In a sieve with a cheesecloth, put the ricotta then place the sieve on top of a bowl. Use plastic wrap to cover then refrigerate for at least 8hrs to a day. Remove the liquid in the bowl.
- Push the tomatoes on a food mill with a fine disc attachment or process the seeded tomatoes with quick pulses in a food processor until ground finely. Avoid overprocessing or the tomatoes will change in color and texture because of the air. In the meantime, on high heat, boil 6-qt salted water in an 8-qt pot.
- Thinly slice 1/2 of the mozzarella then slice the rest into quarter-inch cubes. In a mixing bowl, put the drained ricotta then stir in parsley, grated cheese, and mozzarella cubes. Sprinkle white pepper and salt to taste. Whisk the egg well then mix into the ricotta mixture.

- On medium heat, heat olive oil in a big pan. Spread garlic on the oil then cook for 2mins while shaking the pan until golden. Bring the tomatoes near the pan then pour carefully. Put in crushed red pepper then lightly season with salt. Boil the sauce quickly then lower heat to a simmer. Cook for half an hour until the sauce is a bit thick. Mix in basil a couple of minutes before the sauce is done.
- In the meantime, mix the shells in boiling water; boil again while frequently mixing. Cook for 7mins, mixing from time to time while slightly covered until soft yet a bit firm. Using a big skimmer, take the shells out of water then lower them carefully in a bowl of cold water. Carefully drain.
- Preheat oven to 425 degrees F. Spread 3/4 cup of tomato sauce on a 15x10-in baking dish. In each shell, scoop 2tbsp ricotta mixture until just filled but not overstuffed. Arrange the shells side by side in a baking dish. Scoop the rest of the sauce on top of shells until coated. Evenly layer the mozzarella slices on top of the shells. Bake for 25mins until the mozzarella is bubbling and brown. Take it out of the oven then let it sit for 5mins. Serve.
- There are 36 shells in 1lbs of jumbo pasta shells. This recipe is just enough to fill just 30 shells so you'll have some leftovers. Some will break while cooking or in the box so you can use them. Before filling, cook the shells to al dente or the shells will tear when stuffed.

Nutrition Information

- Calories: 902
- Total Carbohydrate: 27 g
- Cholesterol: 175 mg
- Total Fat: 52 g
- Fiber: 6 g
- Protein: 81 g
- Sodium: 1101 mg
- Saturated Fat: 26 g

6. Barbecue Chicken Meatballs

"To easily roll the chicken mixture into a balls, just chill it up for half an hour or you can also add extra quarter cup of crumbs."
Serving: Makes 6 servings | Prep: 30m

Ingredients

- 1 lb. ground chicken
- 2/3 cup corn-bread crumbs or bread crumbs
- 1 egg
- 1 tsp. chili powder
- 1 small onion, grated and drained
- 1/2 tsp. paprika (optional)
- 1 tsp. kosher salt
- 2 tbsps. applesauce
- 2 tbsps. olive oil
- 1 cup barbecue sauce (we like Trader Joe's)

Direction

- Mix together the first 8 ingredients. Shape the mixture into 1-inch balls.
- Pour the oil in a wide frying pan. Drop the meatballs and fry them for about 8 to 10 minutes until browned all over and until completely cooked.
- Pour the barbecue sauce. Let it cook for roughly a minute until it evaporates and sticks to the meatballs. Serve.
- Take note that when making meatballs, prepare a bowl of water nearby to dip your hands in, to prevent the mixture from sticking to your hands.

Nutrition Information

- Calories: 296
- Total Carbohydrate: 30 g
- Cholesterol: 92 mg
- Total Fat: 12 g
- Fiber: 1 g
- Protein: 16 g
- Sodium: 646 mg
- Saturated Fat: 3 g

7. Black Cod With Fennel Chowder And Smoked Oyster Panzanella

"A rich chowder!"
Serving: Makes 4 servings

Ingredients

- 3 tbsps. butter
- 3/4 cup 1/4-inch cubes fresh fennel bulb
- 3/4 cup 1/4- to 1/3-inch cubes peeled Yukon Gold potato
- 1/2 cup chopped onion
- 1/4 cup finely chopped leek (white and pale green parts only)
- 1 tbsp. all purpose flour
- 2 small bay leaves
- 1 1/2 tsps. chopped fresh thyme
- 1 8-oz. bottle clam juice
- 3/4 cup whipping cream
- 3/4 cup whole milk
- 1 tsp. finely grated lemon peel
- 1/4 cup finely chopped celery
- 1/4 cup finely chopped shallot
- 2 tbsps. chopped fresh parsley
- 4 1/2 tsps. fresh lemon juice, divided
- 1/2 tsp. finely grated lemon peel
- 1/4 cup minced smoked canned oysters
- 5 tbsps. unsalted butter, divided
- 1 tbsp. chopped fresh thyme
- 4 black cod fillets with skin
- Coarse kosher salt
- 1/4 cup panko (Japanese breadcrumbs),* toasted

Direction

- Chowder: Melt butter in big saucepan on medium low heat. Add leek, onion, potato and fennel then cover; cook for about 8 minutes till veggies are just tender yet not brown. Add thyme, bay leaves and flour; mix for 1 minute. Mix milk, cream and clam juice in. Simmer for about 10 minutes till flavors blend and chowder slightly thickens. Mix lemon peel in; season with pepper and salt to taste. You can make this 1 day in advance, cool for 30 minutes then cover and refrigerate.
- Panzanella and fihs: Toss smoked oysters, lemon peel, 1 1/2 tsp. lemon juice, parsley, shallot and celery in medium bowl. Season shallot-celery mixture with pepper and salt to taste.
- Mix 3 tsp. lemon juice, thyme and 3 tbsp. butter in small saucepan; whisk on low heat till sauce simmers and butter melts. Season with pepper and coarse salt. Take off heat. Melt 2 tbsp. butter in big nonstick skillet on high heat. Sprinkle pepper and coarse salt on fish. Add fish to skillet, skin side down. Cook for 6-7 minutes, drizzling lemon-butter sauce on, till fish is just opaque in middle and skin is crispy.
- Rewarm chowder on low heat; throw bay leaves. Divide chowder to 4 shallow bowls. Put fish in middle of chowder, skin side down. Mix panko into shallot-celery mixture. Put on dish; serve.

Nutrition Information

- Calories: 649
- Total Carbohydrate: 20 g
- Cholesterol: 223 mg
- Total Fat: 41 g
- Fiber: 3 g
- Protein: 51 g
- Sodium: 1221 mg
- Saturated Fat: 25 g

8. Breakfast Risotto

Serving: Makes 4 servings

Ingredients

- 4 tbsps. (1/2 stick) butter, divided
- 4 hot Italian sausages, casings removed
- 1 small onion, chopped (about 1 cup)
- 2 small bay leaves
- 1 cup arborio rice or medium-grain white rice
- 1/2 cup dry white wine

- 3 cups (or more) low-salt chicken broth
- Pinch of saffron threads
- 1/3 cup freshly grated Parmesan cheese plus additional for serving
- 1/3 cup chopped fresh Italian parsley

Direction

- Add 2 tbsps. butter in big saucepan and melt over medium-high heat. Drop the sausages; break them up using a fork. Stir in the next 2 ingredients. Sauté for roughly 4 minutes until the onion turns translucent. Mix in the rice. Add wine; let the mixture boil for a minute until the liquid evaporates. Stir in 3 cups of saffron and broth; let the mixture boil. Adjust the heat to medium-low; make it to a simmer and stir from time to time until the risotto has softened. Add an extra broth if it turns too dry, roughly 18 minutes. Dispose the bay leaves; stir in 1/3 cup of cheese and parsley. Spice it up with pepper and salt. Pass the cheese alongside.

Nutrition Information

- Calories: 725
- Total Carbohydrate: 45 g
- Cholesterol: 116 mg
- Total Fat: 48 g
- Fiber: 1 g
- Protein: 24 g
- Sodium: 887 mg
- Saturated Fat: 20 g

9. Broccoli Sautéed In Wine And Garlic (broccoli Al Frascati)

"In this recipe, you don't need to boil the heady and fragrant veggies."
Serving: Makes 6 servings

Ingredients

- 6 tbsps. extra-virgin olive oil
- 4 cloves garlic, thinly sliced
- 3 lbs. broccoli, cut into spears
- 1 cup Frascati or other dry white wine
- 1 tbsp. hot red pepper flakes
- Grated zest of 1 lemon
- Grated zest of 1 orange

Direction

- On medium-high heat, heat garlic and olive oil in a 10-12-in. sauté pan until sizzling. Put in broccoli; cook white frequently mixing and pouring wine gradually to avoid browning the garlic for 8-10mins until the stalks are tender. Toss in zests and red pepper flakes. Serve right away.

Nutrition Information

- Calories: 235
- Total Carbohydrate: 20 g
- Total Fat: 15 g
- Fiber: 7 g
- Protein: 7 g
- Sodium: 77 mg
- Saturated Fat: 2 g

10. Bruschetta With Fava Beans, Greens, And Blood Oranges

"A version of bruschetta toast with fava puree spread and fresh salad on top."
Serving: Makes 6 appetizer servings

Ingredients

- 1 3/4 cups frozen double-peeled fava beans (about one 14-oz. bag), thawed, divided
- 1 cup water
- 1 garlic clove, minced
- 6 tbsps. extra-virgin olive oil, divided
- 2 tbsps. fresh lemon juice
- 3 blood oranges or navel oranges
- 1 tbsp. white balsamic vinegar
- 6 cups mixed baby greens (about 3 oz.)
- 18 slices sourdough or French baguette, toasted

Direction

- In a small bowl, put 1/4 cup fava beans and reserve for salad later. In a big pot, mix 1 cup of water, garlic and 1 1/2 cups fava beans. Cook to a boil then lower heat to medium and continue to simmer, uncovered, stirring form time to time, for about 10 minutes until fava beans are soft. Remove the fava beans and reserve the cooking liquid. Pour favas to a food processor and stir in lemon juice and 3 tbsps. oil. Pulse until you achieve a smooth puree. Drizzle by tablespoonfuls of the reserved cooking liquid to moisten puree as necessary. Sprinkle with salt and pepper to taste then pour the fava puree to another small bowl. This step can be done 1 day ahead. Store the whole fava beans and fava puree separately, covered and chilled. When it's time to use, take the puree out to room temperature first.
- From one orange, finely grate enough peel equivalent to 1 tsp.. From the same orange, squeeze 2 tbsps. juice. Peel and cut off the white pith from the 2 oranges that remains. Using a small sharp knife, slice between membranes to release orange segments over a bowl. In a small bowl, whisk together 2 tbsps. orange juice, 3 tbsps. oil, orange peel and vinegar. Sprinkle with salt and pepper.
- In a big serving bowl, combine greens, 1/4 cup favas and orange segments. Drizzle with the orange vinaigrette.
- Lay out warm baguette toasts and spread with fava bean puree, dividing equally. Serve toasts with the salad on top.
- Ingredient tip: You can find frozen double-peeled fava beans at Middle Eastern markets or some specialty foods stores.

Nutrition Information

- Calories: 299
- Total Carbohydrate: 37 g
- Total Fat: 15 g
- Fiber: 7 g
- Protein: 9 g
- Sodium: 204 mg
- Saturated Fat: 2 g

11. Caramelized-onion And Gorgonzola Grilled Pizza

"The charred crust of this pizza is topped with Gorgonzola, toasted walnuts, and sweet onions."
Serving: Makes 6 (appetizer) servings | Prep: 30m

Ingredients

- 6 tbsp. extra-virgin olive oil, divided
- 1 1/4 lbs. onions (2 large), halved lengthwise and thinly sliced
- 14 to 16 oz. pizza dough, thawed if frozen
- 1/4 lb. Gorgonzola dolce, crumbled (1 cup)
- 1/2 cup walnuts, toasted and coarsely chopped
- 1/4 cup chopped flat-leaf parsley

Direction

- On medium-low heat, heat a quarter cup of oil in a 12-in heavy skillet until shimmering. Cook onions, quarter tsp. pepper, and half tsp. salt while mixing from time to time for 15-20mins, covered, until golden. Move to a small bowl; cover and keep warm.
- Set a grill on top of low charcoal for direct heat or medium heat for gas.
- On a big baking sheet, stretch dough into a 12x10-in rectangle; brush with a tbsp. of oil.
- On the grill area, put the remaining tbsp. of oil, dough, parsley, onions, nuts, and cheese.
- Grease the grill rack then place the dough on the grill with the oiled-side down then brush the remaining tbsp. of oil on top. Grill for 1 1/2-3 mins while covering until the bottom is golden brown.
- Place the crust back in the baking sheet using tongs flip the crust so the grilled side is facing up. Evenly scatter parsley, onions, nuts, and cheese. Slide the pizza from the sheet to the grill; grill for around 3 mins while covering until the underside is golden brown and the

- cheese is partially melted. Move to a cutting board then slice into portions,
- You need to replenish the coals if you plan on making all dishes using the grill prior to grilling the veal.
- The onions can be prepared a day in advance; refrigerate.
- The nuts can be toasted a day in advance; cool then store at room temperature in an airtight container.

Nutrition Information

- Calories: 445
- Total Carbohydrate: 45 g
- Cholesterol: 17 mg
- Total Fat: 24 g
- Fiber: 4 g
- Protein: 13 g
- Sodium: 698 mg
- Saturated Fat: 7 g

12. Carrot Pizza With Fontina And Red Onion

"This amazing pizza makes use of creamy and delicious sweet carrot puree instead of tomato sauce. Purchase the carrots with the green since the bitter carrot fronts can be a delicious pizza topping too."
Serving: Makes 2 pizzas, serves 4–6 | Prep: 35m

Ingredients

- 2 tbsps. olive oil
- 1/2 medium onion, chopped
- 1/2 lb. carrots (about 3-4 medium carrots), peeled and thinly sliced
- 1/2 cup white wine
- 1/2 tsp. kosher salt
- 1/4 cup mascarpone
- 1/8 tsp. cayenne pepper
- 1/2 lb. prepared pizza dough, room temperature
- All-purpose flour (for surface)
- Olive oil (for brushing)
- 8 oz. Fontina cheese, grated (about 2 cups)
- 1/2 medium red onion, root intact and thinly sliced lengthwise into wedges
- 1 cup (loosely packed) carrot fronds or baby arugula

Direction

- Prepare the carrot puree. On medium-high heat, heat oil in a big pan until it shimmers. Put onions; cook while mixing regularly for 2mins until translucent. Put in carrots; cook while mixing from time to time for 5mins until it starts to brown. Pour in wine; cook while mixing regularly for 2mins until it reduces by 1/2.
- Turn to medium-low heat, mix in a cup of water and salt until blended; cover. Let it simmer for 15mins until most of the liquid evaporates and the carrots are tender.
- Move the mixture to a blender; put in a quarter cup water, cayenne, and mascarpone. Take out the stopper on the lid or keep the lid slightly open. Use a towel to cover to avoid splattering hot liquid; puree the mixture until smooth.
- Prepare the pizza. Put two upturned rimmed baking sheets on the top and bottom thirds of the oven then preheat to 450 degrees F.
- On a lightly floured surface, halve the dough then shape into two balls. Roll each ball into 6x10-in ovals that can hit the baking sheets. Take the preheated sheets out of the oven then slather oil on the bottoms. Put the dough carefully on the sheets then slather with additional oil. Bake for 5mins until the dough starts to brown.
- Evenly slather the reserved carrot puree on the pizzas then top with onion and cheese. Bake for 10-12mins until the cheese is bubbling and melted, turn the sheets and swap the places on the racks halfway through baking. Move pizzas on cutting boards; add carrot fronds on top then slice.
- The carrot puree can be prepared up to two days ahead; chill until ready to make the pizza.

Nutrition Information

- Calories: 605
- Total Carbohydrate: 40 g
- Cholesterol: 92 mg
- Total Fat: 38 g
- Fiber: 4 g
- Protein: 24 g
- Sodium: 967 mg
- Saturated Fat: 17 g

13. Castellane Pasta With Sausage, Peppers, Cherry Tomaotes, And Marjoram

"This dish that is made with some filling ingredients is perfect for a cold night."
Serving: Makes 4 to 6 servings

Ingredients

- 1 tbsp. extra-virgin olive oil
- 1 lb. hot Italian sausages, casings removed
- 2 red bell peppers, chopped (about 2 cups)
- 1 large onion, chopped (about 2 cups)
- 2 1/2 tsps. chopped fresh marjoram
- 2 12-oz. packages cherry tomatoes
- 12 oz. castellane (long oval shells) or fusilli pasta
- 5 oz. crumbled goat cheese

Direction

- On medium-high heat, heat oil in a big non-stick pan. Sauté sausages in hot oil while crumbling using the back of a fork for 5mins until brown. Put in onion and peppers; sauté for 13mins until the onion is golden brown and soft. Mix in marjoram then the tomatoes. Let it simmer for 5mins while crumbling using the back of fork until the tomatoes release their juices and are soft. Generously sprinkle pepper and salt to taste.
- In the meantime, cook pasta until just tender but firm to chew in a big pot with boiling salted water; drain.
- Place the pasta back in the pot; mix in goat cheese and sausage mixture to combine. Serve pasta on plates.

Nutrition Information

- Calories: 918
- Total Carbohydrate: 83 g
- Cholesterol: 102 mg
- Total Fat: 48 g
- Fiber: 8 g
- Protein: 37 g
- Sodium: 1012 mg
- Saturated Fat: 19 g

14. Chicken Scarpariella

"Nobody knows where this common dish in Italo-American restaurants came from. Scarpariella is an Italian slang that means shoemaker. Shoemaker means shortcutting things at hand in kitchen lingo. Basically, this Chicken Scarpariella features spring chicken that is cut into tiny pieces then cooked with a couple of basic ingredients."
Serving: Makes 4 servings

Ingredients

- 1 3 1/2 lb. chicken
- Salt and pepper
- 1 tsp. dried oregano
- 1/2 cup extra-virgin olive oil
- 3 cloves garlic, thinly sliced or slivered
- 1/2 of a fresh lemon
- 1/2 cup white wine
- 1/2 cup red wine vinegar
- 1 cup chicken broth
- 3 sprigs fresh rosemary, leaves only
- 1/2 cup chopped fresh flat-leaf (or Italian) parsley leaves, washed and dried
- 3 tbsp. butter

Direction

- In cold running water, wash the chicken then put in a big bowl; pour in fresh water to cover then add 2tbsp salt. Chill for an hour to brine and improve the moistness and texture. Take

the chicken out of the water then rinse. Use paper towels to dry.
- Slice the chicken to at least ten portions then season with oregano, pepper, and salt. If desired, put additional oregano.
- On low heat, heat oil in a lidded Dutch oven or 12-in heavy and straight-sided pan. In batches, shallow fry the chicken until golden brown while gently flipping the pieces using tongs. Move to a platter.
- Put in slices of garlic in the pan on low heat. Gently cook but don't brown the garlic. Move to the platter with chicken using a slotted spoon.
- Squeeze the lemon half juice in the pan then drop the lemon as well. Pour in stock, vinegar, and wine; boil on medium heat. Scrape the brown bits in the pan.
- Place the chicken and accumulated juices in the pan; simmer the liquid. Braise the chicken for 8mins while covered until completely cooked. Watch carefully to avoid overcooking since small chicken pieces cook faster than big ones.
- Move cooked chicken to a serving platter. In the pan, mix in butter, parsley, and rosemary to combine. Drizzle the sauce all over the chicken then serve right away.

Nutrition Information

- Calories: 956
- Total Carbohydrate: 7 g
- Cholesterol: 227 mg
- Total Fat: 77 g
- Fiber: 2 g
- Protein: 53 g
- Sodium: 1315 mg
- Saturated Fat: 21 g

15. Classic Marinara Sauce

"The little black dress of Italian-American cooking."
Serving: Makes about 5 cups

Ingredients

- 1/4 cup olive oil
- 1 small onion, finely chopped
- 4 garlic cloves, thinly sliced
- 2 sprigs basil
- 2 (28-oz.) cans whole peeled tomatoes

Direction

- Put the oil in a medium heavy pot placed over medium heat. Add the onion, and cook while stirring from time to time for 8–10 minutes until it turns very soft. Add the garlic and sauté. Stir the mixture from time to time for roughly 5 minutes until very soft then stir in the basil. Drop the tomatoes and crush them using your hands as you go; spice it up with pepper and salt; make it to a simmer. Lessen the heat and gently simmer while stirring it from time to time for roughly an hour until the sauce turns thick. Spice up with pepper and salt. Allow to cool.
- Take note that the sauce can be prepared a week in advanced. Chill it while covered, or freeze up to 3 months.

Nutrition Information

- Calories: 78
- Total Carbohydrate: 7 g
- Total Fat: 6 g
- Fiber: 3 g
- Protein: 1 g
- Sodium: 183 mg
- Saturated Fat: 1 g

16. Eggplant Marinara Flatbread

Serving: Makes 6 appetizer servings | Prep: 30m

Ingredients

- 4 tbsps. (about) olive oil, divided
- 6 1/3- to 1/2-inch-thick eggplant rounds (3 to 4 inches in diameter; from 1 large)
- 1 loaf ciabatta or pain rustique, cut horizontally in half, trimmed to 9-inch length
- 1 1/4 cups purchased fresh marinara sauce
- 2 oz. soft fresh goat cheese
- 1/3 cup chopped fresh basil plus 6 whole leaves (for garnish)
- 1 cup coarsely grated mozzarella cheese (about 4 oz.)

Direction

- Preheat the oven to 400 degrees F. On medium-high heat, heat 2 tbsp. oil in a big skillet. Sprinkle pepper and salt over the eggplant then place in the skillet; cover. Cook for 10 mins, flipping until tender. Move to plate. Brush the rest of the oil on the bottom half of bread's cut-side. Cook for a minute with the cut-side down on the skillet until golden.
- Arrange the bread on baking sheet with the cut-side up; spread 3/4 cup sauce. Break the goat cheese into crumbles then add on top; scatter chopped basil. Put eggplant on top then mound mozzarella over. Scoop the rest of the sauce on top.
- Bake for approximately 12 mins until the crust is crisp and the topping is hot; slice into six portions. Top with basil leaves to garnish.

17. Eggplant Parmesan Rolls With Swiss Chard And Fresh Mint

"This broiled eggplant dish is filled with ricotta then wrapped in mint. It originally came from a fried eggplant recipe with oregano-tomato sauce."
Serving: Makes 6 servings

Ingredients

- 2 medium eggplants (about 2 1/4 lbs. total), trimmed, cut lengthwise into 1/4-inch-thick slices
- Coarse kosher salt
- Extra-virgin olive oil
- 1 1-lb. bunch Swiss chard, center ribs removed
- 2 large eggs
- 1 15-oz. container whole-milk ricotta cheese
- 1 1/4 cups finely grated Parmesan cheese, divided
- 2 tbsps. chopped fresh mint
- 3/4 tsp. freshly ground black pepper
- 1 15- to 16-oz. can tomato sauce
- 1 8-oz. ball fresh water-packed mozzarella,* drained, thinly sliced

Direction

- Put one layer of eggplant slice on the sides and bottom of two big colanders until covered; generously scatter coarse salt. Keep on adding eggplant layer in both colanders until all the eggplant slices are gone, scatter coarse salt on each layer. Put each colander on top of a big bowl; let it sit for at least half to a maximum of full hour. Run the eggplant slices in water to get rid of the extra salt. Use paper towels to dry well.
- Place oven rack 5 to 6-in from heat then preheat the broiler. Put parchment paper on three big rimmed baking sheets. Put the eggplant slices on the prepared baking sheets in one layer. Slather olive oil on each side of the slices. Broil one sheet at a time for 3-4mins on each side until the eggplant slices are starting to brown and are tender, keep an eye

on the slices and remove as necessary if cooking too fast. Take the sheet out of the oven then let the eggplant cool as you make the filling.

- Boil a big pot of salted water. Put in chard then boil for 2mins until tender; drain then run in cold water. Squeeze the chard to release the excess moisture until dry then coarsely chop. Squeeze again in the middle of paper towel until dry. In a medium bowl, beat a pinch of coarse salt and eggs. Mix in black pepper, chopped chard, mint, a cup of parmesan, and ricotta cheese.
- Grease a 15-in by 10-in by 2-in glass baking dish lightly. Evenly slather 1/2 of the tomato sauce on the dish. Split the ricotta-chard filling between the eggplant slices, putting one tablespoonful of filling in the middle of each. Roll the eggplant slices up beginning on one short end of each to enfold the filling. Place the rolls over the sauce in the dish with the seam-side down. Spread the remaining tomato sauce all over. Arrange the mozzarella slices on top of the roll in one layer. Top with the remaining quarter cup Parmesan cheese. You can make this a day in advance; use foil to cover then refrigerate.
- Preheat the oven to 350 degrees F. Bake the rolls for half an hour if freshly made or 40mins if chilled while covered in foil until completely heated. Remove the foil then bake for another 15-20mins until the sauce is bubbling and there are brown spots. Serve hot.
- You can use regular mozzarella in this dish. You can find the cheese used in this dish at Italian markets, supermarkets, and specialty food stores.

18. Eggplant, Tomato, And Fontina Pizza

"As the dough rises, prepare the toppings and eggplant then heat the pizza stone."
Serving: Makes 2 (10-inch) pizzas | Prep: 45m

Ingredients

- 1 (1 1/2-lb.) eggplant, cut crosswise into 1/4-inch-thick slices
- 1 3/4 tsps. salt
- 3/4 cup packed fresh basil leaves
- 1/4 cup packed fresh mint leaves
- 2 garlic cloves
- 10 oz. grape tomatoes (2 cups), quartered
- 5 tbsps. extra-virgin olive oil plus additional for brushing dough
- Pizza dough
- Flour for dredging
- 1/4 lb. Italian Fontina, rind discarded and cheese cut into 1/4-inch dice (1 cup)
- a pizza stone; parchment paper; a baking peel or rimless baking sheet

Direction

- Prepare the pizza toppings. In a colander, sprinkle 1 1/2 tsp salt on the eggplant; drain in the sink for half an hour while turning the eggplants from time to time.
- Chop the garlic, mint, and basil together finely; mix with tomatoes in a bowl. Put in a sieve set on top of a bowl to drain.
- Preheat the broiler.
- Rinse then pat the eggplant dry in batches between paper towels; firmly press to get rid of the excess moisture. Brush around of 4 tbsp. oil on both side of the slices then cut small stacks; slice the stack into quarters. On two shallow heavy baking pans, put the eggplant pieces in one layer; broil one pan at a time for 7-8mins, around five to six inches from heat until golden brown. Turn the eggplants one time. Bring the eggplant to cool at room temperature.

- Place the pizza stone on the lower third of the oven then preheat to 500 degrees F. Heat the stone for an hour.
- Make the pizzas. Don't punch the dough down. Dredge one dough piece gently in flour until coated then move to a parchment paper sheet placed on a baking sheet or baking peel. Hold one edge of the floured dough using both your hands in the air then allow the bottom to touch the parchment paper. Move your hands carefully around the edges of the dough like turning a steering wheel. Let the dough weight stretch the dough roughly to a round of 10-in diameter. Place the round on the parchment then adjust the shape as necessary.
- Get rid of all the exuded liquid from tomatoes. In a bowl, mix tomatoes, the remaining a quarter tsp. salt, and remaining tbsp. oil. Brush oil on the dough round then sprinkle 1/2 of tomatoes, 1/2 of cheese, and 1/2 of cheese on top, keep an inch of border around the edge. Line the far edge of the peel with the far edge of the pizza stone; tilt the peel down then gently jerk to begin moving the pizza. Slide the pizza and parchment onto the stone; bake for 12-15mins until the cheese is bubbling and the crust is golden brown. Take the pizza out of the oven by sliding the peel beneath the paper. Move to a cutting board then get rid of the parchment paper.
- As you bake the first pizza, prepare the second one on another parchment sheet. Bake in the same way.

Nutrition Information

- Calories: 2529
- Total Carbohydrate: 386 g
- Cholesterol: 97 mg
- Total Fat: 66 g
- Fiber: 32 g
- Protein: 94 g
- Sodium: 4977 mg
- Saturated Fat: 26 g

19. Farfalle With Chicken, Tomatoes, Caramelized Onions, And Goat Cheese

"This flavorful pasta features earthy spinach, tangy goat cheese, and sweet tomatoes and onions."
Serving: Makes 4 to 6 servings

Ingredients

- 2 tbsps. olive oil
- 2 large red onions, thinly sliced
- 2 tbsps. Sherry wine vinegar
- 1 tsp. sugar
- 8 oz. farfalle
- 1 cup dry white wine
- 1 cup low-salt chicken broth
- 6 heirloom tomatoes, cored, chopped (about 5 cups)
- 2 cups shredded cooked chicken (from 1/2 rotisserie chicken)
- 1/2 cup thinly sliced basil leaves
- 2 tbsps. chopped fresh marjoram
- 3 cups baby spinach
- 3 oz. soft fresh goat cheese, crumbled

Direction

- On medium-high heat, heat oil in a big heavy pan. Cook onions with salt for 8mins while mixing regularly until it starts to brown. Turn to medium-low heat. Mix in sugar and vinegar; cook for 15mins while mixing often until the onions are brown; move to a bowl. Reserve the pan.
- In the meantime, cook pasta while mixing from time to time until tender yet still firm to chew in a big pot with boiling salted water; drain.
- Pour wine in the reserved pan; boil for 3mins until it reduces to a half cup. Add broth, onions, pasta, and the next four ingredients; sprinkle pepper and salt. On medium heat, mix for 3mins until completely heated.
- Split the spinach between plates; top with pasta. Sprinkle crumbled goat cheese on top.

Nutrition Information

- Calories: 557
- Total Carbohydrate: 60 g
- Cholesterol: 62 mg
- Total Fat: 18 g
- Fiber: 6 g
- Protein: 33 g
- Sodium: 204 mg
- Saturated Fat: 6 g

20. Fastest Chicken Parm

"A different take on a classic dish where the stacked ingredients are broiled instead of dredging and frying them. Through this method, the bread crumbs will stay crunchy and you'll get the lightly roasted tomatoes."
Serving: Serves 4

Ingredients

- 5 tbsps. olive oil
- 3 medium ripe tomatoes
- 4 boneless, skinless chicken breasts (about 2 lbs.)
- Salt and pepper
- 8 oz. fresh mozzarella cheese
- 2 oz. Parmesan cheese (1/2 cup grated)
- 1 bunch fresh basil
- 1 cup bread crumbs

Direction

- Set the broiler on high then place the rack 6-in from heat. On a rimmed baking sheet, spread 2tbsp olive oil all over then place in the broiler. Remove the core then chop the tomatoes. Halve the chicken breast horizontally to form two thin cutlets on each. Use the heel of your hand to flatten each cutlet.
- Take the baking sheet out of the broiler carefully; arrange the cutlets then season with pepper and salt. Add tomatoes on top; broil one side for 5-10mins until the chicken is not pink in the middle, turn the pan as needed. Grate the Parmesan and mozzarella cheese. Get 16-20 leaves from the basil stems. In a small bowl, mix the Parmesan, mozzarella, and bread crumbs.
- Take the baking sheet out of the broiler once the chicken is completely cooked. Put the basil leaves over the tomatoes then spread the cheese and bread crumbs mixture. Drizzle with 3tbsp olive oil.
- Place the sheet back in the broiler; cook for 2-4mins until the cheese and bread crumbs are bubbly and brown. Serve right away.

Nutrition Information

- Calories: 787
- Total Carbohydrate: 26 g
- Cholesterol: 226 mg
- Total Fat: 42 g
- Fiber: 3 g
- Protein: 73 g
- Sodium: 1041 mg
- Saturated Fat: 15 g

21. Four-cheese Manicotti

"You may use a usual spoon for stuffing the manicotti noodles. But for me, I prefer using a piping bag for a slightly faster fill instead."
Serving: 6 servings | Prep: 1h10m

Ingredients

- 6 tbsps. unsalted butter, divided
- 1 medium onion, chopped
- 2 garlic cloves, finely chopped
- 2 tsps. kosher salt, divided, plus more
- 3/4 tsp. freshly ground pepper, divided
- 1 (28-oz.) can whole peeled tomatoes
- 1 (14-oz.) can whole peeled or diced tomatoes
- 1 1/4 cups (packed) basil leaves, coarsely chopped, divided
- 8 oz. dried manicotti noodles
- Olive or vegetable oil (for greasing)
- 1/4 cup all-purpose flour
- 2 cups whole milk
- 1 cup grated Parmesan (about 3 oz.), divided

- 2/3 cup grated Pecorino Romano (about 2 oz.), divided
- 1 lb. fresh ricotta
- 8 oz. fresh mozzarella, cut into 1/2" pieces
- 1 shallot, finely chopped
- 1 large egg

Direction

- Set the oven for preheating to 400°F. Add 2 tbsp. of butter in a big skillet and melt over medium heat. Sauté the garlic and onion and stir it from time to time for about 3 minutes until softened. Sprinkle with a tsp of salt and half a tsp of pepper. Drop tomatoes from both cans and mash them up using a wooden spoon, then adjust the heat to medium-high. Put half a cup of basil, make it to a simmer, and cook while stirring from time to time for roughly 15–20 minutes until slightly evaporated.
- Add the noodles in a big pot of boiling salted water and cook while stirring from time to time until al dente. Drain and place on a lightly greased rimmed baking sheet.
- Meanwhile, add the remaining 4 tbsp. of butter in a medium saucepan and melt over medium-low heat. Drop the flour and cook while stirring continuously for roughly 1-2 minutes until foamy and it produces a nutty smell. Whisk it continuously and add the milk little by little; make it to a simmer. Cook for about 3 minutes while whisking regularly until the mixture can coat the back of a spoon. Mix in third cup of Pecorino and 1/3 cup of Parmesan; spice it up with the remaining quarter tsp. of pepper and half a tsp. salt.
- Mix ricotta, shallot, 1/3 cup Parmesan, mozzarella, egg, remaining third cup of Pecorino, half a tsp. of salt and half a cup of basil in a medium bowl.
- Put the ricotta mixture using a spoon into manicotti noodles at both ends. Scatter 1/2 of tomato sauce then 1/2 of the cheese sauce (keep them separate yet they'll blend together) on bottom of a 13 x 9" or other 3 quarts baking dish. Assemble manicotti over, then top it off with the rest of the cheese sauce, tomato sauce and third cup of Parmesan. Let the manicotti bake inside the oven for 30-35 minutes until it turns bubbly and browns lightly on top. Allow to cool for 5 minutes. Garnish with the remaining quarter cup of basil and serve.

Nutrition Information

- Calories: 709
- Total Carbohydrate: 51 g
- Cholesterol: 158 mg
- Total Fat: 41 g
- Fiber: 6 g
- Protein: 36 g
- Sodium: 1202 mg
- Saturated Fat: 24 g

22. Fresh Tomato Sauce

"This is a yummy and fresh pasta that is really easy to prepare."
Serving: 6 | Prep: 5m | Ready in: 35m

Ingredients

- 1/4 cup olive oil
- 6 tomatoes, chopped
- 3 onions, minced
- 2 green bell peppers, minced
- 4 cloves garlic, minced
- 3 tbsps. white wine
- salt and pepper to taste

Direction

- In a big saucepan, heat oil over medium heat and add white wine, garlic, green bell peppers, onions, and tomatoes, then pepper and salt to taste.
- Mix all the ingredients well and cover, then simmer for 30 minutes and serve.

Nutrition Information

- Calories: 144 calories;
- Total Carbohydrate: 13.4 g

- Cholesterol: 0 mg
- Total Fat: 9.4 g
- Protein: 2.2 g
- Sodium: 10 mg

23. Fried Egg And Sausage Ciabatta Breakfast Pizzas

"You can use different cheeses and sausages that you want for this pizza recipe that is best served with hot sauce. If you want a Middle Eastern version, use feta and lamb sausage."
Serving: Makes 8 servings | Prep: 25m

Ingredients

- 1 loaf ciabatta bread (about 1 lb.)
- 1 cup chopped green onions
- 8 tbsps. olive oil, divided
- 8 oz. sliced hot pepper Monterey Jack cheese
- 1 lb. spicy or sweet Italian sausages, casings removed
- 8 large eggs

Direction

- Preheat the oven to 450 degrees F. Halve the bread horizontally; arrange bread halves on separate baking sheets with the cut-side up. In a small bowl, combine 6 tbsp. oil and onions; sprinkle pepper and salt to season. Set aside 2 tbsp. of onion oil then spread the rest on the bread. Add cheese on top.
- On medium-high heat, sauté and crumble Italian sausages with a spoon for around 7 mins in a big non-stick skillet until thoroughly cooked. Divide the sausage between the bread halves. Bake the pizza for around 10mins until the bread starts to crisp and the cheese melts.
- In the meantime, on medium-high heat, heat 1 tbsp. oil each in two big skillets. Crack four eggs in each skillet then sprinkle with pepper and salt; cook for 2 mins Take off the heat then let the eggs sit in the skillets while baking the pizza.
- Put four eggs over each pizza. Scoop the reserved onion oil on top of the eggs. Slice each pizza into four portions between the eggs.
- You can assemble and refrigerate the pizzas a day in advance if you want to prepare it for brunch. Bake them and put the fried eggs on top at mealtime.

Nutrition Information

- Calories: 539
- Total Carbohydrate: 31 g
- Cholesterol: 228 mg
- Total Fat: 34 g
- Fiber: 2 g
- Protein: 28 g
- Sodium: 914 mg
- Saturated Fat: 11 g

24. Garlic-and-herb-braised Squid

"Simple and garlicky seafood dish."
Serving: Makes 6 servings | Prep: 15m

Ingredients

- 1 1/2 lbs. cleaned squid
- 2 cups flat-leaf parsley sprigs, divided
- 5 garlic cloves
- 3 tbsps. olive oil
- 1/4 tsp. hot red-pepper flakes
- 3/4 cup Chardonnay
- 1 (28-oz.) can whole tomatoes in juice, coarsely chopped
- 1/4 cup water
- Accompaniment: crusty bread

Direction

- Rinse squid in cold water. Pat dry. Cut big tentacles to half, lengthwise. Cut bodies and flaps, if they're there, to 1/2-inch-wide rings, crosswise.
- Chop parsley to get 2 tbsp. Put aside. Chop leftover garlic and parsley together. In a 4-

quart heavy pot, heat oil over low heat until hot. Cook red pepper flakes and garlic-parsley mixture for about 2 minutes, mixing, until garlic starts to sizzle. Bring heat up to medium-high, add the squid, for about 1 minute, cook and stir occasionally until it is barely opaque. Put the wine, simmering briskly and occasionally stirring, uncovered, for about 10 minutes until it reduces slightly. With their juice add tomatoes, 1/2 tsp. pepper, 1 1/4 tsps. salt, and water. Simmer, occasionally stirring, covered, for 30-40 minutes until squid is very tender.
- Season with extra pepper and salt. Stir in leftover parsley.

Nutrition Information

- Calories: 221
- Total Carbohydrate: 11 g
- Cholesterol: 264 mg
- Total Fat: 9 g
- Fiber: 3 g
- Protein: 19 g
- Sodium: 216 mg
- Saturated Fat: 1 g

25. Grilled Eggplant With Caponata Salsa

"A twist on the Sicilian caponata featuring olives, onions, tomatoes, with the eggplant slices topped with tomato salsa."
Serving: Makes 6 servings

Ingredients

- 1 12-oz. container grape or cherry tomatoes, quartered lengthwise
- 2 celery stalks, finely diced
- 1/2 cup chopped Vidalia or Maui onion
- 5 large green olives, pitted, thinly sliced (about 2 tbsps.)
- 2 tbsps. coarsely chopped fresh oregano plus sprigs for garnish
- 1 tbsp. drained capers, rinsed
- 1 garlic clove, minced
- Pinch of dried crushed red pepper
- 3 tbsps. red wine vinegar
- 1 tbsp. extra-virgin olive oil plus additional for brushing
- 1 large eggplant (1 1/2 to 1 3/4 lbs.), trimmed

Direction

- In a medium bowl, combine crushed red pepper, tomatoes, celery, capers, onion, chopped oregano, garlic and olives. In a small bowl, mix a tbsp. of extra-virgin olive oil and red wine vinegar; toss with the tomato mixture to coat. Sprinkle pepper and salt to taste. You can make the caponata two hours in advance. Let it sit on room temperature.
- Preheat the barbecue on medium-high heat. Skin the eggplant lengthwise to make alternating two-inch wide breaks of unpeeled and peeled skin. Slice the eggplant crosswise into six 1-in thick portions. Slather oil on the slices then season with pepper and salt. Grill the slices for 8mins on each side until very tender when poked with a knife and a bit charred.
- On each of six plates, put one grilled eggplant slice. Spread caponata then top with oregano sprigs. Serve at room temperature or warm.

Nutrition Information

- Calories: 70
- Total Carbohydrate: 10 g
- Total Fat: 3 g
- Fiber: 4 g
- Protein: 2 g
- Sodium: 99 mg
- Saturated Fat: 0 g

26. Hoagies

"These Italian version of meat and cheese sandwiches are ready in less than 45 minutes."
Serving: Serves 2

Ingredients

- 2 Italian sandwich rolls or one 9-inch loaf of Italian bread
- 2 tbsps. mayonnaise if desired
- 3/4 cup finely shredded lettuce
- 1/2 small onion, sliced very thin
- 6 slices of hard salami
- 6 thin slices of capicola (seasoned smoked ham) or other cooked ham
- 4 thin slices of provolone
- 6 thin slices of tomato
- 3 tbsps. olive oil
- 1 tbsp. red-wine vinegar
- 1/2 tsp. dried orégano, crumbled
- 2 bottled hot cherry peppers, or to taste, sliced thin

Direction

- Chop the rolls in half horizontally and leave on the edge cut to make a hinge. Spread mayonnaise onto the cut sides of rolls. Layer the lettuce, the onion, the salami, the capicola, the provolone, and the tomato onto the bottom halves of the rolls. Whisk together the cherry peppers, the oregano, the vinegar and the oil in a small bowl. Season with pepper and salt to taste. Sprinkle the dressing atop the fillings and then add the top halves of the rolls to cover the fillings. Chop each sandwich in half.

Nutrition Information

- Calories: 698
- Total Carbohydrate: 29 g
- Cholesterol: 81 mg
- Total Fat: 54 g
- Fiber: 4 g
- Protein: 25 g
- Sodium: 1558 mg
- Saturated Fat: 14 g

27. Homemade Pappardelle With Bolognese Sauce

"Beef, venison and antelope are the top main ingredients of this interesting, wild dish. Enjoy it thoroughly with a glass of medium-bodied red wine."
Serving: Makes 10 servings

Ingredients

- 5 tbsps. butter
- 7 tbsps. extra-virgin olive oil
- 2 cups chopped onions
- 1 1/4 cups chopped celery
- 3/4 cup chopped carrot
- 2 large garlic cloves, chopped
- 1 1/2 lbs. ground beef (15% fat)
- 1 1/2 lbs. antelope sausages or spicy Italian sausages, casings removed
- 3/4 lb. ground venison or ground beef (15% fat)
- 3/4 lb. bacon, chopped
- 1 1/2 cups whole milk
- 1 1/2 cups dry white wine
- 3/4 cup tomato paste (about 7 1/2 oz.)
- Homemade Pappardelle
- 1 cup freshly grated Parmesan cheese plus additional for passing

Direction

- In a big, heavy pot over moderate heat, heat the butter in oil until melted before inserting the following 4 ingredients. For 12 to 14 minutes, sauté the vegetables until they soften but aren't browned. Stir in the bacon, venison, sausage and beef before turning the heat up to a high. Cook for around 15 minutes until the meat turns brown. During the process, use the back of a spoon to break the meat up into smaller pieces. Pour in the tomato paste, wine and milk and whisk together. Turn the heat down to a low and leave it simmering for around 75 minutes, stirring every now and then. It is ready when the juices lessen, the

- flavors are blended and the sauce has thickened.
- Add pepper and salt. (This part of the recipe can be prepared 2 days in advance. After cooking, leave to rest for an hour chilled uncovered until cold. When ready to serve, heat it up over low heat.)
- In a very huge pot, cook pasta in a salted boiling water until just tender but still firm to bite. Cook and stir consistently about 4-5 minutes. If cooking pasta that was chilled, do it for around 5 to 6 minutes.
- Drain, keep 1 cup of the cooking liquid and insert the pasta right back into the same pot. Pour in 1 cup of cheese and warm Bolognese. Over moderate heat, toss in until it is thoroughly heated. In the case that it turns dry, pour in 1/4-cup of reserved cooking liquid. Add pepper and salt to taste. Move the pasta into a shallow, big bowl. Serve the dish passing additional cheese.

28. Inside-out Eggplant Parmigiana

"Any eggplant parmigiana leftover ingredients can be used to make these crisp and delicious pan-fried patties with bread crumbs and eggs."
Serving: Serves 4 (Main course) | Prep: 40m

Ingredients

- 2 tbsps. olive oil
- 1 small onion, finely chopped
- 1 garlic clove, minced
- 1 (14-oz.) can whole tomatoes in juice
- 1/2 cup water
- 1/2 tsp. sugar
- 3 tbsps. finely chopped basil
- 2 (1-lb.) eggplants
- 6 tbsps. olive oil, divided, plus additional for drizzling
- 3/4 cup plain dry bread crumbs
- 1/2 cup grated Parmigiano-Reggiano
- 1/2 cup finely chopped flat-leaf parsley
- 2 garlic cloves, minced, divided
- 6 large eggs, lightly beaten
- 1/2 cup water
- 1/4 tsp. hot red-pepper flakes
- 1/2 lb. arugula, coarse stems discarded, coarsely chopped
- 1 cup packed basil leaves, coarsely chopped
- 1/2 lb. cold fresh mozzarella, ends trimmed and remainder cut into 4 (1/2-inch-thick) slices

Direction

- Prepare the tomato sauce. On medium heat, heat oil in a heavy medium pot until shimmering; cook garlic and onion for 6mins while mixing from time to time until soft.
- In the meantime, in a blender, combine tomatoes with juice until nearly smooth. Pour into the pot with onion mixture then add quarter tsp. salt, sugar, and water. Let it simmer for 10min, mixing from time to time while slightly covered until a bit thick. Mix in basil. Cover then keep warm.
- Bake the eggplant. Place rack at the bottom part of the oven then preheat to 450 degrees F.
- Slice a dozen of 1/3-in thick eggplant rounds on the widest part. Slather 2tbsp oil on both sides then sprinkle a total of half tsp. salt; arrange on a greased baking sheet. Bake for 20-30mins until tender and golden, turn one time. Move to a plate then cover to keep warm. Keep the oven on.
- Prepare the arugula and egg patties. Combine a quarter tsp. each of pepper and salt, bread crumbs, 1/2 of garlic, parsley, and parmesan; mix in water and eggs.
- On medium heat, heat 3tbsp oil in a 12-in heavy pan until shimmering. Put four rounded 1/3 cup egg mixture in the pan; cook for 5mins until puffed and golden, turn one time. Drain patties on paper towels.
- Pour the remaining tbsp. of oil in the pan; cook and stir red pepper flakes and the remaining garlic for half a minute until the garlic is golden. Stir in basil and arugula until just wilted. Mix in 1/8tsp salt.

- Make the stacks. On a baking sheet, put four eggs patties, 3-in apart. Add 2tbsp tomato sauce, a slice each of mozzarella and eggplant, another 2tbsp tomato sauce, a slice of eggplant, the arugula mixture and the rest of the eggplant. Bake for 5-10mins until the cheese is melted. Dribble more oil then serve the rest of the sauce on the side.

Nutrition Information

- Calories: 745
- Total Carbohydrate: 37 g
- Cholesterol: 333 mg
- Total Fat: 53 g
- Fiber: 10 g
- Protein: 35 g
- Sodium: 946 mg
- Saturated Fat: 16 g

- Stir the remaining one tbsp. of marjoram into the dressing. Scoop the dressing onto the cut sides of the bread and divide equally. Arrange meats, cheeses, and onion on the bottom half of the bread. Place in the top half of bread to cover. Chop diagonally into four sandwiches. (You can make sandwiches 4 hours ahead and then chill while wrapped tightly in foil).

Nutrition Information

- Calories: 575
- Total Carbohydrate: 44 g
- Cholesterol: 54 mg
- Total Fat: 33 g
- Fiber: 3 g
- Protein: 27 g
- Sodium: 693 mg
- Saturated Fat: 6 g

29. Italian Deli Sandwiches With Marjoram-caper Dressing

"This is an ideal picnic sandwich during summer."
Serving: Makes 4 servings

Ingredients

- 1/2 cup olive oil
- 1/4 cup chopped fresh Italian parsley
- 1/4 cup drained capers
- 4 tbsps. chopped fresh marjoram
- 2 tbsps. red wine vinegar
- 1 22-inch-long sourdough baguette, halved lengthwise
- 12 oz. assorted sliced deli meats and cheeses (such as mortadella, salami, and provolone)
- 1 cup thinly sliced Vidalia onion

Direction

- In food processor, blend vinegar, 3 tbsps. marjoram, capers, parsley, and olive oil until the herbs are chopped finely. Add pepper and salt to taste. Pour the dressing into a small bowl. Allow to sit for 30 minutes.

30. Italian Sausage With Grilled Broccolini, Kale, And Lemon

"It is a must to avoid the sausage from overcooking as it can dry out. Just have them browned over direct heat and just quickly move to a cooler place to finish cooking."
Serving: 4 servings

Ingredients

- 5 tbsps. olive oil, divided, plus more for grill
- 3 tbsps. crushed unsalted, roasted almonds
- 2 tbsps. fresh lemon juice
- 1 tbsp. drained capers
- 1 tsp. honey
- Kosher salt, freshly ground pepper
- 2 bunches broccolini (about 1 1/2 lbs.)
- 1 bunch small Tuscan kale, tough stems removed
- 1 1/2 lbs. coiled Italian sausage, preferably skewered, or links
- 1 lemon, thinly sliced into rounds, seeds removed
- 2 oz. mild Pecorino, shaved

Direction

- Set a grill for preheating to medium-high, indirect heat (if using a charcoal grill, bank the coals just on one side of the grill; if using a gas grill, leave one or two burners off); grease the grate. Stir together the lemon juice, almonds, capers, 4 Tbsp. oil and honey in a small bowl; spice the dressing with pepper and salt.
- Mix together the kale and broccolini in a big bowl and add the remaining 1 tbsp. of oil. Stir them well to equally coat vegetables; spice up with salt.
- Place the sausage on the grill over direct heat and cook them for roughly 3 minutes per side until it turns brown all over. Place on indirect heat and continue to cook while flipping and rotating from time to time for 8-10 minutes until completely cooked. Put the sausages on a platter.
- Meanwhile, cook the kale and broccolini over direct heat until the kale turns brown lightly and crisp all over the edges and the broccolini stem turns crisp yet tender, roughly for a minute for kale and about 3 minutes for broccolini. Put it back to the bowl.
- Place the lemon slices on the grill and cook for a minute for each side over direct heat until it turns brown lightly. Put on a bowl with kale and broccolini and then add half of Pecorino and half of dressing. Stir them to combine; spice the salad with pepper and salt.
- Mound some of the salad over the sausage and leave some in the bowl. Pour the remaining dressing all over the salad and garnish with the rest of the Pecorino.

Nutrition Information

- Calories: 919
- Total Carbohydrate: 21 g
- Cholesterol: 144 mg
- Total Fat: 78 g
- Fiber: 7 g
- Protein: 37 g
- Sodium: 1600 mg
- Saturated Fat: 24 g

31. Italian Spoon Biscuits With Tomato Sauce And Cheese

"This odd dish is like a combination of pizza bread and lasagna with no meat. It is made with mozzarella cheese, tomato sauce, and biscuits."
Serving: Makes 8 Servings

Ingredients

- 3 10- to 11-oz. cans refrigerated buttermilk biscuits
- 2 cups prepared tomato pasta sauce
- 1 cup sliced green onions
- 1 green bell pepper, chopped
- 2 cups (packed) grated mozzarella cheese (about 8 oz.)

Direction

- Preheat the oven to 350 degrees F. Grease butter on a 13-in by 9-in by 2-in glass baking dish. Slice each biscuit into eight portions then arrange in the buttered dish. Mix in bell pepper, green onions, and sauce until combined.
- Bake for approximately 35 mins until the top is nearly firm to the touch and set. Evenly scatter cheese on top. Bake for around another 5 mins until the cheese melts. Let it sit for 10 mins Slice into squares to serve.

Nutrition Information

- Calories: 464
- Total Carbohydrate: 54 g
- Cholesterol: 25 mg
- Total Fat: 22 g
- Fiber: 3 g
- Protein: 14 g
- Sodium: 1519 mg
- Saturated Fat: 9 g

32. Lasagna With Turkey Sausage Bolognese

Serving: Makes 8 to 10 servings | Prep: 45m

Ingredients

- 2 tbsps. olive oil
- 2 cups chopped onions
- 1/2 cup diced carrot
- 1 tbsp. fennel seeds, crushed in spice mill or in mortar with pestle
- 1 lb. spicy Italian turkey sausages, casings removed
- 3 large garlic cloves, pressed
- 1/2 cup dry white wine
- 5 cups crushed tomatoes with added puree (from two 28-oz. cans)
- 1 cup chopped fresh basil, divided
- 2 tbsps. chopped fresh oregano
- 1 15-oz. container whole-milk ricotta cheese
- 3 cups (packed) coarsely grated whole-milk mozzarella cheese (12 oz.)
- 1 1/4 cups freshly grated Parmesan cheese, divided
- 16 6 1/2 x 3 1/4-inch no-boil lasagna noodles

Direction

- On medium-high heat, heat oil in a big non-stick pan. Sauté fennel seeds, carrot, and onion in hot oil for 5mins. Put in garlic and sausage; sauté for 8-10mins while crumbling until the sausage is completely cooked. Pour in wine; boil for a minute. Put oregano, half cup basil, and tomatoes; boil. Lower heat; let it simmer for 10mins until thick. Sprinkle pepper and salt.
- In a medium bowl, combine half cup basil, ricotta, a cup of Parmesan, and mozzarella well; sprinkle pepper. You can make the cheese mixture and sauce a day in advance; separately cover then refrigerate.
- Put noodles in a big bowl then pour in hot water to cover; soak for about half an hour while separating from time to time. Drain thoroughly.
- Preheat the oven to 375 degrees F. In a 13-in by 9-in by 2-in baking dish, spread a cup of sauce at the bottom then top with four noodles crosswise. Spread a quarter of the cheese mixture by tablespoonfuls. Add a cup of sauce, four noodles, and a third of the remaining cheese mixture on top. Repeat for another two times with a cup of sauce, four noodles, and half of the cheese mixture. Slather the rest of the sauce on top. Spread a quarter cup of Parmesan.
- Bake for 50mins without cover until puffed and completely heated. Let it sit for 10-15mins then serve.

Nutrition Information

- Calories: 678
- Total Carbohydrate: 59 g
- Cholesterol: 115 mg
- Total Fat: 30 g
- Fiber: 6 g
- Protein: 42 g
- Sodium: 1184 mg
- Saturated Fat: 15 g

33. Lasagne Bolognese With Spinach

"This lasagne Bolognese is made with the combination of the Italian-American version and the classic version that is usually made in Emilia-Romagna Italy. The pseudo-besciamella sauce is made by whisking ricotta and milk. You can use a Barilla no-boil dried noodles or an egg pasta in this dish."
Serving: Makes 8 servings | Prep: 1h

Ingredients

- 1/4 cup olive oil
- 3 oz. sliced pancetta, finely chopped
- 1 medium onion, finely chopped
- 1 large carrot, finely chopped
- 1 celery rib, finely chopped
- 2 garlic cloves, chopped
- 2 lbs. ground beef chuck (not lean)

- 1 1/2 cups dry white wine
- 1 1/2 cups whole milk
- 1/4 cup tomato paste
- 1 1/2 tsp. thyme leaves
- 2 (10-oz.) packages frozen chopped spinach, thawed
- 2 (15-oz.) containers whole-milk ricotta
- 4 large eggs, lightly beaten
- 1/2 cup grated Parmigiano-Reggiano
- 1/2 tsp. grated nutmeg
- 3/4 cup whole milk, divided
- 12 Barilla no-boil dried lasagne noodles (from 1 box)
- 1/2 cup grated Parmigiano-Reggiano
- Equipment: a 13- by 9-inch baking pan (3 inches deep)

Direction

- Prepare the sauce. On medium heat, heat oil in a 12-14 inch heavy pan until shimmering. Cook garlic, pancetta, celery, onion and carrot for 12-15mins while mixing from time to time until the veggies are soft and golden. Put in beef, cook for 6-10mins while mixing from time to time to break the lumps until the meat is not pink. Mix in 3/4tsp pepper, wine, quarter tsp. salt, milk, thyme, and tomato paste. Let it simmer for an hour without cover while mixing from time to time until nearly all the liquid evaporates yet the sauce is still moist.
- Prepare the ricotta filling. In a kitchen towel that is not terry cloth, put and squeeze the spinach to release as much liquid as possible.
- Beat a tsp. of pepper, ricotta, 1 1/4tsp salt, eggs, nutmeg, and parmesan. Move 1 1/2 cup of the mixture to a separate bowl then beat in a quarter cup milk; set it aside. Mix spinach and the remaining half cup milk into the rest of the filling.
- Prepare and bake the lasagne. Place the rack in the center of the oven then preheat to 375 degrees.
- Soak noodles for 3-5mins until pliable yet not soft in a bowl with very warm water. Put the noodles on a kitchen towel. You don't need to pat them dry.
- In a baking pan, slather 1 1/2 cup Bolognese sauce then top with a tbsp. of parmesan. Layer three noodles, keeping space in the middle of each. Slather 1/2 of the spinach filling over the noodles, a cup of Bolognese sauce then 1tbsp parmesan. Place the remaining three noodles on top. Spread the reserved ricotta mixture on top then sprinkle with the remaining quarter cup parmesan.
- Use butterred foil or parchment paper and foil to tightly cover the pan; bake for 50mins. Discard the foil; bake for another 15mins until there are brown spots on top. Let it sit for 15-30mins before slicing.
- The Bolognese sauce can be prepared two days in advance; cover once cool then refrigerate.
- You can prepare the lasagne a day in advance; refrigerate. Reheat in a 350 degrees F oven while covered loosely with a foil.

Nutrition Information

- Calories: 766
- Total Carbohydrate: 43 g
- Cholesterol: 242 mg
- Total Fat: 39 g
- Fiber: 4 g
- Protein: 56 g
- Sodium: 644 mg
- Saturated Fat: 18 g

34. Leaving-home Penne Rigate With Broccoli

"You can get the kids to eat broccoli by making this delicious and easy to make Parmesan and broccoli pasta dish. When cooked long enough, the broccoli will turn buttery and soft. It will become a sauce if you mix it with cheese and olive oil using a wooden spoon. When you drain the pasta, be sure to use a mesh strainer or a colander with small holes so that broccoli buds won't be drained too."
Serving: Serves 4

Ingredients

- Salt
- 1 1/2 lbs. broccoli, washed, stems discarded, cut into bite-size florets
- 1 lb. penne rigate
- 3/4 cup extra-virgin olive oil
- 2/3 cup finely grated pecorino cheese, plus extra for serving
- Freshly ground pepper

Direction

- Boil a big pot of water. Add a quarter cup or a handful of salt just enough to taste. Place a fine strainer over the sink.
- Put the broccoli in boiling water then return to boil. Put in pasta; prepare the timer according to the minutes suggested on the box. Drain the broccoli and penne in the colander once the timer is up; move to a big serving bowl. Use a wooden spoon to mix in olive oil until the broccoli bits are evenly distributed and the pasta is coated. Stir in the cheese until you get a nice, green-speckled sauce, then sprinkle a bit more cheese together with some pepper.

Nutrition Information

- Calories: 839
- Total Carbohydrate: 97 g
- Total Fat: 43 g
- Fiber: 8 g
- Protein: 20 g
- Sodium: 756 mg
- Saturated Fat: 6 g

35. Lemon Pepper Acini Di Pepe

"This round and tiny pasta gets its name because it looks a bit like peppercorns. In this dish, it is paired with parmesan, lemon, and pepper."
Serving: Serves 6 (side dish) | Prep: 10m

Ingredients

- 2 cups acini di pepe (less than 1 lb.)
- 2 tbsps. unsalted butter
- 1 tbsp. olive oil
- 1/2 cup grated Parmigiano-Reggiano
- 1 tbsp. grated lemon zest
- 1 tsp. freshly ground black pepper

Direction

- In a 4-qt pot, cook acini di pepe in boiling salted water until al dente. Use 2tsp salt for 3-qt water. Set aside one cup of cooking water; drain the acini di pepe.
- In the same pot, melt butter with oil; take off heat. Mix in half cup of cooking water, pasta, half tsp. salt, cheese, pepper, and zest. If needed, pour in more cooking water to moisten.

36. Limoncello Champagne Cocktails With Mint

Serving: Makes 2 | Prep: 15m

Ingredients

- 1/4 cup fresh mint leaves
- 1/4 cup limoncello
- 2 tbsps. sugar plus additional for dipping Champagne flutes
- Lemon peel strips from 1 lemon
- 4 tsps. fresh lemon juice plus 1 lemon wedge
- 1 cup (about) chilled Champagne or sparkling wine

Direction

- In a blender, add 2 tbsps. sugar, limoncello, lemon strips, and mint. Process mixture until mint is sliced finely and lemon peel must be coarsely chopped for 10 seconds. Strain mixture over a small cup and throw away solids. In the rim of 2 Champagne flutes, run around lemon wedge then dip in sugar. Distribute lemon juice and limoncello mixture between flutes. Top off with Champagne.
- Per serving: 257.9 kcal calories, 0.0 % calories from fat, 0.0 g fat, 0.0 g saturated fat, 0 mg cholesterol, 19.4 g carbohydrates, 0.4 g dietary fiber, 15.9 g total sugars, 19.0 g net carbohydrates, 0.3 g protein.

37. Limoncello Gelato

"Drizzle a not-too-sweet gelato with limoncello for a perfect ending. Place purchased cookies around the dessert."
Serving: Makes about 4 cups

Ingredients

- 2 cups heavy whipping cream
- 1/2 cup whole milk
- 1/4 cup buttermilk
- 1/4 cup mascarpone cheese*
- 4 coffee beans
- 1 tsp. finely grated lemon peel
- 1 vanilla bean, split lengthwise
- 4 large egg yolks
- 1/2 cup sugar
- 2 tbsps. fresh lemon juice
- 1/4 cup limoncello or other lemon liqueur plus additional for serving

Direction

- In a large saucepan, whisk the initial 6 ingredients. Scrape seeds from the vanilla bean then add in together with bean. Cook and stir occasionally over medium-high heat till it forms bubbles at the edges. Take away from the heat and allow to steep for 15 minutes, covered.
- In a large bowl, whisk lemon juice, sugar and egg yolk. Gradually whisk the warm cream mixture into the yolk mixture. Bring the custard back to the same saucepan. Stir for 6 minutes over medium heat till it reads 180°F on a thermometer and the custard is thick enough to coat a spoon; don't boil. Transfer the custard into a medium bowl then add in 1/4 cup of limoncello stir. Let the custard chill for at least 4 hours till cold; stirring constantly. You can make this 1 day ahead then keep chilled and covered.
- Follow the instructions to process the custard in an ice cream maker. Place into a container and allow to freeze up to 2 days, covered. Place gelato into the glasses then drizzle additional limoncello over to serve.

Nutrition Information

- Calories: 278
- Total Carbohydrate: 9 g
- Cholesterol: 141 mg
- Total Fat: 27 g
- Fiber: 0 g
- Protein: 3 g
- Sodium: 46 mg
- Saturated Fat: 15 g

38. Linguine With Herb Broth And Clams

"A more flavorful pasta cooked in herb broth. Best paired with a warm rustic slice of bread."
Serving: Makes 4 servings

Ingredients

- 1/4 cup (1/2 stick) butter
- 2 tbsps. olive oil
- 2 onions, chopped
- 6 garlic cloves, peeled, smashed
- 2 medium tomatoes, cored, chopped
- 3 cups dry white wine
- 1 cup (or more) water

- 3 lbs. Manila clams or small littleneck clams, scrubbed
- 1/3 cup thinly sliced fresh basil leaves
- 1/4 cup chopped fresh parsley
- 1/4 cup chopped fresh oregano
- 2 pinches of dried crushed red pepper
- 8 oz. linguine

Direction

- Put the butter in olive oil in a hefty big pot and melt over medium heat. Stir in the onions and let it cook until it turns soft. Stir it from time to time for roughly 5 minutes. Drop the garlic and stir for a minute. Add the tomatoes and stir from time to time while it cooks until it starts to get soft, roughly 2 minutes. Stir in the white wine and a cup water. Allow the mixture to boil. Adjust the heat to low and make it to a simmer while covered for about 20 minutes for the flavors to blend well. Take note that the broth is best prepared a day in advanced. Cool it a bit, cover and store in the fridge.
- Allow the broth to boil. Drop the clams and let it cook for about 3 to 5 minutes while covered until the clams open (dispose any clams that remains closed). Place the clams on a big bowl; make a tent using a foil to keep the clams warm.
- Mix in the parsley, basil, crushed red pepper and oregano in the broth in pot. Drop the linguine. Let it boil until the pasta is nearly softened yet still very firm to the bite. Stir the pasta from time to time while adding some water by tablespoonfuls if it ended up too dry. Place the clams back with any juices collected to pot. Make it to a simmer for about 3 minutes longer while covered until the clams are completely heated and the pasta has softened yet still firm to bite. Spice it up with pepper and salt.
- Serve the clam and linguine mixture in a big shallow serving platter.

Nutrition Information

- Calories: 33
- Total Carbohydrate: 3 g
- Cholesterol: 5 mg
- Total Fat: 1 g
- Fiber: 0 g
- Protein: 2 g
- Sodium: 85 mg
- Saturated Fat: 0 g

39. Linguine With Pesto Trapanese

Ingredients

- 3/4 cup slivered almonds
- 1 large handful fresh basil leaves
- 1 to 2 large garlic cloves
- Several sprinkles of sea salt
- 6 ripe plum tomatoes
- Handful of grated Pecorino (about 1/2 cup)
- A generous splash of olive oil (about 1/3 cup)
- 1 lb. linguine

Direction

- In a bit of olive oil, sauté almonds until light brown.
- Chop salt, garlic, and basil in a food processor; set aside.
- Add almonds then pulse until orzo-sized.
- Add olive oil, tomatoes, cheese, basil garlic, and almonds back in the food processor then pulse for a bit. Sprinkle fresh-ground coarse pepper.
- Boil the linguine. You can be appalled with the idea of overcooking pasta if you're Sicilian. Split a strand open every minute, drain immediately if there's a small white speck in the middle. Reserve a cupful of pasta water.
- Quickly stir pasta with pesto. If needed, pour in a bit of pasta water. Serve the pasta at room temperature or lukewarm.

Nutrition Information

- Calories: 253

- Total Carbohydrate: 38 g
- Cholesterol: 7 mg
- Total Fat: 7 g
- Fiber: 3 g
- Protein: 10 g
- Sodium: 241 mg
- Saturated Fat: 2 g

40. Linguine With Rustic "meatballs"

"This pasta dish features delicious and satisfying free-form meatball."
Serving: Makes 6 servings | Prep: 20m

Ingredients

- 1 1/4 lbs. meatloaf mix (ground beef, pork, and veal; preferably not mixed together)
- 4 tbsps. extra-virgin olive oil, divided
- 1 tsp. ground cumin
- 1 large red onion, chopped
- 2 medium carrots, finely chopped
- 2 garlic cloves, finely chopped
- 1 cup sweet (red) vermouth
- Rounded 1/8 tsp. hot red-pepper flakes
- 1 tbsp. cornstarch
- 1 3/4 cups reduced-sodium chicken broth
- 2 celery ribs, finely chopped
- 1 tbsp. fresh lemon juice
- 1 lb. thin linguine or spaghetti
- 1/3 cup celery leaves, coarsely chopped
- Accompaniment: grated Parmigiano-Reggiano

Direction

- Crumble the meat into 1 1/2-in masses but avoid mixing the meats. On medium-high heat, heat 2tbsp oil in a 12-in heavy pan until shimmering. On medium-high heat, cook meat with quarter tsp. pepper, half tsp. salt, and cumin for 3mins while mixing from time to time until there are light golden spots. The inside of the meat will not be cooked completely. With a slotted spoon, move the meat to a plate.
- Pour the remaining 2tbsp oil in the pan. On medium-high heat, cook garlic, carrots, and onion for 5-8mins while mixing from time to time until the onion starts to turn golden.
- Put in red pepper flakes and vermouth; boil. Stir cornstarch in broth then mix in the onion mixture; boil while mixing. Lower heat; let it simmer for 3mins while mixing from time to time until a bit thick.
- Mix in lemon juice, celery, and meat with the accumulated juices; let it simmer for 3mins until the meat is completely cooked.
- In a pasta pot, cook linguine until al dente in boiling salted water. Use 2tbsp salt for 6-qt water. Set aside a half cup of the pasta water; drain pasta. Put pasta in the meat with celery leaves. On medium-low heat, cook until completely heated. If needed, pour in the reserved cooking water to moisten. Sprinkle with pepper and salt to taste.

Nutrition Information

- Calories: 615
- Total Carbohydrate: 65 g
- Cholesterol: 60 mg
- Total Fat: 22 g
- Fiber: 4 g
- Protein: 30 g
- Sodium: 244 mg
- Saturated Fat: 6 g

41. Meatballs With Parsley And Parmesan

"You'll never go wrong with these savory meatballs on their own. Try them in a tomato sauce or in a submarine sandwich."
Serving: Makes about 44

Ingredients

- 4 large eggs
- 1/2 cup fresh French breadcrumbs

- 6 tbsps. grated Parmesan cheese
- 3 tbsps. olive oil
- 1/4 cup chopped fresh parsley
- 3 large garlic cloves, minced
- 2 tsps. salt
- 1 tsp. ground black pepper
- 2 lbs. lean ground beef
- Additional olive oil (for frying)

Direction

- Mix together the eggs, Parmesan cheese, breadcrumbs, 3 tbsps. olive oil, pepper, garlic, parsley and 2 tsps. of salt in big bowl to combine. Stir in the ground beef and mix thoroughly. Form the mixture into meatballs having 1 1/2-inch diameter in size.
- Add enough oil in a heavy big skillet to fully coat the bottom; set and let it heat over medium-low heat. Work in batches. Fry the meatballs until turned brown and completely cooked, turning regularly while adding more oil as necessary, fry for roughly 15 minutes per batch. Put on a plate.

Nutrition Information

- Calories: 103
- Total Carbohydrate: 1 g
- Cholesterol: 32 mg
- Total Fat: 8 g
- Fiber: 0 g
- Protein: 6 g
- Sodium: 80 mg
- Saturated Fat: 2 g

42. Microwave Lasagna With Spinach, Mushrooms, And Three Cheeses

"Why spend an hour doing a pasta dish when you can make a hearty and flavorful microwave lasagna in just 15 minutes? This can be a perfect snack for the kids or a welcome food for your guests because it's very easy to make!"

Serving: Serves 4 | Prep: 15m

Ingredients

- 1 (15–16-oz.) container part-skim ricotta
- 1 (10-oz.) package frozen chopped spinach, thawed, squeezed in paper towels to remove excess moisture
- 1 garlic clove, very finely chopped
- 1 tsp. kosher salt
- 1/4 tsp. crushed red pepper flakes (optional)
- 1/4 tsp. freshly ground black pepper
- 2 1/4 cups grated mozzarella (about 9 oz.), divided
- 1/2 cup grated Parmesan (about 2 oz.), divided
- 1 (24-oz.) jar marinara sauce
- 6 no-boil lasagna noodles
- 8 oz. crimini mushrooms, trimmed, sliced 1/4-inch thick, divided
- 1 tbsp. coarsely chopped flat-leaf parsley leaves
- A deep 8x8-inch microwave-proof baking dish

Direction

- In a large bowl, combine ricotta, spinach, salt, pepper, garlic, red pepper flakes (if you're using), 1/4 cup Parmesan cheese, and 1 1/2 cups mozzarella cheese.
- Prepare baking dish and evenly spread 1/2 cup of marinara at the bottom. Put 2 lasagna noodles. Spread 1/2 cup marinara over the noodles. Add half of the ricotta mixture then add half of the mushrooms. Add another layer of 2 lasagna noodles, 1/2 cup marinara, half ricotta mixture and half mushrooms.

- Top with 2 more lasagna noodles, marinara sauce, and 3/4 cup mozzarella cheese. Finish it up by sprinkling 2 tbsps. of Parmesan cheese.
- Cover your baking dish using parchment, then enclose it with a large, overturned microwave-safe tray or plate.
- Pop it in the microwave and cook for 15 minutes on high power. Occasionally check if noodles are tender; otherwise, cover and cook again in the microwave at 1-minute intervals until it becomes tender.
- While still covered, let it stand for 10 minutes. Remove the parchment carefully. To garnish, sprinkle more Parmesan cheese and parsley, then serve.
- Cook's Note: The above recipe is intended for a 1200-watt microwave. If your microwave oven has lower wattage, you may need to extend the cooking time.
- If you prefer to do a meaty lasagna, simply add your favorite sausage, cooked and sliced, to the 2 mushroom layers.

Nutrition Information

- Calories: 652
- Total Carbohydrate: 54 g
- Cholesterol: 97 mg
- Total Fat: 30 g
- Fiber: 6 g
- Protein: 43 g
- Sodium: 1479 mg
- Saturated Fat: 17 g

43. Minted Green Salad

"This light and satisfying American-style salad features cucumber slices and fresh mint."
Serving: Makes 12 servings | Prep: 20m

Ingredients

- 2 carrots
- 3 Kirby cucumbers, halved lengthwise and thinly sliced crosswise
- 2 heads Boston lettuce (1 1/2 lbs.), torn into bite-size pieces
- 1 heart of romaine, torn into bite-size pieces
- 1 1/2 cups packed small mint leaves
- 1/4 cup extra-virgin olive oil
- 1/2 tsp. fine sea salt or kosher salt
- 2 tbsps. red-wine vinegar

Direction

- Slice the carrots in half crosswise. Use a vegetable peeler to shear into wider ribbons. In a big bowl, combine carrot ribbons with oil, cucumbers, mint, and lettuces.
- Toss in sea salt then vinegar.

Nutrition Information

- Calories: 70
- Total Carbohydrate: 6 g
- Total Fat: 5 g
- Fiber: 2 g
- Protein: 2 g
- Sodium: 113 mg
- Saturated Fat: 1 g

44. Mixed-berry Tiramisù With Lime Curd

"This fancy dessert with the brightness of lime is like a combination of summer pudding, tiramisu, and a trifle."
Serving: Makes 12 servings

Ingredients

- 3 cups fresh blueberries (17 oz.)
- 1 cup fresh raspberries (4 1/2 to 5 oz.)
- 1 cup fresh blackberries (5 to 6 oz.)
- 1 cup powdered sugar
- 1/2 cup water
- 3 tbsps. fresh lime juice
- 1 cup thinly sliced fresh strawberries
- 1/3 cup water
- 1/3 cup sugar
- 3 1 1/2-inch-long strips lime peel (green part only; shaved with vegetable peeler)

- 1 7-oz. package crisp ladyfingers (savoiardi, Boudoirs, or Champagne biscuits; do not use soft ladyfingers)*
- 2 1/2 8-oz. containers mascarpone cheese**
- 1/2 cup chilled heavy whipping cream
- Lime Curd

Direction

- Prepare the berries. In a big pot, simmer and stir half cup water, blueberries, powdered sugar, blackberries, and raspberries until the sugar dissolves. Turn to medium heat; simmer for 8mins while mixing from time to time until the berries are soft yet unbroken. Move to a big bowl then mix in lime juice; cool mixture to room temperature. Mix in strawberries then refrigerate for about 4hrs until cold. You can make this a day in advance; cover then keep refrigerated.
- Make the ladyfinger layer and syrup. On medium heat, boil and stir lime peel strips, 1/3 cup sugar, and 1/3 cup water in a small pot until the sugar dissolves. Move to a bowl then cool to room temperature; remove the lime peel.
- Slather syrup on each side of the ladyfingers using a pastry brush. Arrange in a 13-in by 9-in by 2-in glass baking dish in one layer, trim to fit if needed to completely cover the bottom of the dish. Spread the chilled berry mixture all over.
- Prepare the mascarpone topping. In a big bowl, beat cream and mascarpone with an electric mixer until slightly thick and smooth. Avoid overbeating since it may curdle. Beat in lime curd until just combined. Put heaping spoonfuls of mascarpone topping on top of the berry mixture; evenly spread until the berries are covered completely. Cover then place in the refrigerator for at least 8hrs. You can make this a day in advance. Keep refrigerated.
- Serve the tiramisu in bowls.
- You can find this at Italian markets, specialty foods stores, and some supermarkets.
- You can find Italian cream cheese in Italian markets and other supermarkets.

Nutrition Information

- Calories: 359
- Total Carbohydrate: 39 g
- Cholesterol: 102 mg
- Total Fat: 22 g
- Fiber: 3 g
- Protein: 6 g
- Sodium: 203 mg
- Saturated Fat: 12 g

45. Mueller's Classic Lasagna

"This Mueller's lasagna recipe features a delicious tomato and meat sauce to make every bite memorable."
Serving: 8 servings

Ingredients

- 1 lb. ground beef
- 3/4 cup chopped onion
- 2 tbsps. salad or olive oil
- 1 (15-oz.) can tomatoes
- 2 (6-oz.) cans tomato paste
- 2 cups water
- 1 tbsp. chopped parsley
- 2 tsps. salt
- 1 tsp. sugar
- 1 tsp. garlic powder
- 1/2 tsp. pepper
- 1/2 tsp. oregano leaves
- 1/2 package (8 oz.) Mueller's lasagna noodles
- 1 lb. ricotta
- 8 oz. mozzarella cheese, shredded or thinly sliced
- 1 cup grated Parmesan cheese

Direction

- Brown the onion and beef in a big heavy pan lightly. Put in oregano, tomatoes that are blended or mashed with the side of a spoon, tomato paste, pepper, garlic powder, water, sugar, salt, and parsley; simmer for half an hour without cover while mixing from time to time. In the meantime, cook the lasagne

noodles following the box directions; drain. Slather about a cup of sauce in a 13-in by 9-in baking pan. Place the noodles, sauce, mozzarella, ricotta, and Parmesan cheese in alternating layers. End the layer with sauce, mozzarella, and Parmesan cheese.
- Bake for 40-50mins in a 350 degrees F oven until bubbling and pale brown. Let it sit for 15mins. Slice in squares then serve.

Nutrition Information

- Calories: 577
- Total Carbohydrate: 36 g
- Cholesterol: 104 mg
- Total Fat: 33 g
- Fiber: 4 g
- Protein: 34 g
- Sodium: 883 mg
- Saturated Fat: 16 g

46. My Hero

"Prior adding to sandwich, ensure to drain the salad."

Ingredients

- 1 French or Italian bread (7 to 8 inches long)
- 1 tbsp. plus 2 tsps. olive oil
- 8 tender arugula leaves
- 1 ripe plum tomato, cut into 1/4-inch strips
- 1 tbsp. balsamic vinegar
- Salt and pepper, to taste
- 3 slices mozzarella (about 1/8 inch thick)
- 4 whole fresh basil leaves, rinsed and patted dry
- 2 thin slices (2 oz.) prosciutto di Parma
- 4 thin slices (1 oz.) Genoa salami

Direction

- Cut bread lengthwise and remove some of the insides. With 2 tsps. of olive oil, brush insides of bread.
- For salad: In a bowl, toss tomato strips and arugula with balsamic vinegar and leftover tbsp. olive oil. Put pepper and salt to season.
- Set salami, prosciutto, basil and mozzarella on bread bottom. Put salad on top. Cover using top of bread. Diagonally halve the sandwich and wrap thoroughly for the road.

47. New Chicken Parmesan

"Instead of breadcrumbs, use grated Parmesan to coat the chicken breasts for a delicious upgrade on your chicken Parm."
Serving: Makes 4 servings

Ingredients

- 1/3 cup extra-virgin olive oil
- 2 large garlic cloves, pressed
- 1/2 tsp. salt
- 1 12-oz. container grape tomatoes
- 1 1/2 tsps. dried oregano
- Large pinch of dried crushed red pepper
- 4 skinless boneless chicken breast halves (about 6 oz. each)
- 1 1/4 cups finely grated Parmesan cheese, divided
- 6 oz. fresh mozzarella cheese in water, drained, thinly sliced

Direction

- Preheat the oven to 500 degrees F. In a big bowl, beat the first three ingredients. In a medium bowl, put the tomatoes then stir in crushed red pepper, oregano, and 2tbsp garlic oil. In the big bowl, toss chicken with the remaining garlic oil until coated.
- In a pie dish, scatter one cup of Parmesan. Coat one side on each chicken piece in cheese. Place the chicken on one half of a big rimmed baking sheet with the cheese-side up. Spread tomatoes on the sheet's other half.
- Roast chicken for 10mins until firm to touch and completely cooked. Top chicken with slices of mozzarella then place it back in the oven; roast for another 1-2mins until the

cheese melts. Move the tomatoes and chicken on four plates. Top with the remaining quarter cup Parmesan cheese.

Nutrition Information

- Calories: 657
- Total Carbohydrate: 7 g
- Cholesterol: 186 mg
- Total Fat: 42 g
- Fiber: 1 g
- Protein: 61 g
- Sodium: 870 mg
- Saturated Fat: 16 g

48. Orecchiette With Salsa Cruda And Ricotta

"I suggest using a plump late-summer tomatoes to produce ripe juices to infuse this quick, tasty pasta."
Serving: Makes 4 servings | Prep: 10m

Ingredients

- 1 medium shallot, minced
- 2 small garlic cloves, forced through a garlic press
- 2 tbsps. extra-virgin olive oil
- 1 1/2 lbs. tomatoes, chopped
- 1/4 tsp. hot red-pepper flakes
- 1/3 cup coarsely chopped basil
- 1 lb. dried orecchiette
- 3/4 cup ricotta (preferably fresh)
- Small basil leaves

Direction

- Combine all ingredients together except ricotta and pasta in a big bowl with half a tsp. of pepper and 3/4 tsp. of salt. Let it sit, while stirring from time to time for roughly 20 minutes.
- Meanwhile, fill in the pasta pot with salted water (put 3 tbsps. of salt for each 6 qt of water) and let it boil. Add the orecchiette and let it cook until al dente.
- Drain it well and mix with tomato salsa. Spice it up with pepper and salt and spoonful with ricotta.

49. Our Favorite Lasagna With Sausage, Spinach, And Three Cheeses

"This easy one-pan dish can feed a big crowd. It features the perfect blend of three cheese, spinach, and sausage. The sauce is really easy to make and you don't need to boil the noodles."
Serving: Makes 8 to 10 servings | Prep: 40m

Ingredients

- 1 tbsp. extra-virgin olive oil
- 1 lb. sweet Italian sausage, casings removed
- 1 medium onion, chopped
- 3/4 tsp. kosher salt
- 1/4 tsp. freshly ground black pepper
- 4 garlic cloves, minced
- 1/2 tsp. red-pepper flakes, plus more to taste
- 2 tbsps. tomato paste
- Two 28-oz. cans whole tomatoes
- 2 tsps. dried oregano
- Two 15-oz. containers part-skim ricotta cheese
- 1 1/2 cups packed basil leaves
- 1/2 cup grated Parmesan (about 2 oz.)
- 2 large egg yolks
- 3/4 tsp. kosher salt
- 1/4 tsp. freshly ground black pepper
- 2 10-oz. packages frozen chopped spinach, thawed, or 1 1/2 lbs. fresh spinach, steamed
- Pinch kosher salt
- Vegetable-oil cooking spray
- 9 no-boil lasagna noodles (such as Barilla)
- 1 lb. fresh mozzarella, grated (about 4 cups)
- 9 x 13 x 2-inch baking dish, preferably glass

Direction

- Place the rack in the top third of the oven then preheat to 375 degrees F.
- Prepare the sauce. On medium-high heat, heat oil in a big pot. Cook a quarter tsp. pepper,

sausage, 3/4tsp salt, and onion for 8-10mins while crumbling the sausage using a wooden spoon until completely cooked and brown. Turn to medium heat; add tomato paste, red pepper flakes, and garlic. Cook and stir for 1-2mins while mixing often until aromatic. Add oregano and the tomatoes with the juices; simmer and cook for 5mins while crumbling the tomatoes into small pieces using a wooden spoon. Taste and tweak the seasoning. If desired, put in more red pepper flakes.
- Prepare the filling. Process all the filling ingredients in a food processor until mostly smooth.
- Make the lasagna. In a clean dishcloth or paper towel, squeeze the spinach until very dry. Move to a bowl then sprinkle with a pinch of salt.
- Use cooking spray to coat a baking dish; spread two cups of sauce at the bottom. Add three noodles in a layer, 1/3 of ricotta mixture or 1 1/3 cups, then 1/3 of the spinach or 2/3 cups. Spread a cup of grated mozzarella on top.
- Repeat for another two times except the mozzarella on the 3rd layer. Spread the remaining sauce on top of the lasagna. Spread the remaining two cups mozzarella in bunches to let some sauce peek out.
- Put the pan on a rimmed baking sheet. Coat a piece of foil lightly with cooking spray then use to cover the lasagna; bake for 45mins. Discard the foil then bake for another 20mins until bubbly and light brown. Cool for at least 10mins then serve.
- You can make the sauce up to two days ahead then chilled. The filling can be made a day ahead then chilled.

Nutrition Information

- Calories: 726
- Total Carbohydrate: 39 g
- Cholesterol: 166 mg
- Total Fat: 45 g
- Fiber: 7 g
- Protein: 45 g
- Sodium: 1305 mg
- Saturated Fat: 21 g

50. Our Favorite Spaghetti And Meatballs

"The ultimate family dinner recipe."
Serving: Serves 6 | Prep: 1h45m

Ingredients

- 1/2 cup olive oil
- 12 garlic cloves, peeled
- 4 (28-oz.) cans whole tomatoes
- 1/2 tsp. red pepper flakes
- 2 dried bay leaves
- 2 tsps. kosher salt
- 1 1/2 tsps. dried oregano
- 1/2 teapoon freshly ground pepper
- 2/3 cup (packed) basil leaves
- 1 cup roughly torn day-old Italian bread
- 1 cup whole milk
- 8 oz. ground beef
- 8 oz. ground pork
- 8 oz. ground veal
- 3 large eggs, beaten to blend
- 4 garlic cloves, finely chopped
- 1 1/4 cups grated Parmesan, divided
- 3/4 cup coarsely chopped fresh parsley, divided
- 1 tsp. kosher salt, plus more
- 1 tsp. dried oregano
- 1/2 tsp. freshly ground black pepper
- 1/2 tsp. ground fennel seeds
- 1/2 tsp. red pepper flakes
- 1/4 cup olive oil
- 1 lb. spaghetti

Direction

- Tomato sauce: Heat wide big pot on medium low heat then add garlic and oil; cook for 8-10 minutes till all garlic sides are golden brown, occasionally mixing; if it begins to burn, lower heat. Break tomatoes up to smaller pieces with

- kitchen shears/paring knife as garlic cooks. When garlic is nearly ready, add red pepper flakes; cook for 30 seconds till fragrant and toasted, occasionally mixing. Add pepper, oregano, salt, bay leaves and tomatoes; mix till combined well, breaking tomatoes up with wooden spoon.
- Slightly increase heat; simmer gently for a minimum of 2-3 hours till flavors concentrate and sauce thickens, occasionally mixing.
- Meanwhile, make meatballs. Put bread in medium bowl and add milk; rest for 5 minutes till moist. Use your hands to squeeze bread to remove extra milk; discard milk then tear bread to smaller pea-sized pieces. Put back in medium bowl.
- Mix red pepper flakes, fennel, pepper, oregano, 1 tsp. salt, 1/2 cup parsley, 1 cup parmesan, garlic, eggs, veal, pork and beef in big bowl. Mix bread in gently with your hands till ingredients are distributed evenly; don't overmix.
- Use cool water to fill small bowl. Moisten your hands; shape meat between palms to golf ball-sized balls; moisten hands as needed occasionally. Put meatballs, you should have 24, on rimmed baking sheet; chill till sauce is finished.
- Finish sauce and cook pasta and meatballs: Pluck bay leaves out after 2-3 hours of simmering; add basil. Puree till slightly chunky yet not smooth with immersion blender/put sauce in blender/food processor, in batches if needed. Keep 1 1/2 cups sauce; keep leftover sauce in pot warm on very low heat.
- Heat big skillet on medium high heat; add oil. Add meatballs to skillet when hot; don't overcrowd. Brown on all sides in batches for 5 minutes per batch, frequently turning. As you brown the, put meatballs back on baking sheet.
- Add all meatballs when browned to pot with tomato sauce. Divide meatballs and sauce to 2 pots if pot isn't big enough. Put heat on medium low and cover; simmer for 10-15 minutes till meatballs cook through.
- Meanwhile, in big pot with boiling salted water, cook spaghetti till al dente, occasionally mixing. Drain; keep 1 cup pasta cooking liquid. Put pasta in pot on medium low heat. Put reserved 1 1/2 cups sauce on pasta; toss to coat. Add pasta cooking liquid as needed, quarter cup at one time, to coat pasta and loosen sauce.
- Divide pasta to plates; put leftover sauce and meatballs over. Sprinkle 1/4 cup parsley and leftover 1/4 cup parmesan.
- You can make sauce ahead, cooled and frozen for 3 months or refrigerated for 5 days; you can shape meatballs 1 day ahead, refrigerated. You can cook meatballs in sauce, cooled then refrigerated for 3 months frozen or 5 days refrigerated.
- You can increase beef and pork amounts to 12-oz. each if you can't get veal.

Nutrition Information

- Calories: 1062
- Total Carbohydrate: 85 g
- Cholesterol: 186 mg
- Total Fat: 60 g
- Fiber: 14 g
- Protein: 48 g
- Sodium: 2000 mg
- Saturated Fat: 17 g

51. Pan-fried Hawaiian Pizza

Serving: Makes 2 pizzas

Ingredients

- Olive oil, for frying and brushing
- 4 oz. ham or prosciutto, chopped
- 1 (16-oz. ball) homemade pizza dough or your favorite store-bought variety, split into 2 8-oz. balls
- 1 cup Pizza Sauce or your favorite store-bought variety
- 1 (8-oz. ball) fresh mozzarella, thinly sliced
- 1 1/2 cups pineapple cubes

- 4 or 5 fresh basil leaves, shredded

Direction

- Set the broiler for preheating.
- Pour a bit of oil on a medium cast-iron pan and add the ham, fry for roughly 3 minutes over medium-low heat until it turns a little brown and crispy. Set aside.
- Flatten every half of the pizza dough in to circles in the size of your cast-iron pan. The dough will most likely be a bit thicker than what you're used to.
- Set the pan over medium heat and pour about a tbsp. of olive oil. Put a piece of the rolled-out dough. Let it cook for roughly 2-3 minutes until the dough turns bubbly on top and the underneath have browned. Turn, put 1/2 of the sauce, 1/2 of the mozzarella, 1/2 of the pineapple, and half of the ham. Let it cook for additional 2 minutes, until the bottom is completely cooked. Slip under the broiler for roughly 2-3 minutes. Let it cook until the cheese appears bubbly and the pineapple is a little caramelized. Top if off with basil. Take the pizza off from the pan, and do the same with the remaining piece of dough.

52. Pan-seared Steak Pizzaiola

"I use an Italian tomato-based sauce for steak on this pizzaiola. It becomes amped up with crushed red pepper and fennel seeds. Serve this alongside a soft polenta."
Serving: Makes 4 servings | Prep: 20m

Ingredients

- 2 1/2 tbsps. extra-virgin olive oil, divided
- 1 1/2 tsps. dried oregano, divided
- 1/4 tsp. fennel seeds, crushed
- 1/4 tsp. dried crushed red pepper
- 2 large garlic cloves, pressed
- 1 14- to 16-oz. can diced organic tomatoes in juice
- 2 16-oz. boneless rib-eye steaks, each about 3/4 inch thick

Direction

- Add 2 tbsps. of oil in medium saucepan set over medium heat. Drop a tsp. of oregano and the next 3 ingredients; stir for half a minute. Put the tomatoes with its juices and make it to simmer while crushing them using the back of a fork. Lessen the heat and make it to simmer until it turns thick. Stir it from time to time for roughly 10 minutes. Spice it up with pepper and salt.
- Meanwhile, rub the pepper and salt on each sides of the steak, then crush a half a tsp. of the oregano finely using your fingertips and rub over steaks. Pour half a tbsp. of the olive oil in a hefty medium skillet placed over medium-high heat. Place the ribeye steaks and sauté until the steaks are cooked according to your preferred doneness, roughly 6 minutes each side for medium-rare.
- Slice the steaks into pieces and distribute between 4 plates. Pour the sauce on the skillet. Make it to a simmer while scraping up browned bits; pour the sauce over steaks using a spoon.

53. Pancetta And Taleggio Lasagna With Treviso

Ingredients

- 3 tbsps. extra-virgin olive oil
- 8 oz. thinly sliced pancetta (Italian bacon), chopped
- 2 cups thinly sliced celery hearts
- 1 2/3 cups chopped onion
- 1 lb. Treviso radicchio or red endive (4 medium heads), quartered lengthwise, cored, then cut on diagonal into thin strips (about 6 cups), divided
- 3 tsps. chopped fresh thyme, divided
- 1 garlic clove, finely chopped
- 9 lasagna noodles (each 7 x 3 inches)
- 1/4 cup (1/2 stick) unsalted butter

- 2 1/2 tbsps. all purpose flour
- 2 cups whole milk
- Pinch of ground nutmeg
- Pinch of ground white pepper
- 12 oz. Taleggio cheese,* rind removed, cheese cut into 1/2-inch cubes
- 1/2 cup finely grated Parmesan cheese, divided
- 2 tbsps. coarse dry breadcrumbs (preferably from crustless Italian bread)
- Olive oil

Direction

- Prepare the pasta and filling. On medium heat, heat oil in a big heavy pan. Sauté onion, celery, and pancetta in hot oil for 12mins until the veggies are soft yet not brown. Move half cup of Treviso slices to a small bowl then set aside for topping. Put garlic, 2tsp thyme, and the rest of the Treviso on the pan; stir for 3mins until it wilts. Sprinkle pepper and salt.
- In a big pot, cook lasagna noodles in boiling water while mixing from time to time until just tender yet firm to chew; drain. On a big plastic wrap sheet, place the noodles in one layer then use another sheet to cover to prevent from drying. You can make the pasta and filling 2hrs in advance. Let it sit at room temperature.
- Prepare the sauce. On medium-low heat, melt butter in a heavy medium pot. Whisk in flour for 2mins until the roux is light gold. Stir in milk gradually then add white pepper and nutmeg. Turn to medium heat then cook for 2-3mins while mixing regularly until the sauce is boiling and thick. Turn to low heat. In four batches, whisk in Taleggio cheese for 4mins, melt well before adding another. Sprinkle pepper and salt to taste.
- In a 13-in by 9-in by 2-in glass baking dish, spread half cup sauce to thinly cover the bottom. In the dish, lay three noodles side by side crosswise. Trim the noodle ends if needed to fit. Set aside 3/4 cup filling to a separate small bowl for topping. Scoop 1/2 of the remaining filling on top of the noodles. Spread 2/3 cup sauce then top with quarter cup Parmesan cheese. Repeat with the filling, noodles, Parmesan, and sauce. Put a 3rd layer of noodles on top then spread 2/3 cup sauce. Spread the reserved 3/4 cup filling lengthwise down the middle of the lasagna in 2-in wide strip. Use the remaining sauce to drizzle the strip then add breadcrumbs on top. You can make this a day in advance; cover then refrigerate. Let it sit for an hour at room temperature before resuming.
- Preheat the oven to 375 degrees F. Bake for 35mins without cover until the sauce is bubbling and completely heated. Take it out of the oven then cool the lasagna for 15mins.
- In a small bowl, mix the reserved Treviso, a sprinkle of pepper and salt, and a splash of olive oil. Spread on top of the filling strip. Top with the remaining 1tsp thyme.
- You can find the semisoft cheese at Italian markets and specialty food stores.

54. Pappardelle With Chicken And Mushroom Ragù

"Cheap and flavorful ragu with chicken thigh and cremini mushrooms."
Serving: Makes 4 servings | Prep: 30m

Ingredients

- 6 oz. cremini mushrooms
- 3 garlic cloves
- 1/4 cup extra-virgin olive oil
- 1 1/4 lbs. skinless boneless chicken thighs, cut into 1/2-inch pieces
- 1 small onion, chopped
- 3/4 tsp. chopped rosemary
- 3 tbsps. balsamic vinegar
- 1 (28-oz.) can whole tomatoes in juice
- 1/2 lb. dried pappardelle
- 5 oz. baby arugula (about 8 cups)
- Accompaniment: Grated Parmigiano-Reggiano

Direction

- In a food processor, finely chop the garlic and mushrooms.
- On medium-high heat, heat oil in a 12-in heavy pan until shimmering. Sprinkle quarter tsp. pepper and half tsp. salt over the chicken; cook for 3mins while mixing from time to time until just golden. Move to a bowl using a slotted spoon.
- Turn to medium heat; cook onion for 3mins while mixing from time to time until soft.
- Add a quarter tsp. pepper, the mushroom mixture, half tsp. salt, and rosemary; cook for 4mins while constantly mixing until it starts to brown.
- Pour in vinegar then cook until it evaporates. Add tomatoes with juice and chicken; let it simmer for 15mins while mixing from time to time and breaking the tomatoes using a spoon until the sauce is thick.
- In the meantime, cook pappardelle until al dente in a pasta pot with boiling salted water. For 6-qt water, there should be 2tbsp salt.
- Stir arugula in the sauce until it wilts. Mix in drained pasta then cook for another minute.

Nutrition Information

- Calories: 498
- Total Carbohydrate: 14 g
- Cholesterol: 139 mg
- Total Fat: 38 g
- Fiber: 5 g
- Protein: 27 g
- Sodium: 353 mg
- Saturated Fat: 8 g

55. Parmesan Toasts

Serving: Makes 4 servings

Ingredients

- 8 3/4-inch-thick slices Italian bread
- 1 medium garlic clove, halved
- Extra-virgin olive oil
- 1/2 cup finely grated Parmesan cheese
- Fleur de sel or course kosher salt

Direction

- Set the oven for preheating to 400°F. Assemble the bread on baking sheet. Rub each bread with garlic; drizzle with oil. Top it off with cheese. Scatter with fleur de sel. Let it bake for about 12 minutes until the edges turns lightly browned.

Nutrition Information

- Calories: 166
- Total Carbohydrate: 20 g
- Cholesterol: 10 mg
- Total Fat: 6 g
- Fiber: 1 g
- Protein: 8 g
- Sodium: 429 mg
- Saturated Fat: 3 g

56. Pasta Shells With Prosciutto, Ricotta And Mushrooms

Serving: Serves 2

Ingredients

- 12 jumbo pasta shells
- 3 tbsps. butter
- 2 oz. prosciutto, fat trimmed, chopped
- 2 large shallots, chopped
- 8 oz. cremini or button mushrooms, chopped (about 3 cups)
- 1/2 cup ricotta cheese
- 3 tbsps. chopped fresh basil or 1 tbsp. dried, crumbled
- 3 tbsps. chopped fresh parsley
- 1 15-oz. container prepared marinara sauce (about 2 cups)
- 1/2 cup freshly grated Parmesan cheese (about 2 oz.)

Direction

- Preheat the oven to 350 degrees F. In a big pot with boiling salted water, cook pasta until just tender but still firm to the bite. Mix from time to time to avoid sticking; drain.
- In the meantime, on medium-high heat, melt butter in a big heavy skillet. Put in chopped shallots and prosciutto and cook for around 4mins while frequently mixing until the shallots are translucent. Put in chopped mushrooms; cook for approximately 8mins until the juices evaporate and the mushrooms are tender. Take off the heat; mix in parsley, basil, and ricotta. Sprinkle pepper and salt to taste.
- In the bottom of an 8-in by 8-in baking dish, pour marinara sauce. Scoop one rounded tbsp. of mushroom mixture in each pasta shell; arrange in the prepared dish then add grated parmesan on top. You can prepare this a day in advance; cover then chill. Bake for around 20mins until thoroughly heated. Move shells to plates. Scoop sauce on top then serve.

Nutrition Information

- Calories: 1016
- Total Carbohydrate: 114 g
- Cholesterol: 131 mg
- Total Fat: 42 g
- Fiber: 12 g
- Protein: 49 g
- Sodium: 2374 mg
- Saturated Fat: 23 g

57. Pasta Tonnato Nests

Serving: 2 Servings, Can be doubled

Ingredients

- 8 to 9 oz. fresh or dried herb flavored fettuccine
- 1 1/2 tbsps. olive oil
- 1 cup purchased chunky garden style pasta sauce
- 1/4 cup dry red wine
- 1 6-oz. can solid white tuna packed in water, drained
- 1/4 cup sliced pitted brine-cured olives (such as Kalamata)
- 2 tbsps. chopped fresh basil

Direction

- Cook pasta for 10 minutes for dried, 2 minutes for fresh, till just tender yet firm to bite in big pot of boiling salted water; drain pasta. Put in same pot, tossing with oil.
- Simmer wine and sauce in medium heavy saucepan on medium heat; mix olives and tuna in, keeping tuna in fairly big pieces. Season with pepper and salt.
- Divide pasta to 2 plates; create indentation in middles of pasta to make "nests" with big spoon. Put sauce in middles and sprinkle basil on each.

Nutrition Information

- Calories: 708
- Total Carbohydrate: 101 g
- Cholesterol: 33 mg
- Total Fat: 16 g
- Fiber: 7 g
- Protein: 34 g
- Sodium: 882 mg
- Saturated Fat: 2 g

58. Pasta With 10-minute Pesto

"A vibrant pesto."
Serving: 4–6 servings | Prep: 10m

Ingredients

- 1 lb. pasta
- Kosher salt
- 1/3 cup plus 2 tbsps. pine nuts, divided

- 5 cups (loosely packed) basil leaves (about 2 oz.), plus more for serving
- 1 garlic clove, peeled, cut in half
- 1/2 cup extra-virgin olive oil
- 1 cup finely grated Parmesan, plus more for serving

Direction

- Cook pasta till al dente in a big pot of boiling salted water, occasionally mixing. Drain; keep 2 tbsp. of pasta cooking liquid.
- Meanwhile in a small skillet, toast 2 tbsp. of pine nuts on medium low heat for 2-3 minutes till lightly toasted, shaking skillet back and forth; put aside.
- Blanch 5 cups of basil for 30 seconds in a small pot with boiling water. Put into a big bowl with ice water using spider or slotted spoon.
- Puree leftover 1/3 cup of pine nuts, 1/2 tsp. of salt, oil and garlic till mixture is creamy and nuts are chopped very finely in a blender. Lift basil from ice water with your hands; shake excess yet not all water off leaves (a little of water will aid emulsification). Add to blender; puree just to combine then add 1 cup of parmesan and puree just to combine.
- Put pesto in medium bowl; mix in reserved pasta cooking liquid. Put pasta on a platter or a big serving bowl; toss with pesto. Put reserved toasted pine nuts and parmesan over; garnish with basil.

Nutrition Information

- Calories: 586
- Total Carbohydrate: 59 g
- Cholesterol: 13 mg
- Total Fat: 31 g
- Fiber: 3 g
- Protein: 18 g
- Sodium: 309 mg
- Saturated Fat: 6 g

59. Pasta With 15-minute Ham, Pea, And Cream Sauce

"This traditional creamy dish gets a bit of flair and added flavor from grated lemon zest."
Serving: 4-6 servings | Prep: 15m

Ingredients

- 1 lb. farfalle or other short pasta
- Kosher salt
- 3 tbsps. olive oil
- 1 cup thinly sliced shallots (about 2 large)
- 4 oz. thick-cut ham (about 4 slices), cut into thin strips
- 1 cup frozen or fresh shelled peas
- 1 cup heavy cream
- 1 tbsp. plus 1 1/2 tsps. finely grated lemon zest (from about 1 large lemon)
- 2 tbsps. finely chopped fresh flat-leaf parsley, plus more for serving
- Freshly ground black pepper
- Freshly grated Parmesan (for serving)

Direction

- In a big pot, cook the farfalle until al dente in boiling salted water while mixing from time to time; drain. Set aside two tbsps. of pasta cooking liquid.
- In the meantime, on medium-high heat, heat oil in a medium skillet. Cook half tsp. salt and shallots for approximately 5 mins while mixing from time to time until tender; avoid browning. Put in cream, peas, and ham; simmer. Cook for around 5 mins while mixing from time to time until the sauce is slightly thick. Take off the heat; mix in half tsp. pepper, two tbsps. parsley, and lemon zest.
- Put the pasta back in the pot. Mix with the reserved cooking liquid and sauce; sprinkle pepper and salt to season. Split between plates; add Parmesan and parsley on top. Sprinkle more pepper to season.

Nutrition Information

- Calories: 823

- Total Carbohydrate: 100 g
- Cholesterol: 97 mg
- Total Fat: 36 g
- Fiber: 8 g
- Protein: 24 g
- Sodium: 680 mg
- Saturated Fat: 16 g

60. Pasticciata Bolognese— Lasagna With Spinach Noodles And Bolognese Sauce

Serving: Serves 8-10 or more

Ingredients

- 1 recipe fresh Spinach Pasta Dough (page 178)
- 2 recipes (4 cups) besciamella (recipe follows)
- 4 cups Ragù alla Bolognese, either variety (page 143)*
- 2 to 3 tbsps. butter, for the baking pan
- 8 oz. freshly grated Parmigiano-Reggiano or Grana Padano (1 1/2 cups)
- 12 oz. Muenster cheese or low-moisture mozzarella, shredded or very thinly sliced (3 cups)

Direction

- Roll the pasta dough to wide thin sheets; cook briefly.
- Slightly warm Bolognese and besciamella in separate saucepans until spreadable and loose but not hot.
- If baking the pasticciata immediately, place a rack in the middle of the oven then preheat to 375 degrees F.
- Prepare the Base Layers: Use 1/3 cup besciamella to thinly coat the sides and bottom of the dish.
- Spread 1/3 Bolognese on top of the besciamella, over the bottom.
- Drape the pasta sheets along the length of the pan following the illustration until they completely cover the bottom of the dish and going over the short pan sides by about 6 in.
- Spread 1/3 cup besciamella on top of the pasta.
- Spread 1/3 cup Bolognese on top of the besciamella.
- Drape the pasta sheets across the pan width and perpendicular to the first sheets with the ends going over the pan sides by about 6-in. The sheets should completely cover the sides of the pan by now.
- Prepare the filling layers: Spread 2/3 cup besciamella on top of the pasta then top all over with a quarter cup grated cheese. In a thick layer, spread a cup of Bolognese then put 1/3 of the mozzarella or Muenster in slices or shredded to cover.
- Put another pasta layer on top to fit. It should now cover the inside of the pan only. Trim the sheets as needed to fit. Make another thick layer of filling using a cup of Bolognese, 2/3 cup besciamella, another 1/3 shredded cheese, and a quarter cup grated cheese.
- Place another pasta sheets layer then trim to fit. Add a final layer of filling over using a cup of Bolognese, 2/3 cup besciamella, last 1/3 shredded cheese, and a quarter cup grated cheese.
- Put another pasta layer on top of the filling, trim to fit.
- Prepare the topping layers: Spread one-third cup of besciamella on top of the pasta then scatter all over with 2 tbsp. grated cheese.
- Repeat with the last pasta layer followed by the besciamella and grated cheese.
- Fold all the overhanging pasta flaps over the pasticciata.
- Slice a pasta piece or use all the remaining pasta here to fit if the overhanging flaps don't meet and cover the surface.
- Spread the remaining Bolognese and besciamella then scatter all over with 2 tbsp. grated cheese.
- Tent then bake the dish: You can bake the dish later or on the following day, if wished. Use plastic wrap to cover then chill in the meantime.

- Tear a long foil sheet to make a tent then cover the pan before baking in the oven. It will allow the dish to cook inside before the surface turns brown. The foil should not touch the pasticciata in any part by arching the foil, crimp it against the outsides and rim of the pan to secure the pan position and make a good seal. Make 5-6 small holes on the foil using the tip of a sharp knife to poke so as to vent the steam.
- Place the pan on a baking sheet then place the sheet in the oven; bake for 45 mins or until bubbling. Check by peeking under the foil, the bubbling juices means that it's cooking through. Take the pan on the baking sheet out of the oven then discard the foil tent.
- Loosen at sides and carefully lift the foil to avoid from touching the surface of the sticky pasticciata. Place the pan back in the oven; bake for 20 mins more or so until the surface is crisp and deep-colored.
- Set it aside for 20min without a cover to settle. Slice into squares then serve.

61. Penne With Meat Sauce

Serving: Makes 4 servings

Ingredients

- 12 oz. whole-wheat penne
- Vegetable oil cooking spray
- 1/4 cup diced onion
- 1/2 cup diced green bell pepper
- 14 oz. lean (7% fat) ground turkey
- 2 1/4 cups prepared marinara
- 1 tbsp. freshly grated Parmesan

Direction

- Cook the pasta following the package instructions; set aside a quarter cup of cooking water. On medium-low heat, heat cooking spray in a big pan. Sauté pepper and onion in for 7mins until tender. Turn to medium heat then put in turkey; cook for 8mins until brown. Mix in marinara then lower heat. Mix from time to time for 6mins until it comes to a low simmer. In a bowl, combine the reserved water and half cup sauce; mix in sauce and pasta. Split between four bowls then evenly top with the rest of the sauce. Scatter Parmesan on top.

62. Pickled Fig, Robiola, & Pistachio Oil Crostini

"Bruschetta with pickled figs has a sweet and tangy taste."
Serving: Makes 12 servings

Ingredients

- 12 slices ciabatta bread
- 1/2 cup red wine vinegar
- 2 tbsps. sugar
- 6 dried figs
- 1/4 cup water
- 2 tbsps. pistachios, toasted and shelled
- 1/4 cup extra-virgin olive oil
- Robiola cheese

Direction

- In a saucepan, combine sugar, dried figs, a 1/4 cup of water, and red wine vinegar. Let the mixture simmer. Remove from the heat. Let it sit for half an hour until the figs soften.
- Cut the figs in half lengthwise. (You can also use 6 fresh figs and halve them lengthwise.)
- Crush the pistachios finely and combine them with extra-virgin olive oil.
- Grill the bread slices.
- In a warm toast, smear the room temperature Robiola cheese and top it with halved pigs. Drizzle over pistachio oil.

63. Pizza Bianca With Rosemary And Sea Salt

"You might think that from its name Pizza Blanca or white pizza that this Roman dish is like the usual pizza. In reality, it's just like seasoned flatbread that is best enjoyed with cheese and salami."
Serving: Makes 8 servings

Ingredients

- 1 1/2 lbs. fresh pizza dough or two 10-oz. purchased fully baked thin pizza crusts (such as Boboli)
- Extra-virgin olive oil
- 2 tsps. minced fresh rosemary, divided
- Sea salt

Direction

- Set the barbeque to medium-high heat. Halve the dough; spread each half to a ten-in round. Slather oil on one side of each baked crust or round dough; scatter half tsp. each of pepper, sea salt, and rosemary. Arrange with the seasoned side down on the grill. Slather oil on top then scatter half tsp. each of pepper, sea salt, and rosemary. Grill for 4mins on each side for fresh dough until golden or 2min on each side for the baked crust.
- Slice into wedges then serve.
- Enjoy this pizza with Arnaldo-Caprai 2006 "Grecante," Grechetto dei Colli Martani

Nutrition Information

- Calories: 241
- Total Carbohydrate: 43 g
- Total Fat: 4 g
- Fiber: 2 g
- Protein: 7 g
- Sodium: 521 mg
- Saturated Fat: 1 g

64. Pizza Dough

Ingredients

- 6 cups Flour
- 1 1/4 cups Semolina Flour
- 1 tsp. Salt
- 650 milliliters Warm Water
- 1/4 cup Olive Oil
- 3 tsp. Sugar
- 2 tsp. Yeast

Direction

- Preparation
- In a big bowl, mix salt and flour.
- Combine yeast, 150ml warm water, sugar, and olive oil.
- Pour the yeast, oil, and water into the bowl with salt and flour.
- Mix in 500ml warm water into the mixture; blend well.
- Let the dough sit for an hour.
- It can make four pizzas.

65. Pizza Margherita

"A good pizza shouldn't be overwhelmed with too much toppings. Even basic dough is enough to make a tasty grilled bread for the base. Form it like individual pizza then grill for two minutes per side on hot coals. After flipping, add olive oil, rosemary, oregano, thyme, and basil."
Serving: Makes 4 individual pizzas or 1 large pizza

Ingredients

- 3/4 cup warm (105-115°F) water
- 2 1/2 tsp (1 package) dry yeast
- 1 tsp honey
- 1 1/3 cups bread flour
- 1 cup semolina flour
- 1/4 tsp salt
- Vegetable oil for coating
- Cornmeal for sprinkling (optional)
- 1 Tbsp extra-virgin olive oil

- 1 Tbsp chopped fresh basil
- 1 tsp chopped fresh oregano
- 1 clove garlic, minced
- Freshly ground pepper
- 1 cup tomato purée
- 4 plum (Roma) tomatoes, sliced
- 4 1/4 oz part-skim mozzarella, thinly sliced
- 1/4 cup grated Parmesan

Direction

- In a big bowl, mix honey, yeast and water. Mix in enough bread flour until you have a batter with buttermilk consistency; cover. Store in a warm area for an hour until the top is puffy.
- Add salt, semolina flour, and the remaining bread flour. Knead by hand for 10mins or on medium speed in a stand mixer fitted with dough hook or by hand, 4 minutes with the mixer until the dough is elastic, springy, and smooth. Lightly massage oil all over the dough then put in a clean bowl; use cloth to cover. Store at room temperature for 1 1/2hrs until it rises and doubles in size.
- Press the dough down, sinking your fist into it until it deflates; leave it whole to make a big pizza or split equally into four parts for individual pizzas. Shape the dough into smooth ball(s) then cover; let it rise again for 45-60mins until it doubles in size.
- Preheat an oven to 450 degrees F. Grease a 16-in pizza pan or a big baking sheet lightly using vegetable oil or spread with cornmeal.
- Roll and stretch out the ball of doughs on a lightly floured surface evenly until a quarter inch thick. Stretch and spin simultaneously the dough to help in relax properly so it wouldn't spring back as you stretch it. You can do this on a flat surface or by tossing and spinning it in the air and catching it using the back of your hands. Avoid from making very thin patches or tearing the dough. Move the dough round to the prepared pan.
- To make the topping, combine pepper, garlic, oregano, basil and olive oil together to taste; evenly spread the mixture over the pizza dough. Evenly spread tomato purée then add mozzarella and sliced tomatoes on top; sprinkle with parmesan on top.
- Bake the individual pizza for 10-12mins or one large pizza for 20-30mins until the toppings are very hot and the dough is golden brown. Slice into wedges then serve right away or cool for 5-10mins then serve warm.

Nutrition Information

- Calories: 538
- Total Carbohydrate: 76 g
- Cholesterol: 24 mg
- Total Fat: 16 g
- Fiber: 6 g
- Protein: 23 g
- Sodium: 454 mg
- Saturated Fat: 5 g

66. Polenta Cacio E Pepe

"Cook this dish the old-fashioned way if you don't have any pressure cooker to use."
Serving: 4 servings

Ingredients

- 1 cup polenta (not quick-cooking)
- 1 tsp. kosher salt, plus more
- Freshly ground black pepper
- 3 tbsps. unsalted butter
- 4 oz. Pecorino and/or Parmesan, finely grated, plus more
- A pressure cooker

Direction

- Stir 4 cups of water with the polenta in pressure cooker until mixed well. Spice it up with several grinds of pepper and 1 tsp. of salt. Make the mixture to a simmer over medium-high, stir again and secure the pressure cooker following the manufacturer's instructions. Once the cooker hits its high pressure, set the timer for 9 minutes. Once the timer is done, take it off the heat and release the pressure

manually. Open the lid carefully and stir the polenta until creamy and homogenous.
- Stir the butter into polenta, then add 4 oz. Pecorino little by little, stirring until it melts. Taste and spice up with extra salt, if necessary, and lots of pepper.
- Place the polenta to a wide shallow bowl and garnish with additional cheese and grind more pepper coarsely on top.

67. Pressure-cooker Mini Meatballs With Radiatori

"Radiatori, from the name itself, is a small pasta that resembles radiators. In this recipe, the firm pasta complements the texture of meatballs."
Serving: Serves 4

Ingredients

- 1 lb. lean ground beef (preferably 93% lean)
- 1 tbsp. dried basil
- 1 tsp. dried marjoram
- 1/2 tsp. dried thyme
- 2 tbsps. olive oil
- 1 large fennel bulb, trimmed and chopped
- 1 medium yellow onion, chopped
- 1 medium red bell pepper, stemmed, cored, and chopped
- 8 oz. dried radiatori
- 1 (28-oz.) can diced tomatoes (about 3 1/2 cups)
- 1 cup chicken broth
- 1/2 cup dry white wine, such as Chardonnay
- 1 tbsp. dried oregano
- 1/2 tsp. dried rosemary
- 1/2 tsp. grated nutmeg
- 1/4 tsp. salt

Direction

- In a bowl, thoroughly combine thyme, beef, marjoram, and basil. Make 20 1-inch meatballs from the mixture.
- If using a stove top 6 qt. pressure cooker, heat oil on medium heat. If not, set the 6 qt. electric pressure cooker to the browning mode. Cook bell pepper, onion, and fennel for 5 minutes until the onion is translucent; stir regularly.
- Mix in pasta, salt, tomatoes, nutmeg, broth, rosemary, wine, and oregano. Cover the meatballs in sauce.
- Secure the pot's lid.
- If using a stovetop, turn heat to high and set to high pressure, about 15 lbs. per square inch. Once at this pressure, adjust the heat to maintain it; cook for 5 minutes.
- If using an electric cooker, program it to cook at the maximum pressure, about 9 to 11 lbs. per square inch. Keep the pressure at high and set the timer for 8 minutes.
- Release the pressure using the quick-release method.
- Uncover. Mix gently and serve.
- One important note is to make sure that the meatballs are completely covered in sauce before locking the cooker. This way, it can absorb more flavors.

Nutrition Information

- Calories: 600
- Total Carbohydrate: 64 g
- Cholesterol: 76 mg
- Total Fat: 21 g
- Fiber: 10 g
- Protein: 35 g
- Sodium: 373 mg
- Saturated Fat: 6 g

68. Presto Pesto Pizza

Serving: Serves 4 to 6

Ingredients

- 1 1/2 cups (packed) stemmed spinach leaves
- 1/2 cup (packed) fresh basil leaves (about 1 bunch)
- 1 1/2 tbsps. oil from oil-packed sun-dried tomatoes or olive oil
- 1 large garlic clove

- Nonstick vegetable oil spray
- 1 1-lb. loaf frozen bread dough, thawed, room temperature
- 1/3 cup sliced drained oil-packed sun-dried tomatoes
- 2 cups (packed) grated mozzarella cheese (about 8 oz.)
- 1 cup grated Parmesan cheese

Direction

- In a processor, blend the first four ingredients to form coarse puree. Place the pesto in a small bowl. (You can prepare one day ahead. Push plastic directly on the surface of the pesto to cover and then chill).
- Preheat the oven to 375 degrees F. Use vegetable oil spray to spritz a 12-inch-diameter pizza pan. Press the dough out onto the prepared pan to cover completely using moistened fingertips (in case the dough shrinks, allow to stand five minutes and then press out once again). Pour all of pesto atop dough. Drizzle with sun-dried tomatoes and then add the cheeses. Bake the pizza for about 35 minutes until the cheeses have melted and the crust turns brown.

Nutrition Information

- Calories: 659
- Total Carbohydrate: 63 g
- Cholesterol: 70 mg
- Total Fat: 30 g
- Fiber: 4 g
- Protein: 34 g
- Sodium: 1527 mg
- Saturated Fat: 15 g

69. Prosciutto And Fig Panini

"This sweet and savory pressed sandwich features dried figs and prosciutto."
Serving: Makes 8 servings

Ingredients

- 1 cup water
- 1 cup Port
- 1 cup (lightly packed) dried black Mission figs (about 7 oz.), stemmed, halved
- 1 tbsp. dried rosemary
- 2 medium red onions, cut crosswise into 1/4-inch-thick rounds
- 2 tbsps. chilled butter, diced
- 8 ciabatta rolls, halved horizontally
- 8 thin slices prosciutto (3 to 4 oz.)
- 7 oz. shaved Asiago cheese

Direction

- In a small saucepan, boil rosemary, a cup of water, figs, and Port. Turn to medium-low heat; let it simmer for approximately 20 mins while mixing from time to time until the mixture reduces to a generous 1 1/4 cup; slightly cool. In a processor, puree the mixture until smooth. You can prepare the Fig jam three days in advance; cover then refrigerate.
- Preheat the oven to 400 degrees F. On a rimmed baking sheet, arrange the onion rounds then dot with butter; sprinkle pepper and salt. Roast for around 45 mins until golden and tender. This can be made two hours in advance. Let it sit at room temperature.
- At the bottom of each ciabatta roll, spread approximately 1 1/2 tbsp. fig jam. Add cheese, prosciutto, and onions on top then put on each with the roll tops. This can be prepared 2 hrs. in advance. Let it sit at room temperature.
- In a Panini press, cook the Panini following the manufacturer's directions. Or you can also heat a big heavy skillet on medium heat. In batches, put the Panini in the skillet. Put a big cast iron pan or other heavy skillet over the Panini. Weigh the pan down with big cans or bricks. Cook for around 4 mins until the rolls

are golden at the bottom. Remove the skillet on top then flip over the Panini; replace the pan on top the panini. Cook for around another 4 mins until the cheese melts and the Panini is golden. Slice in half to serve.

Nutrition Information

- Calories: 523
- Total Carbohydrate: 66 g
- Cholesterol: 33 mg
- Total Fat: 10 g
- Fiber: 6 g
- Protein: 22 g
- Sodium: 1214 mg
- Saturated Fat: 6 g

70. Quick Tomato Sauce

"If you have tomatoes, olive oil, and garlic in the pantry, you're always sure to make a great sauce. This basic sauce can be given so much variation by mix and matching herbs and the like."
Serving: 9 | Ready in: 25m

Ingredients

- 1 tbsp. extra-virgin olive oil
- 4 cloves garlic, minced
- 1/8 tsp. crushed red pepper
- 2 14-oz. cans diced tomatoes, (not drained)
- Pinch of salt
- Freshly ground pepper to taste

Direction

- In a large and heavy saucepan, heat oil over medium-low heat until it becomes warm. Put in the crushed red pepper and garlic; cook and stir for 30-60 seconds, until they turn fragrant and soft. Place the tomatoes into the pan and use a potato masher to mash. Let it simmer over medium-high heat. Lower the heat to medium. Allow it to cook without the cover, making sure to stir and mash once in a while, for about 20 to 25 minutes until thickened. Season to taste with salt and pepper.

Nutrition Information

- Calories: 34 calories;
- Total Carbohydrate: 5 g
- Cholesterol: 0 mg
- Total Fat: 2 g
- Fiber: 1 g
- Protein: 1 g
- Sodium: 156 mg
- Sugar: 3 g
- Saturated Fat: 0 g

71. Ramp And Sausage Risotto

"This spring risotto features sausage but you can also use the sweet variations if you don't like it spicy."
Serving: Makes 4 servings

Ingredients

- 2 tbsps. (1/4 stick) butter
- 1/2 lb. hot Italian sausages, casings removed
- 12 ramps, trimmed; bulbs and slender stems sliced, green tops thinly sliced
- 1 cup arborio rice
- 1/2 cup dry vermouth
- 3 cups (or more) low-salt chicken broth
- 1/2 cup freshly grated Parmesan cheese plus additional for passing

Direction

- On medium heat, melt butter in a big heavy saucepan. Cook and crumble sausage with a spoon for approximately 5 mins until the sausage is not pink anymore. Add the sliced ramp stems and bulbs; sauté for around 2 mins until nearly tender. Mix in rice for a minute the pour in the vermouth; let it simmer for around a minute until the liquid is absorbed. A cup at a time, pour in three cups of chicken broth; simmer and stir frequently until nearly absorbed before adding the next cup. Keep cooking for approximately 18 mins until the risotto is creamy and the rice is just tender, pour more broth if it looks dry. Stir in half cup grated Parmesan cheese and green tops; sprinkle pepper and salt to taste into the risotto. Serve separately with more grated cheese.

Nutrition Information

- Calories: 549
- Total Carbohydrate: 47 g
- Cholesterol: 68 mg
- Total Fat: 29 g
- Fiber: 3 g
- Protein: 21 g
- Sodium: 673 mg
- Saturated Fat: 13 g

72. Rigatoni With Eggplant And Pine Nut Crunch

"It might take a bit of effort to make this filling rigatoni that is packed with vegetables but the flavor is definitely worth it."
Serving: 8 servings | Prep: 40m

Ingredients

- Nonstick vegetable oil spray
- 1 unpeeled large eggplant (1 1/2 to 1 3/4 lbs.), cut into 1/2-inch cubes
- 2 medium yellow bell peppers, cut into 1/2-inch squares
- 2 cups grape tomatoes
- 3 large garlic cloves, divided
- 1/3 cup olive oil
- 2 cups (firmly packed) fresh basil leaves, divided
- 1 cup freshly grated Parmesan cheese, divided
- 1/4 cup pine nuts
- 1 28-oz. can whole tomatoes in juice
- 1 cup heavy whipping cream
- 1 lb. rigatoni
- 1 lb. whole-milk mozzarella cheese, cut into 1/2-inch cubes

Direction

- Preheat the oven to 425 degrees F. Use a non-stick spray to coat a big rimmed baking sheet; put in peppers and eggplant. Halve the tomatoes lengthwise then place on the sheet. Squeeze a clove of garlic in a garlic press then add over the veggies. Dribble with oil then mix. Season with pepper and salt. Roast for 35-45mins while mixing often until the veggies are tender.
- In a mini processor, blend one garlic clove, 2/3 cup basil, pine nuts, and half cup parmesan until crumbly; sprinkle salt.
- In a processor, blend one garlic clove, tomatoes with juice, 1 1/3 cup basil, and cream until smooth; sprinkle pepper and salt.
- In a pot with boiling salted water, cook pasta while mixing from time to time until tender yet firm to chew; drain. Put the pasta back in the pot then mix with half cup Parmesan, sauce, and the vegetables. Move to a 13-in by 9-in by 2-in baking dish. Top with pine nut topping and mozzarella.
- Bake for 25-35mins until completely heated. Let it sit for 10mins. Serve.

Nutrition Information

- Calories: 892
- Total Carbohydrate: 60 g
- Cholesterol: 150 mg
- Total Fat: 62 g
- Fiber: 7 g
- Protein: 30 g
- Sodium: 740 mg
- Saturated Fat: 27 g

73. Salmon Panzanella With Green Beans

"You can get your dose of omega 3 fatty acids and vitamin c in this filling Italian bread salad with rich green beans."
Serving: Makes 4 servings

Ingredients

- Vegetable oil cooking spray
- 1 lb. salmon fillet, skin removed
- 1/2 tsp. salt, divided
- 1/4 tsp. black pepper, divided
- 1/2 lb. green beans, cut into 1-inch pieces
- 3 tbsps. extra-virgin olive oil
- 1 tbsp. plus 1 teasoon red wine vinegar
- 2 cups cherry tomatoes, halved
- 1 cup thinly sliced red onion
- 8 oz. whole-wheat baguette, cut into 1-inch cubes
- 1/2 cup fresh basil, cut into thin strips

Direction

- Preheat the broiler to low. Use cooking spray to grease a baking sheet. Sprinkle 1/8tsp pepper and quarter tsp. salt over the salmon; broil for 5mins on each side until completely cooked. Cool the salmon. Boil water in a small pot. Cook beans for 3mins in boiling water until tender-crisp and bright green; drain then set the beans aside. In a serving bowl, stir the remaining 1/8tsp pepper, oil, remaining quarter tsp. salt, and vinegar; toss in basil, beans, bread cubes, onion, and tomatoes. Flake the salmon then gently toss in the salad. Let it stand for 10mins. Serve.

74. Sausage Meatball Sandwiches

"This dish features the perfect combination of sweet and spicy Italian sausage. You can also use your preferred uncooked sausage in this recipe."
Serving: Serves 4 | Prep: 1h15m

Ingredients

- 1 1/2 lbs. hot and/or sweet Italian sausage, casings removed
- 8 tbsps. olive oil, divided
- 1 fennel bulb, core removed, thinly sliced
- 1 large onion, chopped
- 10 cloves garlic, thinly sliced, divided
- Kosher salt, freshly ground pepper
- 1 28-oz. can whole peeled tomatoes
- 1 cup (packed) basil leaves
- 4 soft hoagie rolls, split lengthwise down tops
- 4 oz. fresh mozzarella, sliced

Direction

- Roll the sausage lightly into a dozen balls with the size of a golf ball using damp hands. On medium heat, heat two tbsps. oil in another heavy pot or a big Dutch oven. Cook meatballs for 10-12 mins until all over is browned, turning from time to time; move to a plate.
- In the same pot, put two tbsps. oil, fennel, 1/2 of garlic, and onion; sprinkle pepper and salt to season. Cook for 8-10 mins while mixing frequently until the onion is golden brown on the edges and translucent.
- Put in tomatoes, use your hands to crush as you put in the pot; simmer. Sprinkle pepper and salt to season. Cook for 5-8 mins while mixing from time to time until the sauce just starts to become thick.
- Place the meatballs back in the pot; simmer. Cook for 15-20 mins while mixing from time to time until the meatballs are thoroughly cooked and coated and the sauce is reduced by half.
- In the meantime, preheat the broiler. In a food processor, process the remaining four tbsp. oil, the remaining garlic, and basil until it turns to

a smooth paste. Sprinkle pepper and salt to season. Smear 1/2 of the basil mixture on the cut sides of the rolls; arrange on a rimmed baking sheet. Broil for around 2 mins until golden brown.
- Put meatballs inside the rolls then add mozzarella and sauce on top. Broil for approximately 5 mins until the mozzarella is bubbling and melted. Scoop the rest of the basil mixture on top of the sandwiches.

75. Shaved Raw Brussels Sprouts With Castelrosso

"This fresh Italian-style salad has the basic ingredients that you can find in an Italian kitchen like olive oil, Italian cheese, fresh veggies, and Brussels sprouts."
Serving: Serves 4

Ingredients

- 2 pints Brussels sprouts
- 1/2 cup plus 1 tbsp. olive oil
- 1/2 cup freshly squeezed lemon juice
- 1/2 tsp. fine sea salt
- 1/4 tsp. freshly ground white pepper
- 1 cup crumbled Castelrosso cheese (about 4 oz.)
- Black pepper

Direction

- Remove the limp and dark leaves from the sprouts then slice the bottoms off. Halve the sprouts through the core then cut widthwise as thin as possible. Make sure to use a sharp knife to make the shaved sprouts.
- Move to a mixing bowl. You can shave the sprouts a few hours ahead, cover then chill until ready to serve.
- In a wide mixing bowl, beat white pepper, olive oil, salt, and lemon juice. By handful, toss in the shredded sprouts. Once coated, split the sprouts among salad bowls then top with a quarter cup crumbled cheese on each. Put a

grinder with black pepper on the table to serve.

Nutrition Information

- Calories: 430
- Total Carbohydrate: 11 g
- Cholesterol: 29 mg
- Total Fat: 40 g
- Fiber: 4 g
- Protein: 10 g
- Sodium: 414 mg
- Saturated Fat: 10 g

76. Shrimp And Pancetta On Polenta

"The combination of the pancetta and shrimp join forces with rich instant polenta in an Italian twist on a southern favorite, grits and shrimp."
Serving: Makes 4 servings | Prep: 25m

Ingredients

- 1/2 cup instant polenta
- 1/4 lb. pancetta, chopped
- 2 garlic cloves, minced
- 1/4 tsp. hot red pepper flakes
- 3 tbsps. extra-virgin olive oil, divided
- 1 (14-oz.) can diced tomatoes in juice
- 1 lb. cleaned large shrimp
- 1 tbsp. chopped flat-leaf parsley

Direction

- Prepare the polenta and cook following the package instructions in a heavy medium saucepan until it gets thick and creamy, cook for roughly 5 minutes. Take off the heat and spice it up with salt, and place a cover.
- Cook the garlic, red pepper flakes and pancetta in 2 tbsp. of oil in a 12-inch hefty skillet set over medium heat. Stir for about 2 to 3 minutes until the garlic turns golden pale. Add the tomatoes with its juices and make it to simmer for 6 to 8 minutes until the liquid

has evaporates to about a quarter cup. Drop the shrimp and stir from time to time while it cooks, until the shrimp are just cooked well, roughly 3 minutes. Spice it up with salt.
- Put the polenta into shallow bowls and top it off with shrimp mixture. Pour the remaining tbsp. of oil, sprinkle with pepper, and garnish with parsley.

Nutrition Information

- Calories: 380
- Total Carbohydrate: 21 g
- Cholesterol: 162 mg
- Total Fat: 23 g
- Fiber: 3 g
- Protein: 21 g
- Sodium: 842 mg
- Saturated Fat: 6 g

77. Smoked Trout Crostini With Grilled Fennel And Red Onion

Serving: Makes 10 servings

Ingredients

- 20 1/2-inch-thick diagonal slices crusty baguette
- 20 1/2-inch wedges fresh fennel bulb (from about 2 large bulbs), fronds reserved for garnish
- 20 1/2-inch wedges red onion (from 2 large onions)
- Olive oil
- 3 4 1/2-oz. packages skinless smoked trout fillets,* broken into chunks

Direction

- Arrange the vegetables and bread on separate baking sheets; brush each side with oil and season with pepper and salt.
- Preheat the barbecue to medium-high heat or you can also use a broiler. Broil or grill the bread for roughly 2 minutes for each side if grilling until crisp and 1 to 2 minutes per side if broiling. Grill or broil the vegetables for roughly 4 minutes each side if grilling until just softened and golden; 3 to 4 minutes for each side if broiled. Take note that this can be prepared 2 hours in advanced. Let it sit at room temperature.
- Arrange the vegetables, trout and bread on big serving platter. Top it off with fennel fronds. Serve while letting the guests to assemble crostini.
- This can be bought at some supermarkets and at delicatessens and specialty foods stores.

78. Spaghetti Pie

"Beef and pasta casserole made with low-fat cottage cheese and lean ground beef."
Serving: 6 | Prep: 35m | Ready in: 1h25m

Ingredients

- Nonstick cooking spray
- 4 oz. dried spaghetti
- 2 egg whites, lightly beaten
- ⅓ cup grated Parmesan cheese
- 1 tbsp. olive oil
- 2 egg whites, lightly beaten
- 1 (12 oz.) container (1¼ cups) low-fat cottage cheese, drained
- 8 oz. uncooked ground turkey breast or 90% or higher lean ground beef
- 1 cup sliced fresh mushrooms
- ½ cup chopped onion
- ½ cup chopped green and/or red sweet pepper
- 2 cloves garlic, minced
- 1 (8 oz.) can no-salt-added tomato sauce
- 1½ tsps. dried Italian seasoning, crushed
- ⅛ tsp. salt
- ½ cup shredded part-skim mozzarella cheese (2 oz.)

Direction

- Set an oven to preheat to 350 degrees F. Use nonstick cooking spray to coat a 9-inch pie plate, then put aside. To make the crust: Cook the spaghetti following the package instructions but omit the cooking oil and salt. In the meantime, mix together the olive oil, Parmesan cheese and 2 turkey egg whites in a medium bowl. Drain the spaghetti well, then add it to the egg white mixture and toss until coated. Evenly press the spaghetti mixture into the bottom and up the side of the prepped pie plate, then put aside.
- Mix together the drained cottage cheese and 2 egg whites in a small bowl. Spread the cottage cheese mixture on top of the crust in the pie plate, then put aside.
- Cook the garlic, sweet pepper, onion, mushrooms and turkey in a big frying pan until the meat turns brown, then drain off the fat. Stir the salt, Italian seasoning and tomato sauce into the meat mixture in the frying pan. In the crust, spoon over the cottage cheese mixture.
- Let it bake until heated through or for about 20 minutes, then sprinkle mozzarella cheese on top. Let it bake until the cheese melts or for around 5 more minutes. Allow it to stand for 15 minutes prior to serving and slice it into 6 wedges, then serve.

Nutrition Information

- Calories: 256 calories;
- Total Carbohydrate: 23 g
- Cholesterol: 27 mg
- Total Fat: 7 g
- Fiber: 2 g
- Protein: 26 g
- Sodium: 479 mg
- Sugar: 6 g
- Saturated Fat: 3 g

79. Spaghetti With Cremini Mushrooms, Lemon, And Thyme

Serving: Makes 4 servings | Prep: 45m

Ingredients

- 1 lb spaghetti
- 1 cup coarse fresh bread crumbs (from 2 slices firm white sandwich bread)
- 3 tbsps. olive oil
- 1 tsp. salt
- 1/2 stick (1/4 cup) unsalted butter
- 1 1/2 lb cremini mushrooms, trimmed and cut into 1/4-inch-thick slices (6 cups)
- 1 tsp. freshly grated lemon zest
- 3 garlic cloves, chopped (1 tbsp.)
- 1 tsp. Worcestershire sauce
- 2 tbsps. fresh lemon juice
- 1 tsp. minced fresh thyme
- 1/2 tsp. black pepper
- 2 tbsps. minced fresh parsley
- 1 oz finely grated Parmigiano-Reggiano (1/2 cup) plus additional for serving
- Garnish: lemon wedges

Direction

- In a big pot, cook pasta until almost al dente in boiling salted water.
- Meanwhile, in a bowl, combine quarter tsp. salt, 1tbsp olive oil, and bread crumbs. Move to a 12-in heavy pan. On medium heat, cook and stir for 3-5mins until golden; return to the bowl.
- On medium-high heat, heat the remaining 2tbsp oil and 2tbsp butter in a pan until the foam is gone; sauté and stir mushrooms for 4mins until golden. Put in garlic and zest; sauté and stir for 3mins until it releases liquid. Pour in lemon juice and Worcestershire sauce; cook for 2mins until almost all the liquid evaporates. Mix in the remaining 3/4tsp salt, pepper, and thyme.
- Set aside one cup of pasta water. Use a colander to drain the pasta.

- Move mushrooms in the pasta pot; pour in half cup of the reserved pasta water then boil. Mix in the remaining 2tbsp butter and parsley. Put the pasta back in the pot then toss with cheese to blend. Pour more cooking water to moisten if the pasta looks dry.
- Serve pasta with more cheese and bread crumbs on top.

Nutrition Information

- Calories: 764
- Total Carbohydrate: 113 g
- Cholesterol: 31 mg
- Total Fat: 25 g
- Fiber: 6 g
- Protein: 23 g
- Sodium: 810 mg
- Saturated Fat: 9 g

and toss for 4mins until all the mussels open up.
- In the meantime, cook pasta in boiling water until al dente; drain thoroughly.
- Put pasta into the mussels then cook for a minute on high heat; put in parsley. Sprinkle pepper and salt to taste. Add red pepper flakes then serve right away.

Nutrition Information

- Calories: 659
- Total Carbohydrate: 97 g
- Cholesterol: 64 mg
- Total Fat: 7 g
- Fiber: 4 g
- Protein: 42 g
- Sodium: 899 mg
- Saturated Fat: 1 g

80. Spaghetti With Mussels (spaghetti Con Le Cozze)

"This tasty Italian pasta dish features fresh shellfish with parsley, garlic, and white wine sauce."
Serving: Serves 4

Ingredients

- 1/2 extra-virgin olive oil
- 4 cloves garlic, thinly sliced
- 1 cup dry white wine
- 2 lbs. small mussels, scrubbed and debearded
- 1 lb. spaghetti
- 1/4 cup finely chopped Italian parsley
- Salt and freshly ground black pepper
- 1 tbsp. hot red pepper flakes

Direction

- Boil 6-qt. water and 2tbsp salt in a big pot.
- On medium-high heat, heat olive oil in a 12-in sauté pan. Cook garlic in hot oil for a minute until golden brown; pour in wine. Turn the heat up then boil; put in mussels. Cook, stir

81. Spaghetti With No-cook Tomato Sauce And Hazelnuts

"The body and texture of this tomato sauce came from toasted nuts that are incorporated in the base plus the zucchini. You can also use hazelnuts in place of the almonds."
Serving: 4 Servings

Ingredients

- 1/2 cup blanched hazelnuts
- 1 lb. cherry tomatoes, halved
- 1 tsp. kosher salt, plus more
- 12 oz. spaghetti or linguine
- 1 beefsteak tomato, chopped
- 2 garlic cloves, crushed
- 1 tsp. crushed red pepper flakes
- 1 cup basil leaves, divided
- 2 small zucchini (about 8 oz.), coarsely grated
- 1/4 cup olive oil, plus more for drizzling
- Freshly ground black pepper
- 1 oz. ricotta salata (salted dry ricotta), shaved

Direction

- Preheat the oven to 350 degrees F. On a rimmed baking sheet, toast the hazelnuts for 8-10 mins until golden brown, toss one time. Cool the hazelnuts then chop coarsely.
- In a big bowl, put the cherry tomatoes then sprinkle salt to season.
- In a big pot, cook the spaghetti until al dente while mixing from time to time in boiling salted water; drain. Set aside a quarter cup of the pasta cooking liquid.
- Meanwhile, in a food processor, puree 1 tsp. salt, beefsteak tomato, 3 tbsp. chopped hazelnuts, garlic, half-cup basil, and red pepper flakes until smooth. Move to the bowl with salted cherry tomatoes. Toss in zucchini, remaining half cup basil leaves, spaghetti, a quarter cup oil, and pasta cooking liquid and mix to combine. Sprinkle pepper and salt to season.
- Split the pasta between bowls then drizzle with additional oil. Add the remaining hazelnuts and ricotta salata on top.

Nutrition Information

- Calories: 596
- Total Carbohydrate: 75 g
- Cholesterol: 4 mg
- Total Fat: 27 g
- Fiber: 7 g
- Protein: 17 g
- Sodium: 494 mg
- Saturated Fat: 4 g

82. Spaghetti With Red Clam Sauce

"Break out your usual red-checkered tablecloth once you make this briny, spicy and excellently balanced variation of the Italian-American staple at home."
Serving: Makes 4 to 6 servings | Prep: 20m

Ingredients

- 1/3 cup olive oil
- 3 large garlic cloves, chopped
- 1/2 tsp. dried hot red-pepper flakes
- 1 (28- to 32-oz.) can whole tomatoes in juice, coarsely chopped, reserving juice
- 2 tsps. sugar
- 1 lb. spaghetti
- 3 dozen hard-shelled clams such as littlenecks

Direction

- Pour the oil in a 12-14-inch hefty skillet set over medium heat. Heat the oil until it shimmers; drop the garlic with red-pepper flakes, cooking them while stirring for 1 to 2 minutes until it turns pale golden. Drop the tomatoes with its juices, 1/2 tsp. salt and sugar then simmer briskly without any cover. Stir the mixture from time to time for about 7-10 minutes until the consistency turns thick.
- Fill a pasta pot of salted water and allow to boil (place about 3 tbsps. of salt for each 6 quarts of water) Place the spaghetti and let it cook until al dente.
- Meanwhile, drop the clams (in shells) in the sauce mixture and cook while covered. Shake the skillet from time to time for about 6 to 10 minutes until each clams open wide (dispose any clams that remain unopened after 10 minutes). Place the clams (still in shells) as cooked on a big shallow bowl. If the sauce ended up too watery, let it boil for about 2 minutes until slightly thickened.
- Drain the spaghetti. Place the clams back to the sauce and add the pasta. Toss them well.

83. Spicy Cheese Pizza Bread

"This tasty and filling dish with three cheeses is perfect if you want an easy meal to make after a busy day at work. You can also serve it as an appetizer or a side for pasta, salad, or soup."
Serving: Makes 4 to 6 servings

Ingredients

- 1 2-lb. uncut sourdough or Italian bread round (about 9-inch diameter)

- Olive oil
- 1 1/4 cups grated Fontina cheese
- 1 1/4 cups grated provolone cheese
- 1 1/4 cups crumbled feta cheese
- 1 1/2 tsps. dried oregano
- 1/2 tsp. (generous) dried crushed red pepper
- 2/3 cup chopped seeded tomatoes
- 1/2 cup chopped pitted Kalamata olives or other brine-cured black olives

Direction

- Preheat the oven to 350 degrees F. Slice two half-inch thick circles crosswise from the middle of the bread. Set the remaining bread aside for another use. Lightly brush oil on each side of the bread rounds; arrange on a baking sheet. Bake for 15mins until starting to crisp; cool bread for 5mins. Put 1/2 of cheeses, crushed red pepper, and oregano on top of each round. Scatter 1/2 of tomatoes and olives on each. Bake for 15mins until crisp at the bottom and the cheeses melt. Slice into wedges.

Nutrition Information

- Calories: 1106
- Total Carbohydrate: 116 g
- Cholesterol: 118 mg
- Total Fat: 48 g
- Fiber: 10 g
- Protein: 52 g
- Sodium: 2385 mg
- Saturated Fat: 25 g

84. Spinach, Pesto, And Fontina Lasagna

"This vegetarian main dish features delicious homemade mixed herb pesto."
Serving: Makes 8 servings

Ingredients

- 2 tbsps. (1/4 stick) unsalted butter
- 1/4 cup all purpose flour
- 2 1/2 cups reduced-fat (2%) milk
- 1/2 cup dry white wine
- 1 cup freshly grated Parmesan cheese
- 1/2 tsp. salt
- 2 tbsps. olive oil
- 1/2 cup finely chopped shallots
- 4 large garlic cloves, finely chopped
- 3 6-oz. packages baby spinach
- 15 no-boil 7 x 3 1/2-inch lasagna noodles (from two 9-oz. packages)
- 3 1/2 cups fresh ricotta cheese* (28 oz.)
- 1 cup freshly grated Parmesan cheese
- 1/2 tsp. finely grated lemon peel
- 1 large egg
- 2 cups coarsely grated Italian Fontina cheese (8 to 9 oz.), divided
- Herb Pesto

Direction

- Prepare the sauce. On medium heat, melt butter in a big heavy saucepan. Whisk in flour for a minute but avoid browning. Whisk in wine and milk until smooth; cook for 4-5 mins while constantly stirring until the sauce boils and thickens. Take off the heat. Stir in salt and Parmesan cheese. Sprinkle pepper to taste. The sauce can be prepared a day in advance; chill while covering.
- Prepare the spinach. On medium-high heat, heat oil in a big pot. Sauté shallots and garlic for approximately 2 mins until the shallots are soft. Put in all the spinach, the pot should be full. Cook for around 3 mins while mixing often until the spinach wilts but still bright green. Move the spinach to a big sieve placed on top of a bowl using tongs; set the pot aside. Press the excess moisture out of the spinach. Drain for another 10-15 mins
- Place the drained spinach liquid back in the reserved pot; boil until it reduces to a glaze. Put the spinach back in the pot then mix for a minute. Take off the heat then stir in 1 1/2 cup sauce. Sprinkle pepper on the spinach to taste.
- Prepare the lasagna: Put noodles in a big bowl. Pour hot tap water to fill. Soak noodles for

around 15 mins while mixing from time to time to separate until the noodles are pliable. On a work surface, put a big parchment paper sheet; move noodles in one layer on the sheet. Shake the excess water off.

- Preheat the oven to 350 degrees F. Spread butter in a 13-in by 9-in by 2-in glass baking dish. In a medium bowl, combine lemon peel, Parmesan, and ricotta; sprinkle salt to taste. Stir in egg.
- On the prepared dish bottom, thinly spread half a cup of sauce then put three noodles side by side until most of the bottom of the dish is covered. Spread 1/2 of the spinach mixture on top, about 1 1/2 cups. Scatter 1/3 cup Fontina. Add three noodles on top then 1/2 of the ricotta mixture, a generous 1 3/4 cups. Drop while evenly spacing 1/2 of the pesto on top by teaspoonfuls. Keep on layering with three noodles, the rest of the spinach mixture, a third cup of Fontina, another three noodles, and the rest of the ricotta and pesto. Put the last three noodles on top. Spread the remaining sauce all over then top with the rest of Fontina. Use buttered foil to cover the dish.
- Bake for 50-55mins until the edges of the lasagna are bubbling and the dish is thoroughly heated. Take it out of the oven then discard the foil.
- Preheat the broiler. Broil the lasagna for about 4 mins until there are brown spots on top, turn the dish from time to time to evenly brown. Let it sit for 15 mins to set.

Nutrition Information

- Calories: 686
- Total Carbohydrate: 42 g
- Cholesterol: 143 mg
- Total Fat: 40 g
- Fiber: 4 g
- Protein: 39 g
- Sodium: 864 mg
- Saturated Fat: 23 g

85. Springtime Pasta Primavera

"This pasta calls for the freshest seasonal vegetables. A trip to your native farmers' market might be in order."
Serving: Makes 4 servings

Ingredients

- 12 oz. farfalle pasta
- 1/4 cup unsalted butter
- 1/2 cup haricots verts (thin tender green beans), ends trimmed
- 1/2 cup thin asparagus tips and stalks, sliced in 1-inch pieces
- 1/2 cup fresh peas
- 1/2 cup white mushrooms, thinly sliced
- Salt and freshly ground black pepper
- 1 cup half-and-half
- 1/2 cup grated Parmesan cheese
- 4 seeded and diced ripe plum tomatoes
- 2 tbsps. snipped fresh chives

Direction

- Put the pasta in a big pot of boiling salted water and let it cook for about 12 minutes until just softened. Drain and put aside.
- Add the butter in a big pot and melt it over medium-low heat and sauté the vegetables quickly until just softened. Avoid overcooking. Spice it up well with pepper and salt. Pour the half-and-half and cook for roughly 5 minutes until the sauce turns thick. Season through with pepper. Stir in the drained pasta to toss and sprinkle with Parmesan. Top it off with diced tomatoes and pea shoots or chives, if available. Serve it right away.

Nutrition Information

- Calories: 587
- Total Carbohydrate: 74 g
- Cholesterol: 62 mg
- Total Fat: 24 g
- Fiber: 5 g
- Protein: 20 g
- Sodium: 665 mg

- Saturated Fat: 14 g

86. Sunday Sauce With Braciole, Meatballs, And Sausage

"This dish featuring sausages, meatballs, and braciole in sauce is perfect for feeding a big crowd. You can make the sauce in advance since it freezes well."
Serving: 6–8 servings | Prep: 1h10m

Ingredients

- 2 medium onions, cut into 1" pieces
- 4 garlic cloves, peeled
- 1/4 cup olive oil
- 1 1/2 tsps. kosher salt, divided
- 2 tbsps. tomato paste
- 2 tsps. dried oregano
- 1 tsp. crushed red pepper flakes
- 2 (28-oz.) cans whole peeled tomatoes, crushed
- 3 (packed) cups basil leaves
- 1/2 tsp. freshly ground black pepper
- 1 cup finely grated Parmesan
- 2/3 cup chopped parsley
- 1/2 cup fine breadcrumbs
- 3 garlic cloves, finely chopped
- 6 slices beef top round (about 1 1/2 lbs. total), pounded 1/4" thick
- 1 1/4 tsps. kosher salt, divided
- 3/4 tsp. freshly ground black pepper, divided
- 2 tbsps. olive oil, divided
- 1 lb. ground beef chuck (20% fat)
- 2 large eggs
- 2 tbsps. milk
- 3/4 tsp. kosher salt
- 1/4 tsp. freshly ground black pepper
- 2 tbsps. olive oil, divided
- 6 sweet Italian sausages
- 1 lb. pasta, such as spaghetti
- Kosher salt
- Finely grated Parmesan (for serving)
- Butcher's twine

Direction

- Prepare the sauce: In a food processor, puree the garlic and onions till finely very chopped.
- On medium-high heat, heat oil in a big heavy ovenproof pot or Dutch oven. Cook half tsp. salt and the onion mixture for 10-12 mins while mixing frequently until the bits on the bottom are starting to brown and the liquid is evaporated. Put in red pepper flakes, oregano, and tomato paste; cook and stir for approximately 2 mins until the color is slightly darker. Pour in half cup water; cook while scraping up the brown bits in the pot bottom. Mix in a cup of water and the tomatoes with the juices to blend. Mix in basil then sprinkle the remaining tsp. of salt and pepper; simmer to season. Keep warm while mixing from time to time until use.
- Prepare the breadcrumb mixture: In a medium bowl, mix garlic, cheese, breadcrumbs, and parsley.
- Make the braciole: Preheat the oven to 300 degrees F. On a work surface, lay the beef flat then sprinkle with half tsp. pepper and 3/4 tsp. salt to season. Evenly scatter half cup of the breadcrumb mixture. One at a time, roll the beef up beginning at the short end then secure with butcher's twine by binding in a few places. Sprinkle a quarter tsp. pepper and the remaining half tsp. salt on the braciole.
- On medium-high heat, heat a tbsp. of oil in a big skillet. In batches, cook the braciole for approximately 8 mins each batch until all sides are brown, turning from time to time, put in the remaining tbsp. of oil in the pan as necessary.
- Move the braciole to the sauce in the pot; cover. Bake for 1 1/2 hrs. Wipe out the pan then set aside.
- Prepare the sausage and meatballs: In a medium bowl, use a fork to mix the remaining 1 1/4 cup breadcrumb mixture, ground beef, pepper, eggs, salt, and milk; form into a dozen of 1 1/2-inch ball.
- Heat a tbsp. of oil in the reserved skillet. Cook meatballs in batches for around 8 mins each

batch until all sides are brown, turning from time to time; move to a plate. Cook sausages in batches for approximately 8 mins on each batch until all sides are brown, turning from time to time, put in the remaining tbsp. of oil in the pan as needed.

- Lower the sausages and meatballs gently in the sauce using tongs once the braciole has baked for 1 1/2 hours; cover the pot. Keep baking for another 25-30 mins until the sausages and meatballs are thoroughly cooked and the braciole is very tender.
- In a big pot, cook pasta until al dente while mixing from time to time in boiling salted water. Move the braciole, meatballs, and sausages to a platter; discard the strings from the braciole. Scoop warm sauce on top.
- Drain and mix the pasta with a little or the amount of sauce that you prefer; add parmesan on top to serve.
- You can make the sauce three days in advance; cover then chill or freeze for a maximum of six months.
- The sausages, meatballs, and braciole can be prepared three days in advance then submerged in sauce; cover and chill or freeze for up to three months.

Nutrition Information

- Calories: 1160
- Total Carbohydrate: 82 g
- Cholesterol: 265 mg
- Total Fat: 52 g
- Fiber: 10 g
- Protein: 91 g
- Sodium: 1867 mg
- Saturated Fat: 16 g

87. Sunday Stash Marinara Sauce

"This simple tomato sauce is packed with flavor. You can easily make a big batch to freeze for different meals like stews, pastas, soups, and braises."
Serving: Makes about 12 cups | Prep: 25m

Ingredients

- 1/2 cup extra-virgin olive oil
- 2 Vidalia or other sweet onions, peeled, very coarsely chopped
- 6 garlic cloves, peeled
- 2 tsp. dried oregano
- 4 (28-oz.) cans whole peeled tomatoes
- 4 tsp. kosher salt, plus more
- 1 1/2 tsp. freshly ground black pepper, plus more

Direction

- On medium heat, heat oil in a big Dutch oven or pot. Cook garlic and onion for approximately 3 mins while mixing from time to time, avoid browning carefully. Mix in oregano to combine. Crush the tomatoes with your hands then put in the pot with the juices; sprinkle 1 1/2 tsp. pepper and four tsp. salt to season.
- Boil; lower the heat then simmer gently. Cook for around an hour without a cover while mixing from time to time until the sauce reduces slightly. Take off the heat then use an immersion blender to blend until smooth. Sprinkle pepper and salt to season.
- You can make the sauce five days in advance. Chill or freeze in an airtight container for up to six months.

Nutrition Information

- Calories: 71
- Total Carbohydrate: 7 g
- Total Fat: 5 g
- Fiber: 3 g
- Protein: 1 g
- Sodium: 385 mg
- Saturated Fat: 1 g

88. The Duckor Deluxe Wood-fired Pizza

"You can make this wood-fired and perfectly charred pizza at home using any kettle charcoal grill with a special attachment."
Serving: Makes 2 (10") pizzas | Prep: 20m

Ingredients

- 1 (28-oz.) can whole peeled tomatoes (preferably San Marzano)
- Cornmeal (for dusting)
- 1 lb. pizza dough, divided into 2 even balls
- Kosher salt, freshly ground black pepper
- 8 oz. fresh mozzarella, torn into bite-sized pieces, divided
- 4 medium crimini or button mushrooms (about 2 oz.), thinly sliced, divided
- 2 oz. thinly sliced cured meats, such as pepperoni, soppressata, and/or salami, divided
- 1 shallot, thinly sliced into rings, divided
- Honey, crushed red pepper flakes, and basil leaves (for serving)
- A pizza-oven attachment for a charcoal grill, such as a KettlePizza; 2 medium-sized firewood logs; a pizza stone; a pizza peel

Direction

- Set the charcoal grill on high heat. Arrange the lit coals on the grill's rear; add logs to charcoal. On the grill, put the pizza-oven attachment then put pizza stone on the grate.
- Heat the grill for approximately 5 mins until it reaches 800 degrees F. In the meantime, use a colander to drain the tomatoes. Use your hands to crush the tomatoes into small portions then drain again. Move to a medium bowl.
- Lightly dust cornmeal on the pizza peel. Stretch one dough piece at a time, let the dough hang off your fingers then quickly rotate the edge until it turns to around 10-in diameter. It doesn't have to be a perfect circle. Move to the prepared pizza peel; add 1/2 of the tomatoes on top then sprinkle with pepper and salt to season. Add shallot, 1/2 of cheese, meats, and mushrooms on top; sprinkle salt to taste.
- Slide the pizza carefully on the pizza stone directly; cook for 60-90 secs until the crust rear starts to char and bubble. Rotate the pizza to 180 degrees F; keep cooking for another 60-90 secs until the other side of crust is bubbly and charred.
- Move the pizza to a metal pizza tray or cutting board with a very big heatproof spatula or pizza peel and tongs. Drizzle honey all over then add basil and red pepper flakes on top. Cut then serve immediately. Repeat with the rest of the dough, shallot, tomatoes, meats, mushrooms, and cheese.
- The pizza-oven attachment can be used on gas grills too. Omit the firewood then slightly increase the cooking time to fit the lower internal temperature of the gas grill.

89. Tomato Sauce

"This easy and spicy tomato sauce is made from scratch for a lot of dinners."
Serving: 12 | Prep: 15m | Ready in: 1h15m

Ingredients

- 6 1/4 lbs. tomatoes, crushed
- 1/2 cup extra virgin olive oil
- 1 1/2 tbsps. freshly ground black pepper
- 1 tsp. chili seasoning mix
- 1 tsp. salt
- 1 tbsp. minced onion
- 1 tbsp. dried oregano
- 1 tbsp. garlic powder
- 1 tsp. finely minced fresh parsley
- 1 tsp. white sugar

Direction

- In a big saucepan, combine sugar, parsley, garlic powder, oregano, onion, salt, chili seasoning, pepper, olive oil, and tomatoes over low heat. Allow to simmer for 1 hour, and then serve.

Nutrition Information

- Calories: 134 calories;
- Total Carbohydrate: 11.1 g
- Cholesterol: 0 mg
- Total Fat: 9.9 g
- Protein: 2.4 g
- Sodium: 229 mg

90. Tomato, Mozzarella & Thai Basil Crostini

"Rice vinegar and sesame oil twist the caprese eastward."
Serving: Makes 12 servings

Ingredients

- 12 slices seven-grain or sesame bread
- 1/2 garlic clove
- 2 cups (about 10 oz.) halved cherry or grape tomatoes
- 1 small shallot, minced
- 1 tbsp. toasted sesame oil
- 1 tbsp. unseasoned rice vinegar
- Sea salt and freshly ground black pepper
- Sliced fresh mozzarella
- Thai basil leaves

Direction

- Grill the slices of bread and rub them with the garlic clove.
- Mix together the shallot, tomatoes, rice vinegar and sesame oil in a bowl. Sprinkle with pepper and sea salt; let it stand for roughly 15 minutes.
- Place the sliced fresh mozzarella on toasts. Spread the tomato mixture on top of the mozzarella and top it off with Thai basil leaves. Spice up with pepper and sea salt.

91. Tortellini With Italian Sausage, Fennel, And Mushroom

Serving: Makes 8 main-course servings | Prep: 35m

Ingredients

- 1 tbsp. olive oil
- 1 large fennel bulb, trimmed, halved through core, thinly sliced lengthwise (about 3 cups), fronds chopped
- 1 lb. spicy Italian sausages, casings removed, sausage coarsely crumbled
- 1 8-oz. package sliced fresh crimini (baby bella) mushrooms
- 4 large garlic cloves, pressed
- 1 tbsp. fennel seeds, coarsely crushed
- 1/2 cup heavy whipping cream
- 1 cup (or more) low-salt chicken broth
- 1 16-oz. package dried tortellini with pesto filling or fresh tortellini with 3-cheese filling
- 1 5-oz. package fresh baby spinach leaves
- 1/2 cup finely grated Parmesan cheese plus additional (for serving)
- **Test-kitchen tip:**To crush the fennel seeds, enclose the seeds in a heavy-duty resealable plastic bag, then lb. them with a meat mallet or a small heavy skillet.

Direction

- In a big nonstick skillet, heat oil on medium high heat. Put mushrooms, sausage and sliced fennel bulb. Sauté for 12-15 minutes till fennel is nearly tender and sausage is cooked through and brown. Add fennel seeds and garlic. Mix for 1 minute. Mix cream in then a cup of broth. Boil for 2-3 minutes till liquid thickens very slightly and reduces.
- Meanwhile in a big pot, cook tortellini in boiling salted water, occasionally mixing, till tender yet firm to chew. Drain tortellini and put back into the same pot.
- In pot, put sausage mixture into tortellini. Toss till blended on medium heat. Put spinach. Gently toss till spinach wilts. Mix in 1/2 cup

cheese. By 1/4 cupfuls, add more broth to moisten if it's dry. Season with pepper and salt. Sprinkle on chopped fennel fronds. Serve next to some extra cheese.

Nutrition Information

- Calories: 529
- Total Carbohydrate: 34 g
- Cholesterol: 112 mg
- Total Fat: 36 g
- Fiber: 3 g
- Protein: 19 g
- Sodium: 701 mg
- Saturated Fat: 16 g

92. Trenton Tomato Pie Pizza

"The traditional tomato pie in DeLorenzo's is a great inspiration for this crispy and easy tomato pizza."
Serving: Makes 1 (14") pizza | Prep: 20m

Ingredients

- 1 (28-oz.) can whole peeled tomatoes (preferably San Marzano)
- 3/4 tsp. kosher salt
- 8 oz. Food Processor Pizza Dough or prepared pizza dough, room temperature
- All-purpose flour (for surface)
- 5 oz. part-skim milk mozzarella, shredded (about 1 1/2 cups), divided
- 3/4 tsp. extra-virgin olive oil
- Crushed red pepper flakes (for serving; optional)
- A pizza stone or 2 stackable rimmed baking sheets

Direction

- Put the rack in the bottommost part of the oven. Put a two inverted and stacked baking sheets or a pizza stone on the rack then preheat the oven for at least an hour to 500 degrees
- In a colander, drain the tomatoes then use your hands to crumble into small pieces; drain again. Move to a medium bowl then mix in salt; set the tomatoes aside.
- On a lightly floured parchment paper, roll the dough out to a 14-in circle. It should be evenly thin from the middle to the edge. Use plastic wrap to cover the dough if it pulls back when rolling then wait for 5mins.
- Move the parchment paper with the dough on an inverted baking sheet, big cutting board, or a pizza wheel. Spread 1 1/4 cup cheese then the tomatoes on top. Scatter the remaining quarter cup cheese.
- Slide the pizza from the parchment carefully on the hot baking stone. Bake for 10-12mins until the crust is deep golden brown.
- Move to a cutting board then cool the pizza for 2mins; dribble with oil. Slice the pizza into wedges then serve with red pepper flakes, if desired.

Nutrition Information

- Calories: 2540
- Total Carbohydrate: 287 g
- Cholesterol: 196 mg
- Total Fat: 106 g
- Fiber: 32 g
- Protein: 112 g
- Sodium: 5377 mg
- Saturated Fat: 44 g

93. Turkey Meatball Garlic Bread Heroes

"Everyone will love these delicious meatball subs featuring tangy tomato sauce and tender meatballs that are stacked in toasted butter-garlic buns. Instead of grilling, it's better to broil these subs so you can skip the grill baskets and skewers."
Serving: Makes 8 servings | Prep: 1.5h

Ingredients

- 1 (28-oz.) can whole tomatoes in purée
- 2 tbsps. olive oil
- 1 small onion, finely chopped

- 3 garlic cloves, minced
- 1 tsp. sugar
- 1/2 tsp. salt
- 3 cups coarse fresh bread crumbs (from 5 to 6 slices firm white sandwich bread)
- 2/3 cup whole milk
- 2 large eggs, lightly beaten
- 1 1/4 cups grated Pecorino Romano (about 5 oz.)
- 3 garlic cloves, minced
- 3 tbsps. finely chopped flat-leaf parsley
- 1/2 tsp. dried oregano
- 1/2 tsp. salt
- 2 lbs. ground turkey (not breast meat)
- 5 tbsps. unsalted butter, softened
- 2 tbsps. olive oil
- 1 tbsp. minced garlic
- 1/4 tsp. salt
- 2 tbsps. grated Pecorino Romano
- 2 tbsps. finely chopped flat-leaf parsley
- 1/4 tsp. freshly ground black pepper
- 12 hot dog or long potato buns or hoagie rolls
- An instant-read thermometer

Direction

- Prepare the tomato sauce. In a blender, puree the tomatoes along with their puree.
- On medium-high heat, heat oil in a big heavy pot until shimmering; sauté onion for 5-6mins until golden. Put in garlic then sauté for 1min. Put in salt, sugar, and tomato puree; let it simmer for 30-35mins while mixing from time to time without a cover until thick.
- Prepare the meatballs while simmering the sauce. In a big bowl, mix milk and bread crumbs; set aside for 10mins
- Mix in salt, eggs, oregano, cheese, parsley, garlic, and turkey; use your hands to combine until just blended well. Avoid overmixing.
- Shape meatballs from 1 1/2 tbsp. mixture for each then place on two well-oiled big, heavy, rimmed baking sheets.
- Prepare the garlic bread. In a bowl, combine pepper, butter, parsley, oil, cheese, salt, and garlic. On each split sides of every bun, spread two rounded tsps. of garlic butter. Put the buns on a big baking sheet with the buttered-sides up.
- Broil the garlic bread and meatballs. Preheat the broiler.
- Broil meatballs for 5-8 mins, 3-4-in from heat until just thoroughly cooked and golden, turn once. An instant-read thermometer should register 165 degrees F.
- Broil only the buttered-sides of the bun for half to a full minute until golden; watch closely since the buns will brown quickly.
- Make the heroes. Scoop sauce on each bun then add four meatballs on top or according to the size of the buns. Scatter more sauce.
- You can make the tomato sauce up to two days in advance; store in an airtight container in the refrigerate. Reheat before use. If needed, thin the sauce with water until it reaches the preferred consistency.
- You can make the garlic butter up to two days in advance; store in an airtight container while chilling. Bring the garlic butter to room temperature before use.
- You can form the meatballs a day in advance. Arrange on a baking sheet with wax paper then tightly cover with plastic wrap; refrigerate.

Nutrition Information

- Calories: 743
- Total Carbohydrate: 66 g
- Cholesterol: 166 mg
- Total Fat: 35 g
- Fiber: 6 g
- Protein: 42 g
- Sodium: 1117 mg
- Saturated Fat: 13 g

94. Turkey Tonnato

"A fantastic dish for entertaining."
Serving: Makes 6 to 8 (main-course) servings | Prep: 30m

Ingredients

- 3 tbsps. black-olive tapenade
- 1 tbsp. finely grated fresh lemon zest
- 1 tbsp. finely chopped garlic
- 2 tsps. finely chopped fresh rosemary
- 1 (4- to 4 1/2-lb) boneless turkey breast half with skin
- 2 tsps. salt
- 1 tsp. black pepper
- 2 tbsps. extra-virgin olive oil
- 1 cup dry white wine
- 1 (6-oz) can chunk light tuna in olive oil (do not drain)
- 1/2 cup extra-virgin olive oil
- 2 tbsps. water
- 1 tbsp. fresh lemon juice
- 2 tsps. anchovy paste
- Accompaniments: lemon wedges; capers; chopped fresh flat-leaf parsley
- kitchen string; an instant-read thermometer

Direction

- Filling and roast: Place oven rack in center position. Preheat the oven to 350°F.
- In a small bowl, mix rosemary, garlic, zest and tapenade.
- On a work surface, put turkey with pointed, narrower end near you, skin side up. Choose which breast's long side is thickest. Starting from the thickest side, hold a knife parallel to work surface, horizontally cutting breast nearly in half, halting an inch from the other side. Open the breast up like a book. Season 1/2 tsp. pepper and 1 tsp. salt on breast. Evenly spread tapenade mixture on breast using a spoon's back. On all sides, leave an inch border. Beginning with side without the skin, roll turkey up sideways, finishing with the seam side down. The skin should be outside the rolled breast. At 1-in. intervals, use kitchen string to tie the turkey breast crosswise. Pat dry roast. Sprinkle leftover 1 tsp. salt and 1/2 tsp. pepper outside all over the roast.
- Cooking: In a 12-in. heavy skillet, heat 2 tbsp. olive oil till hot yet not smoking. Brown turkey, 8 minutes total, occasionally turning. Put into a 13x9-in. roasting pan. Put wine into pan. Roast turkey for 1 hour till an inserted thermometer diagonally 2-in. into the thickest part reads 160°F.
- On platter, put roast; cool. Keep pan juices. Completely cool roast. Chill, uncovered, wrapped tightly in plastic wrap for 2 hours.
- Sauce: In a blender, puree 4 tbsp. reserved pan juices, anchovy paste, lemon juice, water, 1/2 cup olive oil and tuna and its oil in a blender. Stop to scrape down sides if needed till very smooth. Put into a bowl. Season with pepper and salt. Use a plastic wrap to cover bowl. Chill for 1 hour till cold.
- Turkey tonnato assembly: Slice chilled turkey roast to 1/4-in. thick slices. Throw strings. Put chilled sauce on top. Bring sauce and turkey to room temperature for an hour. Serve with parsley, capers and lemon wedges.
- You can make sauce and turkey roast chilled, separately, for up to 2 days.

Nutrition Information

- Calories: 742
- Total Carbohydrate: 2 g
- Cholesterol: 194 mg
- Total Fat: 46 g
- Fiber: 0 g
- Protein: 72 g
- Sodium: 959 mg
- Saturated Fat: 9 g

95. Veal And Roasted Vegetable Lasagne Anderson

"A great winter recipe."
Serving: Serves 8 to 10

Ingredients

- 1 small onion
- 1/2 lb. mushrooms (about 2 cups)
- 2 garlic cloves
- a 28- to 32-oz. can whole tomatoes
- 1/4 cup drained dried tomatoes packed in oil
- 1 1/2 tbsps. olive oil
- 1/4 cup tomato paste (about half a 6-oz. can)
- 1/2 lb. ground veal
- 1/4 cup chopped fresh basil leaves
- 2 large red bell peppers
- 3 medium onions
- 4 medium carrots
- 8 large garlic cloves
- 2 tbsps. olive oil
- 2 cups grated mozzarella (about 8 oz.)
- a 15-oz. container ricotta (about 1 3/4 cups)
- grated Romano or Parmesan
- 1 large egg
- 1/4 cup finely chopped fresh parsley leaves
- 1 cup packed fresh basil leaves
- twelve 7- by 3 1/2-inch sheets dry no-boil lasagne
- 1/2 cup grated mozzarella (about 2 oz.)
- 1/3 cup grated Romano or Parmesan (about 1 oz.)

Direction

- Veal sauce: Chop mushrooms and onion separately; mince garlic. Drain; chop canned tomatoes and keep juice. Chop dried tomatoes finely. Cook garlic and onion in oil in heavy saucepan on medium low heat till soft, mixing. Add mushrooms; cook till all liquid it gave off evaporates, mixing. Add pepper and salt to taste, canned tomatoes and reserved juice and tomato paste; simmer for 30 minutes, with cover and occasionally mixing.
- Cook veal in nonstick skillet on medium heat as sauce simmers, till cooked through, mixing. Add dried tomatoes and veal to sauce; simmer for 10 minutes. Mix basil in; take off heat. You can make veal sauce 1 day ahead, cover and chill. Before using, bring sauce to room temperature.
- Roast veggies: Preheat an oven to 375°F.
- Cut carrots to 1x1 1/2-inch sticks and onions and bell peppers to 1-inch pieces. Chop garlic coarsely. Toss pepper and salt to taste, oil, garlic and veggies in big shallow baking pan; roast in center of oven for 30-35 minutes till tender, occasionally mixing. You can roast veggies 1 day ahead, cover and chill. Before using, bring veggies to room temperature.
- Ricotta mixture: Mix ricotta mixture ingredients till well combined in bowl.
- Lasagna: Oil 13x9-inch glass baking dish lightly; shred basil leaves coarsely.
- Spread 1 cup veal sauce on bottom of dish; use 3 lasange sheets to cover without touching each other. Drop 1/3 ricotta mixture by spoonfuls on pasta; evenly spread. Put 1/3 veggies over. Spread 1 cup sauce on veggies; sprinkle 1/3 basil on sauce. Create additional layers in exactly the same way; start and end with pasta. Spread leftover sauce on top evenly, covering pasta completely; sprinkle grated cheese.
- Tightly cover dish with foil; slightly tent to avoid foil from touching the top layer. Bake for 40 minutes in center of oven; remove foil. Bake for 10 minutes longer; stand for 5 minutes prior to serving.

Nutrition Information

- Calories: 556
- Total Carbohydrate: 49 g
- Cholesterol: 96 mg
- Total Fat: 27 g
- Fiber: 7 g
- Protein: 30 g
- Sodium: 593 mg
- Saturated Fat: 12 g

96. Veal Cutlets With Mushrooms And Tomatoes

"A lovely recipe for winter and fall."
Serving: Makes 4 servings

Ingredients

- 4 tbsps. olive oil
- 2 large garlic cloves, chopped
- 3/4 tsp. chopped fresh rosemary
- 12 oz. mushrooms, sliced
- 12 oz. plum tomatoes, seeded, chopped
- 1 lb. thin veal cutlets
- All purpose flour
- 1 cup canned low-salt chicken broth
- 1/2 cup dry white wine

Direction

- Heat 2 tbsps. oil in big heavy saucepan on medium high heat then add rosemary and garlic; mix for 30 seconds. Add mushrooms and cover pan; cook for 5 minutes, occasionally mixing. Uncover; sauté for 5 more minutes till mushrooms are golden brown. Add tomatoes; cook for 5 minutes till soft. Put aside.
- Sprinkle pepper and salt on veal; dust using flour. Heat 1 tbsp. oil in big heavy skillet on medium high heat then add 1/2 veal; sauté for 2 minutes per side till cooked through and brown. Put veal on platter; to keep warm, tent with foil. Repeat with leftover veal and 1 tbsp. oil.
- Add wine and broth to same skillet; boil for 4 minutes till reduced by half, scraping browned bits up. Add mushrooms mixture; mix to blend. Season with pepper and salt to taste; scoop on veal and serve.

Nutrition Information

- Calories: 358
- Total Carbohydrate: 11 g
- Cholesterol: 93 mg
- Total Fat: 22 g
- Fiber: 2 g
- Protein: 27 g
- Sodium: 121 mg
- Saturated Fat: 5 g

97. Zeppole

"Yummy cookies that are fried with a cheesy taste."
Serving: 35 | Prep: 15m | Ready in: 40m

Ingredients

- 2 quarts vegetable oil for frying
- 1 cup all-purpose flour
- 2 tsps. baking powder
- 1 pinch salt
- 1 1/2 tsps. white sugar
- 2 eggs, beaten
- 1 cup ricotta cheese
- 1/4 tsp. vanilla extract
- 1/2 cup confectioners' sugar for dusting

Direction

- In a deep-fryer, heat oil to 190 degrees C or 375 degrees F.
- Mix sugar, salt, baking powder, and flour in a medium saucepan. Mix in vanilla, ricotta cheese, and eggs. Gently mix on low heat until incorporated. Batter should be sticky.
- Drop by tbsps. in the hot oil, several at one time. The Zeppole should turn over on their own. Fry for 3 or 4 minutes until golden brown. Drain inside a paper sack then dust with confectioners' sugar. Serve while warm.

Nutrition Information

- Calories: 69 calories;
- Total Carbohydrate: 4.7 g
- Cholesterol: 12 mg
- Total Fat: 5.4 g
- Protein: 0.7 g
- Sodium: 24 mg

98. Zucchini Blossom And Chicken Saltimbocca

"This amazing dinner-party meal features zucchini blossom instead of the classic sage leaf."
Serving: Makes 4 servings

Ingredients

- 12 zucchini blossoms, stems removed
- 2 skinless boneless chicken breast halves (about 1 lb. total)
- 8 thin 6 1/2 x 3 1/2-inch slices prosciutto
- 1 tbsp. unsalted butter
- 1 tbsp. extra-virgin olive oil
- 1/2 cup dry white-wine

Direction

- Rinse the zucchini blossoms gently then dry.
- Put the chicken breast in the middle of 2 of twelve-inch parchment paper squares; lb. with a mallet into 1/4-1/3-inch thick. Take the chicken out of the parchment then slice in half lengthwise.
- Sprinkle pepper and salt on the chicken to season then put three zucchini blossoms on top. Use two slices of prosciutto to wrap each chicken breast then secure the blossoms and prosciutto using toothpick.
- On medium-high heat, melt olive oil and butter in a big heavy skillet. Sauté chicken with the blossom-side down in the skillet for around 3 mins on each side until brown. Pour in white wine; keep cooking for another 2mins until the wine reduces and slightly thickens. Sprinkle pepper and salt to taste. Move the chicken to serving platter; discard the toothpicks. Transfer the sauce all over the chicken.

Nutrition Information

- Calories: 4023
- Total Carbohydrate: 7 g
- Cholesterol: 1439 mg
- Total Fat: 174 g
- Protein: 566 g
- Sodium: 53921 mg
- Saturated Fat: 58 g

Chapter 2: Italian Breakfast Recipes

***

99. Arugula & Mushroom Breakfast Pizza

"Having a kids for breakfast is quite challenging. You need to be creative every morning to make sure that they will have fun and will love the breakfast. Have your kids join you in preparing this recipe. Make it ahead of time for your convenience."
Serving: 6 servings. | Prep: 20m | Ready in: 35m

Ingredients

- 1 prebaked 12-inch thin whole wheat pizza crust
- 3/4 cup reduced-fat ricotta cheese
- 1 tsp. garlic powder
- 1 tsp. paprika, divided
- 1 cup sliced baby portobello mushrooms
- 1/2 cup julienned soft sun-dried tomatoes (not packed in oil)
- 3 cups fresh arugula or baby spinach
- 2 tbsps. balsamic vinegar
- 2 tbsps. olive oil
- 1/4 tsp. salt, divided
- 1/4 tsp. pepper, divided
- 6 large eggs

Direction

- Set the oven for preheating to 450°. Lay the crust on a pizza pan. Scatter the ricotta cheese; sprinkle with half a tsp. of paprika and garlic powder. Top it off with tomatoes and mushrooms.
- Using your clean hands, massage the arugula with oil, vinegar, and 1/8 tsp. each pepper and salt until softened; scatter on top of the pizza.
- Form a six indentations in arugula using a spoon; crack an egg carefully into each. Scatter with remaining paprika, pepper and salt. Let it bake inside the oven for 12-15 minutes until the egg whites are entirely set and yolks start to get thick yet not hard.

Nutrition Information

- Calories: 299 calories
- Total Carbohydrate: 31 g
- Cholesterol: 194 mg
- Total Fat: 13 g
- Fiber: 5 g
- Protein: 15 g
- Sodium: 464 mg

100. Best-of-show Tomato Quiche

"You can use Cajun or Mexican seasoning in this impressive dish in place of the basil. It will still be wonderful no matter what seasoning you use."
Serving: 6-8 servings. | Prep: 20m | Ready in: 01h10m

Ingredients

- 3/4 cup all-purpose flour
- 1/2 cup cornmeal
- 1/2 tsp. salt
- 1/8 tsp. pepper
- 1/3 cup shortening
- 4 to 5 tbsps. cold water
- FILLING:
- 2 cups chopped plum tomatoes
- 1 tsp. salt
- 1/2 tsp. dried basil
- 1/8 tsp. pepper
- 1/2 cup chopped green onions
- 1/2 cup shredded cheddar cheese
- 1/2 cup shredded Swiss cheese
- 2 tbsps. all-purpose flour
- 2 eggs
- 1 cup evaporated milk

Direction

- Mix the first 4 ingredients in a small bowl; mix in shortening until crumbly. Pour in water; use a fork to toss until it forms into a dough ball. Chill for half an hour.
- Roll the dough out on a lightly floured surface until it can fit a 9-inch pie plate; move the dough on the plate. Trim the pastry to half-inch over the edge of the plate then flute the sides. Bake for 10mins in a 375 degrees oven. Completely cool.
- Put tomatoes over the crust then sprinkle cheeses, salt, onions, pepper, and basil. Beat milk, eggs, and flour in a small bowl until smooth; pour on top of the filling.
- Bake for 40-45mins in a 375 degrees oven until an inserted knife in the middle comes out without residue. Let it sit for 10mins then cut.
- Chill any leftovers.

101. Blt Brunch Pie

"This delicious pie features a crust that melts in your mouth, fresh ripe tomatoes, and delicious filling."
Serving: 6-8 servings. | Prep: 20m | Ready in: 60m

Ingredients

- 1-1/4 cups all-purpose flour
- 2 tsps. baking powder
- 1/2 tsp. salt
- 1/2 tsp. dried basil
- 1/2 cup shortening
- 1/2 cup sour cream
- FILLING:
- 3/4 cup mayonnaise
- 1 cup shredded cheddar cheese

- 1 can (4-1/2 oz.) mushroom stems and pieces, drained
- 8 bacon strips, cooked and crumbled
- 1 tbsp. chopped green pepper
- 1 tbsp. chopped onion
- 3 medium tomatoes, peeled and sliced

Direction

- Mix the first 4 ingredients in a big bowl; cut in shortening until the mixture is crumbly. Mix in sour cream; chill for half an hour while covered.
- Push the pastry in a 9-inch pie plate. If desired, flute the sides. Bake for 10mins in a 375 degrees oven then completely cool.
- Mix onion, mayonnaise, green pepper, cheddar cheese, bacon, and mushrooms. In the crust, spread 1/2 of the tomatoes in a layer then add 1/2 of the mayonnaise mixture on top. Repeat the layers.
- Bake for 30-35mins in a 350 degrees oven until an inserted knife in the middle comes out without residue. Chill any leftovers.

Nutrition Information

- Calories: 464 calories
- Total Carbohydrate: 19 g
- Cholesterol: 38 mg
- Total Fat: 39 g
- Fiber: 1 g
- Protein: 8 g
- Sodium: 618 mg

102. Breakfast Pizza Skillet

"Just some changes from the original stovetop dish, I made an instant hit."
Serving: 6 servings. | Prep: 35m | Ready in: 45m

Ingredients

- 1 lb. Johnsonville® Ground Mild Italian sausage
- 5 cups frozen shredded hash brown potatoes
- 1/2 cup chopped onion
- 1/2 cup chopped green pepper
- 1/4 to 1/2 tsp. salt
- Pepper to taste
- 1/2 cup sliced mushrooms
- 4 large eggs, lightly beaten
- 1 medium tomato, thinly sliced
- 1 cup shredded cheddar cheese
- Sour cream and salsa, optional

Direction

- Cook the sausage over medium heat in a large skillet until no longer pink. Add pepper, salt, green pepper, onion and potatoes. Cook for 18-20 minutes over medium-high heat or until the potatoes become brown.
- Stir in mushrooms. Top the potato mixtures with eggs. Arrange sliced tomatoes on top. Top with cheese.
- Cook, covered over medium-low heat until eggs become completely set (do not stir), or for 10-15 minutes. Serve with salsa and sour cream if preferred.

Nutrition Information

- Calories: 445 calories
- Total Carbohydrate: 16 g
- Cholesterol: 219 mg
- Total Fat: 33 g
- Fiber: 2 g
- Protein: 21 g
- Sodium: 873 mg

103. Calico Pepper Frittata

"This frittata that features green and red peppers can fit any meal. Instead of the oven, this is made in the stovetop."
Serving: 4 servings. | Prep: 20m | Ready in: 30m

Ingredients

- 5 large eggs
- 1-1/4 cups egg substitute
- 1 tbsp. grated Romano cheese
- 1/2 tsp. salt

- 1/8 tsp. pepper
- 1 tbsp. olive oil
- 1 medium sweet red pepper, chopped
- 1 medium green pepper, chopped
- 1 jalapeno pepper, seeded and chopped
- 1 medium onion, chopped
- 1 garlic clove, minced

Direction

- Beat the first 5 ingredients in a big bowl until combined.
- On medium-high heat, heat oil in a big non-stick pan. Cook and stir onion and peppers in hot oil until tender. Put in garlic then cook for another minute. Add the egg mixture, it should set at the edges right away. Cook for 8-10mins without cover until the eggs are set completely. Push the cooked part to the middle and let the uncooked eggs flow beneath. Slice into wedges.

Nutrition Information

- Calories: 201 calories
- Total Carbohydrate: 10 g
- Cholesterol: 268 mg
- Total Fat: 10 g
- Fiber: 2 g
- Protein: 17 g
- Sodium: 559 mg

104. Caramelized Mushroom And Onion Frittata

"I remembered how my grandmother make me a buttery sautéed mushrooms when I was still young. Now I am always enjoying them over a rich breakfast frittata."
Serving: 4 servings. | Prep: 15m | Ready in: 60m

Ingredients

- 1 lb. sliced fresh mushrooms
- 1 medium red onion, chopped
- 3 tbsps. butter
- 3 tbsps. olive oil
- 1 shallot, chopped
- 1 garlic clove, minced
- 1/2 cup shredded cheddar cheese
- 1/4 cup shredded Parmesan cheese
- 8 large eggs
- 3 tbsps. heavy whipping cream
- 1/4 tsp. salt
- 1/4 tsp. pepper

Direction

- Add the butter and oil in a 10-in. ovenproof skillet, cook and stir the mushrooms and onion in until tender. Adjust the heat to medium-low; allow them to cook for about half an hour or until it turns deep golden brown. Stir the mixture from time to time. Stir in the garlic and shallot; let it cook for 1 minute more.
- Lessen the heat; top it off with cheeses. Whisk the cream, eggs, pepper and salt in a big bowl; pour over top. Allow to cook for 4-6 minutes while covered or until eggs are almost set.
- Take off the cover of the skillet. Broil, positioning the pan 3-4 in. away from the heat source for 2-3 minutes or until eggs are entirely set. Let it rest for about 5 minutes. Slice into wedges.

Nutrition Information

- Calories: 465 calories
- Total Carbohydrate: 11 g
- Cholesterol: 479 mg
- Total Fat: 38 g
- Fiber: 2 g
- Protein: 22 g
- Sodium: 529 mg

105. Cheesy Vegetable Frittata

""We love making it for brunch or late-night suppers. Eating this dish with some fruits is kind of interesting.""
Serving: 2 servings. | Prep: 15m | Ready in: 35m

Ingredients

- 4 large eggs, beaten

- 1 cup sliced fresh mushrooms
- 1/2 cup chopped fresh broccoli
- 1/4 cup shredded sharp cheddar cheese
- 2 tbsps. finely chopped onion
- 2 tbsps. finely chopped green pepper
- 2 tbsps. grated Parmesan cheese
- 1/8 tsp. salt
- Dash pepper

Direction

- Combine all ingredients in a large bowl. Pour mixture into a shallow 2-cup baking dish coated with cooking spray.
- Bake without a cover at 350° for 20 to 25 minutes or until a knife comes out clean when inserted in the center. Enjoy right away.

Nutrition Information

- Calories: 143 calories
- Total Carbohydrate: 7 g
- Cholesterol: 14 mg
- Total Fat: 5 g
- Fiber: 1 g
- Protein: 19 g
- Sodium: 587 mg

106. Chicken 'n' Ham Frittata

""This hearty egg dish is special and colorful enough to serve for holiday.""
Serving: 6 servings. | Prep: 15m | Ready in: 30m

Ingredients

- 1/2 cup chopped green onions
- 2 garlic cloves, minced
- 2 tbsps. canola oil
- 1-1/4 cups chopped yellow summer squash
- 1 cup chopped zucchini
- 1/2 cup chopped sweet yellow pepper
- 1/2 cup chopped sweet red pepper
- 1 tsp. minced fresh gingerroot
- 2 cups cubed cooked chicken breast
- 1 cup chopped deli ham
- 6 large eggs
- 3/4 cup mayonnaise
- 1/4 tsp. prepared horseradish
- 1/4 tsp. pepper
- 1 cup shredded Monterey Jack cheese

Direction

- In a large ovenproof skillet, sauté the garlic and onions in oil, 1 minute. Include in ginger, peppers, zucchini and yellow squash; cook while stirring till vegetables are crispy-tender, or for 8 minutes. Include in ham and chicken; cook for 1 more minute or till heated through. Take away from the heat.
- In a large bowl, beat pepper, horseradish, mayonnaise and eggs till blended. Pour into the skillet.
- Bake without a cover at 350° till eggs are totally set, or for 25-30 minutes. Top with cheese; cover and let stand till the cheese is melted, or for 5 minutes.

Nutrition Information

- Calories: 504 calories
- Total Carbohydrate: 5 g
- Cholesterol: 286 mg
- Total Fat: 40 g
- Fiber: 1 g
- Protein: 30 g
- Sodium: 669 mg

107. Christmas Morning Frittata

"A wonderful Christmas breakfast for busy people."
Serving: 6-8 servings. | Prep: 15m | Ready in: 40m

Ingredients

- 1 medium onion, chopped
- 1 medium green pepper, chopped
- 1 garlic clove, minced
- 2 tbsps. butter
- 1/2 cup chopped tomatoes
- 1/4 cup minced fresh parsley

- 5 large eggs, lightly beaten
- 2 cups shredded mozzarella cheese
- 1/2 cup soft bread crumbs
- 1 tsp. Worcestershire sauce
- 1/2 to 1 tsp. salt
- 1/4 tsp. pepper

Direction

- Sauté garlic, green pepper, and onion in butter in a skillet until they become tender, or for 5 minutes. Take away from the heat. Stir in parsley and tomatoes; then put aside. Blend the remaining ingredients in a large bowl. Add in the reserved vegetables and stir.
- Add into an ungreased 9-inch pie plate. Uncover and bake at 350 degrees until a knife comes out clean after inserted in the center, or for 25-30 minutes. Before cutting, allow to stand for 5 minutes.

Nutrition Information

- Calories: 174 calories
- Total Carbohydrate: 6 g
- Cholesterol: 162 mg
- Total Fat: 12 g
- Fiber: 1 g
- Protein: 10 g
- Sodium: 345 mg

108. Colorful Frittata

""This egg dish has a unique taste that comes from Dijon mustard. It makes your family to eat more vegetables.""
Serving: 6 servings. | Prep: 5m | Ready in: 30m

Ingredients

- 1 cup broccoli florets
- 3/4 cup sliced fresh mushrooms
- 2 green onions, finely chopped
- 1 tbsp. butter
- 1 cup cubed fully cooked ham
- 8 large eggs
- 1/4 cup water
- 1/4 cup Dijon mustard
- 1/2 tsp. Italian seasoning
- 1/4 tsp. garlic salt
- 1-1/2 cups shredded cheddar cheese
- 1/2 cup chopped tomatoes

Direction

- Sauté onions, mushrooms, and broccoli in butter in a large skill until softened. Add ham and cook until heated through. Turn off the heat and keep warm.
- Whisk garlic salt, Italian seasoning, mustard, water, and eggs together in a bowl until foamy. Mix in broccoli mixture, tomatoes, and cheese.
- Pour the mixture into an oiled shallow 1-1/2-quart baking dish. Bake at 375° for 22 to 27 minutes or until a knife comes out clean when inserted in the center.

Nutrition Information

- Calories: 277 calories
- Total Carbohydrate: 6 g
- Cholesterol: 331 mg
- Total Fat: 20 g
- Fiber: 1 g
- Protein: 20 g
- Sodium: 905 mg

109. Country Oven Omelet

"I love to make this on weekends"
Serving: 4-6 servings. | Prep: 20m | Ready in: 01h10m

Ingredients

- 1 large onion, chopped, divided
- 3 tbsps. canola oil
- 3-1/2 cups frozen shredded hash brown potatoes
- 1-1/2 tsps. salt, divided
- 1/2 tsp. pepper, divided
- 1 lb. ground beef
- 1/4 cup chopped green pepper

- 1/4 cup chopped sweet red pepper
- 1 tbsp. dried parsley flakes
- 1 cup shredded Swiss cheese or shredded part-skim mozzarella cheese
- 4 large eggs
- 1-1/4 cups whole milk
- 1/4 tsp. paprika

Direction

- Sauté 1/2 cup onion in oil in a skillet. Add 1/4 tsp. pepper, 3/4 tsp. salt and harsh browns. Cook for 5 minutes over medium heat until harsh browns are defrosted. Place mixture into an ungreased 10 inch pie plate and press until it forms a shell.
- Bake at 400° for 20 minutes. In the meantime, cook remaining onion, peppers and beef in a skillet over medium heat until meat losses its pink color; drain. Stir in parsley. Place mixture into the potato shell. Add cheese on top.
- Beat paprika, milk, eggs and the leftover salt and pepper in a bowl then pour over the meat mixture. Bake at 400° for 30 minutes until a knife is still clean after being inserted into the center. Allow to rest for 5 minutes before cutting.

Nutrition Information

- Calories: 376 calories
- Total Carbohydrate: 14 g
- Cholesterol: 202 mg
- Total Fat: 24 g
- Fiber: 1 g
- Protein: 26 g
- Sodium: 761 mg

110. Eggs Florentine

"These eggs Florentine recipe is very basic. The important thing is that you don't overcook it."
Serving: 3 | Prep: 10m | Ready in: 20m

Ingredients

- 2 tbsps. butter
- 1/2 cup mushrooms, sliced
- 2 cloves garlic, minced
- 1/2 (10 oz.) package fresh spinach
- 6 large eggs, slightly beaten
- salt and ground black pepper to taste
- 3 tbsps. cream cheese, cut into small pieces

Direction

- In a big frying pan, heat butter over medium heat, stir and cook garlic and mushrooms for 1 minute until garlic is aromatic. Add spinach to the mushroom mixture and cook for 2-3 minutes until spinach wilts.
- Mix eggs into the spinach-mushroom mixture, use pepper and salt to season. Cook, but do not toss, until the eggs begin to firm; turn over. Drizzle the egg mixture with cream cheese and cook for 5 minutes until the cream cheese begins to melt.

Nutrition Information

- Calories: 279 calories;
- Total Carbohydrate: 4.1 g
- Cholesterol: 408 mg
- Total Fat: 22.9 g
- Protein: 15.7 g
- Sodium: 276 mg

111. Flavorful Frittata

"This frittata has the Italian flair from the basil."
Serving: 8 servings. | Prep: 30m | Ready in: 30m

Ingredients

- 1 cup cooked Jones No Sugar Pork Sausage Roll
- 1 small onion, chopped
- 1 jar (4-1/2 oz.) sliced mushrooms, drained
- 1 to 2 tbsps. canola oil
- 12 large eggs
- 1/4 cup half-and-half cream
- 1 tsp. dried basil
- 1/2 tsp. salt

- 1 cup shredded part-skim mozzarella cheese
- 2 cups meatless spaghetti sauce, warmed

Direction

- Sauté mushrooms, onion and sausage in oil in a big nonstick skillet till onion becomes softened. At the same time, mix salt, basil, cream and eggs in a big bowl; add on top of sausage mixture.
- When eggs set, lift the edges, letting uncooked portion flow under. Once eggs are almost set, drizzle with cheese. Cook till the cheese is melted. Chop into wedges; serve along with spaghetti sauce.

Nutrition Information

- Calories: 258 calories
- Total Carbohydrate: 9 g
- Cholesterol: 345 mg
- Total Fat: 16 g
- Fiber: 2 g
- Protein: 18 g
- Sodium: 805 mg

112. Florentine Egg Bake

"You only need some of the practical ingredients like store-bought pesto, biscuit mix and fridge hash browns in making this tasty breakfast bake. You can also use crab meat instead of ham for a seafood version."
Serving: 8 servings. | Prep: 30m | Ready in: 01h20m

Ingredients

- 1 package (20 oz.) refrigerated shredded hash brown potatoes
- 1 tbsp. olive oil
- 1 package (10 oz.) frozen chopped spinach, thawed and squeezed dry
- 4 oz. Swiss cheese, cubed
- 4 oz. thinly sliced deli ham, coarsely chopped
- 8 eggs, lightly beaten
- 1/2 cup buttermilk
- 1 tbsp. prepared pesto
- 1 cup biscuit/baking mix
- 1/4 tsp. salt
- 1/8 tsp. pepper
- 1-1/2 cups shredded Asiago cheese
- 2 tbsps. minced fresh basil

Direction

- Mix oil and hash browns in a big bowl; press in a cooking-spray-coated 13-in by 9-in baking dish. Bake for 25-30 mins in a 350 degrees F oven or until golden brown on the edges.
- Mix Swiss cheese and spinach; scatter on top of the crust then put ham on top. Beat pesto, buttermilk, and eggs in a big bowl. Mix pepper, salt, and biscuit mix; put into the egg mixture. Mix in Asiago cheese. Pour the mixture on top of the ham.
- Bake for 25-30 mins without a cover until an inserted knife in the middle comes out clean. Let it sit for 10-15 mins then slice. Scatter with basil.

Nutrition Information

- Calories: 391 calories
- Total Carbohydrate: 28 g
- Cholesterol: 253 mg
- Total Fat: 21 g
- Fiber: 2 g
- Protein: 23 g
- Sodium: 714 mg

113. Florentine Frittata For Two

"You only need some simple ingredients in this easy weeknight or breakfast dish. You can also add you leftover shrimp or chicken to make this dish even more filling."
Serving: 2 servings. | Prep: 20m | Ready in: 25m

Ingredients

- 3 large eggs
- 3 large egg whites
- 2 tbsps. 2% milk
- 2 tbsps. chopped pitted Greek olives
- 1/4 tsp. salt
- 1/4 tsp. pepper

- 1/4 cup oil-packed sun-dried tomatoes
- 1/2 tsp. dried basil
- 1/4 tsp. dried rosemary, crushed
- 3 cups fresh baby spinach, coarsely chopped
- 1/2 cup crumbled feta cheese

Direction

- Beat the first 6 ingredients in a small bowl; set aside. In an 8-in ovenproof pan, put the tomatoes then top with rosemary and basil; set on medium heat. Add the egg mixture to the pan then put the spinach on top; cover. Cook for 3-5mins until the eggs start to set.
- Remove the cover then top with cheese. Broil for 3-5mins, three to four inches from heat until the eggs are set completely. Let it sit for 5mins then serve.

Nutrition Information

- Calories: 277 calories
- Total Carbohydrate: 9 g
- Cholesterol: 333 mg
- Total Fat: 17 g
- Fiber: 3 g
- Protein: 23 g
- Sodium: 972 mg

114. Fresh Vegetable Frittata

"This recipe is perfect for a breakfast with fresh vegetables."
Serving: 2 servings. | Prep: 15m | Ready in: 35m

Ingredients

- 1 cup egg substitute
- 1 cup sliced fresh mushrooms
- 1/2 cup chopped fresh broccoli
- 1/4 cup shredded reduced-fat cheddar cheese
- 2 tbsps. finely chopped onion
- 2 tbsps. finely chopped green pepper
- 2 tbsps. grated Parmesan cheese
- 1/8 tsp. salt
- Dash pepper

Direction

- Mix all ingredients together in a big bowl. Add to one shallow 2-cup baking plate coated with cooking spray.
- Bake at 350 degrees while uncovered till a knife inserted in the middle comes out clean about 20 to 25 minutes. Serve right away.

Nutrition Information

- Calories: 141 calories
- Total Carbohydrate: 6 g
- Cholesterol: 14 mg
- Total Fat: 5 g
- Fiber: 1 g
- Protein: 19 g
- Sodium: 571 mg

115. Garden Cheddar Frittata

"An easy to make and delicious frittata recipe."
Serving: 6 servings. | Prep: 30m | Ready in: 45m

Ingredients

- 2 small potatoes, peeled and cut into 1/2-inch cubes
- 8 large eggs, lightly beaten
- 2 tbsps. water
- 1/4 tsp. salt
- 1/8 tsp. garlic powder
- 1/8 tsp. chili powder
- 1/8 tsp. pepper
- 1 small zucchini, chopped
- 1/4 cup chopped onion
- 1 tbsp. butter
- 1 tbsp. olive oil
- 2 plum tomatoes, thinly sliced
- 1 cup shredded sharp cheddar cheese
- Minced chives and additional shredded cheddar cheese

Direction

- Set an oven to preheat to 425 degrees. In a small saucepan, put the potatoes and pour

water to cover, then boil. Lower the heat, put cover and let it simmer for 5 minutes, then drain. Whisk the pepper, chili powder, garlic powder, salt, water and eggs in a big bowl, then put aside.
- Sauté the potatoes, onion and zucchini in oil and butter in a 10-inch cast iron or other ovenproof frying pan, until it becomes tender. Lower the heat. Pour 1 1/2 cups of the egg mixture into the frying pan. Lay out 1/2 of the tomatoes on top and sprinkle 1/2 cup of cheese on top. Put the leftover egg mixture and the tomatoes, then the cheese on top.
- Let it bake for 12 to 15 minutes without cover or until the eggs become fully set. Allow it to stand for 5 minutes. Sprinkle it with extra cheddar cheese and chives, then slice it into wedges.

Nutrition Information

- Calories: 251 calories
- Total Carbohydrate: 13 g
- Cholesterol: 307 mg
- Total Fat: 16 g
- Fiber: 2 g
- Protein: 14 g
- Sodium: 325 mg

116. Garlic Zucchini Frittata

"I usually serve dishes that both contrast and complement well with each. This quick savory egg dish can easily double. You may use a leftover chopped ham or taco meat in placed of bacon."

Serving: 4 servings. | Prep: 10m | Ready in: 25m

Ingredients

- 1 tbsp. butter
- 1 tbsp. finely chopped onion
- 4 garlic cloves, minced
- 1 medium zucchini, shredded
- 6 eggs, lightly beaten
- 1/4 tsp. ground mustard
- 4 bacon strips, cooked and crumbled
- 1/4 tsp. salt
- 1/8 tsp. pepper
- 1/4 cup shredded Swiss cheese
- 1/4 cup sliced green onions

Direction

- Place the butter in a 10-in. ovenproof skillet and melt over medium-high heat. Drop the garlic and onion; sauté for a minute. Mix in the zucchini and let it cook for 3 minutes or until softened.
- Beat the eggs and mustard in a big bowl. Pour the mixture in the skillet. Scatter the bacon and season with pepper and salt. As the eggs set, lift the edges while allowing the uncooked portion flow underneath. Let it cook for roughly 7 minutes until the eggs are almost set.
- Position the skillet under the broiler, 6 in. away from the heat source. Broil for 30-60 seconds or until the eggs are entirely set. Top it off with green onions and cheese. Broil for 30 seconds more or until the cheese has melt. Slice into wedges.

Nutrition Information

- Calories: 214 calories
- Total Carbohydrate: 4 g
- Cholesterol: 338 mg
- Total Fat: 15 g
- Fiber: 1 g
- Protein: 14 g
- Sodium: 393 mg

117. Ham And Egg Breakfast Casseroles

"I came up with this breakfast casserole for my family as I tried using things up in my fridge. My kids even loved it!"
Serving: 2 casseroles (12 servings each). | Prep: 25m | Ready in: 55m

Ingredients

- 1 lb. fresh mushrooms, coarsely chopped
- 1/3 cup butter, cubed
- 1/2 tsp. Italian seasoning
- 1/8 tsp. pepper
- 4 cups shredded sharp cheddar cheese
- 1-3/4 cups cubed fully cooked ham
- 1/2 cup shredded Parmesan cheese
- 2 tbsps. all-purpose flour
- 24 large eggs
- 2 cups heavy whipping cream
- 1 tbsp. Dijon mustard
- 1/8 tsp. white pepper

Direction

- Sauté the mushrooms in butter in a Dutch oven until tender. Put an Italian seasoning and pepper; sauté for additional 1 minute. Scatter the mushroom mixture equally between two greased 13x9-in. baking dishes.
- Blend together the cheddar cheese, Parmesan cheese, flour and ham. Top it off over the mushroom mixture. Whisk the eggs, mustard, white pepper and cream in a different big bowl. Drizzle it over the cheese mixture.
- Keep the casserole in the freezer while covered for up to 3 months. Bake the rest of the casserole, without placing any cover, at 350° for roughly 30-35 minutes or until a knife poked in the center comes out clean. Let it rest for about 10 minutes before you slice it.
- In using the frozen casserole: Take it out from the freezer half an hour before baking (Avoid thawing). Let it bake while covered at 350° for 55 minutes. Take off the cover; let it bake for 15 to 20 minutes more or until a knife poked in the middle comes out clean. Let it rest for roughly 10 minutes before you slice it.

Nutrition Information

- Calories: 270 calories
- Total Carbohydrate: 3 g
- Cholesterol: 275 mg
- Total Fat: 22 g
- Fiber: 0 g
- Protein: 15 g
- Sodium: 489 mg

118. Hashbrown And Sausage Breakfast Pizza

"This pizza is a great breakfast, but you can serve it as an appetizer as well."
Serving: 6-8 slices. | Prep: 15m | Ready in: 40m

Ingredients

- 1 tube (8 oz.) refrigerated crescent rolls
- 1 lb. Jones No Sugar Pork Sausage Roll sausage
- 1 cup frozen shredded hash brown potatoes, thawed
- 1 jar (4-1/2 oz.) sliced mushrooms, drained
- 6 bacon strips, cooked and crumbled
- 1/2 cup sliced ripe olives
- 1 cup shredded cheddar cheese
- 1 cup shredded mozzarella cheese
- 5 large eggs
- 1/4 cup whole milk
- 1/2 tsp. salt
- 2 tbsps. grated Parmesan cheese

Direction

- Roll out crescent dough and pull apart into triangles, put on an oiled 12-in. pizza pan. Press the seams together and make edges, put aside.
- Cook sausage in a frying pan over medium heat until no more pink, strain and let cool down slightly. Drizzle over the dough with

olives, bacon, mushrooms, hash browns, and sausage. Put mozzarella and cheddar on top.
- Whisk salt, milk, and eggs in a bowl, put on the pizza. Use Parmesan cheese to drizzle. Bake at 375° until turning golden brown, about 25-30 minutes. Let it sit for 10 minutes before slicing.

Nutrition Information

- Calories: 561 calories
- Total Carbohydrate: 22 g
- Cholesterol: 247 mg
- Total Fat: 41 g
- Fiber: 1 g
- Protein: 25 g
- Sodium: 1366 mg

119. Hearty Potato Frittata

"A flavorful frittata that is so worth the try!"
Serving: 6 servings. | Prep: 20m | Ready in: 40m

Ingredients

- 3/4 lb. lean ground turkey
- 1/2 cup chopped green pepper
- 1/2 tsp. rubbed sage
- 1/2 tsp. crushed red pepper flakes
- 1/8 tsp. ground nutmeg
- 1/2 cup sliced fresh mushrooms
- 2 green onions, chopped
- 4 small red potatoes, thinly sliced
- 4 tsps. butter
- 8 egg whites
- 4 eggs
- 3 tbsps. fat-free milk
- 1 tsp. salt
- 1/4 tsp. pepper

Direction

- Use a cooking spray to grease a 12-inch oven-safe skillet; put in the green pepper, pepper flakes, turkey, nutmeg, and sage then let it cook for 3 minutes over medium heat. Put in the onions and mushrooms and sauté the mixture for 4-5 more minutes until the turkey meat is cooked through and the vegetables have softened. Drain the mixture and put it aside. Put butter in the same skillet and let the potatoes cook in it until they turn light brown in color and are just starting to soften. Put the turkey mixture back into the skillet. Mix the eggs, salt, egg whites, pepper, and milk together in a big bowl. Put it evenly on top of the turkey mixture. Put the lid onto the skillet and let the mixture cook for 8-12 minutes over low heat until the mixture has almost set. Remove the lid from the skillet. Put the mixture in the oven broiler 3-4 inches away from the heat source and let it broil for 3-5 minutes until the eggs have fully set. Allow it to sit for 5 minutes first before slicing.

Nutrition Information

- Calories: 263 calories
- Total Carbohydrate: 20 g
- Cholesterol: 193 mg
- Total Fat: 11 g
- Fiber: 2 g
- Protein: 21 g
- Sodium: 596 mg

120. Impossible Garden Pie

"This delicious and light egg dish features biscuit mix, asparagus and an array of spring garden veggies."
Serving: 6 servings. | Prep: 15m | Ready in: 45m

Ingredients

- 2 cups cut fresh asparagus (1-inch pieces)
- 1-1/2 cups chopped fresh tomatoes
- 1 medium onion, chopped
- 1 garlic clove, minced
- 1/4 tsp. dried basil
- 1/4 tsp. salt
- 1/4 tsp. pepper
- 1 cup shredded part-skim mozzarella cheese
- 1/2 cup grated Parmesan cheese

- 3/4 cup reduced-fat biscuit/baking mix
- 3 large eggs
- 1-1/2 cups fat-free milk

Direction

- Mix the first 7 ingredients in a big bowl. Move to a cooking-spray-coated eight-inch square baking dish. Top with cheese.
- Whisk milk, eggs, and biscuit mix in a separate big bowl until smooth; pour all over the cheese. Bake for 30-35mins in a 400 degrees oven without cover until set and an inserted thermometer in the middle registers 160 degrees. Let it sit for 5mins. Slice.

Nutrition Information

- Calories: 221 calories
- Total Carbohydrate: 20 g
- Cholesterol: 124 mg
- Total Fat: 9 g
- Fiber: 2 g
- Protein: 15 g
- Sodium: 553 mg

121. Individual Italian Frittatas

"This Italian-spired frittata is so delicious with mozzarella, sweet peppers and salami."
Serving: 2 servings. | Prep: 25m | Ready in: 45m

Ingredients

- 1/4 cup finely chopped onion
- 2 tsps. olive oil
- 4 medium fresh mushrooms, chopped
- 4 thin slices hard salami, julienned
- 2 tbsps. finely chopped roasted sweet red pepper
- 4 large eggs
- 1 tbsp. 2% milk
- 1 tbsp. grated Parmesan cheese
- 2 tsps. minced fresh parsley
- 1 tsp. minced fresh chives
- Dash pepper
- 1/4 cup shredded part-skim mozzarella cheese
- Chopped fresh chives, optional

Direction

- On medium heat, cook and stir onion with oil in a small-sized skillet till it becomes soft. Put in mushrooms; cook till softened, 2 to 4 more minutes. Separate among two greased 8-oz. ramekins. Add red pepper and salami on top.
- Mix pepper, minced chives, parsley, Parmesan cheese, milk and eggs in a small-sized bowl; add to the ramekins. Bake for 10 minutes at 400 degrees.
- Drizzle with mozzarella cheese; bake till eggs become set, about 8 to 10 more minutes. Drizzle with chopped chives if you wish.

Nutrition Information

- Calories: 339 calories
- Total Carbohydrate: 6 g
- Cholesterol: 456 mg
- Total Fat: 24 g
- Fiber: 1 g
- Protein: 24 g
- Sodium: 751 mg

122. Italian Apricot-pancetta Strata

"This simple dish is inspired by Italian cuisine and is made of both sweet and savory ingredients. You can serve it as lunch or breakfast."
Serving: 12 servings. | Prep: 35m | Ready in: 01h10m

Ingredients

- 1/3 lb. pancetta, finely chopped
- 2 tbsps. butter, divided
- 1-1/3 cups finely chopped sweet onion
- 2 cups sliced fresh mushrooms
- 3 cups fresh baby spinach, coarsely chopped
- 5 cups cubed multigrain bread
- 1/2 cup sliced almonds, optional
- 6 large eggs
- 1 cup heavy whipping cream

- 1/4 tsp. salt
- 1/4 tsp. pepper
- 1 carton (8 oz.) mascarpone cheese
- 1 cup shredded part-skim mozzarella cheese
- 1/2 cup shredded Asiago cheese
- 1 cup apricot preserves
- 3 tbsps. minced fresh basil

Direction

- Put pancetta in a large skillet and cook till they crisp, remember to stir once in a while. Use a slotted spoon to get pancetta out of the skillet; drain them on paper towels. Throw away the drippings, keep a tbsp. in pan.
- Add a tbsp. of butter to drippings; heat on medium-high heat. Put in onion; cook till onion becomes soft, about 4 to 6 minutes. Move onion to a large bowl.
- Put the remaining butter in pan on heat. Put in mushrooms; cook and stir till mushrooms become soft, about 2 to 3 minutes. Stir in spinach; cook till spinach is wilted, about 30 to 45 seconds.
- Put pancetta, mushroom mixture, cubes of bread and almond according to your liking into onion; toss to mix. Grease a 13x9-in. baking dish and put the mixture into it.
- Beat pepper, salt, cream and eggs in a large bowl till everything is blended. Put in mascarpone cheese and beat just till blended; pour on bread. Use Asiago cheese and mozzarella cheese to sprinkle. Use a spoon to transfer preserves on top. Cover and keep in the fridge for a couple of hours or overnight.
- To preheat: Set oven to 350°. While oven heats, get the strata out of the fridge. Uncover the strata, put it into the oven and bake till it becomes golden brown and a knife comes out clean after being inserted in the center of the strata, about 35 to 45 minutes. Use basil to sprinkle. Allow to sit for 5 to 10 minutes before cutting.

123. Italian Baked Eggs & Sausage

"A rich casserole of fire-roasted tomatoes, Italian sausage, and eggs with butter spread."
Serving: 8 servings. | Prep: 15m | Ready in: 45m

Ingredients

- 1 lb. Johnsonville® Ground Mild Italian sausage
- 1 jar (24 oz.) fire-roasted tomato and garlic pasta sauce
- 1 can (14-1/2 oz.) fire-roasted diced tomatoes, drained
- 3/4 cup part-skim ricotta cheese
- 8 large eggs
- 1/4 tsp. salt
- 1/4 tsp. pepper
- 1/4 cup shredded Parmesan cheese
- 1 tbsp. minced fresh basil
- 1 French bread demi-baguette (4 oz.), cut into 1-inch slices
- 1/4 cup butter, softened

Direction

- Set an oven to 350 degrees and start preheating. Cook the sausage, crumbling the meat in a large skillet over medium heat until not pink anymore; then drain. Stir in tomatoes and pasta sauce. Arrange on a 13x9-inch baking dish.
- Top the meat mixture with a dollop of ricotta cheese. Carefully break an egg in a small bowl; slip the egg onto ricotta. Repeat the process for the remaining eggs. Dust with Parmesan cheese, pepper, and salt.
- Bake until the yolks start to become thick but not hard and the whites are set completely, 30-35 minutes. Take out of the oven and dust with basil.
- At the same time, spread the butter over the bread slices; arrange them on an ungreased baking sheet. Preheat the broiler. Broil 3-4 inches from the heat source for 1-2 minutes per

side until golden brown. Serve right away together with baked eggs.

Nutrition Information

- Calories: 408 calories
- Total Carbohydrate: 22 g
- Cholesterol: 241 mg
- Total Fat: 27 g
- Fiber: 3 g
- Protein: 19 g
- Sodium: 1183 mg

124. Italian Breakfast Casseroles

"You can use your leftover spaghetti sauce for this delicious Italian casserole."
Serving: 4 servings. | Prep: 20m | Ready in: 40m

Ingredients

- 4 medium red potatoes, sliced
- 2 tbsps. vegetable oil
- 8 eggs, lightly beaten
- 1 tbsp. butter
- 1/2 lb. thinly sliced fully cooked ham, diced
- 2 cups spaghetti sauce
- 1/2 cup each shredded cheddar and mozzarella cheese

Direction

- Fry potatoes for approximately 10-15 mins in a skillet with oil until tender; place on the bottom of 4 individual of 16-oz. dish in. Scramble eggs in the same skillet with butter until set; scoop on top of the potatoes. Add ham on top. Put half cup of spaghetti sauce in each casserole; scatter with cheese. Bake for 20 mins in a 350 degrees F oven or until bubbly and hot.

Nutrition Information

- Calories: 566 calories
- Total Carbohydrate: 34 g
- Cholesterol: 482 mg
- Total Fat: 33 g
- Fiber: 4 g
- Protein: 34 g
- Sodium: 1405 mg

125. Italian Brunch Bake

""This is the best dish to be served when you have friends coming over for a brunch.""
Serving: 12 servings. | Prep: 30m | Ready in: 01h25m

Ingredients

- 1 lb. Johnsonville® Ground Mild Italian sausage
- 1 lb. baby portobello mushrooms, quartered
- 1 large onion, chopped
- 1 medium sweet red pepper, chopped
- 1 medium green pepper, chopped
- 2 garlic cloves, minced
- 2 packages (6 oz. each) fresh baby spinach
- 8 slices Italian bread (1 inch thick)
- 12 large eggs
- 1 cup 2% milk
- 1 tsp. Italian seasoning
- 1/2 tsp. salt
- 1/2 tsp. pepper
- 1/4 tsp. ground nutmeg
- 4 cups shredded Italian cheese blend

Direction

- Place a large skillet on medium heat and cook garlic, peppers, onion, mushrooms and sausage till meat is not pink anymore; strain and set aside.
- Coat a large skillet with cooking spray and sauté spinach till wilted. Arrange bread on a baking dish. Allow to broil 2-3 in. from the heat till lightly browned, 1-2 minutes. Move to a greased 13x9-in. baking sheet.
- Combine nutmeg, pepper, salt, Italian seasoning, milk and eggs together in a large bowl. Layer spinach and the sausage mixture over the bread; transfer the egg mixture over

the top. Sprinkle with cheese; refrigerate with a cover overnight.
- Take it out from the refrigerator 30 minutes before baking. Set the oven at 350° and start preheating. Bake with a cover for 50 minutes. Uncover; continue baking for 5-10 more minutes or till a knife comes out clean when inserted in the center. Allow to sit for 10 minutes and start cutting.

Nutrition Information

- Calories: 373 calories
- Total Carbohydrate: 23 g
- Cholesterol: 255 mg
- Total Fat: 20 g
- Fiber: 3 g
- Protein: 24 g
- Sodium: 839 mg

126. Italian Brunch Torte

"This layered breakfast bake is one of our most famous dishes and can be served cold or warm."
Serving: 12 servings. | Prep: 50m | Ready in: 01h50m

Ingredients

- 2 tubes (8 oz. each) refrigerated crescent rolls, divided
- 1 tsp. olive oil
- 1 package (6 oz.) fresh baby spinach
- 1 cup sliced fresh mushrooms
- 7 large eggs
- 1 cup grated Parmesan cheese
- 2 tsps. Italian seasoning
- 1/8 tsp. pepper
- 1/2 lb. thinly sliced deli ham
- 1/2 lb. thinly sliced hard salami
- 1/2 lb. sliced provolone cheese
- 2 jars (12 oz. each) roasted sweet red peppers, drained, sliced and patted dry

Direction

- Set the oven to 350° and start preheating. Grease a 9-in. springform pan and place it on a heavy-duty foil (about 18 in. square) with double thickness. Securely wrap the pan with foil. Unroll and separate 1 tube of crescent dough into triangles. To create a crust, press onto bottom of prepared pan, seal seams well. Bake until set or for 10-15 minutes.
- In the meantime, heat oil over medium-high heat in a large skillet. Add mushrooms and spinach; cook while stirring until mushrooms become tender. Drain on several layers of paper towels, blot well. Beat pepper, Italian seasoning, Parmesan cheese and 6 eggs in a large bowl.
- Layer crust with 1/2 of each of ham, salami, provolone cheese, red peppers and spinach mixture. Pour 1/2 of the egg mixture over top. Repeat layers, place the remaining egg mixture on top.
- On a work surface, unroll the remaining crescent dough and divide them into triangles. Press together to shape a circle, seal seams; put over filling. Beat remaining eggs and brush over dough.
- Bake without a cover until a thermometer reads 160° or for 1 to 1-1/4 hours, loosely cover with foil if necessary to prevent overbrowning. Using a knife, loosen sides from pan carefully; remove the rim from the pan. Allow to sit for 20 minutes.

Nutrition Information

- Calories: 403 calories
- Total Carbohydrate: 19 g
- Cholesterol: 167 mg
- Total Fat: 24 g
- Fiber: 0 g
- Protein: 23 g
- Sodium: 1360 mg

127. Italian Cloud Eggs

"Egg yolks on a nest of whipped Italian-seasoned egg whites that was baked to perfection."
Serving: 4 servings. | Prep: 15m | Ready in: 25m

Ingredients

- 4 large eggs, separated
- 1/4 tsp. Italian seasoning
- 1/8 tsp. salt
- 1/8 tsp. pepper
- 1/4 cup shredded Parmesan cheese
- 1 tbsp. minced fresh basil
- 1 tbsp. finely chopped oil-packed sun-dried tomatoes

Direction

- Set an oven to preheat to 450 degrees. Separate the eggs. In a big bowl, put the whites and place the yolks in another 4 small bowls. Beat the pepper, salt, Italian seasoning and egg whites until it forms stiff peaks.
- Drop the egg white mixture into 4 mounds in a 9-inch cast iron skillet that was generously coated with cooking spray. Make a small well in the middle of each mound using the back of a spoon, then sprinkle cheese on top. Let it bake for around 5 minutes, until it becomes light brown. Slip an egg yolk gently into each of the mounds, then let it bake for another 3-5 minutes until the yolks become set. Sprinkle it with tomatoes and basil, then serve right away.

Nutrition Information

- Calories: 96 calories
- Total Carbohydrate: 1 g
- Cholesterol: 190 mg
- Total Fat: 6 g
- Fiber: 0 g
- Protein: 8 g
- Sodium: 234 mg

128. Italian Egg Bake

"This recipe combines some of my most preferred flavors and my husband enjoys it very much."
Serving: 6 servings. | Prep: 20m | Ready in: 01h05m

Ingredients

- 4 slices sandwich bread, cubed
- 1/4 cup coarsely chopped fresh basil
- 1/4 cup soft sun-dried tomato halves (not packed in oil), finely chopped
- 6 bacon strips, cooked and crumbled
- 1 cup shredded part-skim mozzarella cheese
- 6 large eggs
- 2/3 cup 2% milk
- 1 garlic clove, minced
- 1/2 tsp. salt
- 1/4 tsp. pepper
- 1 tbsp. minced chives

Direction

- Layer 1/2 each of bread, basil, tomatoes, bacon and cheese in a greased 8-in. square baking dish. Repeat layers.
- Beat pepper, salt, garlic, milk and eggs in a small bowl. Place over the layers. Cover and refrigerate for several hours or overnight.
- Turn the oven to 350° and start preheating. Take casserole out of the fridge while oven heats. Bake with a cover for 30 minutes. Bake without a cover for another 15-20 minutes or until golden, puffed and the inserted knife in the center comes out clean. Dust with chives. Allow to sit for 5-10 minutes before cutting.

129. Italian Eggs Benedict With Pesto Hollandaise

"Italian-inspired eggs Benedict with prosciutto and pesto that is perfect for fancy weekend breakfast dates."
Serving: 4 servings. | Prep: 10m | Ready in: 30m

Ingredients

- 1/2 cup butter, cubed

- 1 tbsp. prepared pesto
- 4 large egg yolks
- 2 tbsps. water
- 1 tbsp. lemon juice
- 2 tsps. white vinegar
- 4 large eggs
- 8 thin slices prosciutto or deli ham
- 4 fresh basil leaves
- 4 slices tomato
- 4 slices Italian bread (1 inch thick), toasted

Direction

- Melt butter in a small pot; mix in pesto. Whisk lemon juice, water, and egg yolks in a metal bowl set over simmering water or on top of a double broiler until combined; cook while constantly mixing until it reaches 160 degrees and is thick enough to cover a metal spoon. Turn to very low heat; pour in warm melted butter mixture very slowly while constantly mixing.
- Move to a small bowl then set the bowl in a bigger bowl with warm water. Mix from time to time while keeping warm until serving. Pour 2 to 3 inches of water in a big pot or pan with high sides; pour in vinegar then boil. Adjust heat to keep a gentle simmer. Break one cold egg at a time in a small bowl; keep the bowl close over the water then slide each egg in the water.
- Cook for 3-5mins without cover until the yolks start to thicken yet not hard and the whites are set completely. Lift the eggs out with a slotted spoon.
- On a toast, layer tomato, basil, prosciutto, and eggs. Add hollandaise sauce on top then serve right away.

Nutrition Information

- Calories: 525 calories
- Total Carbohydrate: 24 g
- Cholesterol: 457 mg
- Total Fat: 39 g
- Fiber: 2 g
- Protein: 21 g
- Sodium: 1092 mg

130. Italian Frittata

"The ingredients of these easy-to-make frittatas can be changed depending on your preference. Even the leftovers still taste divine."
Serving: 6 | Prep: 25m | Ready in: 50m

Ingredients

- 1/2 cup diced salami
- 1/2 cup artichoke hearts, drained and chopped
- 1/2 cup chopped cherry tomatoes
- 1 (4.5 oz.) can sliced mushrooms, drained
- 6 eggs
- 1/3 cup milk
- 2 green onions, chopped
- 1 clove garlic, minced
- 1 tsp. dried basil
- 1 tsp. onion powder
- 1 tsp. salt
- ground black pepper to taste
- 1/3 cup grated Parmesan cheese
- 1 cup shredded mozzarella cheese

Direction

- Preheat the oven to 220°C or 425°F; lightly grease a shallow 2qt baking pan.
- On medium heat, heat a pan then add mushrooms, salami, tomatoes, and artichokes. Cook and stir for 4 mins until heated completely; move to the greased baking pan.
- In a big bowl, combine black pepper, eggs, salt, milk, onion powder, green onions, basil, and garlic; spread on top of the salami mixture. Add Parmesan cheese and mozzarella cheese on top.
- Bake in the preheated oven for 20 mins until the cheese melts and the eggs set.

Nutrition Information

- Calories: 211 calories;
- Total Carbohydrate: 5.9 g
- Cholesterol: 216 mg

- Total Fat: 13.4 g
- Protein: 17 g
- Sodium: 1049 mg

131. Italian Mini Frittatas

""Each frittata here looks quite slim because the amounts of each ingredient are quite small. It's very simple to make and great for a brunch.""
Serving: 1 dozen. | Prep: 25m | Ready in: 50m

Ingredients

- 2 tbsps. chopped sun-dried tomatoes (not packed in oil)
- 1/2 cup boiling water
- 2 thin slices prosciutto, finely chopped
- 1/4 cup chopped shallots
- 1 tsp. butter
- 2 garlic cloves, minced
- 1/4 cup all-purpose flour
- 1-1/2 cups fat-free milk
- 4 large egg whites
- 2 large eggs
- 1 cup shredded part-skim mozzarella cheese
- 1/4 cup shredded Asiago cheese
- 1/2 cup canned water-packed artichoke hearts, rinsed, drained and chopped
- 2 tbsps. minced fresh basil or 2 tsps. dried basil
- 3/4 tsp. salt
- 1/2 tsp. white pepper

Direction

- Pour boiling water over tomatoes placed in a small bowl. Cover the bowl and let sit for 5 minutes. Drain off water and set aside.
- Sauté shallots and prosciutto in butter in a small nonstick skillet until shallots are softened. Stir in garlic, cook for 1 more minute. Turn the heat off and put to one side.
- Combine milk and flour in a large bowl until no lumps remain; mix in the eggs and egg whites until incorporated. Mix in prosciutto mixture, reserved tomatoes, pepper, salt, basil, artichokes, and cheeses.
- Grease 12 muffin cups using cooking spray; pour in egg mixture. Bake for 25 to 30 minutes at 350° or until an inserted knife near the middle comes out clean. Gently run a knife around the inside edges to loosen; take out of pan. Serve while warm.

Nutrition Information

- Calories: 172 calories
- Total Carbohydrate: 11 g
- Cholesterol: 93 mg
- Total Fat: 7 g
- Fiber: 0 g
- Protein: 15 g
- Sodium: 642 mg

132. Italian Omelet

"This fast and delicious omelette for four is a cholesterol-free egg product folded with onions and turkey sausage."
Serving: Makes 4 servings. | Prep: 5m | Ready in: 18m

Ingredients

- 1/2 cup chopped onion s
- 4 oz. frozen ground turkey sausage , thawed
- 2 cups cholesterol-free egg product

Direction

- 1. Use cooking spray to coat a medium non-stick frying pan. Add sausage and onions; on medium-high heat, cook and occasionally stir for 5 minutes or up to when sausage is browned on all sides. Remove from skillet.
- 2. Into frying pan, pour the egg product; cook with a lid on for 5 minutes; pour the sausage mixture over.
- 3. Use spatula to fold omelette in half; cover with lid and cook for an additional 3 minutes.

Nutrition Information

- Calories: 110

- Total Carbohydrate: 4 g
- Cholesterol: 20 mg
- Total Fat: 3 g
- Fiber: 0 g
- Protein: 15 g
- Sodium: 620 mg
- Sugar: 2 g
- Saturated Fat: 1 g

133. Italian Pizza Omelet

"This recipe is savory and special and will be a hit everyone will try it."
Serving: 1 serving. | Prep: 10m | Ready in: 20m

Ingredients

- 3/4 cup sliced fresh mushrooms
- 2 tbsps. chopped onion
- 2 tsps. olive oil
- 1 tbsp. butter
- 3 eggs
- 3 tbsps. water
- 1/8 tsp. salt
- 1/8 tsp. pepper
- 1/4 cup shredded part-skim mozzarella cheese
- 1/4 cup marinara sauce or spaghetti sauce, warmed

Direction

- Fry onion and mushrooms in oil in a small skillet until softened. Take out of skillet and reserve. Using the same skillet, put butter to melt on medium-high heat. Mix pepper, salt, water and eggs. Stir mixture into skillet (mixture should set right away at every edge). Push cooked eggs to the middle as eggs set, allowing uncooked pieces to move underneath. Once the eggs are set, scoop mushroom mixture on one side and drizzle with cheese; turn other side on top of filling. Then put omelet on a plate. Pair with marinara sauce.

Nutrition Information

- Calories: 523 calories
- Total Carbohydrate: 14 g
- Cholesterol: 681 mg
- Total Fat: 40 g
- Fiber: 2 g
- Protein: 29 g
- Sodium: 830 mg

134. Italian Sausage Biscuit Bake

"Your morning will be much easier with this tasty and simple dish. My family says it tastes like a fast-food sandwich."
Serving: 10 servings. | Prep: 20m | Ready in: 55m

Ingredients

- 1-1/4 lbs. Johnsonville® Ground Mild Italian sausage
- 2 tubes (12 oz. each) refrigerated buttermilk biscuits, divided
- 1-1/3 cups chopped sweet red peppers
- 8 large eggs, lightly beaten
- 3/4 cup 2% milk
- 1/2 cup minced fresh parsley
- 1-1/2 cups shredded Monterey Jack cheese
- 1 tbsp. butter
- 2 tsps. dried oregano

Direction

- Cook sausage in a big frying pan over medium heat until not pink anymore; strain. In a 13x9-inch baking dish coated with oil, put 10 biscuits. Sprinkle over the biscuits with red peppers and sausage. Combine parsley, milk, and eggs in a big bowl. Add to the sausage. Sprinkle cheese over.
- Bake without a cover at 350°, about 20 minutes. Put the leftover biscuits on top. Brush butter over the biscuits and sprinkle oregano over. Bake until a knife will come out clean when you insert it into the middle and the biscuits turn golden brown, about another 15-

20 minutes. Allow to sit before eating, about 5 minutes.

Nutrition Information

- Calories: 351 calories
- Total Carbohydrate: 19 g
- Cholesterol: 213 mg
- Total Fat: 22 g
- Fiber: 1 g
- Protein: 18 g
- Sodium: 776 mg

135. Italian Sausage Casserole

"Everyone looks forward to this delicious and warm dish that you can easily prepare in advance. It smells really good as it cooks."
Serving: 12 servings. | Prep: 15m | Ready in: 01h15m

Ingredients

- 1 lb. Jones No Sugar Pork Sausage Roll sausage
- 1 lb. bulk Italian sausage
- 1 medium green pepper, chopped
- 1 cup sliced fresh mushrooms
- 1/2 cup chopped onion
- 2-1/2 cups onion and garlic croutons
- 8 large eggs
- 1-1/2 cups whole milk
- 1 cup shredded part-skim mozzarella cheese
- 1 cup shredded cheddar cheese
- 3 to 4 plum tomatoes, thinly sliced
- 1/2 cup shredded Parmesan cheese

Direction

- Cook onion, sausage, mushrooms, and green pepper in a big pan until the veggies are tender and the meat is brown; drain. In a greased 13-in by 9-in baking dish, arrange the croutons then add the sausage mixture on top. Whisk milk and eggs, pour the mixture over the sausage.
- Refrigerate for 8hrs to overnight while covered. Take it out of the fridge about half an hour before baking. Bake for 45mins in a 350 degrees oven without cover.
- Top with cheddar and mozzarella cheese. Arrange slices of tomato on top then scatter Parmesan cheese all over. Bake for another 15-20mins until an inserted knife in the middle comes out without residue. Let it sit for 5mins then slice.

Nutrition Information

- Calories: 329 calories
- Total Carbohydrate: 11 g
- Cholesterol: 195 mg
- Total Fat: 24 g
- Fiber: 1 g
- Protein: 18 g
- Sodium: 643 mg

136. Italian Sausage Egg Bake

"This herb-seasoned and filling entree it perfect for brunch or breakfast."
Serving: 12 servings. | Prep: 20m | Ready in: 01h10m

Ingredients

- 8 slices white bread, cubed
- 1 lb. Johnsonville® Mild Italian Sausage Links, casings removed, sliced
- 2 cups shredded sharp cheddar cheese
- 2 cups shredded part-skim mozzarella cheese
- 9 large eggs, lightly beaten
- 3 cups 2% milk
- 1 tsp. dried basil
- 1 tsp. dried oregano
- 1 tsp. fennel seed, crushed

Direction

- In a greased 13-in by 9-inch baking dish, arrange the bread cubes then set aside. On medium heat, cook sausage in a big pan until it is not pink; drain. Slather the sausage on top of the bread; top with cheeses.

- Combine seasoning, milk, and eggs in a big bowl; pour mixture on the casserole. Cover then chill overnight.
- Take it out of the fridge half an hour before baking. Bake for 50-55mins in a 350 degrees oven without cover until an inserted knife in the middle comes out without residue. Let it sit for 5mins then slice.

Nutrition Information

- Calories: 316 calories
- Total Carbohydrate: 13 g
- Cholesterol: 214 mg
- Total Fat: 20 g
- Fiber: 1 g
- Protein: 21 g
- Sodium: 546 mg

137. Italian Spinach Sausage Pie

"It's a perfectly baked sausage pie that is so amazing for a midnight snack or holiday brunch."
Serving: 8 | Prep: 20m | Ready in: 1h30m

Ingredients

- 1 lb. bulk Italian sausage
- 6 eggs
- 1 (10 oz.) package frozen chopped spinach, thawed and squeezed dry
- 5 cups shredded mozzarella cheese
- 3/4 cup ricotta cheese
- 1/2 tsp. salt
- 1/8 tsp. garlic powder
- 1/8 tsp. ground black pepper
- 1 double crust ready-to-use pie crust
- 1 tbsp. water

Direction

- Prepare the oven and preheat at 375°F or 190°C.
- Place the big skillet on medium-high heat and cook the sausage for 10 minutes until all sides are brown and crumbly. Drain any excess grease. Separate the egg whites and egg yolks. Whisk the egg whites and the leftover eggs in a bowl. Fold in sausage, pepper, ricotta cheese, mozzarella cheese, spinach, salt, and garlic powder.
- Use a pastry to line the bottom of the 10-inch pie plate. Spread the filling into the crust. Lay the leftover rolled out pastry on top of the filling. Cut, seal, and flute its edges, cutting the slits of the pastry. In a small bowl, whisk the water and egg yolk and use the mixture to coat the top of the pie.
- Allow it to bake inside the preheated oven for 50-60 minutes until the crust is golden and the filling is bubbly. Set aside for 10 minutes. Cut it before serving.

Nutrition Information

- Calories: 636 calories;
- Total Carbohydrate: 25.6 g
- Cholesterol: 217 mg
- Total Fat: 45.2 g
- Protein: 31.8 g
- Sodium: 1369 mg

138. Italian Tomato Onion Quiche

"Best prepared in summer with fresh basil and ripe tomatoes, this quiche should be consumed hot while the cheese is still gooey."
Serving: 6 servings. | Prep: 25m | Ready in: 01h15m

Ingredients

- 6 medium fresh mushrooms, thinly sliced
- 2 tsps. canola oil
- 1 sheet refrigerated pie pastry
- 2 cups shredded part-skim mozzarella cheese
- 1 cup sliced sweet onion
- 3 medium plum tomatoes, seeded and thinly sliced
- 1/2 cup shredded Parmesan cheese
- 6 large eggs
- 1 cup half-and-half cream
- 1 tsp. ground mustard

- 1 tsp. dried basil
- 1 tsp. dried oregano
- 1 tsp. dried thyme

Direction

- Heat oil in a big pan; cook mushrooms in hot oil until tender then set aside. Spread pastry until it fits a 9-inch deep-dish pie platter; move pastry in the plate. Cut pastry to half-inch outside the edge of the platter; ridge the edges. Arrange 1/2 of the mozzarella, onion, and tomato in a layer on top of the pastry; add mushrooms then 1/2 of the Parmesan cheese on top.
- Mix herbs, eggs, mustard, and cream together in a small bowl; spread on top of the pastry then add the leftover Parmesan cheese. Bake for 50-60 mins in a 350 degrees F oven until an inserted knife in the middle comes out without residue. If necessary, use a sheet of foil to cover the edges on the final 20 mins of cooking to avoid overbrowning the dish. Set aside for 10 mins then cut.

139. Mascarpone-mushroom Frittata Stack

"This delicious and impressive egg dish is easy to prepare."
Serving: 6 servings. | Prep: 25m | Ready in: 45m

Ingredients

- 8 large eggs
- 1/3 cup heavy whipping cream
- 1/2 cup grated Romano cheese, divided
- 1-1/2 tsps. salt, divided
- 5 tbsps. olive oil, divided
- 3/4 lb. sliced fresh mushrooms
- 1 medium onion, halved and thinly sliced
- 2 tbsps. minced fresh basil
- 2 garlic cloves, minced
- 1/8 tsp. pepper
- 1 carton (8 oz.) Mascarpone cheese

Direction

- Beat 1 tsp. salt, eggs, a quarter cup Romano cheese, and cream in a big bowl.
- On medium-high heat, heat 2 tbsp. oil in a 10-inch skillet. Cook and stir onion and mushrooms until tender. Put in the remaining salt, basil, pepper, and garlic; cook and stir for another minute. Move to a bowl. Mix in the remaining Romano cheese and mascarpone cheese.
- On medium high heat, heat 1 tbsp. oil in the same pan. Add 2/3 cup egg mixture, the mixture on the edges should set immediately. Push the cooked parts to the middle as the eggs set to let the uncooked part flow below.
- Let it sit for 5-7 mins while covering or until set completely; move to a serving platter. Cover then keep warm. Repeat with the rest of the egg mixture to make 2 more frittatas. If needed, add the remaining oil.
- On a serving platter, put a frittata then place 1/2 of the mushroom mixture in a layer. Repeat the layers. Place the remaining frittata on top then slice into wedges.

Nutrition Information

- Calories: 468 calories
- Total Carbohydrate: 6 g
- Cholesterol: 357 mg
- Total Fat: 44 g
- Fiber: 1 g
- Protein: 17 g
- Sodium: 882 mg

140. Mini Frittatas

""This is one spinach recipe even your kids will enjoy. It's easy to make and very tasty.""
Serving: 4

Ingredients

- 6 oz. frozen chopped spinach, thawed and drained

- 1 cup ricotta cheese
- 2 tbsps. sour cream
- 1/2 cup grated Parmesan cheese
- 1/2 cup shredded Cheddar cheese
- 4 eggs
- 1/4 cup milk
- 1/4 tsp. hot pepper sauce
- 1 tsp. ground cumin
- 1/4 tsp. ground black pepper
- 1/2 tsp. lemon pepper
- 2 tbsps. dried parsley
- 3 tbsps. salsa

Direction

- Set oven to 190°C or 375°F. Apply a bit of grease to a 12-cup muffin tin.
- In a medium bowl, mix ricotta cheese, spinach, parmesan cheese, sour cream and cheddar cheese.
- In small mixing bowl, beat eggs, hot sauce, milk, black pepper, cumin, lemon pepper and parsley. Combine the spinach mixture with egg mixture.
- Put mixture into the muffin tin. Let it cook in the oven for 20-25 minutes. Let it cool for 5 minutes before removing the muffins from the cups. Serve while still warm.

Nutrition Information

- Calories: 225 calories;
- Total Carbohydrate: 5.4 g
- Cholesterol: 216 mg
- Total Fat: 15.4 g
- Protein: 17.3 g
- Sodium: 532 mg

141. Mini Italian Frittatas

"A simple and convenient egg dish as a lovely picnic breakfast with your friends."
Serving: 1 dozen. | Prep: 20m | Ready in: 40m

Ingredients

- 1/2 cup boiling water
- 1/4 cup sun-dried tomatoes (not packed in oil)
- 3/4 cup shredded part-skim mozzarella cheese, divided
- 1/2 cup chopped fresh spinach
- 1/3 cup water-packed artichoke hearts, rinsed, drained and chopped
- 1/3 cup chopped roasted sweet red peppers
- 1/4 cup grated Parmesan cheese
- 1/4 cup ricotta cheese
- 2 tbsps. minced fresh basil
- 1 tbsp. prepared pesto
- 2 tsps. Italian seasoning
- 1/4 tsp. garlic powder
- 8 large eggs
- 1/2 tsp. pepper
- 1/4 tsp. salt

Direction

- Set an oven to 350 degrees and start preheating. In a small bowl, pour the boiling water over tomatoes; allow to stand for 5 minutes. Drain the tomatoes and chop.
- Blend tomatoes, garlic powder, Italian seasoning, pesto, basil, ricotta cheese, Parmesan cheese, red peppers, artichokes hearts, spinach, and 1/2 cup of mozzarella cheese in a small bowl. Beat pepper, salt, and eggs in a large bowl until combined; add to the cheese mixture and stir.
- Stuff 3/4 full foil-lined or greased muffin cups. Dust with the remaining mozzarella cheese. Bake until set, about 18-22 minutes. Before taking out of the pan, allow to cool 5 minutes. Serve it warm.

Nutrition Information

- Calories: 95 calories

- Total Carbohydrate: 2 g
- Cholesterol: 149 mg
- Total Fat: 6 g
- Fiber: 0 g
- Protein: 8 g
- Sodium: 233 mg

142. Mini Sausage Quiches

"Fantastic small quiches that are great for potlucks or brunches."
Serving: 4 dozen. | Prep: 25m | Ready in: 45m

Ingredients

- 1/2 lb. Johnsonville® Ground Hot Italian sausage
- 2 tbsps. dried minced onion
- 2 tbsps. minced chives
- 1 tube (8 oz.) refrigerated crescent rolls
- 4 large eggs, lightly beaten
- 2 cups shredded Swiss cheese
- 1 cup 4% cottage cheese
- 1/3 cup grated Parmesan cheese
- Paprika

Direction

- Brown onion and sausage on medium heat in a big skillet until meat isn't pink for 4-5 minutes; drain. Mix chives in.
- Unroll crescent dough on a slightly floured surface to a long rectangle. Seal perforations and seams. Cut to 48 pieces. Up the sides and bottom of greased miniature muffin cups, press it on.
- Fill 2 tsps. sausage mixture in each. Mix cheeses and eggs in a big bowl. Spoon 2 tablespoonfuls on sausage mixture. Sprinkle paprika on.
- Bake for 20-25 minutes at 375 degrees or until an inserted knife in the middle exits cleanly. Cool it for 5 minutes in pan. Transfer out of pans to the wire racks. Sprinkle extra minced chives (optional) serve while warm.

Nutrition Information

- Calories: 66 calories
- Total Carbohydrate: 2 g
- Cholesterol: 27 mg
- Total Fat: 5 g
- Fiber: 0 g
- Protein: 4 g
- Sodium: 116 mg

143. Mushroom Sausage Omelets

"This omelet is filled with garlic, mushrooms, Italian sausage, and cheese and it suits kids very well."
Serving: 4 servings. | Prep: 15m | Ready in: 30m

Ingredients

- 1 fresh Johnsonville® Mild Italian Sausage Links (4 oz.), casing removed
- 1-1/2 cups sliced fresh mushrooms
- 10 large eggs
- 1/2 cup grated Parmesan cheese
- 2 to 4 garlic cloves, minced
- 1/4 tsp. pepper
- 1/4 to 1/2 cup minced fresh parsley
- 4 tsps. olive oil, divided

Direction

- Cook mushrooms and sausage in a 10-in. nonstick frying pan over medium-high heat, until the sausage is no more pink, about 4-6 minutes, crushing the sausage into small pieces. Use a slotted spoon to take out; clean the frying pan.
- Combine pepper, garlic, cheese, and eggs in a big bowl until combined. Mix in parsley.
- Heat 2 tsps. of oil in the same frying pan over medium-high heat. Add half of the egg mixture. The edges of the mixture should set immediately. While the eggs set, let the raw eggs run underneath and push the cooked eggs toward the middle. Once the eggs are hardened and no liquid egg left, put on one

side with half of the sausage mixture; fold omelet in half.
- Slice the omelet into two; put on serving dishes. Cook the rest of the ingredients in the same way.

Nutrition Information

- Calories: 360 calories
- Total Carbohydrate: 5 g
- Cholesterol: 494 mg
- Total Fat: 27 g
- Fiber: 0 g
- Protein: 25 g
- Sodium: 599 mg

144. Pasta Frittata

"This frittata is always a hit on a buffet party."
Serving: 6 servings. | Prep: 15m | Ready in: 30m

Ingredients

- 1 large onion, chopped
- 1 tbsp. vegetable oil
- 12 oz. sliced deli ham, finely chopped
- 4 garlic cloves, minced
- 6 eggs
- 3 egg whites
- 1/2 cup shredded mozzarella cheese
- 2 tbsps. minced fresh parsley
- 1 to 1-1/2 tsps. Italian seasoning
- 1/2 tsp. salt
- 1/2 tsp. pepper
- Dash cayenne pepper
- 2 cups cooked angel hair pasta

Direction

- Sauté onion in oil in the ovenproof skillet. Put in garlic and ham; sauté for 60 seconds more. Take out and put aside. Mix egg whites and eggs together in a big bowl. Put in seasonings, parsley and cheese. Put in the pasta and ham mixture.
- Coat the same skillet using cooking spray if needed. Put in pasta mixture. Keep it covered and cook for 3 minutes over medium heat. Uncover it. Bake at 400 degrees for 13 minutes till becoming set. Allow to rest for 5 minutes prior to cutting.

Nutrition Information

- Calories: 301 calories
- Total Carbohydrate: 18 g
- Cholesterol: 251 mg
- Total Fat: 15 g
- Fiber: 1 g
- Protein: 23 g
- Sodium: 1107 mg

145. Pear-pecan Sausage Quiche

"This great quiche would be a delightful addition to brunch."
Serving: 8 servings. | Prep: 15m | Ready in: 50m

Ingredients

- 1 sheet refrigerated pie pastry
- 1/2 lb. Johnsonville® Ground Hot Italian sausage
- 1/3 cup chopped sweet onion
- 1 medium pear, sliced
- 1/3 cup chopped pecans
- 4 large eggs
- 1-1/2 cups half-and-half cream
- 1/2 tsp. salt
- 1/2 tsp. dried thyme
- 1/8 tsp. ground nutmeg
- 1 cup shredded cheddar cheese
- 8 pecan halves

Direction

- Use pastry to line a 9-inch pie plate and trim pastry to 1/2" beyond edge of pie plate, then flute edges.
- Cook onion and sausage in a big skillet on medium heat until meat is not pink anymore,

about 4 to 5 minutes. Drain. Put pear slices in crust, then put sausage on top. Sprinkle over with pecans. Whisk together nutmeg, thyme, salt, cream and eggs in a big bowl. Stir in cheese and put sausage on.
- Bake at 350° until a knife tucked in the center comes out clean and crust turns golden brown, about 35 to 40 minutes. Use foil to cover edges during the last 15 minutes to avoid overbrowning, if needed. Decorate with pecan halves and allow to stand about 5 minutes before slicing.

Nutrition Information

- Calories: 375 calories
- Total Carbohydrate: 20 g
- Cholesterol: 160 mg
- Total Fat: 27 g
- Fiber: 1 g
- Protein: 12 g
- Sodium: 520 mg

146. Pepperoni Cheese Bake

"You only need a couple of ingredients to make this quick breakfast dish."
Serving: 6-8 servings. | Prep: 10m | Ready in: 30m

Ingredients

- 2 cups shredded part-skim mozzarella cheese
- 1/2 cup diced pepperoni
- 5 large eggs
- 3/4 cup whole milk
- 1/4 tsp. dried basil

Direction

- Arrange mozzarella cheese and pepperoni in a layer in a greased 9-inch pie plate. Beat basil, milk, and eggs in a bowl; pour on top of the cheese. Bake for 20-25 mins in a 400 degrees F oven until an inserted knife in the middle comes out clean. Let it sit for 10 mins then slice.

Nutrition Information

- Calories: 184 calories
- Total Carbohydrate: 2 g
- Cholesterol: 166 mg
- Total Fat: 14 g
- Fiber: 0 g
- Protein: 12 g
- Sodium: 328 mg

147. Pepperoni Frittata

"This frittata should be eaten with toast and fresh fruit."
Serving: 6 servings. | Prep: 5m | Ready in: 25m

Ingredients

- 1-1/4 cups chopped onions
- 2 to 3 tbsps. canola oil
- 1 cup sliced zucchini
- 1/2 cup small cauliflowerets
- 5 eggs, beaten
- 26 slices pepperoni
- 1/3 cup grated Parmesan cheese

Direction

- In one 10-inch ovenproof skillet, sauté the onions in oil till becoming soft. Put in eggs, cauliflower and zucchini. Keep it covered and cook over medium heat for 10 to 15 minutes till eggs become almost set.
- Arrange pepperoni on top of eggs. Broil 6 in. away from the heat for 2 minutes. Drizzle with Parmesan cheese; broil till the top becomes browned a bit and eggs become totally set, about 1 to 2 more minutes. Chop into wedges.

Nutrition Information

- Calories: 181 calories
- Total Carbohydrate: 5 g
- Cholesterol: 188 mg
- Total Fat: 14 g
- Fiber: 1 g
- Protein: 9 g
- Sodium: 299 mg

148. Pesto Chicken Strata

"It is nice to use these rustic strata with some sweeter brunch dishes such as doughnuts and cinnamon rolls, but using it alone is fine as well."
Serving: 12 servings. | Prep: 25m | Ready in: 01h05m

Ingredients

- 1 lb. boneless skinless chicken thighs, cut into 1-inch pieces
- 3/4 tsp. salt, divided
- 3/4 tsp. coarsely ground pepper, divided
- 1 tbsp. plus 1/2 cup olive oil, divided
- 1 cup chopped fresh basil
- 1-1/2 cups grated Parmesan cheese, divided
- 1 cup shredded part-skim mozzarella cheese
- 2/3 cup pine nuts, toasted
- 5 garlic cloves, minced
- 10 large eggs
- 3 cups 2% milk
- 8 cups cubed Italian bread
- Additional chopped fresh basil leaves

Direction

- Season chicken with 1/4 tsp. pepper and 1/4 tsp. salt. Heat 1 tbsp. oil over medium heat in a large skillet. Add chicken, cook while stirring until no longer pink or for 6-8 minutes. Drain.
- Combine garlic, pine nuts, mozzarella cheese, 1 cup Parmesan cheese and basil in a large bowl. Beat milk, eggs, the remaining oil, pepper and salt in another bowl.
- Layer 1/2 of the bread cubes, 1/3 of the cheese mixture and 1/2 of the chicken in a greased 13x9-in. baking dish. Repeat layers. Sprinkle with remaining cheese mixture. Top with egg mixture; scatter remaining Parmesan cheese over. Cover and refrigerate for several hours or overnight.
- Set the oven to 350° and start preheating. Take strata out of the fridge while oven heats. Uncover and bake for 40-50 minutes until golden brown and the inserted knife in the center comes out clean. Allow to sit for 5-10 minutes before serving. Top with additional basil.

Nutrition Information

- Calories: 415 calories
- Total Carbohydrate: 16 g
- Cholesterol: 199 mg
- Total Fat: 29 g
- Fiber: 1 g
- Protein: 24 g
- Sodium: 598 mg

149. Petite Sausage Quiches

"Small quiches loaded with cayenne, Swiss cheese, and sausage to put on your breakfast table."
Serving: 3 dozen. | Prep: 25m | Ready in: 55m

Ingredients

- 1 cup butter, softened
- 6 oz. cream cheese, softened
- 2 cups all-purpose flour
- FILLING:
- 6 oz. Johnsonville® Ground Mild Italian sausage
- 1 cup shredded Swiss cheese
- 1 tbsp. minced chives
- 1 large egg
- 1/2 cup half-and-half cream
- 1/4 tsp. salt
- Dash cayenne pepper

Direction

- Set an oven to 375 degrees. Whisk flour, cream cheese, and butter until they become smooth. Form the tablespoonfuls of dough into balls; press the sides and the bottom of the greased miniature muffin cups.
- Cook the sausage on medium heat in a big skillet until not pink anymore; drain and crumble the sausage. Dust into the muffin cups with chives, Swiss cheese, and sausage.

Whisk pepper, salt, cream, and egg until combined; add into the shells.
- Bake for 28-30 minutes until browned, (bake for a browner bottom crust on a lower rack). Serve it warm.

150. Pizza Omelet

"This pizza-flavored omelet is my son's favorite"
Serving: 1 serving. | Prep: 5m | Ready in: 15m

Ingredients

- 2 eggs
- 2 tbsps. milk
- 1 tbsp. butter
- 1/4 cup pizza sauce
- 10 slices pepperoni
- 1/4 cup shredded part-skim mozzarella cheese
- 1 tbsp. shredded Parmesan cheese

Direction

- Beat milk and eggs together in a bowl. Melt butter in a skillet placed over medium heat. Add egg mixture to the skillet. While eggs are setting, lift edges in order that raw eggs can flow underneath. When eggs are fully set, remove from the heat.
- Spread pizza sauce on one half of omelet; add mozzarella cheese and pepperoni on top, flip the other half to cover filling. Drizzle Parmesan cheese on top. Serve immediately.

151. Poached Eggs With Tarragon Asparagus

"Everyone loves this breakfast dish with toasted bread crumbs on top."
Serving: 4 servings. | Prep: 10m | Ready in: 30m

Ingredients

- 1 lb. fresh asparagus, trimmed
- 1 tbsp. olive oil
- 1 garlic clove, minced
- 1 tbsp. minced fresh tarragon
- 1/2 tsp. salt
- 1/4 tsp. pepper
- 1 tbsp. butter
- 1/4 cup seasoned bread crumbs
- 4 large eggs

Direction

- Boil three inches of water in a big pan with high sides. Cook asparagus in boiling water for 2-4mins without cover until it turns bright green. Take the asparagus out of the pan then drop in ice water right away; drain then pat the asparagus dry.
- On medium heat, heat oil in another big pan. Cook and stir garlic in hot oil for a minute. Put in pepper, asparagus, salt, and tarragon; cook for 2-3mins while turning from time to time until tender-crisp. Take the contents out of the pan then keep warm. On medium heat, melt butter in the same pan; cook and stir bread crumbs for 1-2mins until toasted. Take off heat.
- Pour 2 to 3 inches of fresh water in the pan used to prepare the asparagus; boil. Adjust heat to keep a gentle simmer. Break one cold egg at a time in a small bowl; set the bowl near the top of the water then slide the egg in.
- Cook eggs for 3-4mins without cover until the yolks start to thicken yet not hard and the whites are set completely. Lift the eggs out with a slotted spoon then place on top of the asparagus. Top with toasted bread crumbs.

Nutrition Information

- Calories: 170 calories
- Total Carbohydrate: 8 g
- Cholesterol: 194 mg
- Total Fat: 12 g
- Fiber: 1 g
- Protein: 9 g
- Sodium: 513 mg

152. Potato & Bacon Frittata

"This frittata can be made with any type of cheese, and you can serve it with either salsa or pesto."
Serving: 8 servings. | Prep: 30m | Ready in: 50m

Ingredients

- 10 large eggs
- 1/4 cup minced fresh parsley
- 3 tbsps. 2% milk
- 1/4 tsp. salt
- 1/8 tsp. pepper
- 8 bacon strips, chopped
- 2 medium potatoes, peeled and thinly sliced
- 2 green onions, finely chopped
- 4 fresh sage leaves, thinly sliced
- 1 cup shredded pepper Jack cheese
- 2 plum tomatoes, sliced

Direction

- Turn oven to 400° to preheat. Whisk eggs with pepper, salt, milk, and parsley in a large bowl; put to one side. Cook bacon in a 10-inch oven-safe skillet over medium heat until partly cooked but not crisp.
- Add sage, onions, and potatoes; cook until potatoes are softened. Lower the heat, sprinkle with cheese. Pour egg mixture and put tomato slices on top.
- Uncover and bake for 20 to 25 minutes or until eggs are totally firm. Allow to stand for 15 minutes before cutting into wedges.

Nutrition Information

- Calories: 287 calories
- Total Carbohydrate: 10 g
- Cholesterol: 295 mg
- Total Fat: 21 g
- Fiber: 1 g
- Protein: 15 g
- Sodium: 441 mg

153. Potato Sausage Frittata

"Use potatoes, eggs, bacon and sausage for making this frittata recipe."
Serving: 4 servings. | Prep: 10m | Ready in: 30m

Ingredients

- 1/2 lb. Jones No Sugar Pork Sausage Roll sausage
- 6 bacon strips, diced
- 1-1/2 cups finely chopped red potatoes
- 1 medium onion, finely chopped
- 8 eggs
- 2 tsps. dried parsley flakes
- 3/4 tsp. salt
- 1/8 tsp. pepper

Direction

- On medium heat, cook the sausage in a big ovenproof skillet till not pink anymore. Take out and put aside. On medium heat, cook bacon in the same skillet till crisp. Transfer to paper towels with a slotted spoon; drain off, saving 2 tbsp. of drippings.
- Sauté onion and potatoes in the drippings till soft. Mix pepper, salt, parsley and eggs in a big bowl. Bring sausage and bacon back to the skillet; add egg mixture on top.
- Keep it covered and let cook till eggs become nearly set, 8 to 10 minutes on low heat. Uncover it; broil 6 inches away from the heat source till eggs become set, about 2 minutes. Chop into wedges.

Nutrition Information

- Calories: 518 calories
- Total Carbohydrate: 17 g
- Cholesterol: 468 mg
- Total Fat: 40 g
- Fiber: 2 g
- Protein: 21 g
- Sodium: 1054 mg

154. Prosciutto-pesto Breakfast Strata

"An amazing recipe that you shouldn't miss."
Serving: 10 servings. | Prep: 25m | Ready in: 01h15m

Ingredients

- 2 cups 2% milk
- 1 cup white wine or chicken broth
- 1 loaf (1 lb.) French bread, cut into 1/2-inch slice
- 1/4 cup minced fresh basil
- 1/4 cup minced fresh parsley
- 3 tbsps. olive oil
- 1/2 lb. thinly sliced smoked Gouda cheese
- 1/2 lb. thinly sliced prosciutto
- 3 medium tomatoes, thinly sliced
- 1/2 cup prepared pesto
- 4 large eggs
- 1/2 cup heavy whipping cream
- 1/2 tsp. salt
- 1/4 tsp. pepper

Direction

- Blend wine and milk in a shallow bowl. Plunge both sides of bread into the milk mixture; gently squeeze out the excess liquid. In a 13x9-inch baking dish coated with cooking spray, place the bread slices in a layer.
- Dust with parsley and basil; spritz with oil. Place with all the tomatoes, 1/2 prosciutto, and 1/2 cheese in a layer; drizzle with half of the pesto. Put pesto, prosciutto, and the remaining cheese on top.
- Beat pepper, salt, cream, and eggs in a small bowl until combined; spread over the top. Cover and put in the fridge overnight or for a few hours.
- Set an oven to 350 degrees and start preheating. While heating the oven, take the strata out of the refrigerator. Uncover and bake until turning golden brown and a knife comes out clean after inserted in the center, or for 50-60 minutes. Before serving, allow to stand for 5-10 minutes.

155. Quiche Italiano

"Spices and pepperoni makes this quiche is no ordinary. You will get compliment when serving this dish, taste good and look great too."
Serving: 4-6 servings. | Prep: 30m | Ready in: 60m

Ingredients

- 1 unbaked pastry shell (10 inches)
- 1/2 cup sliced pepperoni, halved
- 3 tbsps. chopped green pepper
- 2 tbsps. chopped onion
- 1 jar (4-1/2 oz.) sliced mushrooms, drained
- 1 tbsp. butter
- 1/2 tsp. dried oregano
- 1/2 tsp. fennel seed, crushed
- 1-1/4 cups shredded part-skim mozzarella cheese
- 3 large eggs
- 1-1/2 cups half-and-half cream
- 1/2 tsp. salt
- 1/8 tsp. pepper
- 1 medium tomato, cut into wedges

Direction

- Line pastry over the pie plate. Trim the edges and then flute. Remember not to prick the shell. Use metal pie weights or dried beans to weight shell to avoid bubbles. Bake 5-7 minutes at 400°. Take out of the oven, remove the weights and leave it aside.
- Use small skillet, cook butter with mushrooms, onion, green pepper, pepperoni until tender. Mix in fennel seeds and oregano. Spread 1 cup of mozzarella cheese in the pastry, put pepperoni mixture on top. Whisk cream, pepper, salt, eggs in a medium bowl. Transfer into the pastry crust.
- Bake for 25-30 minutes at 375° or until insert a knife in the center and it comes out clean. Decorate with tomato wedges. Sprinkle the remaining mozzarella cheese on top. Bake until the cheese is melted, about 2 minutes. Let it sit for 5 minutes before serve

Nutrition Information

- Calories: 428 calories
- Total Carbohydrate: 23 g
- Cholesterol: 176 mg
- Total Fat: 30 g
- Fiber: 1 g
- Protein: 14 g
- Sodium: 768 mg

156. Ratatouille Frittata

"This colorful dish with fluffy eggs, flavorful sausage chunks, veggies, and hash browns is perfect for brunch or dinner."
Serving: 4 servings. | Prep: 10m | Ready in: 25m

Ingredients

- 2 cups frozen cubed hash brown potatoes
- 2 tbsps. olive oil
- 2 cooked Italian sausage links, diced
- 2 cups cooked ratatouille (from the Ratatouille with Sausage)
- 6 eggs
- 1/4 cup milk
- 1/4 tsp. salt
- 1/8 tsp. pepper

Direction

- Cook hash browns in a 10 or 12-inch ovenproof pan with oil until brown. Mix in ratatouille and sausage.
- Whisk pepper, eggs, salt, and milk in a bowl; pour over the veggies then cover. On medium-low heat, cook for 10mins until the eggs are almost set.
- Remove the cover then broil for 2-3mins, six inches from heat until the top is pale brown and the eggs are set completely.

Nutrition Information

- Calories: 426 calories
- Total Carbohydrate: 19 g
- Cholesterol: 359 mg
- Total Fat: 29 g
- Fiber: 3 g
- Protein: 22 g
- Sodium: 817 mg

157. Ratatouille Quiche

""Surely nobody will decline this recipe when served because of its vibrant color. Rich taste that develops when caramelizing the veggies.""
Serving: 6 servings. | Prep: 35m | Ready in: 01h15m

Ingredients

- Pastry for single-crust pie (9 inches)
- 1 small eggplant, peeled
- 1 medium zucchini
- 1 medium green pepper
- 1 medium tomato, seeded
- 1 small onion
- 2 tbsps. olive oil
- 1 garlic clove, minced
- 1 cup shredded Swiss cheese
- 6 large eggs
- 2 cups half-and-half cream
- 1/2 tsp. salt
- 1/4 tsp. pepper

Direction

- Unfold pastry into pie plate that is 9-inch deep-dish; pinch edges. Use a heavy-duty foil that is double thickness to line not pricked pastry. Place inside the oven and for 8 minutes at 450 degrees F. Take off the foil; then bake again for 5 minutes. Let it cool on a wire rack. Mince the onion, tomato, green pepper, zucchini and eggplant. Then fry vegetables in oil in a large skillet until softened. Stir in garlic; cook for 1 more minute. Put in prepared pastry; sprinkle on cheese. Beat pepper, salt, cream and eggs in a large bowl; dump over cheese. Place inside the oven and bake for 40-45 minutes at 350 degrees F or until the knife poked in the middle comes out clean. Before serving, let it stand for 10 minutes.

Nutrition Information

- Calories: 481 calories
- Total Carbohydrate: 29 g
- Cholesterol: 275 mg
- Total Fat: 32 g
- Fiber: 3 g
- Protein: 17 g
- Sodium: 494 mg

158. Ricotta & Cheddar Zucchini Frittata

"A beautiful dish that is great for both breakfast and dinner. Cheddar cheese makes it more cheesy and flavorful."
Serving: 4 servings. | Prep: 25m | Ready in: 50m

Ingredients

- 3 medium zucchini, thinly sliced
- 3 tbsps. whole wheat flour
- 2 tsps. olive oil
- 6 large egg whites
- 3 large eggs
- 1/2 cup reduced-fat ricotta cheese
- 1/2 cup shredded cheddar cheese, divided
- 1/3 cup plain yogurt
- 1 tbsp. dried parsley flakes
- 2 garlic cloves, minced
- 1/2 tsp. salt
- 1/4 tsp. white pepper
- 1/2 tsp. poppy seeds

Direction

- Toss to coat zucchini with flour. Sauté zucchini in oil in a large nonstick skillet coated with cooking spray until lightly browned and crisp-tender. Turn the heat off.
- Whisk pepper, salt, garlic, parsley, yogurt, 1/4 cup Cheddar cheese, ricotta cheese, eggs, and egg whites in a large bowl. Mix in zucchini. Pour mixture into a 9-inch pie plate coated with cooking spray. Sprinkle remaining cheddar cheese and poppy seeds on top.
- Bring to bake at 350° for 25 to 30 minutes or until a knife comes out clean when inserted in the center. Allow to stand for 5 minutes before cutting into smaller pieces.

Nutrition Information

- Calories: 238 calories
- Total Carbohydrate: 13 g
- Cholesterol: 185 mg
- Total Fat: 12 g
- Fiber: 3 g
- Protein: 19 g
- Sodium: 552 mg

159. Rock 'n' River Breakfast Quiche

"This is a great quiche recipe for breakfast outdoors in nice days."
Serving: 6 servings. | Prep: 15m | Ready in: 45m

Ingredients

- 1/2 lb. Johnsonville® Ground Mild Italian sausage
- 1 cup shredded cheddar cheese
- 1 cup shredded Monterey Jack cheese
- Pastry for single-crust pie (9 inches)
- 3 large eggs, lightly beaten
- 1 cup whole milk
- 1/8 tsp. ground mustard
- Dash nutmeg

Direction

- Cook sausage in a skillet on medium heat until the sausage is not pink anymore. Arrange sausage and cheeses in layers in unbaked pastry shell. Mix the rest of ingredients; transfer over cheese and sausage.
- Bake for half an hour at 350°. Allow to sit for 5 minutes then slice and serve.

Nutrition Information

- Calories: 422 calories

- Total Carbohydrate: 21 g
- Cholesterol: 170 mg
- Total Fat: 29 g
- Fiber: 0 g
- Protein: 18 g
- Sodium: 577 mg

160. Sausage & Mushroom Pizza Frittata

"A special frittata with an array of fresh flavors that is ideal for a sunny breakfast in Florida."
Serving: 4 servings. | Prep: 20m | Ready in: 30m

Ingredients

- 4 oz. Johnsonville® Ground Mild Italian sausage
- 2 cups sliced fresh mushrooms
- 2 tbsps. finely chopped red onion
- 2 tbsps. finely chopped green pepper
- 1/4 cup finely chopped fresh pineapple
- 6 large eggs, beaten
- 6 tbsps. marinara sauce
- 2 tbsps. shredded part-skim mozzarella cheese
- 2 tbsps. grated Parmigiano-Reggiano cheese
- 2 tbsps. minced fresh parsley

Direction

- Preheat the broiler. On medium heat, cook pepper, sausage, onion, and mushrooms for 6-8mins while crumbling the sausage in a 10-inch ovenproof pan until the veggies are tender and sausage is not pink; drain.
- Put the sausage mixture back in the pan then mix in pineapple. Add beaten eggs; cook for 4-6mins while covered until almost set. Slather the marinara all over then top with cheeses.
- Broil for 2-3mins, three to four inches from heat until the cheese melts and eggs are set completely. Let it sit for 5mins. Top with parsley then slice into wedges.

161. Sausage 'n' Spinach Eggs

"This recipe also goes great with cilantro and chorizo in place of oregano and Italian sausage"
Serving: 8 servings. | Prep: 25m | Ready in: 25m

Ingredients

- 1 lb. Johnsonville® Ground Hot Italian sausage
- 2 large onions, finely chopped
- 1/2 lb. sliced fresh mushrooms
- 2 garlic cloves, minced
- 1/4 tsp. salt
- 1/4 tsp. ground nutmeg
- 1/4 tsp. dried oregano
- 1/4 tsp. pepper
- 2 tbsps. olive oil
- 8 cups torn fresh spinach (about 1/2 lb.)
- 8 large eggs
- 1/4 tsp. hot pepper sauce
- 1 cup shredded Monterey Jack cheese

Direction

- In a 10 inches ovenproof skillet, crumble sausage and cook over medium heat until sausage loses its pink color. Drain, set aside. In the same skillet sauté seasonings, garlic, mushrooms and onions in oil until vegetables are softened. Add spinach in batches; cook over medium-low heat for 3 to 4 minutes or until spinach is wilted.
- Whisk together hot pepper sauce and eggs in a large bowl. Return sausage to skillet; add egg mixture. When eggs is setting, lift the edges in order that raw eggs can flow underneath. Cook for 8 to 10 minutes or just until the eggs are almost set.
- In the meantime, turn on the oven's broiler and start preheating. Place egg mixture 6 inch from the heat source and broil for 30 to 60 seconds or until completely set. Drizzle cheese on top; broil for an additional 30 seconds or until cheese is fully melted. Cut into wedges and serve right away.

Nutrition Information

- Calories: 280 calories
- Total Carbohydrate: 7 g
- Cholesterol: 248 mg
- Total Fat: 20 g
- Fiber: 2 g
- Protein: 18 g
- Sodium: 506 mg

162. Savory Italian Sausage Strata

"You can make this puffy casserole ahead for later use without affecting its great flavor."
Serving: 12 servings. | Prep: 25m | Ready in: 01h25m

Ingredients

- 1 lb. Johnsonville® Ground Mild Italian sausage
- 1 loaf sourdough bread (1 lb.), cubed
- 1 jar (4-1/2 oz.) sliced mushrooms, drained
- 1/4 cup thinly sliced green onions
- 10 large eggs, lightly beaten
- 3 cups half-and-half cream
- 1 tsp. ground mustard
- 1/2 tsp. salt
- 1 cup shredded Italian cheese blend

Direction

- Cook sausage over medium heat in a large skillet until no longer pink; drain. Put bread cubes in a greased 13x9-in. baking dish. Top with a layer of mushrooms, onions and sausage.
- Beat salt, mustard, cream and eggs in a large bowl. Top over the bread mixture, dust with cheese. Refrigerate, covered, overnight.
- Take the casserole out of the fridge half an hour before baking. Bake without a cover at 350° for 60-65 minutes or until the inserted knife in the center comes out clean. (Use a foil to loosely cover if top browns too quickly.) Allow to sit for 10 minutes before serving.
- Serve immediately or freeze, covered, for up to 3 months before refrigerating and baking.
- To use frozen casserole: Thaw the casserole in the fridge overnight. Take out of the fridge half an hour before baking. Bake as directed.

Nutrition Information

- Calories: 414 calories
- Total Carbohydrate: 25 g
- Cholesterol: 242 mg
- Total Fat: 25 g
- Fiber: 1 g
- Protein: 19 g
- Sodium: 824 mg

163. Savory Salami Strata

"A great brunch dish with a mild Italian flavor."
Serving: 8 servings. | Prep: 15m | Ready in: 01h10m

Ingredients

- Butter, softened
- 16 slices bread, crusts removed
- 1 cup diced fresh tomato
- 1/4 cup diced green pepper
- 8 slices salami or pepperoni
- 2 cups shredded mozzarella cheese
- 6 large eggs, lightly beaten
- 3 cups 2% milk
- 1 tsp. dried basil
- 1/2 tsp. salt
- 1/2 tsp. Italian seasoning

Direction

- Butter 1 side of each bread slice. Put 8 slices in a greased 13x9-inch baking dish, buttered-side facing up. Reserve 1 tbsp of green pepper and 1 tbsp of tomato. Layer it with salami, cheese, leftover tomato and green pepper, then put the leftover bread on top.
- Whisk the Italian seasoning, salt, basil, milk and eggs in a big bowl, then pour it on top of the bread. Sprinkle the reserved green pepper

and tomatoes on top. Put on cover and let it chill in the fridge for a minimum of 4 hours.
- Take it out of the fridge 30 minutes prior to baking. Let it bake for 55 minutes at 325 degrees without cover or until an inserted knife in the middle exits clean. Allow it to stand for 10 minutes prior to serving.

Nutrition Information

- Calories: 294 calories
- Total Carbohydrate: 19 g
- Cholesterol: 203 mg
- Total Fat: 16 g
- Fiber: 1 g
- Protein: 18 g
- Sodium: 653 mg

164. Savory Tomato Pie

"This cheese-less quiche is perfect for breakfasts, brunches, and lunches. Don't go shy on basil!"
Serving: 6-8 servings. | Prep: 25m | Ready in: 01h10m

Ingredients

- 5 green onions, sliced
- 3/4 cup chopped sweet onion
- 2 tbsps. butter
- 2 lbs. tomatoes, peeled, seeded and chopped
- 1 unbaked pastry shell (9 inches)
- 3 eggs
- 1 cup half-and-half cream
- 1-1/2 tsps. salt
- 1 tbsp. minced fresh basil or 1 tsp. dried basil
- 1/2 tsp. white pepper

Direction

- Sauté onions in a big pan with butter until tender; put in tomatoes. On low heat, cook and stir until soft. Take off heat then cool.
- Place a double-thick heavy-duty foil on unbaked pastry shell. Bake for 5mins in a 450 degrees oven. Discard the foil then bake for another 5mins. Lower heat to 350 degrees.
- Beat pepper, eggs, basil, salt, and cream in a bowl until smooth; combine with the tomato mixture. Pour the mixture in the pastry shell then bake for 45-50mins until an inserted knife in the middle comes out without residue. Let it sit for 5mins then slice.

Nutrition Information

- Calories: 246 calories
- Total Carbohydrate: 22 g
- Cholesterol: 107 mg
- Total Fat: 15 g
- Fiber: 2 g
- Protein: 6 g
- Sodium: 622 mg

165. Scrambled Egg Pockets

"These fiber and protein-rich egg pockets are made with an easy homemade pizza dough. You can also use store-brought dough if you want. These are perfect for breakfast or weeknight suppers."
Serving: 4 servings. | Prep: 20m | Ready in: 35m

Ingredients

- 2 cups egg substitute, divided
- 1/2 cup shredded part-skim mozzarella cheese
- 1/4 cup oil-packed sun-dried tomatoes, chopped
- 1 tbsp. minced fresh basil or 1 tsp. dried basil
- 1 portion (1 lb.) Whole Wheat Pizza Dough
- 2 tbsps. grated Parmesan cheese

Direction

- Reserve 2tbsp egg substitute. On medium heat, cook and stir the rest of the egg substitute in a big cooking-spray-coated non-stick skillet until nearly set. Mix in basil, tomatoes and mozzarella cheese; cook and stir until set completely. Take off the heat.
- Roll dough on a floured surface into a 13-inch square; slice into 4 squares. Move to a 15-in by 10-in baking pan greased with cooking spray.

Scoop the egg mixture on 1/2 of each square within half-inch of the edges.
- Brush a tbsp. of the saved eggs substitute on the edges of the dough. Fold one corner to the opposite corner over the filling to make a triangle; use a fork to press the edges and seal. Slice slits in top. Brush the remaining egg substitute then top with sprinkled Parmesan cheese. Bake for 12-15 mins in a 400 degrees F oven or until golden brown.

Nutrition Information

- Calories: 351 calories
- Total Carbohydrate: 47 g
- Cholesterol: 10 mg
- Total Fat: 8 g
- Fiber: 8 g
- Protein: 25 g
- Sodium: 669 mg

166. Scrambled Egg Spinach Casserole

"The nutmeg in this amazing casserole perfectly complements the mild feta cheese, spinach, and sausage."
Serving: 8 servings. | Prep: 40m | Ready in: 01h25m

Ingredients

- 2 tbsps. butter
- 2 tbsps. all-purpose flour
- 1/2 tsp. ground nutmeg
- 1/8 tsp. plus 1/2 tsp. salt, divided
- 1/8 tsp. plus 1/4 tsp. pepper, divided
- 2 cups 2% milk
- 1/2 lb. Johnsonville® Ground Mild Italian sausage
- 1/2 cup chopped sweet onion
- 12 eggs
- 3 tbsps. half-and-half cream
- 1 package (10 oz.) frozen chopped spinach, thawed and squeezed dry
- 1-1/2 cups (6 oz.) crumbled feta cheese
- TOPPING:
- 3/4 cup soft bread crumbs
- 1 tbsp. butter, melted
- 2 tbsps. grated Parmesan cheese
- 1/4 tsp. paprika

Direction

- Melt butter in a small pot; mix in 1/8tsp each of pepper and salt, nutmeg, and flour, until smooth. Pour in milk gradually; boil. Cook and stir for 2mins until thick. Take off heat then completely cool.
- In the meantime, on medium heat, cook the remaining pepper and salt, onion, and sausage in a big pan until the meat is not pink; drain. Move to a greased 13-in by 9-in baking dish then set it aside.
- Beat cream and eggs in a big bowl. Mix in cooled white sauce, feta, and spinach; add on the sausage mixture then cover. Chill overnight.
- Take it out of the fridge half an hour before baking. Mix melted butter and bread crumbs to make the topping; spread on top of the casserole. Add paprika and Parmesan cheese on top.
- Bake for 45-50mins in a 350 degrees oven without cover until an inserted knife in the middle comes out without residue. Let it sit for 10mins then serve.

Nutrition Information

- Calories: 319 calories
- Total Carbohydrate: 11 g
- Cholesterol: 360 mg
- Total Fat: 21 g
- Fiber: 2 g
- Protein: 21 g
- Sodium: 763 mg

167. Six-veggie Bake

"You can assemble this strata-like dish with fresh veggies the night before if you're going to be busy the next day. You just need to make a salad then bake this dish the following day."
Serving: 16 servings. | Prep: 15m | Ready in: 45m

Ingredients

- 1 loaf (1 lb.) Italian bread, cut into 1/2-inch cubes
- 1 can (14-1/2 oz.) diced tomatoes, undrained
- 1 package (10 oz.) frozen chopped spinach, thawed and squeezed dry
- 1 cup chopped fresh mushrooms
- 1 cup shredded part-skim mozzarella cheese
- 1/2 cup chopped green pepper
- 1/2 cup chopped zucchini
- 2 green onions, chopped
- 1 tsp. dried basil
- 1/2 tsp. dried oregano
- 1 cup fat-free milk
- 1 cup egg substitute
- 1 tsp. salt-free seasoning blend
- 1/4 tsp. pepper

Direction

- Mix the first ten ingredients in a big bowl; move to a cooking-spray-coated 13-in by 9-in baking dish.
- Whisk pepper, milk, seasoning blend, and egg substitute in a small bowl; pour all over the veggie mixture then cover. Chill for 2hrs to overnight.
- Take it out of the fridge about half an hour before baking. Bake for 15mins while covered in a 425 degrees oven. Remove the cover then bake for another 15mins until an inserted knife in the middle comes out without residue.

Nutrition Information

- Calories: 128 calories
- Total Carbohydrate: 18 g
- Cholesterol: 5 mg
- Total Fat: 3 g
- Fiber: 2 g
- Protein: 8 g
- Sodium: 292 mg

168. Spinach Bacon Brunch Pizza

"Deep-dish pizza made with spinach, cheese, eggs and bacon."
Serving: 2 servings. | Prep: 20m | Ready in: 01h05m

Ingredients

- 1-1/3 cups biscuit/baking mix
- 1/3 cup water
- 6 large eggs, lightly beaten
- 2/3 cup sour cream
- 3/4 tsp. garlic powder
- 1/2 tsp. pepper
- 2 cups fresh baby spinach, chopped
- 1 cup shredded cheddar cheese
- 2 green onions, chopped
- 8 bacon strips, cooked, crumbled and divided

Direction

- Mix together the water and biscuit mix in a small bowl until a soft dough forms. Press it up the sides and onto the bottom of a cooking spray coated 8-inch deep-dish pie plate.
- Let it bake for 6 minutes at 400 degrees or until it turns golden brown in color. Take it out of the oven. Lower the heat to 375 degrees.
- Mix together the pepper, garlic powder, sour cream and eggs in a small bowl. Stir in 1/2 of the bacon, green onions, cheddar and spinach, then pour it into the crust. Sprinkle the leftover bacon on top. Let it bake for 40 to 45 minutes or until an inserted knife in the middle exits clean.

Nutrition Information

- Calories: 527 calories
- Total Carbohydrate: 29 g
- Cholesterol: 388 mg
- Total Fat: 34 g

- Fiber: 1 g
- Protein: 25 g
- Sodium: 1098 mg

169. Spinach Brunch Pizza

"This pie is so rich that you can serve it for either breakfast or dinner. For a healthier approach, you can use turkey bacon instead of bacon."
Serving: 2 servings. | Prep: 20m | Ready in: 45m

Ingredients

- 2/3 cup reduced-fat biscuit/baking mix
- 2 tbsps. plus 1 tsp. water
- 2 cups fresh baby spinach, chopped
- 1/2 cup egg substitute
- 1/3 cup sour cream
- 1/3 cup shredded reduced-fat cheddar cheese
- 2 green onions, chopped
- 1/2 tsp. garlic powder
- 2 bacon strips, cooked and crumbled

Direction

- Mix water and biscuit mix in a small bowl to make a soft dough. Coat a 7 in. pie plate by cooking spray, press dough up the sides and onto the bottom.
- Bake for 5 minutes at 450 degrees till becomes golden brown. Get out of the oven. Lower the heat to 375 degrees.
- Mix garlic powder, onions, cheese, sour cream, egg substitute, spinach in a small bowl. Transfer the mixture into the crust. Use bacon to sprinkle. Bake till becomes golden brown, about 25 to 30 minutes.

Nutrition Information

- Calories: 365 calories
- Total Carbohydrate: 34 g
- Cholesterol: 45 mg
- Total Fat: 16 g
- Fiber: 2 g
- Protein: 18 g

- Sodium: 857 mg

170. Spinach Omelet Brunch Roll

"A beautiful and delicious dish which is full of veggies."
Serving: 8 servings. | Prep: 20m | Ready in: 35m

Ingredients

- 2 cups egg substitute
- 4 large eggs
- 1/2 tsp. salt
- 1/8 tsp. hot pepper sauce
- 1 package (10 oz.) frozen chopped spinach, thawed and squeezed dry
- 1/4 cup chopped red onion
- 1 tsp. Italian seasoning
- 5 turkey bacon strips, diced and cooked, divided
- 1 lb. sliced fresh mushrooms
- 2 tsps. canola oil
- 1 cup shredded part-skim mozzarella cheese, divided

Direction

- Line parchment paper onto a 15x10x1-inch baking pan; spray cooking spray on the paper; put aside. Whisk pepper sauce, salt, eggs, and egg substitute in a big bowl. Mix in 1/4 cup bacon, Italian seasoning, onion, and spinach.
- Transfer to the prepared pan. Bake 15-20 minutes at 375 degrees until set. At the same time, in a big nonstick skillet, sauté mushrooms in oil until tender, about 6-8 minutes. Place on paper towels to drain; blot to get rid of excess moisture. Keep them warm.
- Turn omelet onto a work surface; take out parchment paper. Sprinkle 3/4 cup cheese and the mushrooms on the omelet; roll up jelly-roll style, beginning with a short side. Remove to a serving plate. Sprinkle with the rest bacon and cheese.

Nutrition Information

- Calories: 160 calories

- Total Carbohydrate: 6 g
- Cholesterol: 122 mg
- Total Fat: 8 g
- Fiber: 2 g
- Protein: 17 g
- Sodium: 505 mg

171. Spinach-sausage Egg Bake

"This filling but quick dish features red peppers, spinach, a lot of cheese, and Italian sausage. You can easily serve this during the holidays."
Serving: 6 servings. | Prep: 15m | Ready in: 35m

Ingredients

- 1 lb. Johnsonville® Ground Mild Italian sausage
- 1/2 cup chopped onion
- 1 jar (7 oz.) roasted red peppers, drained and chopped, divided
- 1 package (10 oz.) frozen chopped spinach, thawed and squeezed dry
- 1 cup all-purpose flour
- 1/4 cup grated Parmesan cheese
- 1 tsp. dried basil
- 1/2 tsp. salt
- 8 large eggs
- 2 cups whole milk
- 1 cup shredded provolone cheese

Direction

- On medium heat, cook onion and sausage in a big skillet until the meat is not pink anymore; drain. Move to a lightly oiled 3-quart baking dish; scatter with 1/2 of red peppers. Add spinach on top.
- Mix salt, flour, basil, and Parmesan cheese in a big bow. Beat milk and eggs; mix into the flour mixture until combined. Spread on top of the spinach.
- Bake for 15-20 mins in a 425 degrees F oven without a cover until an inserted knife in the middle comes out clean. Add the remaining red peppers and provolone cheese on top.

Bake for another 3-5 mins or until the cheese melts. Let it sit for 5 mins Serve.

172. Spiral Omelet Supreme

"A new recipe to make omelet for a delightful brunch."
Serving: 8 servings. | Prep: 08h00m | Ready in: 08h20m

Ingredients

- 4 oz. cream cheese, softened
- 3/4 cup 2% milk
- 1/4 cup plus 2 tbsps. grated Parmesan cheese, divided
- 2 tbsps. all-purpose flour
- 12 large eggs
- 2 tsps. canola oil
- 1 large green pepper, chopped
- 1 cup sliced fresh mushrooms
- 1 small onion, chopped
- 1-1/4 tsps. Italian seasoning, divided
- 1-1/2 cups shredded part-skim mozzarella cheese
- 1 plum tomato, seeded and chopped

Direction

- Set an oven to 375 degrees and start preheating. Use a parchment paper to line sides and the bottom of a greased 15x10x1-inch pan; coat the paper with cooking spray.
- Whisk the cream cheese until it becomes soft; slowly whisk in the milk. Whisk in 1/4 cup of Parmesan cheese and flour. Beat the eggs in a large bowl until combined. Put in the cream cheese mixture; combine thoroughly. Spread over the prepared pan. Bake for 20-25 minutes until set.
- At the same time, heat the oil over medium-high in a large skillet; sauté the onion, mushrooms, and pepper for 3-4 minutes until they are tender-crisp. Add a tsp. of Italian seasoning and stir. Keep it warm.
- Take the omelet out of the oven; put the pepper mixture, tomato, and mozzarella on top right away. Roll the omelet up jelly-roll

style beginning with a short side, lift the parchment and remove it as you roll. Place into a platter. Dust with the remaining Italian seasoning and Parmesan cheese.

Nutrition Information

- Calories: 275 calories
- Total Carbohydrate: 8 g
- Cholesterol: 312 mg
- Total Fat: 19 g
- Fiber: 1 g
- Protein: 18 g
- Sodium: 372 mg

173. Tiramisu Crepes

""Graceful crepes, stuffed with creamy mascarpone cheese and mix with vanilla and a hint of coffee liquor, a flavorful treat all the time. So extra in every way.""
Serving: 22 crepes. | Prep: 30m | Ready in: 35m

Ingredients

- 4 large eggs
- 3/4 cup 2% milk
- 1/4 cup club soda
- 3 tbsps. butter, melted
- 2 tbsps. strong brewed coffee
- 1 tsp. vanilla extract
- 1 cup all-purpose flour
- 3 tbsps. sugar
- 2 tbsps. baking cocoa
- 1/4 tsp. salt
- FILLING:
- 1 carton (8 oz.) mascarpone cheese
- 1 package (8 oz.) cream cheese, softened
- 1 cup sugar
- 1/4 cup coffee liqueur or strong brewed coffee
- 2 tbsps. vanilla extract
- Optional toppings: chocolate syrup, whipped cream and baking cocoa

Direction

- Whisk vanilla, coffee, butter, soda, milk and eggs in a large bowl. Mix salt, cocoa, sugar and flour; stir to milk mixture and combine well. Keep in the refrigerator for 1 hour, covered.
- Prepare an 8-inch nonstick skillet that is lightly greased and place over medium heat; drop 2 tbsps. batter into the middle of skillet. Lift and rotate pan to equally coat bottom. Cook until looks dry on top; flip and cook for 15-20 seconds more. Take to a wire rack. Once cool, pile crepe with paper towels or waxed paper in between.
- To make filling, whisk sugar and cheeses in a large bowl until fluffy. Stir in vanilla and liqueur; whisk until smooth. Scoop about 2 tbsps. filling down the middle of each crepe; then roll up. Top with whipped cream and chocolate syrup and dust with cocoa (optional.)

Nutrition Information

- Calories: 188 calories
- Total Carbohydrate: 18 g
- Cholesterol: 67 mg
- Total Fat: 11 g
- Fiber: 0 g
- Protein: 4 g
- Sodium: 92 mg

174. Tomato Asparagus Frittata

"This hearty garden frittata with tomatoes and asparagus is so quick to make."
Serving: 6-8 servings. | Prep: 10m | Ready in: 25m

Ingredients

- 1/4 lb. fresh asparagus, trimmed and halved
- 6 large eggs
- 8 bacon strips, cooked and crumbled
- 1 cup sliced fresh mushrooms
- 1/3 cup chopped onion
- 1/4 cup butter

- 1 medium tomato, sliced
- 1 cup shredded cheddar cheese

Direction

- Add asparagus to a steamer basket; position into a saucepan over 1 inch of water. Boil; keep it covered and steamed till becoming tender-crisp, about 4 to 5 minutes. Drain off and put aside.
- Beat eggs in a bowl till becoming frothy; mix in bacon. Sauté onion and mushrooms in butter in a big skillet till becoming softened. Pour in egg mixture. When eggs start to set, lift the edges, allowing the uncooked portion to flow underneath till the eggs become soft-set.
- Arrange asparagus on top of the egg mixture to look like wheel spokes. Add tomato slices on top. Keep it covered and cook over medium-low heat till eggs become set. Drizzle with cheese. Take out of the heat. Keep it covered and allow it to rest till cheese is melted a bit, about 3 to 4 minutes.

Nutrition Information

- Calories: 203 calories
- Total Carbohydrate: 3 g
- Cholesterol: 195 mg
- Total Fat: 17 g
- Fiber: 1 g
- Protein: 10 g
- Sodium: 294 mg

175. Tomato Onion Quiche

""I always look forward to summer time when eating quiche with fresh basil and vine-ripe tomatoes.""
Serving: 3 servings. | Prep: 20m | Ready in: 01h05m

Ingredients

- 1 sheet refrigerated pie pastry
- 1 cup shredded part-skim mozzarella cheese
- 1/2 cup sliced sweet onion
- 2 small plum tomatoes, seeded and thinly sliced
- 3 medium fresh mushrooms, thinly sliced
- 1/4 cup shredded Parmesan cheese
- 3 large eggs
- 1/2 cup half-and-half cream
- 1/2 tsp. ground mustard
- 1/2 tsp. dried basil
- 1/2 tsp. dried oregano
- 1/2 tsp. dried thyme

Direction

- Cut pastry sheet in half. Rewrap; refrigerate one half for using later. Roll out the remaining half into an 8-inch circle on a lightly floured surface. Move to a 7-inch pie plate; flute edges.
- Layer tomatoes, onion and half of the mozzarella cheese in pastry. Sprinkle with mushrooms on top; layer with tomatoes, onion and the remaining mozzarella cheese. Dust with Parmesan cheese. In a small bowl, mix herbs, mustard, cream and eggs; spread over top.
- Bake at 350° till a knife comes out clean after being inserted in the center, or for 45-55 minutes. Allow to stand for 10 minutes and start cutting.

Nutrition Information

- Calories: 436 calories
- Total Carbohydrate: 26 g
- Cholesterol: 265 mg
- Total Fat: 26 g
- Fiber: 2 g
- Protein: 22 g
- Sodium: 516 mg

176. Vegetarian Egg Strata

"A delicious recipe to pair nicely with mixed salad and fresh bagels or breads for a delightful brunch."
Serving: 12 servings. | Prep: 25m | Ready in: 01h10m

Ingredients

- 1 medium zucchini, finely chopped
- 1 medium sweet red pepper, finely chopped
- 1 cup sliced baby portobello mushrooms
- 1 medium red onion, finely chopped
- 2 tsps. olive oil
- 3 garlic cloves, minced
- 2 tsps. minced fresh thyme or 1/2 tsp. dried thyme
- 1/2 tsp. salt
- 1/4 tsp. pepper
- 1 loaf (1 lb.) day-old French bread, cubed
- 2 packages (5.3 oz. each) fresh goat cheese, crumbled
- 1-3/4 cups grated Parmesan cheese
- 6 eggs, lightly beaten
- 2 cups fat-free milk
- 1/4 tsp. ground nutmeg

Direction

- Sauté onion, mushrooms, red pepper and zucchini in oil in a large skillet until they become tender. Put in pepper, salt, thyme, and garlic; sauté for 1 more minute.
- In a greased 13x9-inch baking dish, arrange Parmesan cheese, goat cheese, zucchini mixture, and 1/2 bread cubes in a layer in reverse order. Repeat the process.
- Beat together nutmeg, milk, and eggs in a small bowl. Place the blend over the top. Put in the fridge, covered, overnight.
- Before baking, take out from the fridge for half an hour. Set an oven to 350 degrees and start preheating. Uncover and bake until a knife comes out clean after inserted in the center, or for 45-50 minutes. Before cutting, allow to stand for 10 minutes.

Nutrition Information

- Calories: 281 calories
- Total Carbohydrate: 27 g
- Cholesterol: 140 mg
- Total Fat: 12 g
- Fiber: 2 g
- Protein: 17 g
- Sodium: 667 mg

177. Zippy Strata

""This is not pizza, but its taste is quite like pizza's.""
Serving: 6-12 servings. | Prep: 15m | Ready in: 01h30m

Ingredients

- 12 slices white bread, divided
- 6 slices process mozzarella cheese
- 15 thin slices tomato
- 1 can (8 oz.) mushroom stems and pieces, drained
- 3 tbsps. dried minced onion
- 1/4 cup all-purpose flour
- 3/4 tsp. dried oregano
- 1/2 tsp. salt
- 1/2 tsp. dried basil
- 1/4 tsp. garlic powder
- 1/4 tsp. cayenne pepper
- 1/8 tsp. pepper
- 3 cups 2% milk
- 5 eggs, lightly beaten
- 1/2 cup grated Parmesan cheese

Direction

- Line a greased 13x9-inch baking dish with 6 bread slices. Layer with remaining bread, minced onion, mushrooms, tomato and mozzarella cheese.
- Mix eggs, milk, seasonings and flour till smooth in a large bowl. Pour over the bread; dust with Parmesan cheese. Cover and refrigerate overnight.
- Take away from the refrigerator for half an hour before baking. Bake without a cover at

325° till a knife comes out clean after being inserted in the center, or for 1-1/4 hours.

Nutrition Information

- Calories: 214 calories
- Total Carbohydrate: 21 g
- Cholesterol: 111 mg
- Total Fat: 9 g
- Fiber: 1 g
- Protein: 12 g
- Sodium: 476 mg

178. Zucchini Crepes

"*"I can simply reheat them by storing a several of these soft well-filed crepes in the freezer, once friends stop by unpredicted. And, they're excellent way to apply more zucchini."*"

Serving: 6 servings. | Prep: 25m | Ready in: 45m

Ingredients

- 1 cup all-purpose flour
- 2 large eggs
- 1/2 cup egg substitute
- 1-1/2 cups fat-free milk
- 3/4 tsp. salt
- FILLING:
- 1 large onion, chopped
- 1 medium green pepper, chopped
- 1 cup sliced fresh mushrooms
- 1 tbsp. canola oil
- 1 medium zucchini, shredded and squeezed dry
- 2 medium tomatoes, chopped and seeded
- 1-1/2 cups shredded reduced-fat cheddar cheese, divided
- 1/4 tsp. salt
- 1/4 tsp. dried oregano
- 1/8 tsp. pepper
- 1-1/2 cups meatless spaghetti sauce

Direction

- Combine salt, milk, egg substitute, eggs and flour in a large bowl until smooth. Keep in the refrigerator for 1 hour, covered.
- Use cooking spray to coat an 8-inch nonstick skillet then heat; place about 1/4 cup batter into middle of skillet. Lift and rotate pan to equally coat bottom. Cook until top looks dry; flip and cook for 15-20 seconds more. Take to a wire rack. Continue with remaining batter; apply cooking spray to coat as necessary.
- Once cool, pile crepes with paper towels or waxed paper in between. Sauté mushrooms, green pepper and onion in oil in a large skillet until tender. Stir in zucchini; sauté for 2-3 minutes more. Take off from heat; mix in pepper, oregano, salt, 1 cup of cheese and tomatoes.
- Place onto crepes and roll up. Then assemble in a 13x9-inch baking dish coated with cooking spray. Pour spaghetti sauce over crepes and spread. Bake in oven, covered, for 15-20 minutes at 350°F. Sprinkle with remaining cheese. Bake for 5 minutes more, without cover, or until cheese is dissolved.

Nutrition Information

- Calories: 264 calories
- Total Carbohydrate: 33 g
- Cholesterol: 78 mg
- Total Fat: 7 g
- Fiber: 3 g
- Protein: 18 g
- Sodium: 900 mg

Chapter 3: Italian Brunch Recipes

***

179. Artichoke Quiche

"Apparently this tasty quiche is very popular in Oklahoma."
Serving: 6 servings. | Prep: 20m | Ready in: 45m

Ingredients

- 1 small onion, finely chopped
- 1 garlic clove, minced
- 2 tsps. vegetable oil
- 4 large eggs
- 1/4 cup soft bread crumbs
- 2 tbsps. minced fresh parsley
- 1/4 tsp. salt
- 1/8 tsp. dried oregano
- 1/8 tsp. pepper
- 1/8 tsp. hot pepper sauce
- 2 cups shredded cheddar cheese
- 1 can (14 oz.) water-packed artichoke hearts, rinsed, drained and chopped

Direction

- Sauté garlic and onion in oil in a skillet till both become soft; set aside. Put hot pepper sauce, pepper, oregano, salt, parsley, bread crumbs and eggs in a large bowl then whisk. Add the onion mixture, artichokes, cheese and stir. Grease a 9 in. pie plate and pour the mixture in. Bake at 350 degrees till a knife comes out clean after being inserted into the center, about 22 to 26 minutes.

Nutrition Information

- Calories: 232 calories
- Total Carbohydrate: 8 g
- Cholesterol: 182 mg
- Total Fat: 16 g
- Fiber: 0 g
- Protein: 14 g
- Sodium: 544 mg

180. Breakfast Bread Bowls

""You can pack these creative and convenient bread bowls with anything you want which is the best part. Well-loved breakfasts.""
Serving: 4 servings. | Prep: 20m | Ready in: 40m

Ingredients

- 1/2 cup chopped pancetta
- 4 crusty hard rolls (4 inches wide)
- 1/2 cup finely chopped fresh mushrooms
- 4 large eggs
- 1/8 tsp. salt
- 1/3 tsp. pepper
- 1/4 cup shredded Gruyere or fontina cheese

Direction

- Prepare the oven by preheating to 350°F. Cook and occasionally stir the pancetta over medium heat in a small skillet until brown in color. Use a slotted spoon to remove the pancetta and transfer onto paper towels to drain. In the meantime, cut a thin slice on top of each roll. Empty out the bottom of the roll, leave a shell that is 1/2 inch thick (keep the removed bread for other use); put the shells on a baking sheet that is ungreased. Put pancetta and mushrooms into the bread shells. Gently crack an egg into each roll; season eggs with pepper and salt. Top with cheese. Place inside in the preheated oven and bake for 18 to 22 minutes or until the egg whites are fully set and yolks start to thicken but not so hard.

181. Breakfast Pepperoni Pizza

"This fun pizza breakfast dish with cream eggs can also be served as a filling entree for dinner."
Serving: 2 servings. | Prep: 15m | Ready in: 25m

Ingredients

- 2 eggs
- 1 green onion, chopped
- 2 tsps. water

- 1 tsp. butter
- 1 prebaked mini pizza crust
- 1/3 cup shredded cheddar cheese
- 1/4 cup pizza sauce
- 12 slices pepperoni

Direction

- Beat water, onion, and eggs, in a small bowl. Heat butter in a small skillet until hot; pour in the egg mixture. On medium heat, cook and stir until the eggs are partially set.
- On an ungreased baking sheet, put the crust then top with 2 tbsp. of cheese; drizzle with approximately 2 tbsp. pizza sauce. Add scrambled egg mixture on top. Drizzle the rest of the pizza sauce then scatter with the rest of the cheese. Add pepperoni on top.
- Bake for 10-12 mins in a 400 degrees F oven or until the crust is slightly crisp. Let it sit for 5 mins Serve.

Nutrition Information

- Calories: 547 calories
- Total Carbohydrate: 55 g
- Cholesterol: 248 mg
- Total Fat: 26 g
- Fiber: 2 g
- Protein: 24 g
- Sodium: 1142 mg

182. Brunch Lasagna

"Before your guests arrive, you simply put this dish in the oven; add muffins and fresh fruit and you will have a tasty dish that surely will please your guests. You can enjoy it with hearty supper and sprinkle salsa on top."
Serving: 9 servings. | Prep: 25m | Ready in: 01h10m

Ingredients

- 6 lasagna noodles
- 8 large eggs, beaten
- 1/2 cup whole milk
- Butter-flavored cooking spray
- 2 jars (16 oz. each) Alfredo sauce
- 3 cups diced fully cooked ham
- 1/2 cup chopped green pepper
- 1/4 cup chopped green onions
- 1 cup shredded cheddar cheese
- 1/4 cup grated Parmesan cheese

Direction

- Cook noodles as the package direct. In the meantime, whisk milk and eggs in a big bowl. Cook eggs over medium-low heat in a big nonstick frying pan skillet coated with butter-flavored cooking spray until set but moist. Take away from heat. Strain the noodles.
- In an oiled 13x9-in or 10-in. square baking plate, spread 1/2 cup of Alfredo sauce. Put onions, green pepper, ham, and 3 lasagna noodles (cut the noodles to fit the plate if needed).
- Put half of the rest of the noodles and Alfredo sauce on top. Put the rest of Alfredo sauce, cheddar cheese, and scrambled eggs. Use Parmesan cheese to drizzle.
- Bake without a cover at 375° until bubbly, about 45-50 minutes. Let it sit for 10 minutes before eating.

Nutrition Information

- Calories: 408 calories
- Total Carbohydrate: 24 g
- Cholesterol: 257 mg
- Total Fat: 24 g
- Fiber: 2 g
- Protein: 25 g
- Sodium: 1175 mg

183. Brunch Risotto

"This light, flavorful and inexpensive risotto makes a surprising addition to a traditional brunch menu."
Serving: 8 servings. | Prep: 10m | Ready in: 40m

Ingredients

- 5-1/4 to 5-3/4 cups reduced-sodium chicken broth

- 3/4 lb. Italian turkey sausage links, casings removed
- 2 cups uncooked arborio rice
- 1 garlic clove, minced
- 1/4 tsp. pepper
- 1 tbsp. olive oil
- 1 medium tomato, chopped

Direction

- Heat broth in a big saucepan and keep warm. Cook sausage in a big nonstick skillet until it isn't pink anymore, then drain and set aside.
- Sauté pepper, garlic and rice with oil in the same skillet about 2 to 3 minutes. Turn the sausage back to the skillet. Stir in 1 cup heated broth carefully, then cook and stir until entire liquid is absorbed.
- Put in 1/2 cup leftover broth at a time while stirring immediately. Let the liquid absorb between additions. Cook just until rice is nearly softened and risotto is creamy. Cook for about 20 minutes in total. Put in tomato and heat through, then serve promptly.

Nutrition Information

- Calories: 279 calories
- Total Carbohydrate: 42 g
- Cholesterol: 23 mg
- Total Fat: 6 g
- Fiber: 1 g
- Protein: 12 g
- Sodium: 653 mg

184. Christmas Breakfast Casserole

"This tasty casserole is loaded with vegetables, herbs, and sausage. I often make this dish at Christmas."
Serving: 12 servings. | Prep: 20m | Ready in: 45m

Ingredients

- 1 lb. Johnsonville® Ground Mild Italian sausage
- 1 cup chopped onion
- 1 jar (7 oz.) roasted red peppers, drained and chopped, divided
- 1 package (10 oz.) frozen chopped spinach, thawed and well drained
- 1 cup all-purpose flour
- 1/4 cup grated Parmesan cheese
- 1 tsp. dried basil
- 1/2 tsp. salt
- 8 large eggs
- 2 cups whole milk
- 1 cup shredded provolone cheese
- Fresh rosemary sprigs, optional

Direction

- Start preheating the oven to 425°. Cook onion and sausage in a frying pan over medium heat until the sausage is not pink anymore. Remove into a 3-quart baking dish coated with oil. Sprinkle all spinach and 1/2 red peppers over.
- Mix salt, basil, Parmesan cheese, and flour together in a bowl. Stir together milk and eggs, pour over the dry ingredients and stir thoroughly. Add over the spinach.
- Bake until a knife will come out clean when you insert it into the middle, about 20-25 minutes. Sprinkle the provolone cheese and the leftover red peppers over. Bake until the cheese melts, about another 2 minutes. Allow to sit before slicing, about 5 minutes. Use rosemary to garnish if you want.

Nutrition Information

- Calories: 232 calories
- Total Carbohydrate: 13 g
- Cholesterol: 170 mg
- Total Fat: 13 g
- Fiber: 1 g
- Protein: 14 g
- Sodium: 531 mg

185. Egg And Tomato Scramble

"My mother used to make this for me when I was little"
Serving: 1 serving. | Prep: 5m | Ready in: 15m

Ingredients

- 1 plum tomato, peeled and chopped
- 1 tsp. chopped fresh basil or 1/4 tsp. dried basil
- 1 egg or egg substitute equivalent
- 1 tsp. water
- 1 garlic clove, minced
- 1 tsp. olive oil, optional
- Salt and pepper to taste, optional
- 1 slice bread, toasted
- Additional fresh basil, optional

Direction

- Mix together basil and tomato in a small bowl; set aside. Beat garlic, water and egg in another bowl. In a small nonstick skillet, heat oil if desired; add egg mixture. Cook while stirring gently until egg is almost set. Add tomato mixture, and pepper and salt if desired.
- Cook until egg is set completely and tomato is heated through, remember to stir while cooking. Serve with toast. Place basil on top to garnish if desired.

Nutrition Information

- Calories: 152 calories
- Total Carbohydrate: 20 g
- Cholesterol: 1 mg
- Total Fat: 4 g
- Fiber: 0 g
- Protein: 11 g
- Sodium: 289 mg

186. Egg 'n' Pepperoni Bundles

"These flavorful bundles are everyone's gift on Christmas!"
Serving: 4 servings. | Prep: 20m | Ready in: 35m

Ingredients

- 7 sheets phyllo dough (14 inches x 9 inches)
- 1/2 cup butter, melted
- 8 tsps. dry bread crumbs
- 2 oz. cream cheese, cut into 8 cubes
- 4 eggs
- 24 slices pepperoni, quartered or 1-1/2 oz. Jones Canadian Bacon, diced
- 1/3 cup provolone cheese
- 2 tsps. minced chives

Direction

- On a work surface, place one sheet of phyllo dough; brush the sheet with butter. Put another sheet of phyllo on top, brush the sheet with butter. Repeat 5 times. Cut the phyllo in 1/2 widthwise, then cut in 1/2 lengthwise. Place each stack in each of the 4 grease jumbo muffin cups carefully. Brush butter on edges of dough. Sprinkle onto each cup's bottom with 2 tsps. of bread crumbs. Top each with 2 cream cheese cubes.
- Break each egg individually into a custard cup; pour egg gently over cream cheese. Top with chives, provolone cheese and pepperoni. Seal by pinching phyllo's corners together. Bake at 400° until golden brown or for 13-17 minutes. Serve while it is still warm.

Nutrition Information

- Calories: 509 calories
- Total Carbohydrate: 20 g
- Cholesterol: 305 mg
- Total Fat: 42 g
- Fiber: 1 g
- Protein: 16 g
- Sodium: 733 mg

187. Frittata Florentine

"This beautiful Italian omelet is filled with ingredients that is perfect for brunch."
Serving: 4 servings. | Prep: 25m | Ready in: 30m

Ingredients

- 6 large egg whites
- 3 large eggs
- 1/2 tsp. dried oregano
- 1/4 tsp. garlic powder
- 1/4 tsp. salt
- 1/4 tsp. pepper
- 1 tbsp. olive oil
- 1 small onion, finely chopped
- 1/4 cup finely chopped sweet red pepper
- 2 turkey bacon strips, chopped
- 1 cup fresh baby spinach
- 3 tbsps. thinly sliced fresh basil leaves
- 1/2 cup shredded part-skim mozzarella cheese

Direction

- Preheat the broiler. Beat the first 6 ingredients in a small bowl.
- On medium-high heat, heat oil in an 8-inch ovenproof skillet. Cook and stir bacon, red pepper, and onion for 4-5 mins or until the onion is tender. Turn to medium-low heat, add spinach on top.
- Add the egg mixture. Push the cooked parts to the middle as the eggs set to let the uncooked parts flow under. Cook until the eggs are almost thick. Take off the heat; scatter with basil and cheese.
- Broil for 2-3mins, three to four inches from heat or until the eggs are set completely. Let it sit for 5 mins Slice into wedges.

Nutrition Information

- Calories: 176 calories
- Total Carbohydrate: 4 g
- Cholesterol: 174 mg
- Total Fat: 11 g
- Fiber: 1 g
- Protein: 15 g
- Sodium: 451 mg

188. Full Garden Frittata

""Made this recipe for someone that is conscious in health. Added a fresh mozzarella and leftover bruschetta topping to lighten it up. Served at breakfast. Well loved by everyone and pinned in my book of recipes.""
Serving: 2 servings. | Prep: 25m | Ready in: 35m

Ingredients

- 4 large eggs
- 1/3 cup 2% milk
- 1/4 tsp. salt, divided
- 1/8 tsp. coarsely ground pepper
- 2 tsps. olive oil
- 1/2 medium zucchini, chopped
- 1/2 cup chopped baby portobello mushrooms
- 1/4 cup chopped onion
- 1 garlic clove, minced
- 2 tbsps. minced fresh basil
- 1 tsp. minced fresh oregano
- 1 tsp. minced fresh parsley
- Optional toppings: halved grape tomatoes, small fresh mozzarella cheese balls and thinly sliced fresh basil

Direction

- Prepare the oven by preheating to 375°F. Whisk together in a bowl 1/8 tsp. pepper and salt, milk and eggs. Heat oil over medium-high heat in an 8-inch oven proof skillet. Put onion, mushrooms and zucchini then stir and cook until softened. Add in the left salt, herbs and garlic; cook for 1 more minute. Put in the egg mixture. Place inside the preheated oven and bake for 10 to 15 minutes, without cover, or until the eggs are set. Slice into 4 wedges. Serve with toppings if you want.

Nutrition Information

- Calories: 227 calories
- Total Carbohydrate: 7 g
- Cholesterol: 375 mg

- Total Fat: 15 g
- Fiber: 1 g
- Protein: 15 g
- Sodium: 463 mg

189. Italian Garden Frittata

"For a yummy breakfast or brunch, serve this beautiful frittata with melon slices."
Serving: 4 servings. | Prep: 15m | Ready in: 30m

Ingredients

- 4 large eggs
- 6 large egg whites
- 1/2 cup grated Romano cheese, divided
- 1 tbsp. minced fresh sage
- 1/2 tsp. salt
- 1/4 tsp. pepper
- 1 tsp. olive oil
- 1 small zucchini, sliced
- 2 green onions, chopped
- 2 plum tomatoes, thinly sliced

Direction

- Preheat broiler. In a big bowl, beat together 1/4 cup cheese, eggs, egg whites, sage, salt and pepper.
- Coat a 10-inch broiler-safe pan with cooking spray then pour oil to warm over medium-high heat. Toss in green onions and zucchini and stir-fry for 2 minutes. Turn heat down to medium-low. Stir in egg mixture and continue cooking, covered, for 4 to 7 minutes or until eggs are almost firm.
- Remove the cover and place tomatoes and the rest of the cheese on top. Broil 3 to 4 inches from heat for 2 to 3 minutes or until eggs have firmed up. Set aside for 5 minutes to cool then slice into wedges.

Nutrition Information

- Calories: 183 calories
- Total Carbohydrate: 4 g
- Cholesterol: 228 mg

- Total Fat: 11 g
- Fiber: 1 g
- Protein: 18 g
- Sodium: 655 mg

190. Italian Sausage Strata

""This is usually served for breakfast.""
Serving: 12 servings. | Prep: 20m | Ready in: 01h20m

Ingredients

- 1/2 cup butter, softened, divided
- 12 to 16 slices day-old bread, crusts removed
- 1/2 lb. fresh mushrooms, sliced
- 2 cups sliced onions
- Salt and pepper to taste
- 1 lb. Johnsonville® Ground Mild Italian sausage, cooked and drained
- 3 cups shredded cheddar cheese
- 5 large eggs, lightly beaten
- 2-1/2 cups whole milk
- 1 tbsp. Dijon mustard
- 1 tsp. ground nutmeg
- 1 tsp. ground mustard
- 2 tbsps. minced fresh parsley

Direction

- Spread one side of each bread slice with 1/4 cup of butter. In a greased 13x9-inch baking dish, arrange half of the bread with the butter side down.
- In a large skillet, sauté onions and mushrooms in the remaining butter. Sprinkle with pepper and salt. In the prepared pan, use a spoon to pour half of the mushroom mixture over the bread. Sprinkle with cheese and half of the sausage on top. Layer with cheese, sausage, mushroom mixture and remaining bread. In a large bowl, whisk the ground mustard, nutmeg, Dijon mustard, milk and eggs. Pour over the cheese. Use a cover and chill in a refrigerator overnight.
- Take it out from the refrigerator for half an hour before baking. Bake with a cover at 350°,

50 minutes. Bake without a cover for another 10-15 minutes or till a knife comes out clean after being inserted in the center. Top with parsley. Allow to sit for 10 minutes. Serve.

Nutrition Information

- Calories: 340 calories
- Total Carbohydrate: 13 g
- Cholesterol: 161 mg
- Total Fat: 25 g
- Fiber: 1 g
- Protein: 16 g
- Sodium: 574 mg

191. Mini Spinach Frittatas

"Those mouth-watering frittatas are. Irresistibly delicious. They are easy to make, chill well and you can double the recipe to serve a crowd."
Serving: 2 dozen. | Prep: 10m | Ready in: 30m

Ingredients

- 1 cup whole-milk ricotta cheese
- 3/4 cup grated Parmesan cheese
- 2/3 cup chopped fresh mushrooms
- 1 package (10 oz.) frozen chopped spinach, thawed and squeezed dry
- 1 large egg
- 1/2 tsp. dried oregano
- 1/4 tsp. salt
- 1/4 tsp. pepper
- 24 slices pepperoni

Direction

- Turn oven to 375° to preheat. Mix the first 8 ingredients together in a small bowl. Put a pepperoni slice in each of the 24 oiled mini-muffin cups. Pour cheese mixture into each cup to fill 3/4 full.
- Bake for 20 to 25 minutes until totally firm. Use a knife to run around the inside edges of the cup carefully to loosen the frittatas. Serve when still warm.

Nutrition Information

- Calories: 128 calories
- Total Carbohydrate: 4 g
- Cholesterol: 50 mg
- Total Fat: 9 g
- Fiber: 1 g
- Protein: 10 g
- Sodium: 396 mg

192. Mozzarella Vegetable Strata

"A nutritious dish for breakfast or brunch."
Serving: 2 servings. | Prep: 20m | Ready in: 50m

Ingredients

- 1/2 cup sliced zucchini
- 1/3 cup sliced fresh mushrooms
- 1/3 cup chopped onion
- 2 tsps. canola oil
- 1 tbsp. minced fresh parsley or 1-1/2 tsps. dried parsley flakes
- 3/4 tsp. minced fresh basil or 1/4 tsp. dried basil
- 2-3/4 cups cubed bread
- 1/2 cup shredded part-skim mozzarella cheese
- 2 eggs
- 1/2 cup 2% milk
- 1/4 tsp. salt
- 1/8 tsp. pepper
- 1 plum tomato, seeded and chopped

Direction

- In a small skillet, sauté onion, mushrooms, and zucchini in oil until tender. Drain. Mix in basil and parsley.
- Coat an 8x4-inch loaf pan with cooking spray. In the loaf pan, put layers of 1/2 the bread cubes and mozzarella cheese. Arrange vegetables, the rest of bread and cheese on top. Beat pepper, salt, milk, and eggs in a small bowl; spread over cheese then sprinkle tomato over the surface.

- Cover and bake for 20 minutes at 350 degrees. Remove cover and continue to bake until a knife inserted into the center comes out clean, 10-15 minutes. Let sit 5 minutes then slice.

Nutrition Information

- Calories: 371 calories
- Total Carbohydrate: 33 g
- Cholesterol: 234 mg
- Total Fat: 17 g
- Fiber: 3 g
- Protein: 20 g
- Sodium: 785 mg

193. Parmesan Ham Frittata

"This Italian egg dish is the combinations of variety of ingredients."
Serving: 2 servings. | Prep: 15m | Ready in: 20m

Ingredients

- 1/4 cup chopped onion
- 1/4 cup chopped green pepper
- 2 garlic cloves, minced
- 2 tbsps. olive oil
- 4 eggs
- Salt and pepper to taste
- 1/2 cup cubed fully cooked ham
- 1/4 cup grated Parmesan cheese

Direction

- In the 6-inch broiler-proof skillet, sauté garlic, green pepper, and onion in oil. Lower the heat to medium. Whip pepper, salt and eggs in a bowl. Pour ham and egg mixture into vegetables.
- When eggs set, lift the edges, allowing the uncooked portion to flow under. Once eggs become almost set, drizzle with cheese. Broil 4 to 5 inches away from the heat source till eggs become totally set, about 1 to 2 minutes.

Nutrition Information

- Calories: 388 calories
- Total Carbohydrate: 6 g
- Cholesterol: 451 mg
- Total Fat: 30 g
- Fiber: 1 g
- Protein: 24 g
- Sodium: 761 mg

194. Pepper And Fresh Herb Frittata

"This egg dish with herby seasoning with peppers can be eaten for brunch or breakfast."
Serving: 6 servings. | Prep: 25m | Ready in: 30m

Ingredients

- 12 large eggs
- 2 tbsps. minced fresh chives
- 2 tbsps. minced fresh parsley
- 2 tsps. minced fresh basil or 1/2 tsp. dried basil
- 2 tsps. minced fresh oregano or 1/2 tsp. dried oregano
- 1 tsp. salt
- 1/4 tsp. pepper
- 3 tbsps. olive oil
- 1/2 cup sliced pickled peppers
- 1/2 cup crumbled goat cheese

Direction

- Preheat the broiler. Mix pepper, salt, herbs and eggs till become blended in a big bowl.
- On medium-low heat, heat oil in the 10-inch broiler-safe skillet. Add the egg mixture. Cook it while covered till almost set, about 10 to 12 minutes. Add cheese and pickled peppers on top.
- Broil 4-5 inches away from the heat source till eggs become set totally, about 3 to 4 minutes. Allow it to rest for 5 minutes. Chop into wedges.

Nutrition Information

- Calories: 234 calories
- Total Carbohydrate: 2 g
- Cholesterol: 384 mg
- Total Fat: 19 g
- Fiber: 1 g
- Protein: 14 g
- Sodium: 708 mg

195. Quick Anise Fruit Bowl

"Fruits coated in a thick, sweet syrup."
Serving: 18 servings (3/4 cup). | Prep: 25m | Ready in: 25m

Ingredients

- 2 cups water
- 1-1/2 cups sugar
- 3 tbsps. lemon juice
- 2 tbsps. aniseed
- 1/2 tsp. salt
- 1 fresh pineapple, peeled and cubed
- 1 small cantaloupe, peeled, seeded and cubed
- 1/2 lb. seedless red grapes
- 2 large bananas, sliced
- 2 medium nectarines, sliced
- 2 medium oranges, peeled and sectioned
- 2 medium kiwifruit, peeled and sliced
- 1 large pink grapefruit, peeled and sectioned

Direction

- Add salt, aniseed, lemon juice, sugar, and water in a large saucepan and bring to a boil. Lower the heat and simmer until mixture is slightly thick, or for 10 to 15 minutes. Allow to cool slightly; then cover and chill in the refrigerator.
- Combine the leftover ingredients in a large bowl. Pour the syrup on the fruits and toss until coated. Chill before serving. Serve alongside a slotted spoon.

Nutrition Information

- Calories: 151 calories
- Total Carbohydrate: 38 g
- Cholesterol: 0 mg
- Total Fat: 1 g
- Fiber: 2 g
- Protein: 1 g
- Sodium: 69 mg

196. Sausage And Hashbrown Breakfast Pizza

"This tasty meal is made with frozen hash browns and crescent rolls. If you're going to camp, this dish is the best to bring along."
Serving: 6-8 servings. | Prep: 10m | Ready in: 40m

Ingredients

- 1 tube (8 oz.) refrigerated crescent rolls
- 1 lb. Jones No Sugar Pork Sausage Roll sausage
- 1 cup frozen shredded hash brown potatoes, thawed
- 1 cup shredded cheddar cheese
- 3 large eggs
- 1/4 cup whole milk
- 1/4 tsp. pepper
- 1/4 cup grated Parmesan cheese

Direction

- Roll out crescent dough and put on an oiled 12-in. pizza pan, press the seams together and press up sides of the pan to make a crust.
- Brown sausage in a big frying pan over medium heat, strain and let cool down a little. Drizzle over the crust with cheddar cheese, hash browns, and sausage.
- Beat pepper, milk, and eggs in a small bowl, put on the pizza. Use Parmesan cheese to drizzle. Bake at 375° until a knife will come out clean when you stick it in the middle, about 28-30 minutes. Let it sit for 10 minutes before slicing.

Nutrition Information

- Calories: 332 calories
- Total Carbohydrate: 15 g
- Cholesterol: 120 mg
- Total Fat: 24 g
- Fiber: 0 g
- Protein: 13 g
- Sodium: 623 mg

197. Sausage Mushroom Quiche

"Delightful and satisfying, this quiche is one of the best I ever had."
Serving: 6 | Prep: 20m | Ready in: 50m

Ingredients

- 1 lb. small fresh button mushrooms
- 1 lb. ground pork breakfast sausage
- 1/2 cup chopped fresh parsley
- 3 eggs
- 1 cup half-and-half cream
- 1/2 cup grated Parmesan cheese
- 1/4 tsp. salt
- 1 (9 inch) unbaked 9 inch pie crust

Direction

- Preheat oven to 400°F or 200°C. Snip off the stems of the mushroom and cut any large pieces in half.
- In a big pan, crush the sausage and add the mushrooms. Cook on medium-high heat until all the liquid from the mushrooms has evaporated and both mushrooms and meat have lightly browned. Remove the grease then add parsley.
- In a big bowl, whisk the eggs then add the cheese, cream and salt. Pour egg mixture into the pan with the sausage and mushroom. Blend well. Scoop mixture into the pie shell.
- Bake for 25-30 minutes until the filling is firm and crust is well browned. Set aside for 10 minutes before serving.

Nutrition Information

- Calories: 612 calories;
- Total Carbohydrate: 20.6 g
- Cholesterol: 167 mg
- Total Fat: 50.3 g
- Protein: 19.9 g
- Sodium: 1101 mg

198. Super-stuffed Omelet

"This dish is omelet ingredients wrapped in a tortilla. It's great to serve at breakfast."
Serving: 2 servings. | Prep: 15m | Ready in: 30m

Ingredients

- 1/4 cup chopped fresh tomato
- 2 large mushrooms, sliced
- 2 tbsps. finely chopped green or sweet red pepper
- 1 tbsp. diced onion
- 3 large eggs
- 1/4 cup 2% milk
- 2 tsps. minced fresh parsley
- 1/2 tsp. dried basil
- Pepper to taste
- 4 spinach leaves
- 2 slices cheddar cheese
- 1 flour tortilla (10 inches)
- 2 slices deli ham
- 1 cup shredded cheddar cheese, divided
- Sour cream and salsa, optional

Direction

- In a 10-in. nonstick frying pan greased with cooking spray, sauté onion, green pepper, mushrooms, and tomato until soft. Take out and put aside.
- Beat pepper, basil, parsley, milk, and eggs in a small bowl. Add to the frying pan, cook over medium heat. While the eggs set, raise the edges to let the raw portion run underneath. Once the eggs set, put tortilla, cheese slices, and spinach on top.

- Upturn the pan to flip the omelet, put the omelet back to the pan with tortilla side turning down. Put on one side of the omelet with the sautéed vegetables and ham. Use 3/4 cup of shredded cheese to drizzle and fold the other side of the omelet over the filling. Put a cover on and let it sit until the cheese melts, about 1-1/2 minutes. Take away from heat. Put the rest of the shredded cheese on top. Enjoy with salsa and sour cream if you want.

Nutrition Information

- Calories: 629 calories
- Total Carbohydrate: 29 g
- Cholesterol: 423 mg
- Total Fat: 39 g
- Fiber: 3 g
- Protein: 41 g
- Sodium: 1063 mg

199. Tomato Herb Frittata

"Every slice of this egg dish is filled with fresh tomatoes and cheesy eggs, enhanced by garlic and herbs."
Serving: 6 servings. | Prep: 20m | Ready in: 35m

Ingredients

- 9 eggs
- 1-1/4 cups shredded part-skim mozzarella cheese, divided
- 1/2 cup 2% milk
- 1 tbsp. minced fresh basil or 1 tsp. dried basil
- 1 tbsp. minced fresh oregano or 1 tsp. dried oregano
- 1 tsp. minced fresh thyme or 1/4 tsp. dried thyme
- 1/2 tsp. salt
- 1/4 tsp. pepper
- 1-1/2 cups grape tomatoes
- 2 tbsps. olive oil
- 2 garlic cloves, minced
- Thinly sliced fresh basil, optional

Direction

- Beat pepper, salt, herbs, milk, 3/4 cup cheese and eggs in a small bowl; put aside.
- Sauté tomatoes in oil in a 10-in. ovenproof skillet until tender. Add garlic, cook for another 1 minute. Transfer the egg mixture to a pan; top with remaining cheese.
- Bake for 12-15 minutes at 400° or until eggs are set completely. Allow to sit for 5 minutes. Cut into wedges. Decorate with sliced basil if preferred.

Nutrition Information

- Calories: 227 calories
- Total Carbohydrate: 4 g
- Cholesterol: 332 mg
- Total Fat: 16 g
- Fiber: 0 g
- Protein: 16 g
- Sodium: 425 mg

200. Too-yummy-to-share Scramble

"Treat yourself with this delicious single-serving egg breakfast with a fresh flavor from basil."
Serving: 1 serving. | Prep: 5m | Ready in: 15m

Ingredients

- 1/4 cup chopped sweet onion
- 1/4 cup chopped tomato
- 1/8 tsp. dried basil
- Dash salt and pepper
- 1 egg
- 1 tbsp. water
- 2 tbsps. shredded reduced-fat cheddar cheese

Direction

- On medium heat, cook and stir onion in a small cooking-spray-coated non-stick pan until tender. Put in pepper, tomato, salt, and basil; cook for another minute.

- Beat water and egg in a small bowl; pour into the pan with egg mixture. Cook and stir until the egg is set completely. Take off heat then top with cheese. Cover then let it sit until the cheese melts.

Nutrition Information

- Calories: 136 calories
- Total Carbohydrate: 7 g
- Cholesterol: 222 mg
- Total Fat: 8 g
- Fiber: 1 g
- Protein: 11 g
- Sodium: 310 mg

201. Triple-cheese Florentine Frittata

"This ham and cheese frittata has a great deal of my desired ingredients and taste."
Serving: 4 servings. | Prep: 30m | Ready in: 35m

Ingredients

- 3 small red potatoes (about 8 oz.), peeled and cut into 1/4-inch slices
- 2 tbsps. water
- 2 tsps. plus 1 tbsp. canola oil, divided
- 1/2 cup chopped onion
- 1 cup fresh baby spinach
- 5 large eggs
- 1/4 cup white wine or chicken broth
- 1/4 tsp. dried oregano
- 1/4 tsp. pepper
- 1/8 tsp. salt
- 1 cup shredded cheddar cheese
- 1/2 cup cubed fully cooked ham
- 3 tbsps. shredded Swiss cheese
- 1/4 cup grated Parmesan cheese

Direction

- Preheat the broiler. In a microwave-safe bowl, mix water and potatoes; cover and microwave till soft, about 3 to 5 minutes on high heat. Allow to cool down a bit; drain.
- In the 10-inch ovenproof skillet, on medium heat, heat 2 tsp. of oil. Put in onion; cook and stir till soft, about 3 to 4 minutes. Take out of the pan.
- Put spinach into same pan; cook and stir till it becomes wilted, 30 to 45 seconds. Drain off the spinach and squeeze to dry; coarsely chop. Mix salt, pepper, oregano, wine, and eggs in a small-sized bowl; mix in spinach, onion, Swiss cheese, ham and Cheddar cheese. Lightly mix in potatoes.
- In the 10-inch ovenproof skillet, on the medium heat, heat the leftover oil. Add the egg mixture. Cook while covered till almost set, 3 to 5 minutes. Drizzle with Parmesan cheese.
- Broil 3 to 4 inches away from heat source till eggs become totally set, about 2 to 4 minutes. Allow it to rest for 5 minutes. Chop into wedges.

202. Veggie Breakfast Pizza

"A Mexican dish made with a combination of various recipes."
Serving: 8 slices. | Prep: 50m | Ready in: 01h05m

Ingredients

- 1-1/4 tsps. active dry yeast
- 3/4 cup warm water (110° to 115°)
- 1 tbsp. sugar
- 1 tbsp. olive oil
- 1 tsp. salt
- 2-1/4 cups all-purpose flour
- TOPPINGS:
- 1 cup salsa
- 2 medium tomatoes, seeded and chopped
- 1 large onion, chopped
- 1 small green pepper, chopped
- 1 tbsp. olive oil
- 6 large eggs, beaten
- 1/2 tsp. seasoned salt
- 1/4 tsp. salt

- 1/4 tsp. garlic pepper blend
- 1 cup shredded part-skim mozzarella cheese

Direction

- Dissolve the yeast in warm water in a big bowl. Add 1 1/4 cups flour, salt, oil and sugar, then beat it until it becomes smooth. To form a soft dough, mix in enough leftover flour (the dough will get sticky). Flip it onto a lightly floured surface, then knead it for about 6 to 8 minutes, until it becomes pliable and smooth.
- Put it in a cooking spray coated bowl, then flip it once so the top will be coated. Put on cover and allow it to rise for 30 minutes in a warm area.
- Punch down the dough and roll it into a 13-inch round. Move to a cooking spray coated 12-inch pizza pan. Build up the edges a bit. Use a fork to thoroughly prick the dough and let it bake for 8 to 10 minutes at 425 degrees or until it turns golden brown.
- In the meantime, drain the salsa and get rid of the liquid. Cook and stir the green pepper, onion and tomatoes in oil in a big skillet on medium heat, until it becomes crisp-tender. Mix together the seasonings and eggs, then add it into the pan. Let it cook and stir until the eggs become set.
- Scoop the egg mixture and salsa on top of the crust, then sprinkle cheese on top. Let it bake until the cheese melts or for 3 to 5 minutes.

Nutrition Information

- Calories: 285 calories
- Total Carbohydrate: 34 g
- Cholesterol: 168 mg
- Total Fat: 10 g
- Fiber: 2 g
- Protein: 13 g
- Sodium: 731 mg

203. Veggie Sausage Strata

"After my retirement, I have dedicated most of my time to making recipes. This casserole is one of my family's most favorite dishes."
Serving: 12 servings. | Prep: 15m | Ready in: 01h35m

Ingredients

- 2 lbs. Johnsonville® Ground Mild Italian sausage
- 2 medium green peppers, coarsely chopped
- 1 medium onion, chopped
- 8 large eggs
- 2 cups whole milk
- 2 tsps. salt
- 2 tsps. white pepper
- 2 tsps. ground mustard
- 12 slices bread, cut into 1/2-inch pieces
- 1 package (10 oz.) frozen chopped spinach, thawed and squeezed dry
- 2 cups shredded Swiss cheese
- 2 cups shredded cheddar cheese
- 1 medium zucchini, cut into 1/4-inch slices

Direction

- Cook onion, green peppers, and sausage in a big frying pan over medium heat until the meat is not pink anymore; strain. In the meantime, combine mustard, pepper, salt, milk, and eggs in a big bowl. Mix in zucchini, cheeses, spinach, bread, and the sausage mixture.
- Remove the mixture into a 13x9-inch baking dish coated with oil. Put a cover on and chill overnight.
- Take out of the fridge before baking, about 30 minutes. Put a cover on and bake for 40 minutes at 350°. Remove the cover, bake until a knife will come out clean when you insert it into the middle, about another 40-45 minutes.

204. Wine 'n' Cheese Strata

"This dish is a meal in itself! Use two 13x9-inch baking dishes and double the ingredients if you wanna serve it in events or brunch get-togethers."

Serving: 10-12 servings. | Prep: 15m | Ready in: 01h25m

Ingredients

- 1 lb. day-old Italian bread, cubed
- 3 tbsps. butter, melted
- 1-1/3 cups shredded Swiss cheese
- 1 cup shredded Monterey Jack cheese
- 2 oz. salami, coarsely chopped
- 8 large eggs
- 1-1/2 cups milk
- 1/4 cup dry white wine or water
- 2 green onions, chopped
- 1-1/2 tsps. spicy brown mustard
- 1/4 tsp. pepper
- Dash crushed red pepper flakes
- 3/4 cup sour cream
- 1/2 cup shredded Parmesan cheese

Direction

- In a greased 13x9-inch baking dish, put in the bread cubes and sprinkle it evenly with melted butter. Top it off with salami and cheese. Whisk the wine, mustard, pepper flakes, milk, onions, eggs, and pepper together in a bowl. Distribute it evenly on top. Cover the baking dish and keep it in the fridge overnight. Take the chilled mixture out from the fridge 30 minutes prior to baking. Put it in the preheated 325°F oven and let it bake, covered, for 1 hour. Remove the cover then put an even layer of sour cream on top. Top it off with Parmesan cheese. Put it back in the oven and bake for 10 more minutes until the cheese has melted.

Nutrition Information

- Calories: 342 calories
- Total Carbohydrate: 22 g
- Cholesterol: 190 mg
- Total Fat: 19 g
- Fiber: 1 g
- Protein: 17 g
- Sodium: 554 mg

Chapter 4: Italian Dinner Recipes

***

205. Angel Hair Pasta With Sausage & Spinach

Serving: 4 servings. | Prep: 15m | Ready in: 30m

Ingredients

- 4 Johnsonville® Mild Italian Sausage Links (4 oz. each), sliced
- 1 medium onion, chopped
- 2 garlic cloves, minced
- 2 tsps. olive oil
- 2 cans (14-1/2 oz. each) chicken broth
- 8 oz. uncooked angel hair pasta, broken in half
- 2 packages (10 oz. each) fresh spinach, trimmed and coarsely chopped
- 2 tbsps. all-purpose flour
- 1/4 tsp. pepper
- 1/3 cup heavy whipping cream

Direction

- On medium heat, cook garlic, onion, and sausage in a Dutch oven with oil until the meat is not pink; drain. Pour in broth then boil. Put in pasta; cook while frequently mixing for 3mins.
- Put in spinach gradually; cook and stir for 2-3mins until the spinach wilts and the pasta is tender. Mix cream, pepper, and flour in a

small bowl until smooth. Mix into the pasta mixture gradually; boil. Cook and stir for 1-2mins until thick.

Nutrition Information

- Calories: 563 calories
- Total Carbohydrate: 57 g
- Cholesterol: 77 mg
- Total Fat: 26 g
- Fiber: 6 g
- Protein: 25 g
- Sodium: 1546 mg

206. Bacon Bolognese

"This pasta dish with ground beef, juicy tomatoes, white wine, and bacon will bring you back to your childhood memories."
Serving: 10 servings. | Prep: 15m | Ready in: 03h30m

Ingredients

- 1/2 lb. ground beef
- 1/2 lb. ground pork
- 1/2 tsp. salt
- 1/4 tsp. pepper
- 2 medium carrots, chopped
- 1 medium onion, chopped
- 6 thick-sliced bacon strips, chopped
- 8 garlic cloves, minced
- 1 cup dry white wine
- 1 can (28 oz.) whole tomatoes, crushed slightly
- 1-1/2 cups chicken stock or reduced-sodium chicken broth
- 1 package (16 oz.) spaghetti
- 3 tbsps. butter, cubed
- 1 cup grated Parmesan cheese

Direction

- On medium heat, cook pork and beef for 5-7 mins in a six-quart stockpot until the meat is not pink anymore while crumbling. Mix in pepper and salt. Take the meat out of the pot using a slotted spoon; drain the drippings.
- Put bacon, onion, and carrots in the same pot. On medium heat, cook and stir for 6-8 mins or until the veggies are soft. Put in garlic; cook for another minute. Place the meat back in the pot then pour in wine; boil and mix to loosen the brown bits from the pan. Cook until the liquid is nearly evaporated.
- Put in stock and tomatoes; bring back to boil. Lower the heat; let it simmer for 3-4 hrs while mixing from time to time, covered to let the flavors meld.
- In order to serve, cook the spaghetti following the package instructions until al dente; drain, Mix butter in the meat sauce; toss in spaghetti to blend then serve with cheese.

Nutrition Information

- Calories: 483 calories
- Total Carbohydrate: 41 g
- Cholesterol: 61 mg
- Total Fat: 26 g
- Fiber: 3 g
- Protein: 20 g
- Sodium: 686 mg

207. Baked Ziti With Fresh Tomatoes

"I prepared the meat sauce in advance to save time!"
Serving: 6 servings. | Prep: 01h10m | Ready in: 01h40m

Ingredients

- 1 lb. ground beef
- 1 cup chopped onion
- 3 lbs. plum tomatoes, peeled, seeded and chopped (about 15 tomatoes)
- 1-1/2 tsps. salt
- 1 tsp. dried basil
- 1/4 tsp. pepper
- 8 oz. uncooked ziti
- 2 cups shredded part-skim mozzarella cheese, divided
- 2 tbsps. grated Parmesan cheese

Direction

- In a Dutch oven, cook the onion and beef over medium heat till the meat is not pink anymore; let it drain. Mix in the pepper, basil, salt and tomatoes. Decrease heat to low; cook with cover while from time to time stirring for 45 minutes.
- Cook ziti as stated on package directions; let it drain. Put in a large bowl. Whisk in 1 cup of mozzarella cheese and sauce. Move to a greased 3-quart baking dish; scatter top with the leftover mozzarella cheese and Parmesan cheese.
- Bake with cover at 350° for about 15 minutes. Then bake with no cover for 15 more minutes, or up to heated through.

Nutrition Information

- Calories: 375 calories
- Total Carbohydrate: 33 g
- Cholesterol: 60 mg
- Total Fat: 14 g
- Fiber: 2 g
- Protein: 29 g
- Sodium: 851 mg

208. Beef & Bacon Gnocchi Skillet

"You can top this gnocchi with pickles, mustard, and ketchup since it really tastes like bacon cheeseburgers."
Serving: 6 servings. | Prep: 10m | Ready in: 30m

Ingredients

- 1 package (16 oz.) potato gnocchi
- 1-1/4 lbs. lean ground beef (90% lean)
- 1 medium onion, chopped
- 8 cooked bacon strips, crumbled and divided
- 1 cup water
- 1/2 cup heavy whipping cream
- 1 tbsp. ketchup
- 1/4 tsp. salt
- 1/4 tsp. pepper
- 1-1/2 cups shredded cheddar cheese
- 1/2 cup chopped tomatoes
- 2 green onions, sliced

Direction

- Preheat the broiler. Prepare the gnocchi following the package instructions; drain.
- In the meantime, on medium heat, cook onion and beef while breaking the meat into crumble for 4-6 mins in a big ovenproof skillet until the beef is not pink anymore; drain.
- Mix in 1/2 of the bacon, put in ketchup, gnocchi, cream, and water; boil. On medium heat, cook and stir for 3-4 mins until the sauce is thick. Put in seasonings then scatter with cheese.
- Broil for 1-2 mins, three to four inches from heat until the cheese melts. Add the remaining bacon, green onions, and tomatoes on top.

Nutrition Information

- Calories: 573 calories
- Total Carbohydrate: 35 g
- Cholesterol: 136 mg
- Total Fat: 31 g
- Fiber: 2 g
- Protein: 36 g
- Sodium: 961 mg

209. Best Lasagna

""My family and friends rated this lasagna recipe as the best. Light garden salad with Italian vinaigrette could be added and serve to family and friends.""
Serving: 10 | Prep: 30m | Ready in: 1h30m

Ingredients

- 1 (16 oz.) package lasagna noodles
- 1 lb. ground beef
- 1 onion, chopped
- salt and pepper to taste
- 1 tbsp. Italian seasoning
- 4 cups ricotta cheese
- 1 cup grated Romano cheese
- 2 1/2 cups spaghetti sauce

- 1 1/2 cups shredded mozzarella cheese
- 2 medium zucchini, sliced
- 1 cup fresh basil leaves

Direction

- Let water boil fast in a big pot. Then add lasagna noodles and let it boil until it becomes al dente for 6-8 minutes. Discard excess water then rinse it with cold water. Flatten noodles and use paper towel to take out excess water.
- Place skillet on a medium high heat then cook ground beef until it becomes brown. Then mix in Italian seasoning, pepper, and salt. Continue cooking the beef until done and no longer is pink. Discard excess water and put aside.
- Blend well the seasoned ground beef, Romano cheese, two cups of spaghetti sauce, and ricotta cheese in a big bowl. Let oven heat up to 375°F or to 190°C.
- At the bottom of a 9x13 inch baking dish, place a thin layer of spaghetti sauce. Assemble a layer of noodles sideways and a few the other way. On top of the noodles, layer it with a substantial amount of ricotta mixture. Then top it with some basil leaves. Make another layer of noodles sideways. Level it with one cup of mozzarella cheese. Slice up zucchini and layer it on top of the mozzarella cheese. Level it with another thin layer of ricotta cheese. Assemble the last layer of noodles sideways. Level it with what's left of the spaghetti sauce; embellish layer with basil leaves and other half of cup mozzarella cheese.
- Let it bake in a heated oven for 50 to 55 minutes. Cover with a slice of foil if Mozzarella cheese becomes excessively brown.

Nutrition Information

- Calories: 407 calories;
- Total Carbohydrate: 45.2 g
- Cholesterol: 52 mg
- Total Fat: 14.9 g
- Protein: 23.4 g
- Sodium: 626 mg

210. Cabbage Goulash

"Those who don't like cabbages will change their minds once they've tasted this goulash served with hard rolls or French bread."
Serving: 10-12 servings. | Prep: 15m | Ready in: 30m

Ingredients

- 1 lb. Jones No Sugar Pork Sausage Roll sausage
- 1 lb. ground beef
- 1 large onion, chopped
- 1 can (28 oz.) diced tomatoes
- 1 can (6 oz.) tomato paste
- 2 tbsps. cider vinegar
- 1 tbsp. chili powder
- 1 tsp. garlic powder
- 1/4 tsp. crushed red pepper flakes, optional
- 10 cups shredded cabbage

Direction

- On medium heat, cook onion, beef, and sausage on a big kettle until the meat is not pink anymore; drain. Mix in the rest of the ingredients then boil. Lower the heat; let it simmer for 15-20 mins without a cover or until the cabbage is tender.

Nutrition Information

- Calories: 183 calories
- Total Carbohydrate: 11 g
- Cholesterol: 32 mg
- Total Fat: 11 g
- Fiber: 3 g
- Protein: 11 g
- Sodium: 329 mg

211. Caprese Chicken With Bacon

"This delicious chicken breast is topped with gooey mozzarella, smoky bacon, ripe tomatoes, and fresh basil. It smells appetizing as you bake them."
Serving: 4 servings. | Prep: 20m | Ready in: 45m

Ingredients

- 8 bacon strips
- 4 boneless skinless chicken breast halves (6 oz. each)
- 1 tbsp. olive oil
- 1/2 tsp. salt
- 1/4 tsp. pepper
- 2 plum tomatoes, sliced
- 6 fresh basil leaves, thinly sliced
- 4 slices part-skim mozzarella cheese

Direction

- In an ungreased 15-in by 10-in by 1-in baking pan, arrange the bacon then bake for 8-10 mins in a 400 degrees F oven or until partially cooked but not crisp. Move to drain on paper towels.
- In an ungreased 13-in by 9-in baking pan, put the chicken then brush with oil. Scatter with pepper and salt. Add basil and tomatoes on top; use two bacon strips to wrap each in a crisscross pattern.
- Bake for 20-25 mins in a 400 degrees F oven without a cover or until a thermometer registers 170 degrees F. Add cheese on top then bake for another minute or until cheese melts.

Nutrition Information

- Calories: 373 calories
- Total Carbohydrate: 3 g
- Cholesterol: 123 mg
- Total Fat: 18 g
- Fiber: 0 g
- Protein: 47 g
- Sodium: 821 mg

212. Cheese & Prosciutto-stuffed Chicken

"These chicken rolls are filled with herb cream cheese, sun-dried tomatoes, prosciutto and topped with blue cheese sauce."
Serving: 4 servings. | Prep: 20m | Ready in: 45m

Ingredients

- 4 boneless skinless chicken breast halves (6 oz. each)
- 1/2 cup spreadable garlic and herb cream cheese
- 4 thin slices prosciutto
- 1/4 cup chopped oil-packed sun-dried tomatoes
- 8 fresh basil leaves
- 1/4 cup all-purpose flour
- 2 eggs
- 2/3 cup dry bread crumbs
- 3 tbsps. grated Romano cheese
- 3 tbsps. olive oil
- SAUCE:
- 1 cup heavy whipping cream
- 1 tbsp. finely chopped shallot
- 3/4 cup crumbled Gorgonzola cheese
- 1/4 tsp. salt
- 1/4 tsp. pepper
- Minced fresh basil

Direction

- Set the oven to 350° and start preheating. Flatten chicken breasts to 1/4-in. thickness; spread 2 tbsps. of cream cheese down each center. Top with 1 slice of prosciutto, one tbsp. of tomatoes and 2 basil leaves. Roll them up, tuck in their ends and use toothpicks to secure.
- Place eggs and flour in separate shallow bowls. Mix together Romano cheese and bread crumbs in another shallow bowl. Dip chicken in flour, eggs and roll them into bread crumb mixture so that they are fully covered.
- Brown chicken in oil in batches in a large skillet. Place seam side down in a greased 11x7-in. baking dish. Bake without a cover

- until the thermometer reads 165°, about 35-40 minutes.
- Heat shallot and cream in a small saucepan over medium heat until forming bubbles around the pan's sides. Stir in Gorgonzola cheese, pepper and salt. Cook until cheese is melted, about 4-6 minutes, stirring occasionally.
- Remove toothpicks. Drizzle chicken with sauce; top with a sprinkle of minced basil.

Nutrition Information

- Calories: 757 calories
- Total Carbohydrate: 16 g
- Cholesterol: 307 mg
- Total Fat: 55 g
- Fiber: 2 g
- Protein: 50 g
- Sodium: 1111 mg

213. Cheese-stuffed Shells

"This recipe is inspired from one of the menu at an Italian Restaurant in California. The pasta dish is rich and cheesy. I got the recipe and I just made a little changes to it."
Serving: 12 servings. | Prep: 35m | Ready in: 01h25m

Ingredients

- 1 lb. Johnsonville® Ground Mild Italian sausage
- 1 large onion, chopped
- 1 package (10 oz.) frozen chopped spinach, thawed and squeezed dry
- 1 package (8 oz.) cream cheese, cubed
- 1 large egg, lightly beaten
- 2 cups shredded part-skim mozzarella cheese, divided
- 2 cups shredded cheddar cheese
- 1 cup 4% cottage cheese
- 1 cup grated Parmesan cheese
- 1/4 tsp. salt
- 1/4 tsp. pepper
- 1/8 tsp. ground cinnamon, optional
- 24 jumbo pasta shells, cooked and drained
- SAUCE:
- 1 can (29 oz.) tomato sauce
- 1 tbsp. dried minced onion
- 1-1/2 tsps. dried basil
- 1-1/2 tsps. dried parsley flakes
- 2 garlic cloves, minced
- 1 tsp. sugar
- 1 tsp. dried oregano
- 1/2 tsp. salt
- 1/4 tsp. pepper

Direction

- Set a large skillet over medium heat, add the sausage and onion and cook until the sausage's meat is no longer pink; let it drain and place in a big bowl. Add in the cream cheese, spinach and egg; stir. Add a cup of mozzarella cheese, cottage cheese, cheddar cheese, Parmesan cheese, pepper, salt, and cinnamon if preferred.
- Fill the pasta shells with sausage mixture, stuffing it evenly. Assemble in two 11x7-in. baking dishes coated using a cooking spray. Mix together the sauce ingredients and pour over shells.
- Cover and let it bake inside the oven at 350° for 45 minutes. Remove the cover and top it off with the rest of the mozzarella. Allow to bake for additional 5-10 minutes or until bubbly and cheese has melt. Let it sit for 5 minutes before you serve it in.

Nutrition Information

- Calories: 397 calories
- Total Carbohydrate: 24 g
- Cholesterol: 94 mg
- Total Fat: 23 g
- Fiber: 2 g
- Protein: 24 g
- Sodium: 1097 mg

214. Chicken & Spinach Mostaccioli

"A simple but delicious, saucy pasta dish with a sprinkle of fresh basil."

Serving: 4 servings. | Prep: 20m | Ready in: 35m

Ingredients

- 8 oz. uncooked mostaccioli
- 1/2 cup coarsely chopped sun-dried tomatoes (not packed in oil)
- 1 cup boiling water
- 3 tbsps. butter
- 1 large onion, thinly sliced
- 2 garlic cloves, minced
- 2 tbsps. all-purpose flour
- 2-1/4 cups chicken broth
- 1 cup half-and-half cream
- 3 cups coarsely chopped fresh spinach
- 2 cups cubed cooked chicken breast
- 1/4 tsp. salt
- 1/8 tsp. pepper
- Thinly sliced fresh basil

Direction

- Cook mostaccioli as directed on the package until al dente. In the meantime, combine boiling water and tomatoes in a small bowl; let it sit 5 minutes. Drain the tomatoes.
- In a Dutch oven over medium heat, heat butter. Add garlic and onion; cook and stir until tender, for 4-5 minutes. Mix in flour until incorporated; whisk in cream and broth gradually. Heat until boiling, stirring continuously; cook and stir until thickened, or for 2 minutes. Mix in pepper, salt, drained tomatoes, chicken and spinach.
- Drain the mostaccioli; put into the pan. Cook until spinach is wilted and heated through, stir from time to time. Sprinkle basil on top.

Nutrition Information

- Calories: 527 calories
- Total Carbohydrate: 55 g
- Cholesterol: 109 mg
- Total Fat: 19 g
- Fiber: 4 g
- Protein: 33 g
- Sodium: 997 mg

215. Chicken And Tomato Scampi

"Simple ingredients are transformed to a lively dish with this recipe."

Serving: 4 servings. | Prep: 10m | Ready in: 25m

Ingredients

- 2 to 3 garlic cloves, minced
- 1/4 cup chopped green onions
- 2 tbsps. butter
- 1 tbsp. olive oil
- 4 boneless skinless chicken breast halves, cut into 1-inch pieces
- 1 tsp. salt, optional
- 1/2 tsp. pepper
- 1 can (14-1/2 oz.) Italian stewed tomatoes
- 1/4 cup lemon juice
- 1/2 tsp. sugar
- 2 tsps. cornstarch
- 2 tsps. cold water
- 1/4 cup chopped fresh parsley
- Hot cooked rice, optional

Direction

- On medium heat, sauté onions and garlic in a pan with oil and butter until the onions are tender. Put in chicken, pepper, and salt if desired. Cook for 6-8mins until the juices are clear. Put in sugar, lemon juice, and tomatoes; heat completely.
- Mix water and cornstarch; mix into the chicken mixture then boil. Cook and stir for a minute until thick. Put in parsley. If desired, serve chicken over rice.

Nutrition Information

- Calories: 255 calories
- Total Carbohydrate: 8 g

- Cholesterol: 73 mg
- Total Fat: 13 g
- Fiber: 0 g
- Protein: 28 g
- Sodium: 356 mg

216. Chicken Parmesan With Mushrooms

"Everyone will love this chicken dish with bubbly cheese on top."
Serving: 6 servings. | Prep: 15m | Ready in: 45m

Ingredients

- 1 large egg
- 2 tbsps. water
- 2/3 cup dry bread crumbs
- 1 envelope reduced-sodium onion soup mix
- 1/8 tsp. pepper
- 6 boneless skinless chicken breast halves (5 oz. each)
- 1-1/2 cups spaghetti sauce
- 1 can (7 oz.) mushroom stems and pieces, drained
- 1 cup shredded part-skim mozzarella cheese

Direction

- Whisk water and egg in a shallow bowl. Mix pepper, soup mix, and bread crumbs in a separate shallow bowl. Submerge the chicken in egg mixture then coat in crumb mixture.
- Arrange the chicken in a greased 13-in by 9-in baking dish. Bake for 22-25 mins in a 400 degrees F oven without a cover or until the juices are clear.
- Mix mushrooms and spaghetti sauce in a small bowl; scoop on top of the chicken then scatter with cheese. Bake for another 5-7 mins or until the cheese melts and the sauce is bubbly.

Nutrition Information

- Calories: 304 calories
- Total Carbohydrate: 15 g

- Cholesterol: 103 mg
- Total Fat: 9 g
- Fiber: 2 g
- Protein: 37 g
- Sodium: 792 mg

217. Chicken With Red Pepper Sauce And Spinach

"Gorgeous, simple, and fast dish with veggies for a weeknight meal. It's fancy enough to serve for your guests."
Serving: 4 servings. | Prep: 20m | Ready in: 30m

Ingredients

- 1 egg white
- 1/2 cup seasoned bread crumbs
- 1/4 tsp. salt
- 4 boneless skinless chicken breast halves (4 oz. each)
- 1 tbsp. olive oil
- 6 oz. fresh baby spinach (about 7-1/2 cups)
- 1 jar (7 oz.) roasted sweet red peppers, drained
- 1 garlic clove, peeled
- 1/2 tsp. Italian seasoning
- 1/2 cup crumbled feta cheese
- Fresh basil leaves, optional

Direction

- Beat egg white in a shallow bowl. Combine salt and bread crumbs in a separate shallow bowl. Submerge the chicken in egg white then dredge in the crumb mixture.
- On medium heat, heat oil in a big pan. Cook chicken in hot oil for 4-5mins on each side until a thermometer registers 165 degrees F. In the meantime, out the spinach in a steamer basket then set over a big pot with an inch of water; boil. Steam for 3-4mins while covered until tender.
- In a food processor, blend Italian seasoning, garlic, and peppers until smooth; move to a microwaveable bowl. Microwave while covered until completely heated.

- Split the spinach between 4 plates then serve with chicken. Add 2tbsp red pepper sauce, 2tbsp cheese, and basil if desired, on top.

Nutrition Information

- Calories: 245 calories
- Total Carbohydrate: 9 g
- Cholesterol: 70 mg
- Total Fat: 9 g
- Fiber: 2 g
- Protein: 29 g
- Sodium: 600 mg

218. Citrus Garlic Shrimp

"This amazing linguine and shrimp combo features sunny citrus and garlic."
Serving: 6 servings. | Prep: 5m | Ready in: 25m

Ingredients

- 1 package (16 oz.) linguine
- 1/2 cup olive oil
- 1/2 cup orange juice
- 1/3 cup lemon juice
- 3 to 4 garlic cloves, minced
- 5 tsps. grated lemon zest
- 4 tsps. grated orange zest
- 1 tsp. salt
- 1/4 tsp. pepper
- 1 lb. uncooked medium shrimp, peeled and deveined
- Shredded Parmesan cheese and minced fresh parsley, optional

Direction

- Cook the linguine following the package instructions. In the meantime, mix together the next 8 ingredients and process in a blender while covering until combined; move to a big skillet then boil. Lower the heat; mix in shrimp. Let it simmer for 3-4 mins without a cover or until the shrimp is pink.
- Drain and mix the linguine with the shrimp mixture. If desired, scatter with parsley and cheese.

Nutrition Information

- Calories: 504 calories
- Total Carbohydrate: 60 g
- Cholesterol: 112 mg
- Total Fat: 20 g
- Fiber: 3 g
- Protein: 22 g
- Sodium: 526 mg

219. Crab-stuffed Flounder With Herbed Aioli

"You'll surely love this delicious flounder with creamy and light aioli sauce and the flavors of garlic and chives if you're a seafood lover."
Serving: 6 servings. | Prep: 20m | Ready in: 40m

Ingredients

- 1/4 cup egg substitute
- 2 tbsps. fat-free milk
- 1 tbsp. minced chives
- 1 tbsp. reduced-fat mayonnaise
- 1 tbsp. Dijon mustard
- Dash hot pepper sauce
- 1 lb. lump crabmeat
- 6 flounder fillets (6 oz. each)
- Paprika
- AIOLI:
- 1/3 cup reduced-fat mayonnaise
- 2 tsps. minced chives
- 2 tsps. minced fresh parsley
- 2 tsps. lemon juice
- 1 garlic clove, minced

Direction

- Mix the first 6 ingredients in a small bowl; fold in crab gently. Halve the fillets crosswise then arrange the 6 halves in a cooking-spray-coated 15x10x1-inch baking pan. Spread the crab

mixture on top of the fillets then place the remaining fish on top. Season with paprika.
- Bake for 20-24mins in a 400 degrees oven until it easily flakes with a fork. In the meantime, mix the aioli ingredients. Serve aioli with fish.

Nutrition Information

- Calories: 276 calories
- Total Carbohydrate: 3 g
- Cholesterol: 153 mg
- Total Fat: 8 g
- Fiber: 0 g
- Protein: 45 g
- Sodium: 585 mg

220. Creamy Chicken Tetrazzini Casserole

"Even the leftovers of this creamy tetrazzini still taste amazing!"
Serving: 6 servings. | Prep: 30m | Ready in: 60m

Ingredients

- 12 oz. uncooked spaghetti
- 1 small onion, chopped
- 1 celery rib, chopped
- 1/4 cup butter, cubed
- 1 can (14 oz.) chicken broth
- 1-1/2 cups half-and-half cream
- 1 package (8 oz.) cream cheese, cubed
- 2 cups cubed cooked chicken
- 1 can (4 oz.) mushroom stems and pieces, drained
- 2 to 4 tbsps. sliced pimientos
- 1/2 tsp. salt
- 1/4 tsp. pepper
- 1/2 cup sliced almonds, toasted
- 1/4 cup grated Parmesan cheese
- 1/4 cup crushed potato chips

Direction

- Cook the spaghetti following the package instructions. In the meantime, sauté celery and onion in a big pan with butter until tender. Mix in cream cheese, cream, and broth; cook and stir until the cheese melts. Take off heat.
- Mix in pepper, chicken, salt, pimentos, and mushrooms. Drain the spaghetti then toss into the chicken mixture to coat. Move to a greased 13-in by 9-in baking dish.
- Bake for 20mins in a 350 degrees oven without cover; top with chips, Parmesan cheese, and almonds. Bake for another 10-15mins until the topping is golden brown and completely heated.

Nutrition Information

- Calories: 668 calories
- Total Carbohydrate: 51 g
- Cholesterol: 138 mg
- Total Fat: 37 g
- Fiber: 4 g
- Protein: 30 g
- Sodium: 865 mg

221. Creamy Pesto Shrimp Linguine

"Impress your friends with this fantastic but easy pasta dish with pesto cream sauce."
Serving: 4 servings. | Prep: 15m | Ready in: 30m

Ingredients

- 8 oz. linguine
- 1 lb. uncooked large shrimp, peeled and deveined
- 1/4 cup butter, cubed
- 2 cups heavy whipping cream
- 1 cup grated Parmesan cheese
- 1/3 cup prepared pesto
- 1/4 tsp. pepper

Direction

- Cook the linguine following the package instructions.

- In the meantime, sauté shrimp in a big pan with butter until pink; take the shrimp out of the pan then set aside. Pour cream in the pan then boil gently. Lower heat; cook for 4-6mins without cover while mixing from time to time until a bit thick.
- Mix in pepper, pesto, and cheese until smooth. Put the shrimp back in the pan then completely heat. Drain then serve the linguine with sauce.

Nutrition Information

- Calories: 1000 calories
- Total Carbohydrate: 48 g
- Cholesterol: 355 mg
- Total Fat: 73 g
- Fiber: 3 g
- Protein: 40 g
- Sodium: 727 mg

222. Double-duty Chicken With Olives & Artichokes

"Red wine and olives is the star of this delicious chicken dish."

Serving: 4 servings plus leftovers. | Prep: 30m | Ready in: 04h30m

Ingredients

- 1/4 cup all-purpose flour
- 1/2 tsp. garlic salt
- 1/4 tsp. pepper
- 8 bone-in chicken thighs (3 lbs.), skin removed if desired
- 1 tbsp. olive oil
- 4 garlic cloves, thinly sliced
- 1 tbsp. grated lemon zest
- 1 tsp. dried thyme
- 1/2 tsp. dried rosemary, crushed
- 1 can (14 oz.) water-packed quartered artichoke hearts, drained
- 1/2 cup pimiento-stuffed olives
- 1 bay leaf
- 1-1/2 cups orange juice
- 3/4 cup chicken broth
- 2 tbsps. honey
- GREMOLATA:
- 1/4 cup minced fresh basil
- 1 tsp. grated lemon zest
- 1 garlic clove, minced

Direction

- Combine pepper, flour, garlic salt in a shallow bowl; coat each side of the chicken thighs in the mixture then shake off the extra. On medium heat, heat oil in a big pan. Cook chicken in batches until both sides are brown; move to a 4-quart slow cooker.
- Scatter rosemary, garlic, thyme, and lemon zest over the chicken. Add bay leaves, olives, and artichoke hearts on top. Combine honey, broth, and orange juice in a bowl; pour all over. Cook for 4-5hrs on Low while covered until the chicken is tender. Discard the bay leaf.
- Set aside 4 chicken thighs to make the double duty chicken and feta spinach salad; chill while covered. In a small bowl, combine the gremolata ingredients then scatter all over the artichoke mixture and remaining chicken.

Nutrition Information

- Calories: 434 calories
- Total Carbohydrate: 34 g
- Cholesterol: 81 mg
- Total Fat: 21 g
- Fiber: 1 g
- Protein: 26 g
- Sodium: 971 mg

223. Eggplant & Zucchini Rollatini

"You'll get a lot of praises with this simple rollatini dish featuring fried thin eggplant slices that are filled with cheese then topped with tomato sauce."
Serving: 8 servings. | Prep: 60m | Ready in: 01h30m

Ingredients

- 1 large eggplant
- 1/2 tsp. salt
- SAUCE:
- 1/3 cup chopped onion
- 3 garlic cloves, minced
- 1 tbsp. olive oil
- 2 cans (28 oz. each) crushed tomatoes
- 1/4 cup dry red wine or vegetable broth
- 1 tbsp. sugar
- 2 tsps. each dried oregano and dried basil
- 1 tsp. salt
- 1/4 tsp. pepper
- ROLLATINI:
- 4 cups shredded part-skim mozzarella cheese
- 1 package (8 oz.) cream cheese, softened and cubed
- 1 large zucchini, thinly sliced
- 2 tbsps. plus 1/2 cup olive oil, divided
- 2 large eggs, lightly beaten
- 1 cup dry bread crumbs
- 1/2 cup grated Parmesan cheese

Direction

- Peel the eggplant then cut into 16 of 1/8-inch thick portion lengthwise. Put the eggplant slices and scatter with salt in a colander set on top of a plate then mix. Let it sit for half an hour; rinse then drain.
- Sauté garlic and onion in a big saucepan with oil until tender; put in the rest of the sauce ingredients then boil. Lower the heat; let it simmer for 20-25 mins without a cover while mixing from time to time to let the flavors blend.
- Preheat the oven to 350 degrees F. Mix cream cheese and mozzarella well in a big bowl. Sauté zucchini in a big skillet with 2 tbsp. oil until tender; remove the zucchini then set aside.
- In separate shallow bowls, put bread crumbs and eggs. Submerge the eggplant in eggs then dredge in breadcrumbs. Fry in batches for 2-3 mins per side in the remaining oil or until golden brown. Place on paper towels to drain.
- In an ungreased 13-in by 9-in baking dish, scoop a cup of sauce then arrange eggplant slices and zucchini in a layer. Put 3 tbsp. cheese mixture on top of each. Roll up then arrange on the baking dish with the seam-side down. Add the remaining sauce on top; cover. Bake for 30-35 mins until bubbly. Scatter with Parmesan cheese.

Nutrition Information

- Calories: 601 calories
- Total Carbohydrate: 36 g
- Cholesterol: 116 mg
- Total Fat: 41 g
- Fiber: 7 g
- Protein: 26 g
- Sodium: 1244 mg

224. Fast Italian Stew

"Escarole has large wavy jagged-edged green leaves and it makes this dish taste wonderful."
Serving: 6 servings. | Prep: 20m | Ready in: 50m

Ingredients

- 1 lb. ground beef
- 1/2 lb. Johnsonville® Ground Mild Italian sausage
- 1 cup chopped onion
- 1 can (15 oz.) cannellini or white kidney beans, rinsed and drained
- 2 cups cut fresh green beans
- 1 can (14-1/2 oz.) Italian stewed tomatoes, undrained
- 1 cup vegetable broth
- 1 can (6 oz.) tomato paste
- 2 tsps. dried oregano

- 1 tsp. salt
- 1/2 tsp. pepper
- 1 bunch escarole, trimmed and torn
- 1/2 cup shredded Parmesan cheese

Direction

- Cook onion, sausage, and beef in a Dutch oven over medium heat until the meat is not pink anymore; strain. Add pepper, salt, oregano, tomato paste, broth, tomatoes, green beans, and cannellini beans.
- Boil it. Lower the heat, simmer with a cover for 15 minutes. Add escarole; simmer with a cover until wilted, about another 5 minutes. Sprinkle Parmesan cheese over each serving.

Nutrition Information

- Calories: 339 calories
- Total Carbohydrate: 28 g
- Cholesterol: 57 mg
- Total Fat: 14 g
- Fiber: 9 g
- Protein: 26 g
- Sodium: 1252 mg

225. Favorite Chicken Marsala

"Your family will eat up this flavorful dish."
Serving: 6 servings. | Prep: 35m | Ready in: 55m

Ingredients

- 1/2 cup plus 1 tbsp. all-purpose flour, divided
- 1/4 tsp. salt
- 1/4 tsp. pepper
- 1-1/2 lbs. boneless skinless chicken breasts, cut into 1/2-inch strips
- 1/4 cup olive oil
- 1/4 cup butter, divided
- 1 cup sliced fresh shiitake mushrooms
- 1 cup sliced baby portobello mushrooms
- 2 large shallots, chopped
- 1 cup marsala wine
- 1 cup chicken broth
- 1 cup heavy whipping cream
- 2 tbsps. minced fresh parsley
- PASTA:
- 1 package (16 oz.) angel hair pasta
- 1 whole garlic bulb, minced
- 1/4 cup olive oil
- 3 tbsps. butter
- 1/2 cup grated Parmesan cheese
- 1/2 tsp. salt
- 1/4 tsp. pepper
- Dash crushed red pepper flakes

Direction

- Put pepper, salt and 1/2 cup of flour in a large resealable plastic bag. Put in chicken, a few pieces at a time, and shake it to coat. In a large pan, cook the chicken in 2 tbsps. butter and oil in batches until it is no longer pink. Discard and keep warm.
- Sauté shallots and mushrooms in the remaining butter until tender. Pour in wine, stirring to loosen browned bits from skillet. Top with a sprinkle of the remaining flour; mix until blended. Stir in cream and broth gradually. Bring to a boil. Lower heat; cook while stirring until slightly thickened or 5 to 10 mins.
- In the meantime, cook pasta following the package instructions in a Dutch oven. Drain, reserving 1/2 cup of cooking liquid. Sauté garlic in butter and oil for 2 mins in the same Dutch oven. Transfer the pasta into the skillet; mix in reserved cooking liquid, pepper flakes, pepper, salt and cheese.
- Transfer pasta on the serving platter; top with sauce and chicken. Top with a sprinkle of parsley.

Nutrition Information

- Calories: 945 calories
- Total Carbohydrate: 72 g
- Cholesterol: 159 mg
- Total Fat: 52 g
- Fiber: 3 g
- Protein: 38 g
- Sodium: 673 mg

226. Fettuccine With Black Bean Sauce

"Incorporate veggies in your daily meal just like in this meatless spaghetti sauce that pairs well with spinach fettuccine."

Serving: 5 servings. | Prep: 15m | Ready in: 30m

Ingredients

- 6 oz. uncooked fettuccine
- 1 small green pepper, chopped
- 1 small onion, chopped
- 1 tbsp. olive oil
- 2 cups garden-style pasta sauce
- 1 can (15 oz.) black beans, rinsed and drained
- 2 tbsps. minced fresh basil or 2 tsps. dried basil
- 1 tsp. dried oregano
- 1/2 tsp. fennel seed
- 1/4 tsp. garlic salt
- 1 cup shredded part-skim mozzarella cheese

Direction

- Cook the fettuccine following the package instructions. In the meantime, sauté onion and green pepper in a big saucepan with oil until tender. Mix in seasonings, black beans, and pasta sauce.
- Boil then lower the heat. Let it simmer for 5mins without a cover. Drain the fettuccine. Add sauce and sprinkled cheese on top.

Nutrition Information

- Calories: 350 calories
- Total Carbohydrate: 51 g
- Cholesterol: 17 mg
- Total Fat: 10 g
- Fiber: 8 g
- Protein: 16 g
- Sodium: 761 mg

227. Fettuccine With Porter Beer Meat Ragu

"I'm always trying to combine my hobby of making a beer and my passion and love for cooking as often as possible. So here's a must try recipe."

Serving: 6 servings. | Prep: 15m | Ready in: 01h35m

Ingredients

- 1 lb. Johnsonville® Ground Mild Italian sausage
- 1/2 cup chopped sweet onion
- 1/2 cup chopped carrot
- 1/3 cup chopped celery
- 1/3 cup chopped sweet red pepper
- 2 garlic cloves, minced
- 1 can (28 oz.) crushed tomatoes, undrained
- 1 bottle (12 oz.) porter beer
- 1 cup sliced fresh mushrooms
- 2 tbsps. sliced green olives with pimientos
- 1 tbsp. capers, drained
- 2 bay leaves
- 2 tsps. dried basil
- 1/2 tsp. caraway seeds
- 1/2 tsp. pepper
- 12 oz. uncooked fettuccine

Direction

- Add the sausage in a big skillet and cook over medium heat for roughly 6-8 minutes or until the sausage are no longer pink. While it cooks, break them into crumbles; drain.
- Drop the onion, celery, red pepper and carrot; sauté until the vegetables are softened. Put in garlic and cook for additional 1 minute. Mix in the beer, tomatoes, mushrooms, capers, seasonings and olives. Let the mixture boil. Lessen the heat; make it to a simmer without placing any cover, for an hour or until the consistency turns thick. Stir the mixture from time to time. Take away the bay leaves.
- Prepare the fettuccine and cook following the package directions; drain. Serve it alongside the sausage mixture.

Nutrition Information

- Calories: 469 calories
- Total Carbohydrate: 56 g
- Cholesterol: 41 mg
- Total Fat: 19 g
- Fiber: 6 g
- Protein: 19 g
- Sodium: 813 mg

228. French Bread Pizza

"This delicious bread pizza is made with just a loaf of French bread, mozzarella, and meaty tomato sauce."
Serving: 8 servings. | Prep: 30m | Ready in: 42m

Ingredients

- 1 lb. extra-lean ground beef
- 1 onion, chopped
- 1 French bread loaf (1 lb.)
- 1 can (15 oz.) tomato sauce
- 2 tsp. dried oregano leaves
- 1 pkg. (8 oz.) KRAFT Shredded Mozzarella Cheese with a TOUCH OF PHILADELPHIA
- 4 slices cooked OSCAR MAYER Bacon, crumbled

Direction

- In a big pan, cook onions and meat until brown. In the meantime, halve the bread crosswise then slice each portion in half lengthwise. Arrange on a baking sheet that is covered with foil with the cut-sides up.
- Mix oregano and tomato sauce into the meat; let it simmer for 5mins while mixing from time to time. Slather meat over the bread slices; add bacon and cheese on top.
- Bake for 12min until the cheese melts. Slice in half.

Nutrition Information

- Calories: 360
- Total Carbohydrate: 38 g
- Cholesterol: 55 mg

- Total Fat: 11 g
- Fiber: 3 g
- Protein: 27 g
- Sodium: 850 mg
- Sugar: 5 g
- Saturated Fat: 6 g

229. Garlic Shrimp Spaghetti

"Enjoy this delicious dish with garlic bread toast and salad."
Serving: 6 servings. | Prep: 10m | Ready in: 25m

Ingredients

- 1 package (8 oz.) spaghetti
- 2 tbsps. cornstarch
- 1/2 cup water
- 1 can (14-1/2 oz.) chicken broth
- 4 garlic cloves, minced
- 1/8 tsp. cayenne pepper
- 2 tbsps. olive oil
- 1-1/2 lbs. cooked shrimp, peeled and deveined
- 2 tbsps. lemon juice
- 1/4 tsp. grated lemon peel
- 1/4 cup minced fresh parsley

Direction

- Cook the spaghetti following the package instructions. In the meantime, mix broth, water, and cornstarch in a small bowl until smooth. Set it aside.
- Sauté cayenne and garlic in a big pan with oil until the garlic is tender. Mix the broth mixture then pour gradually into the pan; boil. Cook and stir for 2mins until thick.
- Lower heat; put in parsley, shrimp, lemon peel, and lemon juice. Cook for 2 to 4mins until completely heated. Drain then move the spaghetti to a big bowl; toss with the shrimp mixture to coat.

Nutrition Information

- Calories: 320 calories

- Total Carbohydrate: 33 g
- Cholesterol: 172 mg
- Total Fat: 7 g
- Fiber: 1 g
- Protein: 29 g
- Sodium: 444 mg

230. Garlic Tilapia With Mushroom Risotto

"This quick and tasty dish is made with boxed risotto, cheese, shallots, and mushrooms. Serve it with seasoned fish on busy weeknights"
Serving: 4 servings. | Prep: 5m | Ready in: 30m

Ingredients

- 1 package (5-1/2 oz.) Parmesan risotto mix
- 1 cup sliced fresh mushrooms
- 1/4 cup chopped shallots
- 1-1/2 lbs. tilapia fillets
- 1-1/2 tsps. seafood seasoning
- 4 tbsps. butter, divided
- 3 garlic cloves, sliced
- 1/4 cup grated Parmesan cheese

Direction

- Cook the risotto following the package instructions; put shallots and mushrooms with the water.
- In the meantime, scatter seafood seasoning on the tilapia. On medium heat, heat 2tbsp butter in a big non-stick pan. Cook tilapia in batches with garlic for 5mins until the tilapia starts to easily flake with a fork, flip the tilapia halfway through cooking.
- Mix the remaining butter and cheese in the risotto; take off heat. Serve the risotto with tilapia.

Nutrition Information

- Calories: 432 calories
- Total Carbohydrate: 32 g
- Cholesterol: 118 mg

- Total Fat: 18 g
- Fiber: 1 g
- Protein: 39 g
- Sodium: 964 mg

231. Golden Burger Spirals

"The recipe for this convenient dish that everybody loves came from a dental hygienist."
Serving: 4-6 servings. | Prep: 15m | Ready in: 45m

Ingredients

- 1 lb. ground beef
- 1 medium onion, chopped
- 1 medium green pepper, chopped
- 1 can (10-3/4 oz.) condensed golden mushroom soup, undiluted
- 1 can (8 oz.) tomato sauce
- 1-1/2 cups shredded cheddar cheese, divided
- 1/2 tsp. salt
- 1 package (8 oz.) spiral pasta, cooked and drained

Direction

- On medium heat, cook green pepper, onion, and beef in a big pan until the meat is not pink; drain. Add salt, soup, a cup of cheese, and tomato sauce. Mix in pasta.
- Move to a greased 2 1/2-quart baking dish then top with the remaining cheese. Bake for half an hour in a 350 degrees oven without cover until bubbly.

Nutrition Information

- Calories: 416 calories
- Total Carbohydrate: 39 g
- Cholesterol: 69 mg
- Total Fat: 17 g
- Fiber: 2 g
- Protein: 26 g
- Sodium: 975 mg

232. Ham & Sun-dried Tomato Alfredo

"You just need 5 ingredients to make this special, decadent, but easy-to-make Alfredo dish with sun-dried tomatoes."
Serving: 4 servings. | Prep: 10m | Ready in: 20m

Ingredients

- 8 oz. uncooked linguine
- 1/4 cup chopped oil-packed sun-dried tomatoes
- 1 cup heavy whipping cream
- 1/2 cup grated Parmesan cheese
- 1 cup cubed fully cooked ham

Direction

- Cook the linguine following the package instructions.
- In the meantime, sauté tomatoes in a cooking-spray-coated big pan for a minute. Lower heat then mix in cheese and cream. Boil gently on medium heat. Let it simmer for 5-7mins without cover until thick.
- Drain the linguine then mix into the sauce mixture. Put in ham then heat completely.

Nutrition Information

- Calories: 523 calories
- Total Carbohydrate: 46 g
- Cholesterol: 109 mg
- Total Fat: 30 g
- Fiber: 2 g
- Protein: 19 g
- Sodium: 644 mg

233. Hawaiian Pizza

"This Hawaiian Pizza recipe featuring fresh pineapple chunks, bacon, and ham, will be your newest addiction."
Serving: Makes 20 servings. | Prep: 15m | Ready in: 33m

Ingredients

- 1 can (13.8 oz.) refrigerated pizza dough
- 1/3 cup KRAFT Original Barbecue Sauce
- 1-1/2 cups KRAFT Shredded Mozzarella Cheese with a TOUCH OF PHILADELPHIA
- 4 slices OSCAR MAYER Deli Fresh Smoked Ham, chopped
- 4 slices OSCAR MAYER Bacon, cooked, crumbled
- 1/2 cup chopped fresh pineapple

Direction

- On a cooking-spray-coated baking sheet, unroll the pizza dough then press into a 15-in by 10-in rectangle. Bake for 10 mins. The crust won't be cooked.
- Spread barbeque sauce on the crust the put the remaining ingredients on top.
- Bake for 8 mins or until the crust is deep golden brown and the cheese is melted.

Nutrition Information

- Calories: 80
- Total Carbohydrate: 12 g
- Cholesterol: 5 mg
- Total Fat: 2.5 g
- Fiber: 0 g
- Protein: 4 g
- Sodium: 290 mg
- Sugar: 3 g
- Saturated Fat: 1 g

234. Healthy Shrimp Piccata Pasta

"Easy and flavorful shrimp and capers recipe."
Serving: 4 servings. | Prep: 10m | Ready in: 20m

Ingredients

- 6 oz. uncooked spaghetti
- 2 shallots, chopped
- 1 tbsp. olive oil
- 1 lb. uncooked medium shrimp, peeled and deveined
- 1 jar (3 oz.) capers, drained
- 3 tbsps. lemon juice

- 1/2 tsp. garlic powder

Direction

- Cook the spaghetti following the directions on packaging. Meanwhile, sauté shallots in oil in a big nonstick skillet until tender. Put in garlic powder, lemon juice, capers and shrimp; cook and stir for 5 to 6 minutes or until the shrimp is pink.
- Drain the spaghetti; add shrimp mixture and toss.

Nutrition Information

- Calories: 293 calories
- Total Carbohydrate: 37 g
- Cholesterol: 168 mg
- Total Fat: 5 g
- Fiber: 2 g
- Protein: 24 g
- Sodium: 453 mg

235. Hearty Lasagna

"Here is a recipe that is flawless for sharing with a loved one! This lasagna is made extra special with a heart on top as a finishing touch. You won't feel the need to rush when it's time to dig in as you can prepare it earlier."

Serving: 12 servings. | Prep: 01h45m | Ready in: 02h30m

Ingredients

- 1-1/2 lbs. ground beef
- 1 medium onion, chopped
- 1 garlic clove, minced
- 3 tbsps. olive oil
- 1 can (28 oz.) Italian diced tomatoes, undrained
- 1 can (8 oz.) tomato sauce
- 1 can (6 oz.) tomato paste
- 1 tsp. dried oregano
- 1 tsp. sugar
- 1 tsp. salt
- 1/4 tsp. pepper
- 2 carrots, halved
- 2 celery ribs, halved
- 12 oz. lasagna noodles
- 1 carton (15 oz.) ricotta cheese
- 2 cups shredded part-skim mozzarella cheese
- 1/2 cup grated Parmesan cheese

Direction

- Cook garlic, onion, and beef in oil using a large skillet, until the onion is tenderized, and the meat turns brown. Strain. Add tomato paste, tomato sauce, tomatoes, oregano, salt, pepper, and sugar and mix evenly. Add in celery and carrots into the sauce. Simmer without covering for 1-1/2 hours, periodically stirring the sauce. In the meantime, follow package instructions to prepare the lasagna noodles. Strain and run under cold water. Dispose celery and carrots. Grease a 13x9-inch baking tray and layer as follows; 1/3 of noodles, 1/3 of meat sauce, 1/3 ricotta cheese, 1/3 mozzarella cheese, and 1/3 Parmesan cheese. Repeat the arrangement again. Cover with excess noodles and meat sauce. Cut a piece of aluminum foil into a heart and place at the center of the sauce. Distribute remainder of ricotta around the heart. Scatter remaining Parmesan and mozzarella. Bake while uncovered for 45 minutes at 350 degrees. Dispose the heart-shaped foil. Let the dish sit for 10-15 minutes before slicing.

Nutrition Information

- Calories: 391 calories
- Total Carbohydrate: 36 g
- Cholesterol: 56 mg
- Total Fat: 16 g
- Fiber: 3 g
- Protein: 25 g
- Sodium: 790 mg

236. Homemade Spaghetti And Meatballs

"Since my passion is on cooking, I always cook for my family more than my wife. She loves this dish!"
Serving: 8-10 servings. | Prep: 20m | Ready in: 03h20m

Ingredients

- SAUCE:
- 2 cans (10-3/4 oz. each) condensed tomato soup, undiluted
- 2-2/3 cups water
- 1 can (12 oz.) tomato paste
- 1 jar (4-1/2 oz.) sliced mushrooms, undrained
- 1 medium onion, chopped
- 3 tbsps. Worcestershire sauce
- 3 tbsps. chili powder
- 1 tsp. salt
- 1/2 tsp. cayenne pepper
- 2 garlic cloves, minced
- Pinch pepper
- MEATBALLS:
- 2 large eggs, beaten
- 1/4 cup chopped onion
- 1 tsp. garlic salt
- 1/3 tsp. pepper
- 2 lbs. ground beef
- Hot cooked spaghetti

Direction

- Mix together all the sauce ingredients in a big Dutch oven or you can also use a kettle. Make it to a simmer for 2 hours, without placing any cover. Combine the onion, eggs, pepper and garlic salt in a bowl; crumble the beef on top of the mixture and mix thoroughly. Form into small meatballs; fry in a skillet, a few at a time until browned. Transfer the meatballs on the sauce and make it to a simmer for an hour. Serve alongside spaghetti.

Nutrition Information

- Calories: 266 calories
- Total Carbohydrate: 17 g
- Cholesterol: 103 mg
- Total Fat: 13 g
- Fiber: 4 g
- Protein: 22 g
- Sodium: 807 mg

237. Italian Baked Chicken Breasts

"This baked chicken is juicy and soft. You can enjoy it with a salad, Italian bread, or green beans."
Serving: 2 servings. | Prep: 15m | Ready in: 35m

Ingredients

- 2 egg whites
- 2 tsps. balsamic vinegar
- 1/3 cup dry bread crumbs
- 1/2 tsp. dried parsley flakes
- 1/4 tsp. garlic powder
- 1/4 tsp. garlic salt
- 2 boneless skinless chicken breast halves (4 oz. each)
- Butter-flavored cooking spray
- 1/8 tsp. salt
- 1/8 tsp. pepper

Direction

- Whisk vinegar and egg whites in a shallow bowl. Mix together garlic salt, garlic powder, parsley, and bread crumbs in a second shallow bowl. In the egg mixture, put the chicken to dip, and then in the crumb mixture to coat.
- Put in a greased 8-inch square baking dish; lightly spray butter-flavored spray over the chicken to coat. Sprinkle pepper and salt over. Bake without a cover at 375° until a thermometer displays 170°, about 20-25 minutes.

Nutrition Information

- Calories: 191 calories
- Total Carbohydrate: 9 g
- Cholesterol: 63 mg
- Total Fat: 4 g
- Fiber: 1 g

- Protein: 28 g
- Sodium: 560 mg

238. Italian Cabbage And Rice

"Everyone loves to help in making this delicious dish!"
Serving: 6 servings. | Prep: 15m | Ready in: 30m

Ingredients

- 1-1/2 lbs. ground pork
- 1 cup chopped onion
- 2 garlic cloves, minced
- 4 cups shredded cabbage
- 1 can (8 oz.) tomato sauce
- 1 cup chicken broth
- 2 tbsps. red wine vinegar
- 1/2 tsp. dried oregano
- 1/2 tsp. dried basil
- 1/2 tsp. fennel seed
- 1/4 tsp. pepper
- 1/4 tsp. sugar
- 3 cups cooked long grain rice
- 6 bacon strips, cooked and crumbled
- 1/4 tsp. crushed red pepper flakes, optional
- Grated Parmesan cheese, optional

Direction

- Cook garlic, onion, and pork in a big pan until the meat is brown; drain. Put in the next 9 ingredients then cover; let it simmer for 5mins. Mix in red pepper flakes if desired, bacon, and rice; cover. Let it simmer for another 5mins until the cabbage is tender. If desired, top with Parmesan cheese.

Nutrition Information

- Calories: 380 calories
- Total Carbohydrate: 30 g
- Cholesterol: 76 mg
- Total Fat: 17 g
- Fiber: 2 g
- Protein: 25 g
- Sodium: 398 mg

239. Italian Meatball Mix

"I keep this mix for clammy meatballs in the refrigerator for a brisk Italian supper."
Serving: 16 meatballs per batch. | Prep: 15m | Ready in: 35m

Ingredients

- 2-1/2 cups dry bread crumbs
- 2/3 cup dried minced onion
- 2/3 cup grated Parmesan cheese
- 1/3 cup dried parsley flakes
- 1 tbsp. garlic powder
- 1 tbsp. garlic salt
- ADDITIONAL INGREDIENTS (for each batch):
- 1 egg, lightly beaten
- 1 lb. ground beef

Direction

- Blend the first 6 ingredients in a big bowl. Store for up to 2 months in the refrigerator. Yield: 4 batches (around total of 4 cups).
- To prepare meatballs: Mix 1 cup meatball mix and egg in a big bowl. Crumble beef over the blend and stir well. Form into balls of 1-1/2 inch.
- Brown meatballs in a skillet; drain. Move to a baking dish of 13 x 9-inch. Bake for 20 to 25 minutes at 400°, until meat is not pink anymore.

Nutrition Information

- Calories: 83 calories
- Total Carbohydrate: 4 g
- Cholesterol: 33 mg
- Total Fat: 4 g
- Fiber: 0 g
- Protein: 7 g
- Sodium: 155 mg

240. Italian Sausage Lasagna Rolls

"Another exciting way to eat your lasagna. Keep a pan of these lasagna goodies in the freezer for a quick meal for unexpected guests and family dinners."
Serving: 10 servings. | Prep: 30m | Ready in: 01h15m

Ingredients

- 1 tbsp. olive oil
- 1 medium onion, finely chopped
- 2 garlic cloves, minced
- 1 can (28 oz.) crushed tomatoes, undrained
- 1 can (15 oz.) tomato sauce
- 1 can (6 oz.) tomato paste
- 1 tsp. each dried basil, marjoram, oregano, parsley flakes and thyme
- 1/2 tsp. pepper
- 1/4 tsp. salt
- 1 can (2-1/4 oz.) sliced ripe olives, drained
- 10 uncooked lasagna noodles
- 1 package (19 oz.) Johnsonville® Mild Italian Sausage Links
- 1 package (6 oz.) fresh baby spinach
- 1 package (8 oz.) cream cheese, softened
- 2 cups shredded part-skim mozzarella cheese

Direction

- Preheat the oven at 350°F. Heat oil in a big saucepan over medium heat. Sauté onion for 4-6 minutes or until soft. Put in the garlic and sauté for a minute. Mix in the seasonings, tomato paste, tomato sauce and tomatoes and let it boil. Lower the heat and simmer without the cover for 40 minutes. Add in the olives.
- While the sauce is simmering, follow package instructions in cooking the lasagna noodles until al dente. In a big skillet, cook the sausage following the package instructions then drain excess oil. Cut the cooked sausages in half, widthwise. Cook the spinach in the same skillet over medium-high heat for 2 to 3 minutes or until the spinach is wilted then squeeze out excess liquid from the spinach.
- Mix spinach and cream cheese together in a small bowl. In a 13x9-inch baking dish, pour 3 cups of sauce mixture evenly at the bottom. On each lasagna noodle, spread 2 tbsps. of cream cheese mixture evenly at the middle of each noodle. Put a halved sausage on the short end and gently roll the lasagna noodle up. Cut each stuffed lasagna noodle widthwise in half and put it in the sauce mixture on the baking dish, ruffle side up. Do the whole stuffing and rolling process again for the remaining lasagna noodles.
- Put 1 1/2 cups of sauce mixture on top of the stuffed lasagna rolls then put mozzarella cheese on top of each roll. Cover the baking dish, put in the preheated oven and bake for 40 minutes. Remove the cover and bake for 5-10 more minutes or until the cheese has melted. Top with the remaining sauce mixture before serving it warm.

241. Italian Sausage Skillet

"The combination of Italian sausage, tomato sauce, stuffing and vegetables makes this cheesy, easy, weeknight-fast skillet deliciously good."
Serving: Makes 6 servings. | Prep: 10m | Ready in: 40m

Ingredients

- 1-1/2 lb. Italian sausage, cut into 2-inch-thick slices
- 1 large red pepper, sliced
- 1 large green pepper, sliced
- 1 large onion, sliced
- 1 can (8 oz.) tomato sauce
- 1 pkg. (6 oz.) STOVE TOP Savory Herbs Stuffing Mix, prepared
- 1 cup KRAFT Shredded Mozzarella Cheese

Direction

- Sauté the sausage in a big skillet over medium-high heat until it turns evenly browned and completely cooked; drain.
- Stir in the onions and peppers; cover. Adjust the heat to medium and let it cook for roughly 10 minutes while stirring from time to time. Add the tomato sauce. Stir and allow the mixture to boil.

- Top it off with the sausage mixture with stuffing; garnish with cheese. Adjust the heat to low; cover. Let it cook for about 5 minutes or until cheese has melt.

Nutrition Information

- Calories: 460
- Total Carbohydrate: 32 g
- Cholesterol: 55 mg
- Total Fat: 27 g
- Fiber: 3 g
- Protein: 22 g
- Sodium: 1440 mg
- Sugar: 9 g
- Saturated Fat: 9 g

242. Lasagna With White Sauce

"This recipe uses ingredients that are normally kept in stock in the household. You don't need to pre-cook the noodles in this recipe. It's very easy to make that even kids could participate in the making of this lovely lasagna dish."
Serving: 10-12 servings. | Prep: 40m | Ready in: 01h20m

Ingredients

- 1 lb. ground beef
- 1 large onion, chopped
- 1 can (14-1/2 oz.) diced tomatoes, undrained
- 2 tbsps. tomato paste
- 1 tsp. beef bouillon granules
- 1-1/2 tsps. Italian seasoning
- 1 tsp. salt
- 1/2 tsp. pepper
- 1/4 tsp. cayenne pepper
- WHITE SAUCE:
- 2 tbsps. butter
- 3 tbsps. all-purpose flour
- 1 tsp. salt
- 1/4 tsp. pepper
- 2 cups 2% milk
- 1-1/4 cups shredded mozzarella cheese, divided
- 10 to 12 uncooked lasagna noodles

Direction

- Put onion and beef in a Dutch oven and cook over medium heat until the meat is not pink; then drain excess oil. Mix in the bouillon, seasonings, tomatoes and tomato paste. Cover the Dutch oven and cook for about 20 minutes over medium-low heat while occasionally stirring.
- While the meat sauce is cooking, melt butter in a big pan then mix in the salt, pepper and flour until fully combined. Slowly put in the milk. Let it boil and cook for 1 minute or until sauce is thick in consistency. Remove the pan from heat then add 1/2 of cheese and mix; put aside.
- In an ungreased 13x9-inch pan, put in 1/2 of meat sauce on bottom. Layer on 1/2 of the lasagna noodles and the remaining meat sauce. Put the remaining lasagna noodles on top. Put the white sauce evenly on top of the noodles. Finish with the remaining cheese on top.
- Put the covered baking dish in the preheated oven at 400°F and bake for 40 minutes or until bubbling and the noodles are soft.

Nutrition Information

- Calories: 232 calories
- Total Carbohydrate: 22 g
- Cholesterol: 38 mg
- Total Fat: 10 g
- Fiber: 1 g
- Protein: 14 g
- Sodium: 639 mg

243. Make Once, Eat Twice Lasagna

"Make this freezer-friendly lasagna dish that you can easily heat up during impromptu lunches and dinners. This is perfect with a side of garlic bread or salad."
Serving: 2 lasagnas (12 servings each). | Prep: 35m | Ready in: 01h30m

Ingredients

- 18 lasagna noodles
- 3 lbs. ground beef
- 3 jars (26 oz. each) spaghetti sauce
- 2 large eggs, lightly beaten
- 1-1/2 lbs. ricotta cheese
- 6 cups shredded part-skim mozzarella cheese, divided
- 1 tbsp. dried parsley flakes
- 1 tsp. salt
- 1/2 tsp. pepper
- 1 cup grated Parmesan cheese

Direction

- Follow the packet directions in cooking the noodles. Set a Dutch oven over medium heat and cook beef until brown. Drain the beef; mix in the spaghetti sauce and set aside. Mix 4 1/2 cups of mozzarella cheese, salt and pepper, eggs, parsley, and ricotta cheese in a large bowl.
- Drain the cooked noodles. Prepare two greased 13x9-inch baking pans. At the bottom of each pan, layer a cup of meat sauce, three pieces of noodles, a cup of the made ricotta mixture, and a cup and a half of meat sauce. Repeat the layers two times; then top with Parmesan cheese and remaining mozzarella cheese. Cover one of the lasagna pans and freeze for up to 3 months. Bake the leftover covered pan in a preheated oven at 375°F for 45 minutes. Remove aluminum foil and bake until the top becomes bubbly or for 10 minutes longer. Leave to cool for 10 minutes before serving.

Nutrition Information

- Calories: 365 calories
- Total Carbohydrate: 25 g
- Cholesterol: 78 mg
- Total Fat: 17 g
- Fiber: 2 g
- Protein: 27 g
- Sodium: 820 mg

244. Meatless Spaghetti

"You might mistake this deliciously chunky sauce as being filled with meat but it actually comprises a whole heap of amazing produce. On busy days, it's great to have uncomplicated and unfussy recipes like this one to turn to. I can start preparing the sauce in the early afternoon and leave it simmering slowly on the stove until dinnertime."
Serving: 14 servings. | Prep: 25m | Ready in: 01h25m

Ingredients

- 6 garlic cloves, minced
- 1 cup chopped celery
- 1 medium onion, chopped
- 2 tbsps. canola oil
- 6 small zucchini, chopped (about 2 lbs.)
- 1 medium green pepper
- 1 can (6 oz.) pitted ripe olives, drained and sliced
- 4 beef bouillon cubes or 2 vegetable bouillon cubes
- 1 cup hot water
- 1 jar (6 oz.) sliced mushrooms, drained
- 1 can (28 oz.) diced tomatoes, undrained
- 2 cans (15 oz. each) tomato sauce
- 1 can (6 oz.) tomato paste
- 1 tbsp. brown sugar, optional
- 2 tsps. dried basil
- 2 tsps. dried oregano
- 2 tsps. dried parsley flakes
- 1 tsps. salt, optional
- 1/2 tsp. pepper
- 2 lbs. spaghetti, cooked and drained

Direction

- In a Dutch oven or a big saucepan, heat oil and sauté the onion, celery and garlic until they become tender. Stir the olives, green pepper and zucchini in then sauté them for 2 to 3 minutes.
- Stir bouillon in water until dissolved then pour it on the vegetables. Place the following 10 ingredients in and boil. Lower the heat and cover it. Let it simmer for 1 hour, stirring from time to time. Eat with spaghetti.

Nutrition Information

- Calories: 102 calories
- Total Carbohydrate: 14 g
- Cholesterol: 0 mg
- Total Fat: 5 g
- Fiber: 0 g
- Protein: 4 g
- Sodium: 624 mg

245. No-bake Mushroom Lasagna

"This summer lasagna with a simple layer of sauce and noodles can be made even without an oven."
Serving: 1 serving. | Prep: 20m | Ready in: 30m

Ingredients

- 2 lasagna noodles
- 1/4 cup sliced fresh mushrooms
- 2 tbsps. chopped onion
- 1 tsp. canola oil
- 1/2 cup spaghetti sauce
- 1/4 cup chopped tomato
- 1/8 tsp. dried basil
- Dash pepper
- 1/4 cup shredded part-skim mozzarella cheese
- 2 tsps. shredded Parmesan cheese

Direction

- Prepare the lasagna noodles following the package instructions. Sauté onions and mushroom in a small pan until tender. Put in pepper, spaghetti sauce, basil, and tomato; boil. Lower heat and let it simmer, covered, for 10 mins; mix from time to time. On low heat, cook in mozzarella cheese until it melts
- Cut drained noodles into thirds. Spread 2 tbsps. sauce on a plate and top with 2 noodle pieces. Repeat the process for another two times. Add the leftover sauce and top with Parmesan cheese.

Nutrition Information

- Calories: 430 calories
- Total Carbohydrate: 55 g
- Cholesterol: 22 mg
- Total Fat: 15 g
- Fiber: 5 g
- Protein: 19 g
- Sodium: 814 mg

246. Pasta Arrabbiata (angry Pasta)

"I came up with this recipe while back in Italy. Give this pasta some kick by adding more crushed red pepper."
Serving: 6 servings. | Prep: 15m | Ready in: 40m

Ingredients

- 1/2 lb. bacon strips, chopped
- 2 garlic cloves, minced
- 1/3 cup olive oil
- 3 cans (15 oz. each) tomato puree
- 6 fresh basil leaves, thinly sliced
- 1/2 to 1 tsp. crushed red pepper flakes
- 3 cups uncooked penne pasta
- Grated Parmesan cheese

Direction

- Put the bacon in a big skillet over medium heat and let it cook until crisp. Place on paper towels using a slotted spoon; dispose the drippings.
- Using the same skillet, add the garlic in olive oil and give it a stir for a minute. Stir in the

tomato puree, pepper flakes, bacon and basil. Allow the mixture to boil; adjust the heat and make it to a simmer for roughly 15 minutes for the flavors to blend. Stir the mixture from time to time.
- Meanwhile, prepare the pasta and cook following the package directions; drain. Serve it with the sauce and top it off with Parmesan cheese.

Nutrition Information

- Calories: 460 calories
- Total Carbohydrate: 31 g
- Cholesterol: 42 mg
- Total Fat: 28 g
- Fiber: 3 g
- Protein: 20 g
- Sodium: 925 mg

247. Pasta With Sausage And Tomatoes

"This recipe is perfect if you're looking for a quick way to make spaghetti sauce."
Serving: 4 servings. | Prep: 20m | Ready in: 20m

Ingredients

- 1 lb. Johnsonville® Ground Mild Italian sausage
- 2 cans (16 oz. each) diced tomatoes, undrained
- 1-1/2 tsps. chopped fresh basil or 1/2 tsp. dried basil
- 1 package (12 oz.) pasta, cooked and drained

Direction

- Cook sausage in a pan until brown; drain. Put it basil and tomatoes; let it simmer for 10mins without cover. Serve over paste right away.

Nutrition Information

- Calories: 525 calories
- Total Carbohydrate: 70 g
- Cholesterol: 45 mg
- Total Fat: 16 g
- Fiber: 4 g
- Protein: 23 g
- Sodium: 683 mg

248. Penne & Sausage Casseroles

"This casserole featuring mushrooms, sausage, and cheese is always a hit."
Serving: 2 casseroles (8 servings each). | Prep: 50m | Ready in: 01h20m

Ingredients

- 1-1/2 lbs. uncooked penne pasta
- 1 lb. Johnsonville® Ground Mild Italian sausage
- 1 lb. sliced fresh mushrooms
- 1 large onion, chopped
- 3 tbsps. olive oil
- 6 garlic cloves, minced
- 1 tbsp. dried oregano
- 1-1/2 cups dry red wine or beef broth, divided
- 2 cans (14-1/2 oz. each) stewed tomatoes, cut up
- 1 can (15 oz.) tomato sauce
- 1 cup beef broth
- 4 cups shredded part-skim mozzarella cheese
- 4 cups shredded fontina cheese
- Minced fresh parsley, optional

Direction

- Cook the pasta following the package instructions. In the meantime, on medium heat, cook sausage in a Dutch oven until it is not pink; drain and set the sausage aside.
- Sauté onion and mushrooms in the same Dutch oven with oil until tender. Put it oregano and garlic; cook for another minute. Mix in a cup of wine then boil. Cook until the liquid reduces by 1/2. Mix in the remaining wine, tomatoes, sausage, broth, and tomato sauce; boil. Lower heat; let it simmer while covered for 15mins.

- Drain the pasta. In each of two greased 13-in by 9-in baking dish, slather half cup of sauce. Split 1/2 of the pasta among the dishes; arrange each in a layer with 2 1/2 cups sauce and a cup each of the cheeses. Repeat the layers.
- Bake for 25mins in a 350 degrees while covered. Remove the cover then bake for another 5-10mins until the cheese is melted and bubbly. If desired, garnish with parsley.

Nutrition Information

- Calories: 460 calories
- Total Carbohydrate: 41 g
- Cholesterol: 59 mg
- Total Fat: 21 g
- Fiber: 3 g
- Protein: 24 g
- Sodium: 756 mg

249. Penne With Tomatoes & White Beans

"If you like a bit of Greek taste, you can use feta cheese in this tasty dish featuring the delicious combo of beans, pasta, and vegetables."

Serving: 4 servings. | Prep: 15m | Ready in: 30m

Ingredients

- 8 oz. uncooked penne pasta
- 2 tbsps. olive oil
- 1 garlic clove, minced
- 2 cans (14-1/2 oz. each) Italian diced tomatoes, undrained
- 1 can (15 oz.) white kidney or cannellini beans, rinsed and drained
- 1 package (10 oz.) fresh spinach, trimmed
- 1/4 cup sliced ripe olives
- 1/2 tsp. salt
- 1/4 tsp. pepper
- 1/2 cup grated Parmesan cheese

Direction

- Cook the pasta following the package instructions. In the meantime, on medium high heat, heat oil in a big skillet. Cook and stir in garlic for a minute. Put in beans and tomatoes; boil. Lower the heat; let it simmer for 5-7mins without a cover to let the flavors blend.
- Add pepper, spinach, salt, and olives. On medium heat, cook and stir until the spinach wilts. Drain the pasta then add tomato mixture and cheese on top.

Nutrition Information

- Calories: 491 calories
- Total Carbohydrate: 77 g
- Cholesterol: 9 mg
- Total Fat: 13 g
- Fiber: 9 g
- Protein: 19 g
- Sodium: 1505 mg

250. Penne With Veggies And Black Beans

"Use your bountiful harvest of carrots, zucchini, sweet pepper, and tomatoes in this filling pasta dish. You can use 1/2 cup thick teriyaki sauce or 1/2 cup salsa in this dish for a change."

Serving: 2 servings. | Prep: 15m | Ready in: 25m

Ingredients

- 3/4 cup uncooked penne pasta
- 1/3 cup sliced zucchini
- 1/3 cup sliced fresh carrot
- 4 medium fresh mushrooms, sliced
- 1/2 small green pepper, thinly sliced
- 1/2 small onion, thinly sliced
- 1 small garlic clove, minced
- 1/4 tsp. each dried basil, oregano and thyme
- 1/4 tsp. salt
- 1/8 tsp. pepper
- 2 tsps. olive oil, divided

- 1 cup canned black beans, rinsed and drained
- 1/4 cup chopped seeded tomato
- 2 tbsps. shredded Parmesan cheese
- 2 tsps. minced fresh parsley

Direction

- Cook the pasta following the package instructions. In the meantime, sauté seasonings, zucchini, garlic, carrot, onion, green pepper, and mushrooms in a big non-stick pan with 1tsp oil until tender-crisp. Mix in beans.
- Drain the pasta then toss into the vegetable mixture. Gently mix in the remaining olive oil and tomato. Top with parsley and Parmesan cheese.

Nutrition Information

- Calories: 300 calories
- Total Carbohydrate: 47 g
- Cholesterol: 4 mg
- Total Fat: 7 g
- Fiber: 8 g
- Protein: 14 g
- Sodium: 643 mg

251. Pepperoni Pasta

"You can use wagon wheel pasta in place of 1/2 the rotini for a fun twist in this recipe."
Serving: 6-8 servings. | Prep: 25m | Ready in: 55m

Ingredients

- 1 lb. ground beef
- 1 medium onion, chopped
- 1 medium green pepper, chopped
- 1 garlic clove, minced
- 3-1/2 cups spaghetti sauce
- 1 can (4 oz.) mushroom stems and pieces, drained
- 1 package (3-1/2 oz.) sliced pepperoni
- 8 oz. uncooked spiral pasta, wagon wheel pasta or pastas of your choice
- 1 cup shredded part-skim mozzarella cheese
- 1 cup shredded provolone cheese
- Grated Parmesan cheese

Direction

- On medium heat, cook green pepper, onion, and beef in a big skillet until the meat is not pink anymore. Put in garlic then cook for another minute; drain. Put in pepperoni, mushrooms, and spaghetti sauce.
- Put 1/2 of the pasta and meat mixture in a layer in a greased 13-in by 9-in baking dish. Top with half cup each of provolone and mozzarella cheeses. Repeat the layers then scatter with Parmesan cheese.
- Bake for 30-35 mins in a 400 degrees F oven without a cover or until thoroughly heated. Let it sit for 15 mins Serve.

Nutrition Information

- Calories: 372 calories
- Total Carbohydrate: 22 g
- Cholesterol: 61 mg
- Total Fat: 21 g
- Fiber: 3 g
- Protein: 23 g
- Sodium: 992 mg

252. Personal Pizzas

Serving: 1 serving. | Prep: 5m | Ready in: 15m

Ingredients

- 2 Rhodes™ Dinner Rolls, thawed to room temperature

Direction

- Spray cooking spray lightly on counter or surface. Blend the rolls to make a ball. Roll dough into a 6 to 7-inch circle. Move dough to a greased cookie sheet. Use the tines of a fork, to prick the dough several times. Bring to bake

for 8-10 minutes at 350°F. Take it out from the oven and allow to cool.
- Use your favorite toppings to top. Bake in a 350-degree oven until cheese is melted and ingredients are cooked through, 5-7 minutes.

253. Pesto-olive Chicken

"This gorgeous and hearty chicken entree is made with just some basic ingredients that you can find in the pantry."
Serving: 4 servings. | Prep: 10m | Ready in: 30m

Ingredients

- 4 boneless skinless chicken breast halves (6 oz. each)
- 1/2 cup prepared pesto
- 2 jars (4-1/2 oz. each) sliced mushrooms, drained
- 1 can (4-1/2 oz.) chopped ripe olives
- 1 cup shredded provolone cheese

Direction

- Preheat the oven to 400 degrees F. Slightly flatten the chicken then arrange in an ungreased 13-in by 9-in baking dish. Scoop pesto on top of the chicken; add olives and mushrooms on top.
- Bake for 15-18mins without a cover or until a thermometer registers 165 degrees F. Top with sprinkled cheese then bake for another 1-2mins or until the cheese melts.

Nutrition Information

- Calories: 490 calories
- Total Carbohydrate: 8 g
- Cholesterol: 124 mg
- Total Fat: 29 g
- Fiber: 3 g
- Protein: 49 g
- Sodium: 1117 mg

254. Pizza Pancakes

"This filling and delicious treat is perfect for people who have such big appetites. You might want to double the recipe for this one."
Serving: 14 pancakes. | Prep: 20m | Ready in: 30m

Ingredients

- 2 cups biscuit/baking mix
- 2 tsps. Italian seasoning
- 2 large eggs
- 1 cup 2% milk
- 1/2 cup shredded part-skim mozzarella cheese
- 1/2 cup chopped pepperoni
- 1 plum tomato, chopped and seeded
- 1/4 cup chopped green pepper
- 1 can (8 oz.) pizza sauce, warmed

Direction

- Mix Italian seasoning and biscuit mix in a bowl. Beat milk and eggs in a separate bowl until combined; mix with the dry ingredients until just moistened. Mix in pepper, cheese, tomato, and pepperoni.
- On medium heat, preheat the griddle then lightly grease. Pour quarter cupfuls of butter on the griddle; cook until the bottoms are golden and the bubbles on the surface start to pop. Flip then cook the other side until golden. Serve with pizza sauce.

Nutrition Information

- Calories: 272 calories
- Total Carbohydrate: 28 g
- Cholesterol: 70 mg
- Total Fat: 13 g
- Fiber: 2 g
- Protein: 10 g
- Sodium: 827 mg

255. Pizza With Wheat Crust

"Try this huge change over a classic pizza crust. It's a whole wheat version and it's perfect for your favorite pizza toppings. You'll never go wrong with this tender, thick and tasty homemade crust."

Serving: 2 pizzas (8 slices each). | Prep: 15m | Ready in: 35m

Ingredients

- 1 cup water (70° to 80°)
- 2 tbsps. olive oil
- 1 tbsp. sugar
- 1-1/2 tsps. salt
- 1/2 tsp. dried oregano
- 1/2 tsp. dried basil
- 1/4 tsp. garlic powder
- 2 cups all-purpose flour
- 1 cup whole wheat flour
- 2-1/4 tsps. active dry yeast
- 1 can (15 oz.) pizza sauce
- 3 cups shredded mozzarella cheese
- Pizza toppings of your choice, optional

Direction

- Put the first 10 ingredients in a bread machine pan respectively suggested by manufacturer. Set the machine to its' dough setting (monitor the dough every after 5 minutes of mixing; add 1 to 2 tbsps. of flour or water if necessary).
- Once the cycle is completed, lay the dough on a lightly floured work area. Cover the dough and let it rest for about 10 minutes. Split the dough into half; flatten every portion into a 12-in. pizza pan that's greased. Spread the pizza sauce and scatter the cheese over. Add your favorite pizza toppings if preferred. Let it bake at 400° for roughly 18-20 minutes or until the cheese and the crust becomes lightly brown.

Nutrition Information

- Calories: 170 calories
- Total Carbohydrate: 21 g
- Cholesterol: 16 mg
- Total Fat: 7 g
- Fiber: 2 g
- Protein: 7 g
- Sodium: 375 mg

256. Pork With Gorgonzola Sauce

"A delicious roast pork tenderloin nicely served with Gorgonzola cheese sauce."

Serving: Makes 6 servings

Ingredients

- 1/4 cup Dijon mustard
- 1 tbsp. olive oil
- 1 tbsp. dried thyme
- 2 3/4-lb. pork tenderloins
- 1 tbsp. butter
- 1 tbsp. all purpose flour
- 1 cup whipping cream
- 1/4 cup dry white wine
- 1/4 cup canned low-salt chicken broth
- 1 cup crumbled Gorgonzola cheese (about 4 oz.)

Direction

- Preparation for pork: Oil a large rimmed baking sheet. In a small bowl, whisk thyme, olive oil, and Dijon mustard to combine. Sprinkle pepper and salt over the pork tenderloins. Heat the heavy large non-stick skillet on high. Put in pork and sear, turning from time to time, for about 10 minutes until they are browned all over. Place the seared pork into the oiled baking sheet. Spread the Dijon mustard mixture on all sides of pork. (This can be made up to 2 hours ahead. Uncover and put the pork in the fridge).
- Set an oven to 425°F and start preheating. Roast the pork for about half an hour until a thermometer inserted into the thickest part of the meat reads 150°F. Take away from the oven and allow to stand for 5 minutes.
- At the same time, prepare the sauce: In a heavy small saucepan, melt a tbsp. butter on medium heat. Put in a tbsp. of flour and whisk

for a minute. Slowly whisk in chicken broth, white wine, and whipping cream. Boil, regularly whisking, for about a minute until the mixture thickens enough to coat the spoon. Put in the crumbled Gorgonzola, then whisk for about 5 minutes until the sauce reduces to the desired degree of consistency and the cheese melts and becomes smooth.
- Cut the pork and place into the plates. Ladle some sauce over the pork. Serve and pass additional sauce separately.

Nutrition Information

- Calories: 488
- Total Carbohydrate: 4 g
- Cholesterol: 199 mg
- Total Fat: 30 g
- Fiber: 1 g
- Protein: 49 g
- Sodium: 457 mg
- Saturated Fat: 15 g

257. Potato Pizza Casserole

"Pizza lovers will surely love this delicious one-dish meal."
Serving: 8 | Prep: 5m | Ready in: 50m

Ingredients

- 1 lb. ground beef
- 1 small onion, chopped
- salt and pepper to taste
- 1/4 tsp. garlic powder
- 5 cups peeled and thinly sliced potatoes
- 1 (3 oz.) package chopped pepperoni
- 1 (10.75 oz.) can condensed tomato soup
- 1 (10.75 oz.) can condensed Cheddar cheese soup
- 1/2 cup milk
- 1/2 tsp. dried oregano
- 1/4 tsp. Italian seasoning
- 1/2 tsp. brown sugar
- 8 oz. shredded mozzarella cheese

Direction

- Preheat oven to 175°C or 350°Fahrenheit. On medium heat, cook onion and ground beef in a big skillet until brown evenly; drain grease. Sprinkle garlic powder, pepper, and salt to season.
- In a 9-in by 13-in baking dish, spread a layer of sliced potatoes. Spread onion and ground beef on top of the potatoes. Top over the ground beef with pepperoni slices. On medium heat, mix milk, Cheddar cheese soup, and tomato soup in a saucepan; sprinkle brown sugar, Italian seasoning, and oregano to season. Stir well and cook until thoroughly heated; pour on top of the contents in the baking dish.
- Use an aluminum foil to cover the dish; bake in the preheated oven for half an hour. Uncover then top with sprinkled mozzarella cheese. Bake for another 15 mins until the cheese is bubbly and melted.

Nutrition Information

- Calories: 383 calories;
- Total Carbohydrate: 27.7 g
- Cholesterol: 74 mg
- Total Fat: 19.9 g
- Protein: 23.6 g
- Sodium: 888 mg

258. Puffed Pan Pizza

"This quick and saucy recipe will surely please everyone."
Serving: 8 servings. | Prep: 25m | Ready in: 01h15m

Ingredients

- 1/2 lb. ground beef
- 1 medium onion, chopped
- 1 tsp. Italian seasoning
- Salt and pepper to taste
- 4 tubes (12 oz. each) refrigerated buttermilk biscuits
- 1/2 cup chopped green pepper
- 4 oz. fresh mushrooms, sliced

- 3-1/2 cups spaghetti sauce
- 2 cups shredded cheddar cheese

Direction

- On medium heat, cook onion and beef in a big pan until the meat is not pink. Put in pepper, salt, and Italian seasoning; let it simmer for a minute. Split the biscuits into quarters then transfer 1/2 of the biscuits in a big bowl. Gently fold in 1/2 of the spaghetti sauce, cheese, mushrooms, and green pepper until blended. Move to a greased 13-in by 9-in baking dish. Repeat. Add the rest of the sauce all over the biscuit mixture. Top with the rest of the cheese. Bake for 50mins in a 350 degrees oven until puffed in the middle. Let it sit for 5-10mins. Serve.

Nutrition Information

- Calories: 341 calories
- Total Carbohydrate: 34 g
- Cholesterol: 46 mg
- Total Fat: 15 g
- Fiber: 2 g
- Protein: 17 g
- Sodium: 1050 mg

259. Reynolds Italian Meatballs

Serving: 8 to 9 large meatballs. | Prep: 15m | Ready in: 45m

Ingredients

- 1 Reynolds® Oven Bag, Large Size
- 1 tbsp. flour
- 1 jar (about 26 oz.) pasta sauce, divided
- 1 lb. ground beef
- 1/2 small red bell pepper, finely chopped
- 1/4 cup bread crumbs
- 1 egg
- 1-1/2 tsps. Italian seasoning
- 1 tsp. salt
- 1 tsp. garlic powder
- Hot cooked pasta or hoagie rolls
- Shredded Parmesan cheese, (optional)

Direction

- Preheat the oven to 350 degrees F.
- In a Reynolds® Oven bag shake flour then put the bag in a 13-in by 9-in by 2-in baking pan that's at least 2-in deep. In a big bowl, put 2/3 cup pasta sauce then set aside. Pour the rest of the pasta sauce in the bag then squeeze to combine with the flour.
- In the bowl with pasta sauce, mix in garlic powder, ground beef, salt, bell pepper, Italian seasoning, egg, and bread crumbs until combined. Make each meatball using about one-third cup of mixture. In an even layer, arrange the meatballs in the oven bag.
- Use a nylon tie to secure the oven bag; make 6 half-inch slits on top. Slip the ends of the bag in pan.
- Bake for 30-35mins until the meat thermometer registers 160 degrees F. Serve sauce and meatballs on top of hot cooked pasta or halve the meatballs then serve as meatball subs on hoagie rolls. If desired, top meatballs with shredded Parmesan cheese.

260. Rich Italian Beef Roll Ups

"This dish originally doesn't have a recipe but it still turned up really delicious."
Serving: 12 servings. | Prep: 20m | Ready in: 01h10m

Ingredients

- 2 lbs. lean ground beef
- 2 eggs, lightly beaten
- 1 cup Italian-seasoned bread crumbs
- 1/2 cup milk
- 5 tsps. dried minced onion
- 1-1/2 tsps. salt
- 1/4 tsp. pepper
- 3 to 3-1/2 lbs. beef top round steak
- 2 tbsps. canola oil
- 4 cups spaghetti sauce, divided

- Hot cooked spaghetti, optional

Direction

- Combine pepper, ground chuck, salt, eggs, onion, milk, and crumbs thoroughly in a big bowl; form into a dozen 3-inch rolls.
- Slice the steak into a dozen 6 1/2 by 3 1/2-inch portions. Wrap a piece of steak on each roll then secure using toothpicks. On medium heat, brown the roll-ups in a big pan.
- In a 13x9-inch baking dish, slather two cups of spaghetti sauce then top with roll-ups. Use the remaining sauce to cover. Bake for 50-55mins in a 350 degrees oven while covered until the steak is tender. Discard the toothpicks. If desired, serve on top of pasta.

Nutrition Information

- Calories: 400 calories
- Total Carbohydrate: 16 g
- Cholesterol: 149 mg
- Total Fat: 16 g
- Fiber: 2 g
- Protein: 45 g
- Sodium: 932 mg

261. Romano Basil Turkey Breast

"Impress your guests with this grilled and golden turkey that is made flavorful with cheese and basil beneath the skin."
Serving: 8 servings. | Prep: 15m | Ready in: 01h45m

Ingredients

- 4 oz. Romano cheese, shredded
- 1/2 cup fresh basil leaves, chopped
- 4 lemon slices
- 4 garlic cloves, minced
- 1 bone-in turkey breast (4 to 5 lbs.)
- 2 tbsps. olive oil
- 1/2 tsp. salt
- 1/4 tsp. pepper

Direction

- Mix garlic, cheese, lemon slices, and basil. Loosen the turkey breast skin carefully with fingers then put the mixture beneath the skin. Secure the skin to underside the breast using toothpicks. Rub oil on the skin then scatter with pepper and salt.
- Use a drip pan to set the grill for indirect heat. Put the turkey on top of the drip pan. On indirect medium heat, grill the chicken for 1 1/2-2hrs while covering or until a thermometer registers 170 degrees F. Discard the toothpicks then cover. Let it sit for 10 mins then cut.

Nutrition Information

- Calories: 402 calories
- Total Carbohydrate: 1 g
- Cholesterol: 136 mg
- Total Fat: 20 g
- Fiber: 0 g
- Protein: 53 g
- Sodium: 493 mg

262. Saucy Chicken & Tortellini

"This detectable dish will comfort your heart in those gloomy, bad days."
Serving: 8 servings. | Prep: 10m | Ready in: 06h25m

Ingredients

- 1-1/2 lbs. boneless skinless chicken breasts, cut into 1-inch cubes
- 1/2 lb. sliced fresh mushrooms
- 1 large onion, chopped
- 1 medium sweet red pepper, cut into 1/2-inch pieces
- 1 medium green pepper, cut into 1/2-inch pieces
- 1 can (2-1/4 oz.) sliced ripe olives, drained
- 1 jar (24 oz.) marinara sauce
- 1 jar (15 oz.) Alfredo sauce

- 2 packages (9 oz. each) refrigerated cheese tortellini
- Grated Parmesan cheese, optional
- Torn fresh basil, optional

Direction

- Mix first seven ingredients together in a 5-qt. slow cooker. Cook without covering on low heat for 6-8 hours, until chicken is tender.
- Mix in tortellini and Alfredo sauce. Cook while covering for about 15-20 minutes, until tortellini is tender. Add basil and Parmesan cheese on top, if desired.
- Freeze option: Put vegetables and chicken in freezer containers; add sauce on top. Let cool and freeze. When using, thaw partially in fridge overnight. Place in a microwave-safe dish with a cover and microwave on high until heated through, gently stirring and adding in a little water if needed.

Nutrition Information

- Calories: 437 calories
- Total Carbohydrate: 44 g
- Cholesterol: 91 mg
- Total Fat: 15 g
- Fiber: 5 g
- Protein: 31 g
- Sodium: 922 mg

263. Saucy Garlic Chicken For Two

"This appetizing and rich spinach entree features roasted garlic. You can make this ahead then place in the oven when you're ready to serve it on special gatherings."
Serving: 2 servings. | Prep: 40m | Ready in: 01h15m

Ingredients

- 2 whole garlic bulb
- 1 tbsp. olive oil, divided
- 4-1/2 cups fresh baby spinach
- 1/2 tsp. salt, divided
- 1/4 tsp. coarsely ground pepper, divided
- 2 boneless skinless chicken breast halves (6 oz. each)
- 2 tbsps. butter, cubed
- 2 tbsps. all-purpose flour
- 1-1/2 cups 2% milk
- 1-1/4 cups grated Parmesan cheese, divided
- Dash ground nutmeg
- Hot cooked pasta
- Chopped tomato and minced fresh parsley, optional

Direction

- Discard the garlic's papery outer skin but do not separate the cloves or peel. Slice off the garlic bulb tops; slather 1/2 of oil on the bulbs. Use heavy-duty foil to wrap each bulb; bake for 30-35mins in a 425 degrees oven until soft. Let bulbs cool for 10-15mins.
- In the meantime, put spinach in an oiled 11-in by 7-in baking dish; scatter 1/2 the pepper and salt. Brown each side of the chicken in a big pan with the remaining oil; nestle on top of the spinach.
- Melt butter in a big pot. Mix in flour until the mixture is smooth; pour in milk gradually then boil. Cook and stir for 1-2mins until thick. Mix in the remaining salt, nutmeg, and a cup of cheese. Move to a blender and squeeze into blender with softened garlic. Pour the mixture all over the chicken.
- Bake for 30-35mins in a 425 degrees while covered until the sauce is bubbly and a thermometer registers 170 degrees. Remove the cover then top with the remaining cheese; bake for another 5mins. Serve with pasta. If desired, add parsley and tomato on top.

264. Saucy Stuffed Zucchini

"If you have a load of zucchini supply from your garden, use them up in this vegetable recipe."
Serving: 3-4 servings. | Prep: 30m | Ready in: 55m

Ingredients

- 3 to 4 medium zucchini (1-3/4 to 2 lbs.)

- 12 oz. Johnsonville® Ground Mild Italian sausage, cooked and drained
- 1/2 cup chopped sweet red pepper
- 1/2 cup chopped green pepper
- 2 tbsps. chopped onion
- 1-1/2 tsps. Italian seasoning
- 1 can (8 oz.) tomato sauce
- 2 tbsps. butter
- 2 tbsps. all-purpose flour
- 1/4 tsp. salt
- 1-1/4 cups milk
- 1/2 cup grated Parmesan cheese, divided
- 1 tsp. Dijon mustard

Direction

- Halve the zucchini lengthwise; scoop the pulp out and set it aside, keep a quarter-inch shell. In salted water, cook shells for 2mins; remove the shells then drain. Set the shells aside.
- Chop the pulp then put it in a pot; boil with tomato sauce, sausage, Italian seasoning, onion, and peppers. Lower heat; let it simmer for 5mins while covered. Put the shells in a greased 13x9-in baking dish; put the filling in the shells.
- Melt butter in a pot; stir in salt and flour until smooth. Pour in milk gradually then boil; cook and mix for 2mins until bubbly and thick. Take off heat. Put in mustard and quarter cup Parmesan cheese.
- Pour the mixture on top of the zucchini then top with the remaining Parmesan. Bake for 25-30mins in a 350 degrees oven without cover until completely heated.

Nutrition Information

- Calories: 346 calories
- Total Carbohydrate: 18 g
- Cholesterol: 67 mg
- Total Fat: 23 g
- Fiber: 3 g
- Protein: 19 g
- Sodium: 1126 mg

265. Sausage, Artichoke & Sun-dried Tomato Ragu

"This easy, hearty, and thick spaghetti sauce tastes even better the following day. You can add bell pepper and celery in it if you want."
Serving: 2 quarts. | Prep: 20m | Ready in: 06h20m

Ingredients

- 1 lb. Johnsonville® Ground Mild Italian sausage
- 1/2 lb. lean ground beef (90% lean)
- 1 medium onion, finely chopped
- 3 cans (14-1/2 oz. each) diced tomatoes, undrained
- 1 cup oil-packed sun-dried tomatoes, chopped
- 2 cans (6 oz. each) Italian tomato paste
- 1 jar (7-1/2 oz.) marinated quartered artichoke hearts, drained and chopped
- 3 garlic cloves, minced
- 2 tsps. minced fresh rosemary
- 1 tsp. pepper
- 1/2 tsp. salt
- 1 bay leaf
- 3 tbsps. minced fresh parsley
- Hot cooked spaghetti
- Grated Parmesan cheese, optional

Direction

- On medium-high heat, cook onion, beef, and sausage for 4-6mins in a big pan while crumbling until the meat it is not pink; drain. Move to a 5-6 quart slow cooker; mix in bay leaf, tomatoes, tomato paste, pepper, artichokes, rosemary, salt and garlic.
- Cook for 6-8hrs on low while covered until completely heated. Discard the bay leaf then mix in parsley. Serve sauce with spaghetti. Add grated Parmesan on top if desired. You can put the cooled sauce in freezer containers then freeze. Thaw the sauce partially overnight in the fridge to use. Heat in a pot while mixing from time to time.

Nutrition Information

- Calories: 259 calories
- Total Carbohydrate: 17 g
- Cholesterol: 39 mg
- Total Fat: 17 g
- Fiber: 3 g
- Protein: 11 g
- Sodium: 1535 mg

266. Sautéed Scallops & Shrimp Pasta

"This mouth-watering seafood pasta is best enjoyed with crusty sourdough. You can omit the red pepper flakes if you don't like the added heat."
Serving: 2 servings. | Prep: 20m | Ready in: 35m

Ingredients

- 8 uncooked shrimp (16-20 per lb.), peeled and deveined
- 6 sea scallops (about 12 oz.)
- 1/2 tsp. seafood seasoning
- 3 tbsps. unsalted butter, divided
- 1-1/2 cups (about 3 to 4 oz.) small fresh mushrooms, halved
- 1/2 cup frozen peas, thawed
- 1/4 cup finely chopped shallots
- 1/3 cup white wine or chicken broth
- 4 oz. uncooked angel hair pasta
- 1/4 cup plus 1 tbsp. chopped fresh parsley, divided
- 2 large garlic cloves, minced
- 1/4 to 1/2 tsp. crushed red pepper flakes
- 1/4 tsp. salt
- 2 tbsps. grapeseed oil

Direction

- Pat the scallops and shrimp dry then scatter with seafood seasoning.
- On medium heat, melt 1 tbsp. butter in a small skillet. Cook and stir mushrooms for around 3 mins; put in peas. Cook for 3-4 mins until the veggies are tender; take them out of the pan. Put 1 tbsp. butter and shallots into the pan; cook and stir for 1-2 mins until beginning to turn soft. Mix in wine. Turn to medium-low heat; let it simmer without a cover until serving.
- In the meantime, cook the pasta following the package instructions in a big saucepan; set aside half a cup of pasta cooking water. Put the pasta back into the pan. Mix in the remaining butter, a quarter cup of parsley, mushroom mixture, garlic, salt, and pepper flakes on low heat. Pour in enough saved pasta cooking water to moisten.
- On medium-high heat, heat oil in a big skillet. Add and sear shrimp and scallops for around 2-3 mins per side until the shrimp is pink and the scallops are firm and golden brown. Mix with sauce and pasta. Scatter with the remaining parsley.

Nutrition Information

- Calories: 733 calories
- Total Carbohydrate: 56 g
- Cholesterol: 210 mg
- Total Fat: 35 g
- Fiber: 3 g
- Protein: 47 g
- Sodium: 1263 mg

267. Savory Spaghetti Sauce

"The freshness of the spaghetti sauce is pleasing to all. I use this recipe often especially in the summer and it tastes best with fresh herbs."
Serving: 4-6 servings (about 1 quart). | Prep: 5m | Ready in: 01h15m

Ingredients

- 1 lb. ground beef
- 1 large onion, chopped
- 2 cans (15 oz. each) tomato sauce
- 1 garlic clove, minced
- 1 bay leaf
- 1 tbsp. minced fresh basil or 1 tsp. dried basil

- 2 tsps. minced fresh oregano or 3/4 tsp. dried oregano
- 2 tsp. sugar
- 1/2 to 1 tsp. salt
- 1/2 tsp. pepper
- Hot cooked spaghetti
- Fresh oregano, optional

Direction

- Cook onion until tender and beef until not pink in a Dutch oven. Drain excess grease. Mix in the next eight ingredients. Heat to a boil. Cover, decrease heat, and gently boil for 1 hour, stirring sporadically. Take the bay leaf out. Serve over spaghetti. You can put oregano on as a garnish.

Nutrition Information

- Calories: 182 calories
- Total Carbohydrate: 7 g
- Cholesterol: 50 mg
- Total Fat: 9 g
- Fiber: 1 g
- Protein: 17 g
- Sodium: 559 mg

268. Seafood-stuffed Shells

"Even if you're not a fan of fish, you'll still love these delicious stuffed shells."
Serving: 10 servings. | Prep: 35m | Ready in: 01h05m

Ingredients

- 30 uncooked jumbo pasta shells
- 1/2 lb. bay scallops
- 2 tsps. butter
- 2 eggs
- 2 cups (16 oz.) cream-style cottage cheese
- 1 carton (15 oz.) ricotta cheese
- 1/2 tsp. ground nutmeg
- 1/4 tsp. pepper
- 1 can (6 oz.) lump crabmeat, drained
- 3/4 lb. cooked small shrimp, peeled and deveined
- 1 jar (15 oz.) Alfredo sauce

Direction

- Prepare the pasta shells following the package instructions.
- In the meantime, on medium heat, cook scallops for 1-2 mins in a small skillet or until opaque; move to a big bowl.
- Preheat the oven to 350 degrees F. In a blender, process pepper, 1 egg, nutmeg, ricotta, and 1/2 of the cottage cheese until smooth; put in the bowl with scallops. Repeat with the rest of the pepper, egg, nutmeg, ricotta, and cottage cheese. Put into the scallops. Mix in shrimp and crab.
- Drain and rinse the shells in cold water; stuff the seafood mixture in the shells. Arrange in a greased 13-in by 9-in baking dish then add Alfredo sauce on top.
- Bake for 30-35 mins while covering or until bubbly.

269. Shrimp And Pasta Supper

"Prepare this delicious and easy-to-make pan dish on your busy days."
Serving: 4-6 servings. | Prep: 15m | Ready in: 30m

Ingredients

- 12 oz. linguine
- 1 lb. fresh shrimp, peeled and deveined
- 1 cup sliced celery
- 3 tbsps. butter
- 1 jar (28 oz.) chunky spaghetti sauce
- Hot pepper sauce to taste
- 1 cup frozen peas, thawed
- 1 tbsp. minced fresh parsley
- 1 cup shredded part-skim mozzarella cheese

Direction

- Cook the pasta following the package instructions. In the meantime, sauté celery and

shrimp in a big skillet with butter until the shrimp is pink. Mix in pepper and spaghetti sauces; boil. Lower the heat; let it simmer for 15 mins while covering.
- Drain linguine then place the linguine and peas into the shrimp mixture, mix to coat. Scatter with cheese and parsley. Heat until the cheese melts.

Nutrition Information

- Calories: 491 calories
- Total Carbohydrate: 59 g
- Cholesterol: 145 mg
- Total Fat: 17 g
- Fiber: 6 g
- Protein: 28 g
- Sodium: 965 mg

270. Simple Chicken Parmesan

"A simple and yummy recipe. You can freeze half the sauce for another time."
Serving: 4

Ingredients

- 2 medium garlic cloves, peeled and crushed
- 2 tbsps. extra-virgin olive oil
- 1 (28 oz.) can crushed tomatoes (quality varies dramatically; I prefer Redpack, Progresso and Muir Glen brands)
- 1/2 tsp. dried basil
- 1/4 tsp. dried oregano
- 1/4 tsp. sugar
- Salt and freshly ground pepper, to taste
- 2 large boneless, skinless chicken breasts (6 to 8 oz. each), halved crosswise
- 1 large egg
- 1/2 cup dry bread crumbs
- 8 oz. spaghetti or linguine
- 1/4 cup extra-virgin olive oil
- 1/2 cup grated part-skim mozzarella cheese
- 1/4 cup grated Parmesan cheese, plus extra for passing at the table

Direction

- Heat 2 tbsp. of oil and garlic in big saucepan on medium high heat till garlic begins to sizzle. Mix in a few grinds of pepper, a pinch of salt, sugar, oregano, basil and tomatoes; simmer for 10-12 minutes till flavors meld and sauce thickens a bit. Cover; keep warm. Put aside 1/2 for another time.
- Put chicken pieces between 2 plastic wrap sheets; lb. cutlets to 1/4-in. thick with a heavy pan or your fists.
- Boil 2-qt. of salted water in a big soup kettle.
- Beat egg till blended well in a pie pan. Mix more black pepper and breadcrumbs in another pie pan. Preheat the broiler.
- Dip both sides of each cutlet in beaten egg, one by one, then into breadcrumbs; put on wire rack above a cookie sheet to adhere breading.
- Heat leftover 1/4 cup of oil in a 12-in. skillet on medium high heat. Add cutlet when oil begins to shimmer; sauté for 5 minutes in total till golden brown on each side. Wash then dry the wire rack; put back on the cookie sheet. Cook pasta following package directions in boiling water as cutlets sauté.
- Put cutlets on clean wire rack on a cookie sheet; put portion of cheeses over each. Broil cutlets till it is spotty brown and cheese melts 4-5-in. away from the heat source.
- Drain pasta; place a portion of pasta and cutlet on each of 4 plates. Put 2 or 3 tbsp. of sauce on part of every cutlet; sauce the pasta as you please. Serve with more Parmesan.

Nutrition Information

- Calories: 715 calories;
- Total Carbohydrate: 67.4 g
- Cholesterol: 126 mg
- Total Fat: 29.2 g
- Protein: 45.6 g
- Sodium: 655 mg

271. Simple Italian Pork Chops

"The delicious sauce in this dish is perfect over mashed potatoes and keeps the Italian pork chops juicy and flavorful. You only need 5 ingredients in this recipe and it's really easy to make!"
Serving: 4 servings. | Prep: 10m | Ready in: 30m

Ingredients

- 4 boneless pork loin chops (1 inch thick and 6 oz. each)
- 1/4 tsp. pepper
- 4 tsps. butter
- 1/3 cup white wine or chicken broth
- 1/3 cup prepared Italian salad dressing

Direction

- Sprinkle pepper on the pork chops. On medium heat, cook the chops in a big pan until brown. Pour in salad dressing and wine; cover. Cook for 10-12mins until a thermometer registers 160 degrees F.
- Take the pork chops out of the pan then keep warm. Boil the cooking juices and cook until it reduces to a half cup. Serve the sauce with pork.

Nutrition Information

- Calories: 343 calories
- Total Carbohydrate: 2 g
- Cholesterol: 92 mg
- Total Fat: 21 g
- Fiber: 0 g
- Protein: 33 g
- Sodium: 411 mg

272. Simply Great Chicken

"This delicious and hearty baked chicken is perfect for busy days."
Serving: 4 servings. | Prep: 5m | Ready in: 60m

Ingredients

- 1 broiler/fryer chicken (3-1/2 to 4 lbs.), cut up and skin removed
- 1 envelope Italian salad dressing mix
- 1/2 cup packed brown sugar

Direction

- In one layer, arrange the chicken in a greased 13x9-inch baking dish. Scatter sugar and salad dressing mix on top. Bake for 55-60 mins in a 350 degrees F oven without a cover or until the juices are clear.

Nutrition Information

- Calories: 544 calories
- Total Carbohydrate: 29 g
- Cholesterol: 153 mg
- Total Fat: 25 g
- Fiber: 0 g
- Protein: 48 g
- Sodium: 777 mg

273. Skillet-roasted Lemon Chicken With Potatoes

"This simple and nutritious meal has that herb-lemon taste."
Serving: 4 servings. | Prep: 20m | Ready in: 45m

Ingredients

- 1 tbsp. olive oil, divided
- 1 medium lemon, thinly sliced
- 4 garlic cloves, minced and divided
- 1/4 tsp. grated lemon peel
- 1/2 tsp. salt, divided
- 1/4 tsp. pepper, divided
- 8 boneless skinless chicken thighs (4 oz. each)

- 1/4 tsp. dried rosemary, crushed
- 1 lb. fingerling potatoes, halved lengthwise
- 8 cherry tomatoes
- Minced fresh parsley, optional

Direction

- Preheat the oven to 450 degrees F. Grease 1 tsp. oil on a 10-in cast iron or other ovenproof skillet. Place the lemon slices in one layer on the skillet.
- Mix 1/8 tsp. pepper, 1 tsp. oil, a quarter tsp. salt, lemon peel, and two minced garlic cloves; rub on the chicken. Top chicken with the lemon.
- Mix pepper, rosemary, salt, garlic, and the remaining oil in a big bowl. Toss in tomatoes and potatoes to coat; arrange on top of the chicken. Bake for 25-30 mins without a cover until the potatoes are tender and the chicken is not pink anymore. Scatter with minced parsley if desired. Serve.

Nutrition Information

- Calories: 446 calories
- Total Carbohydrate: 18 g
- Cholesterol: 151 mg
- Total Fat: 20 g
- Fiber: 3 g
- Protein: 45 g
- Sodium: 429 mg

274. Slow Cooker Sweet Sour Meatballs

"Just slow cook the frozen meatballs and you'll surely come back to an aromatic and soothing Asian-style dish."
Serving: 2 servings. | Prep: 10m | Ready in: 05h10m

Ingredients

- 16 frozen fully cooked homestyle meatballs (1/2 oz. each), thawed
- 1/2 cup sugar
- 2 tbsps. plus 2 tsps. cornstarch
- 1/3 cup white vinegar
- 1 tbsp. reduced-sodium soy sauce
- 1/2 medium green pepper, cut into 1-inch pieces
- 1 can (8 oz.) pineapple chunks, undrained
- Hot cooked rice, optional

Direction

- Put the meatballs in a 1 1/2-quart slow cooker. Combine soy sauce, sugar, vinegar, and cornstarch in a small bowl; pour all over the meatballs then put in green pepper. Cook for 4 1/2hrs on low while covered until the pepper is tender-crisp.
- Mix in pineapple, cover then cook for another half hour. If desired, serve over rice.

Nutrition Information

- Calories: 794 calories
- Total Carbohydrate: 94 g
- Cholesterol: 186 mg
- Total Fat: 29 g
- Fiber: 2 g
- Protein: 39 g
- Sodium: 582 mg

275. Slow-cooked Chicken Cacciatore

"This Italian chicken entree with the aroma of fresh garlic and dried herbs can be easily prepared in a slow cooker. It also features diced tomatoes, sliced mushrooms, and green pepper."
Serving: 6 servings. | Prep: 20m | Ready in: 04h20m

Ingredients

- 1/3 cup all-purpose flour
- 1 broiler/fryer chicken (3 to 4 lbs.), cut up
- 2 tbsps. canola oil
- 2 medium onions, cut into wedges
- 1 medium green pepper, cut into strips
- 1 jar (6 oz.) sliced mushrooms, drained
- 1 can (14-1/2 oz.) diced tomatoes, undrained

- 2 garlic cloves, minced
- 1/2 tsp. salt
- 1/2 tsp. dried oregano
- 1/4 tsp. dried basil
- 1/2 cup shredded Parmesan cheese

Direction

- Put flour in a big ziplock bag. Place a few chicken pieces at a time then shake the bag to coat. Brown the chicken on all sides in a big pan with oil.
- Move to a five-quart slow cooker. Add mushrooms, green pepper, and onions on top. Mix basil, tomatoes, oregano, salt, and garlic in a small bowl; pour on top of the veggies. Cook for 4-5hrs on low while covered until the veggies are tender and the chicken juices are clear. Serve with cheese.

Nutrition Information

- Calories: 296 calories
- Total Carbohydrate: 16 g
- Cholesterol: 78 mg
- Total Fat: 12 g
- Fiber: 3 g
- Protein: 29 g
- Sodium: 582 mg

276. Smoked Turkey Sausage Pizza

"This cheesy and easy-to-make dish features a smoky flavor from the turkey sausage."
Serving: 6 servings. | Prep: 25m | Ready in: 35m

Ingredients

- 1 package (6-1/2 oz.) pizza crust mix
- 1/2 cup chopped green pepper
- 1/2 cup chopped sweet red pepper
- 2/3 cup pizza sauce
- 1 package (14 oz.) smoked turkey sausage, sliced
- 1 jar (6 oz.) sliced mushrooms, drained
- 1/4 cup chopped green onions
- 1/2 cup shredded part-skim mozzarella cheese
- 1/2 cup shredded cheddar cheese
- 1/4 cup grated Parmesan cheese
- 1/2 tsp. dried oregano

Direction

- Prepare the pizza dough following the package instructions then place on a greased baking sheet. Press the dough into a 12x10-in rectangle with your floured hands; bake for 3mins in a 425 degrees oven.
- In the meantime, sauté peppers in a small non-stick pan covered in cooking spray until tender-crisp.
- Slather pizza sauce on the crust within an inch of the sides. Add sautéed veggies, onions, mushrooms, and sausage on top. Mix oregano and cheeses; spread over the pizza.
- Bake until the crust is golden brown and the cheese melts for 10-15mins.

Nutrition Information

- Calories: 285 calories
- Total Carbohydrate: 28 g
- Cholesterol: 60 mg
- Total Fat: 9 g
- Fiber: 2 g
- Protein: 21 g
- Sodium: 1166 mg

277. Spaghetti Sauce

"This dish with the tomato sauce is so wonderful."
Serving: 4 | Prep: 10m | Ready in: 30m

Ingredients

- 2 tsps. olive oil
- 1/2 small onion, chopped
- 2 green onions, chopped
- 2 tsps. crushed garlic
- 1 (28 oz.) can peeled and diced tomatoes
- 4 tsps. dried basil

- 4 tsps. dried oregano
- 1 tsp. white sugar

Direction

- In a big sauce pan, heat the oil on medium heat. Sauté the garlic, green onion and onion. Once the onions become clear, whisk in the sugar, oregano, basil and tomatoes. Boil, turn the heat to low, and let simmer for 20 minutes.

Nutrition Information

- Calories: 81 calories;
- Total Carbohydrate: 11.1 g
- Cholesterol: 0 mg
- Total Fat: 2.6 g
- Protein: 2.3 g
- Sodium: 310 mg

---

278. Spicy Sausage Linguine

Serving: Serves 4

Ingredients

- 2 tbsps. olive oil
- 1 lb. fully cooked smoked sausages (such as hot links), cut diagonally into 1/4-inch-thick slices
- 1 large onion, chopped
- 6 large garlic cloves, minced
- 1 tsp. dried crushed red pepper
- 1 tsp. dried basil
- 1 tsp. dried oregano
- 1 tsp. rosemary
- 1 lb. linguine
- 1 1/2 cups canned low-salt chicken broth
- 1/4 cup freshly grated Parmesan cheese
- 2 tbsps. chopped fresh parsley

Direction

- On medium-high heat, heat oil in a big heavy pan. Sauté sausages in hot oil for 5mins until brown. Move sausages on paper towels using a slotted spoon to drain. In the same pan, sauté rosemary, chopped onion, oregano, minced garlic, basil, and dried crushed pepper for 5mins until the onion is golden. Put the sausage back in the pot; sprinkle pepper and salt. Take off heat.
- In the meantime, in a big pot, cook pasta until tender yet still firm to chew in boiling water; drain. Add broth in the pot then boil. Toss the pasta back in the pot to coat.
- Move broth and pasta to a big bowl. Scoop the sausage mixture on top of the pasta. Top with parsley and Parmesan cheese to serve.

Nutrition Information

- Calories: 878
- Total Carbohydrate: 94 g
- Cholesterol: 84 mg
- Total Fat: 39 g
- Fiber: 5 g
- Protein: 38 g
- Sodium: 974 mg
- Saturated Fat: 11 g

---

279. Spicy Shrimp & Peppers With Pasta

"Enjoy this dish at any weeknight. This one is filling and tasty family dish and best paired with tender shrimp, whole wheat pasta, veggies and just the right amount of heat."
Serving: 4 servings. | Prep: 20m | Ready in: 45m

Ingredients

- 1 cup sliced baby portobello mushrooms
- 1 medium sweet yellow pepper, cut into 1/2-inch pieces
- 1 medium green pepper, cut into 1/2-inch pieces
- 1 shallot, minced
- 2 tbsps. olive oil
- 1 garlic clove, minced
- 1/2 tsp. crushed red pepper flakes
- 1 can (28 oz.) crushed tomatoes
- 1 tsp. Italian seasoning
- 1/2 tsp. salt

- 6 oz. uncooked whole wheat linguine
- 1 lb. uncooked medium shrimp, peeled and deveined
- 3 tbsps. minced fresh parsley or 1 tbsp. dried parsley flakes

Direction

- Coat a big nonstick skillet with cooking spray. Sauté the mushrooms, shallot and peppers in oil until softened. Stir in pepper flakes and garlic; let it cook for additional 1 minute.
- Add in the Italian seasoning, tomatoes and salt; stir. Allow the mixture to boil. Lessen the heat; make it to a simmer without any cover for 12-15 minutes or until vegetables are softened.
- Meanwhile, prepare the linguine and cook following the package directions. Drop the shrimp to sauce; let it cook and stir for roughly 5-7 minutes or until it turns pink.
- Drain the linguine and toss it into the sauce. Heat well. Top it off with parsley.

Nutrition Information

- Calories: 385 calories
- Total Carbohydrate: 53 g
- Cholesterol: 138 mg
- Total Fat: 10 g
- Fiber: 10 g
- Protein: 28 g
- Sodium: 697 mg

280. Spinach Pasta Sauce

"Everyone is surprised when they heard the secret ingredient on this sauce. I just added a hint of anise and it perfectly matches the zippy Italian sausage and tomatoes." Serving: 8-10 servings. | Prep: 25m | Ready in: 01h25m

Ingredients

- 1-1/2 lbs. Johnsonville® Ground Mild Italian sausage
- 3 cups sliced fresh mushrooms
- 1/2 cup each chopped carrot, green pepper and onion
- 1 can (28 oz.) crushed tomatoes
- 1 can (15 oz.) tomato sauce
- 1 can (6 oz.) tomato paste
- 1/2 cup grated Parmesan cheese
- 1/2 cup beef broth or red wine
- 3/4 tsp. each aniseed, seasoned salt, pepper, garlic powder, brown sugar, dried basil and oregano
- 4 cups coarsely chopped fresh spinach
- Hot cooked pasta
- 2 cups shredded mozzarella cheese
- 1/4 cup crumbled cooked bacon

Direction

- Cook and crumble the sausage in a Dutch oven until it turns brown; drain. Add the carrot, mushrooms, onion and green pepper; sauté for about 5 minutes. Stir in the sauce, tomatoes, paste, broth, seasonings and Parmesan; make it to simmer for an hour while covered. Add the spinach and completely heat. Serve alongside the pasta; garnish with bacon and mozzarella.

Nutrition Information

- Calories: 274 calories
- Total Carbohydrate: 17 g
- Cholesterol: 50 mg
- Total Fat: 16 g
- Fiber: 4 g
- Protein: 18 g
- Sodium: 1049 mg

281. Spinach-stuffed Chicken Parmesan

"This fast recipe uses homemade breadcrumbs that are made with heels of bread loaves that are toasted and crushed."
Serving: 4 servings. | Prep: 25m | Ready in: 55m

Ingredients

- 4 cups fresh spinach
- 2 garlic cloves, minced
- 2 tsps. olive oil
- 2 tbsps. grated Parmesan cheese, divided
- 1/4 tsp. salt
- 1/4 tsp. pepper
- 4 boneless skinless chicken breast halves (4 oz. each)
- 1/2 cup dry whole wheat bread crumbs
- 1 large egg, lightly beaten
- 2 cans (8 oz. each) no-salt-added tomato sauce
- 1 tsp. dried basil
- 1 tsp. dried oregano
- 3/4 cup shredded part-skim mozzarella cheese

Direction

- Preheat the oven to 375 degrees. Cook and stir garlic and spinach in a big pan with oil until just wilted; drain. Mix in pepper, salt, and 1tsbp Parmesan cheese.
- Use a meat mallet to lb. the chicken breast until a quarter-inch thick. Slather 1tsbp spinach mixture on each. Fold the chicken over the filling to enclose; use toothpicks to secure.
- In separate shallow bowls, put egg and breadcrumbs. Submerge the chicken in egg then coat in crumbs. Arrange in an 8-inch cooking-spray-coated baking dish with the seam-side down. Bake for 20mins without cover.
- In the meantime, mix oregano, basil, and tomato sauce in a big bowl; pour all over the chicken. Top with the remaining Parmesan cheese and mozzarella cheese. Bake for another 10-15mins without cover until a thermometer registers 165 degrees. Remove the toothpicks then serve.

Nutrition Information

- Calories: 281 calories
- Total Carbohydrate: 14 g
- Cholesterol: 104 mg
- Total Fat: 10 g
- Fiber: 2 g
- Protein: 31 g
- Sodium: 432 mg

282. Spooky Pizza

"You can never go wrong with pizza and this recipe is one that's perfect for the Halloween!"
Serving: 8 servings. | Prep: 15m | Ready in: 25m

Ingredients

- 1 loaf (1 lb.) frozen bread dough, thawed
- 1 cup pizza sauce
- 1 cup shredded part-skim mozzarella cheese
- 4 slices Jones Canadian Bacon
- 3 slices pineapple
- 1 pitted ripe olive, cut in half lengthwise

Direction

- Roll out the dough in the shape of a circle that is 15 inches in size. Place the dough circle on a 14-inch pizza pan that is not greased, build the edges of the dough circle up a little bit. Put it in a 425° oven and let it bake for 10-12 minutes or until it turns light brown in color.
- Spread the sauce evenly on top of the baked pizza dough then top it off evenly with cheese. Put it in the oven and let it bake for 5 minutes. Slice each of the Canadian bacon slices into strips that are 1/4 inch in size then put it onto the pizza in such a way that it resembles hair. Put it back in the oven and let it bake for 5-6 minutes or until the cheese turns brown in color.
- Use 2 pineapple slices and olive halves to make the eyes of the pizza. Cut the remaining

pineapple slice into 2 equal portions, then cut 3 thin small pieces from 1 of the pineapple portion. For the teeth and mouth of the pizza, use the thin pieces of pineapple and the other remaining pineapple portion. (Reserve any remaining pineapple for other future use.)

283. Super Spaghetti Sauce

"At my house, we can never tell how many we'll take for dinner. This sauce for a spaghetti is one of my favorites –it is filling, full of flavor and quick. Smoked kielbasa gives it the strong aroma, and the salsa adds the kick."
Serving: 2-1/2 quarts. | Prep: 10m | Ready in: 30m

Ingredients

- 1 lb. ground beef
- 1 lb. Johnsonville® Fully Cooked Polish Kielbasa Sausage Rope, cut into 1/4-inch slices
- 2 jars (24 oz. each) spaghetti sauce with mushrooms
- 1 jar (16 oz.) chunky salsa
- Hot cooked pasta

Direction

- Put the beef in a Dutch oven placed over medium heat. Allow the beef to cook until no visible pink color on the meat; drain and place aside. Using the same pan, cook the sausage for roughly 5-6 minutes over medium heat or until the sausages turned brown.
- Mix in the spaghetti sauce, reserved beef and the salsa; heat well. Serve alongside the pasta.

Nutrition Information

- Calories: 325 calories
- Total Carbohydrate: 18 g
- Cholesterol: 60 mg
- Total Fat: 21 g
- Fiber: 2 g
- Protein: 17 g
- Sodium: 1378 mg

284. Swiss Chicken Rolls

"An impressive and simple entrée."
Serving: 2 servings. | Prep: 20m | Ready in: 40m

Ingredients

- 2 boneless skinless chicken breast halves (5 oz. each)
- 2 slices Swiss cheese (3/4 oz. each)
- 2 thin slices prosciutto or deli ham
- 1 tbsp. butter
- 1 tbsp. olive oil
- 1/4 cup chopped onion
- 1 small garlic clove, minced
- 1 tsp. all-purpose flour
- 1/3 cup Marsala wine or chicken broth
- 2 tsps. minced fresh parsley
- 1 tsp. minced fresh rosemary or 1/4 tsp. dried rosemary, crushed
- 1 tsp. minced fresh thyme or 1/4 tsp. dried thyme
- Dash salt
- Dash pepper

Direction

- Flatten chicken to 1/4-in. thick. Down middle of each, put one prosciutto and cheese slice. Begin with short side, roll up like a jelly roll. Use toothpicks to secure.
- Brown all chicken sides in oil and butter in a small skillet. Put into square 8-in. baking dish coated in cooking spray. Bake for 20-25 minutes, covered, at 350° till a thermometer registers 170°.
- Sauté garlic and onion till tender in same skillet. Mix flour in till blended. Add wine gradually. Boil. Stir and cook till thick for 2 minutes. Mix leftover ingredients in. Throw toothpicks form the chicken rolls. Serve it with the sauce.

Nutrition Information

- Calories: 421 calories
- Total Carbohydrate: 10 g
- Cholesterol: 117 mg

- Total Fat: 20 g
- Fiber: 1 g
- Protein: 38 g
- Sodium: 367 mg

285. Tomato Zucchini Stew

"Everyone will love this winter stew that is perfect for get-together and potlucks."
Serving: 6-8 servings. | Prep: 25m | Ready in: 01h15m

Ingredients

- 1-1/4 lbs. Johnsonville® Ground Mild Italian sausage
- 1-1/2 cups sliced celery (3/4-inch pieces)
- 8 medium fresh tomatoes (about 4 lbs.), peeled and cut into sixths
- 1-1/2 cups tomato juice
- 4 small zucchini, sliced into 1/4-inch pieces
- 2-1/2 tsps. Italian seasoning
- 1-1/2 to 2 tsps. salt
- 1 tsp. sugar
- 1/2 tsp. garlic salt
- 1/2 tsp. pepper
- 3 cups canned whole kernel corn, drained
- 2 medium green peppers, sliced into 1-inch pieces
- 1/4 cup cornstarch
- 1/4 cup water
- Shredded part-skim mozzarella cheese

Direction

- On medium heat, cook and crumble the sausage in a big saucepan or Dutch oven until the meat is not pink anymore; drain. Put in celery; cook for 15 mins then drain.
- Add seasonings, tomatoes, zucchini, and tomato juice; boil. Lower the heat; let it simmer for 20 mins while covering. Put in peppers and corn; let it simmer for 15 mins while covering.
- Mix water and cornstarch; mix into the stew then boil. Cook and stir until the mixture is thick. Scatter with cheese.

Nutrition Information

- Calories: 262 calories
- Total Carbohydrate: 29 g
- Cholesterol: 28 mg
- Total Fat: 11 g
- Fiber: 5 g
- Protein: 12 g
- Sodium: 1344 mg

286. Tortellini With Salmon-ricotta Sauce

"This dish pairs well with veggies like carrots and peas or a tomato salad. It tastes good with canned tuna or salmon too."
Serving: 4 servings. | Prep: 15m | Ready in: 30m

Ingredients

- 1 package (9 oz.) refrigerated cheese tortellini
- 2 green onions, sliced
- 1 tsp. butter
- 2 garlic cloves, minced
- 1 tsp. cornstarch
- 1 cup fat-free milk
- 1/2 cup shredded part-skim mozzarella cheese
- 1 cup fat-free ricotta cheese
- 1 pouch (7.1 oz.) boneless skinless pink salmon
- 2 tbsps. snipped fresh dill or 2 tsps. dill weed
- 1-1/2 tsps. grated lemon peel
- 1-1/2 tsps. lemon juice
- 1/4 tsp. salt

Direction

- Cook the tortellini following the package instructions. In the meantime, sauté onions in a big pan with butter until tender. Put in garlic then cook for another minute. Mix milk and cornstarch until smooth; mix into the pan gradually then boil. Cook and stir for 2mins until a bit thick.
- Mix in mozzarella cheese until it melts. Mix in salt, ricotta cheese, lemon juice, salmon, lemon peel, and dill.

- Drain the tortellini then mix into the ricotta sauce. Cook and stir until completely heated.

Nutrition Information

- Calories: 373 calories
- Total Carbohydrate: 40 g
- Cholesterol: 67 mg
- Total Fat: 11 g
- Fiber: 2 g
- Protein: 28 g
- Sodium: 797 mg

287. Turkey Pasta Toss

"You can make a complete meal with this simple and fresh recipe by serving it with Italian bread and salad."
Serving: 6 servings. | Prep: 15m | Ready in: 35m

Ingredients

- 3 cups uncooked penne pasta
- 2 Italian turkey sausage links, casings removed
- 1 large sweet yellow pepper, cut into 1/2-inch strips
- 1 tbsp. olive oil
- 6 garlic cloves, minced
- 4 plum tomatoes, cut into 1-inch chunks
- 20 pitted ripe olives, halved
- 1/4 cup minced fresh basil
- 1/4 tsp. crushed red pepper flakes
- 1/4 tsp. salt
- 1/4 cup shredded Romano cheese

Direction

- Cook the pasta following the package instructions. In the meantime, on medium heat, cook and crumble sausage in a big skillet until the meat is not pink anymore; drain then keep warm.
- Sauté pepper in the same pan with oil until tender-crisp; put in garlic. Cook for another minute. Mix in sausage, tomatoes, salt, olives, pepper flakes, and basil. Drain the pasta then

mix into the skillet; thoroughly heat. Top with sprinkled cheese.

Nutrition Information

- Calories: 249 calories
- Total Carbohydrate: 32 g
- Cholesterol: 24 mg
- Total Fat: 9 g
- Fiber: 3 g
- Protein: 12 g
- Sodium: 480 mg

288. Turkey Penne With Lemon Cream Sauce

"This pasta dish is alive with color and will please even the picky eaters in your household. It packs a good punch and is loaded with satisfying tastes, it is a great way to get some veggies in your young children too!"
Serving: 4 servings. | Prep: 20m | Ready in: 30m

Ingredients

- 2 cups uncooked penne pasta
- 1/2 lb. turkey breast cutlets, cut into 3/4-inch pieces
- 3 tbsps. butter, divided
- 2 cups fresh broccoli florets
- 3 small carrots, thinly sliced
- 2 garlic cloves, minced
- 2 tbsps. all-purpose flour
- 1-1/2 tsps. chicken bouillon granules
- 1/2 tsp. dried thyme
- 1/4 tsp. pepper
- 1/8 tsp. salt
- 2-1/2 cups half-and-half cream
- 1/4 cup lemon juice
- 2 plum tomatoes, seeded and chopped

Direction

- Follow the directions on the package to cook the pasta. While waiting, put 1 tbsp. of butter in a large frying pan and sauté turkey until not pink. Remove the turkey and keep warm. Put the rest of the butter in the same pan and sauté carrots and broccoli until tender and crispy. Add the garlic and cook 1 more minute. Mix in salt, bouillon granules, flour, pepper, and thyme until combined. In a separate bowl, mix lemon juice and cream. Slowly stir cream mixture into the frying pan with broccoli mixture. Heat to a boil. Stirring constantly, cook until thick, 2-3 minutes. Drain water from pasta. Add the pasta to the frying pan. Finally, mix in tomatoes and turkey and heat until completely hot.

Nutrition Information

- Calories: 528 calories
- Total Carbohydrate: 43 g
- Cholesterol: 136 mg
- Total Fat: 25 g
- Fiber: 4 g
- Protein: 28 g
- Sodium: 594 mg

289. Turkey Spaghetti Sauce

"This is rich, relaxed and savory, yet lower in sodium than the jarred meat sauce."
Serving: 7-1/2 cups. | Prep: 25m | Ready in: 01h05m

Ingredients

- 1 lb. Italian turkey sausage links, casings removed
- 1/2 lb. extra-lean ground turkey
- 1-3/4 cups sliced fresh mushrooms
- 1 medium green pepper, chopped
- 1 medium onion, chopped
- 1 can (29 oz.) tomato puree
- 1 can (14-1/2 oz.) diced tomatoes, undrained
- 1 can (6 oz.) tomato paste
- 2 bay leaves
- 1 tbsp. dried oregano
- 1 tsp. garlic powder
- 1 tsp. dried basil
- 1/2 tsp. salt
- 1/4 tsp. pepper
- Hot cooked multigrain spaghetti

Direction

- Crumble the turkey and sausage into a big nonstick skillet coated using the cooking spray. Stir in the mushrooms, onion and green pepper. Sauté over medium heat until no visible pink color on the meat; drain. Mix in the tomatoes, puree, tomato paste, seasonings and bay leaves. Allow the mixture to boil. Lessen the heat; make it to a simmer for half an hour without placing any cover.
- Dispose the bay leaves. Serve preferred amount with spaghetti. Let the remaining sauce cools; place in a freezer containers. This can be stored in the freezer for up to 3 months.
- To prepare the frozen sauce: Thaw in the fridge over the night. Put in a saucepan and heat well.

Nutrition Information

- Calories: 103 calories
- Total Carbohydrate: 9 g
- Cholesterol: 24 mg
- Total Fat: 3 g
- Fiber: 2 g
- Protein: 10 g
- Sodium: 325 mg

290. Tuscan Chicken And Beans

"A great rustic Italian meal."
Serving: 4 servings. | Prep: 15m | Ready in: 30m

Ingredients

- 1 lb. boneless skinless chicken breasts, cut into 3/4-inch pieces
- 2 tsps. minced fresh rosemary or 1/2 tsp. dried rosemary
- 1/4 tsp. salt
- 1/4 tsp. coarsely ground pepper
- 1 cup reduced-sodium chicken broth
- 2 tbsps. sun-dried tomatoes (not packed in oil), chopped

- 1 can (15-1/2 oz.) white kidney or cannellini beans, rinsed and drained

Direction

- Mix pepper, salt, rosemary and chicken in a small bowl. In a big nonstick skillet coated in cooking spray, cook the chicken on medium heat till browned.
- Mix tomatoes and broth in; boil. Lower heat. Simmer for 3-5 minutes, uncovered, till juices are clear. Put beans then heat through.

Nutrition Information

- Calories: 216 calories
- Total Carbohydrate: 17 g
- Cholesterol: 63 mg
- Total Fat: 3 g
- Fiber: 4 g
- Protein: 28 g
- Sodium: 517 mg

291. Where's The Squash Lasagna

"A revised recipe so that the zucchini goes unnoticed."
Serving: 12 servings. | Prep: 40m | Ready in: 01h40m

Ingredients

- 1 lb. ground beef
- 2 large zucchini (about 1 lb.), shredded
- 3/4 cup chopped onion
- 2 garlic cloves, minced
- 1 can (14-1/2 oz.) stewed tomatoes
- 2 cups water
- 1 can (12 oz.) tomato paste
- 1 tbsp. minced fresh parsley
- 1-1/2 tsps. salt
- 1 tsp. sugar
- 1/2 tsp. dried oregano
- 1/2 tsp. pepper
- 9 lasagna noodles, cooked, rinsed and drained
- 1 carton (15 oz.) ricotta cheese
- 2 cups shredded part-skim mozzarella cheese
- 1 cup grated Parmesan cheese

Direction

- Cook the beef, onion, and zucchini in a pan on medium heat until meat is not pink. Put in garlic and cook one minute more. Drain excess grease.
- Mix tomatoes, with lid on, in an electric blender or food processor until smooth. Add to beef mixture. Pour in the tomato paste, water, seasonings and parsley. Let it boil. Turn heat down and let simmer without the lid for half an hour, stirring every now and then.
- Slightly grease a 13x 9-inch baking tray, pour in 1 cup meat sauce. Layer with 3 pastas, 1/3 of meat sauce, 1/2 of ricotta cheese, 1/3 of Parmesan and mozzarella cheeses. Make the layers again. Finish with the remaining pasta, meat sauce, and the cheeses.
- Cover the tray and bake 45 minutes at 350°. Remove cover and bake 15 minutes more until bubbling. Let it sit for 15 minutes before slicing.

Nutrition Information

- Calories: 309 calories
- Total Carbohydrate: 27 g
- Cholesterol: 53 mg
- Total Fat: 13 g
- Fiber: 3 g
- Protein: 21 g
- Sodium: 642 mg

292. White Lasagna

"Chicken, ham, cheese, and asparagus have flavors that are combined well in this one-of-a-kind entrée. This recipe gives an out-of-the-box solution for holiday turkey leftovers! I prefer serving it with a salad and garlic bread."
Serving: 8-10 servings. | Prep: 25m | Ready in: 60m

Ingredients

- 9 lasagna noodles
- 1/4 cup butter, cubed
- 1/3 cup all-purpose flour
- 1 tbsp. minced dried onion

- 1/4 tsp. garlic powder
- 1/8 tsp. pepper
- 2 cups chicken or turkey broth
- 1 cup milk
- 1 cup grated Parmesan or Romano cheese, divided
- 1 can (4 oz.) sliced mushrooms, drained
- 1 package (10 oz.) frozen cut asparagus or 3/4 lb. fresh cut asparagus, cooked and drained
- 2 cups cubed cooked chicken or turkey
- 1 package (6 oz.) sliced or shredded mozzarella cheese
- 6 oz. thinly sliced cooked ham, chopped

Direction

- Follow package instructions to cook noodles. Strain the water. Melt butter in a large saucepan and add onions, flour, garlic powder and pepper. Introduce in milk and broth, and stir until consistency is thick and bubbles appear. Stir into saucepan 1/2 cup of Parmesan cheese. Grease a 13x9-in baking tray, and pour 1/2 cup of sauce into bottom of the tray, making sure it is spread evenly. Mix the remaining sauce with the mushrooms. Layer the tray with 3 noodles. Followed by asparagus, chicken, mozzarella, and approximately a cup of sauce. Continue layering with 3 more noodles, the cooked ham, and half of sauce that remain. Cover with the excess noodles and sauce. Scatter the remaining Parmesan cheese on top. Leave the tray uncovered and bake for 35 minutes at 350 degrees, or until it is thoroughly heated.

Nutrition Information

- Calories: 322 calories
- Total Carbohydrate: 25 g
- Cholesterol: 66 mg
- Total Fat: 15 g
- Fiber: 2 g
- Protein: 24 g
- Sodium: 678 mg

293. Ziti Supper For Two

"This healthy and easy-to-make pasta entree is made with store-bought spaghetti sauce improved with cheese, crisp vegetables, fresh parsley, and olives."
Serving: 2 servings. | Prep: 10m | Ready in: 30m

Ingredients

- 2/3 cup uncooked ziti or small tube pasta
- 1/3 cup chopped green pepper
- 1/4 cup finely chopped onion
- 1/4 cup finely chopped celery
- 1/4 tsp. minced garlic
- 1 tbsp. olive oil
- 1 tbsp. butter
- 1 cup spaghetti sauce with meat
- 2 tbsps. chopped pimiento-stuffed olives
- 2 tbsps. minced fresh parsley
- 1/4 cup shredded cheddar cheese

Direction

- Cook the pasta following the package instructions. In the meantime, sauté garlic, green pepper, celery, and onion for 4-5 mins in a big skillet with butter and oil or until tender.
- Mix in parsley, olives, and spaghetti sauce; boil. Lower the heat; let it simmer for 10-12 mins without a cover or until thoroughly heated. Drain then mix the pasta into the skillet. Scatter with cheese.

Nutrition Information

- Calories: 372 calories
- Total Carbohydrate: 33 g
- Cholesterol: 38 mg
- Total Fat: 23 g
- Fiber: 4 g
- Protein: 11 g
- Sodium: 813 mg

294. Zucchini And Corn-stuffed Chicken

"Serve this easy and flavorful dish with rice or pasta."
Serving: 2 servings. | Prep: 15m | Ready in: 45m

Ingredients

- 1 small zucchini, finely chopped
- 1/4 cup fresh or frozen corn, thawed
- 3 tbsps. grated Parmesan cheese, divided
- 2 boneless skinless chicken breast halves (6 oz. each)
- 1 tsp. olive oil
- 1/8 tsp. salt
- 1/8 tsp. pepper

Direction

- Mix 2 tbsp. cheese, corn, and zucchini in a small bowl. Slice a pocket in each chicken breast; stuff with half cup zucchini mixture on each pocket. Use toothpicks to secure.
- Move to a cooking-spray-coated 8-inch square baking dish. Drizzle with oil then scatter salt, remaining cheese, and pepper. Scoop the rest of the zucchini mixture surrounding the chicken. Bake for 30-35mins in a 350 degrees F oven without a cover or until a thermometer registers 170 degrees F.

Nutrition Information

- Calories: 262 calories
- Total Carbohydrate: 7 g
- Cholesterol: 101 mg
- Total Fat: 9 g
- Fiber: 1 g
- Protein: 39 g
- Sodium: 351 mg

295. Zucchini Pesto With Shrimp And Farfalle

"This summer, use the bountiful produce in making this flavorful and fancy pasta with basil-zucchini pesto."
Serving: 6 servings. | Prep: 25m | Ready in: 40m

Ingredients

- 8 oz. uncooked multigrain bow tie pasta
- 1 lb. zucchini, sliced
- 2 tbsps. olive oil, divided
- 1 cup loosely packed basil leaves
- 1/2 cup shredded Parmigiano-Reggiano or Parmesan cheese, divided
- 3 tbsps. pine nuts, toasted
- 4 garlic cloves, peeled and halved
- 1 large sweet onion, chopped
- 1 lb. peeled and deveined cooked medium shrimp
- 1/2 cup reduced-fat evaporated milk
- 1 tsp. lemon juice
- 1-3/4 tsps. kosher salt
- 1/2 tsp. grated lemon peel
- 1/2 tsp. coarsely ground pepper

Direction

- Cook the pasta following the package instructions. In the meantime, sauté zucchini in a Dutch oven with 1tbsp oil until tender. Take it out of the pan then slightly cool.
- Drain the pasta then set aside 1/3 cup of the pasta liquid. Puree 2/3 cup cooked zucchini, basil, reserved cooking liquid, quarter cup cheese, garlic, and pine nuts in a food processor.
- Cook onion in the same Dutch oven with the remaining oil until tender. Mix in the remaining zucchini, pasta, and shrimp. Toss in the purees mixture, pepper, milk, lemon peel, salt, and lemon juice to coat; completely heat. Top with the remaining cheese.

Nutrition Information

- Calories: 368 calories
- Total Carbohydrate: 37 g

- Cholesterol: 121 mg
- Total Fat: 12 g
- Fiber: 5 g
- Protein: 29 g
- Sodium: 827 mg

Chapter 5: Italian Vegetarian Recipes

***

296. Artichoke Crostini

"Best when basil is fresh, and tomatoes are vine-ripened."
Serving: 32 appetizers. | Prep: 30m | Ready in: 30m

Ingredients

- 1 sourdough baguette (1 lb.)
- 2 cups chopped seeded tomatoes
- 1 can (14 oz.) water-packed artichoke hearts, rinsed, drained and chopped
- 2 tbsps. minced fresh basil
- 2 tbsps. olive oil
- 1/2 tsp. seasoned salt
- 1/8 tsp. pepper

Direction

- Slice the baguette into 32 pieces. Arrange on a baking sheet with no grease. Coat the bread with cooking spray. Bake until bread is crisp for 7 to 10 minutes at 325 degrees. Transfer to a wire rack to cool.
- Combine seasoned salt and pepper, oil, basil, artichokes, and tomatoes in a large bowl. Spoon the mixture on the toast.

Nutrition Information

- Calories: 106 calories

- Total Carbohydrate: 17 g
- Cholesterol: 0 mg
- Total Fat: 3 g
- Fiber: 2 g
- Protein: 3 g
- Sodium: 314 mg

297. Artichoke-red Pepper Tossed Salad

"Serve the dressing with artichoke hearts to complete this basic tossed salad."
Serving: 20-25 servings. | Prep: 15m | Ready in: 15m

Ingredients

- 1 head medium head iceberg lettuce
- 1 bunch romaine, torn
- 1 can (14 oz.) water-packed artichoke hearts, rinsed, drained and chopped
- 2 medium sweet red peppers, julienned
- 1/2 cup thinly sliced red onion
- 1/2 cup olive oil
- 1/2 cup red wine vinegar
- 2 tbsps. Dijon mustard
- 2 tsps. sugar
- 1 tsp. seasoned salt
- 1/2 cup shredded Parmesan cheese

Direction

- Combine the initial 5 ingredients in a large bowl. Combine seasoned salt, sugar, mustard, vinegar and oil in a jar, cover with a tight-fitting lid and shake well. Drizzle the salad with dressing and toss till coated. Sprinkle Parmesan cheese over.

298. Arugula Salad With Shaved Parmesan

"This is a great salad with a pretty combination of fresh peppery arugula, golden raisins, shredded Parmesan and crunchy almonds that brings very unique flavor."
Serving: 4 servings. | Prep: 15m | Ready in: 15m

Ingredients

- 6 cups fresh arugula
- 1/4 cup golden raisins
- 1/4 cup sliced almonds, toasted
- 3 tbsps. olive oil
- 1 tbsp. lemon juice
- 1/4 tsp. salt
- 1/4 tsp. freshly ground pepper
- 1/3 cup shaved or shredded Parmesan cheese

Direction

- Mix together almonds, raisins and arugula in a big bowl. Pour lemon juice and oil over. Sprinkle with pepper and salt then toss to coat well. Split among 4 plates and sprinkle with cheese on top.

Nutrition Information

- Calories: 181 calories
- Total Carbohydrate: 10 g
- Cholesterol: 4 mg
- Total Fat: 15 g
- Fiber: 2 g
- Protein: 4 g
- Sodium: 242 mg

299. Asparagus Linguine

"Asparagus and pasta are tumbled together in this mildly-seasoned dish."
Serving: 4 servings. | Prep: 10m | Ready in: 25m

Ingredients

- 6 oz. uncooked linguine
- 1 small onion, chopped
- 2 garlic cloves, minced
- 1 tbsp. olive oil
- 2 tsps. butter
- 1/2 lb. fresh asparagus, trimmed and cut into 1/2-inch pieces
- 2 tbsps. white wine or chicken broth
- 2 tbsps. grated Parmesan cheese
- 1 tbsp. lemon juice
- 1/4 tsp. salt
- 1/8 tsp. pepper

Direction

- Cook linguine following the package directions. In the meantime, sauté garlic and onion in butter and oil in a nonstick skillet until softened. Add asparagus; cook and stir until crisp-tender for about 2 minutes. Next, pour in the broth or wine; continue to cook and stir until the liquid is reduced for 1-2 minutes. Then, remove from the heat.
- Allow the linguine to drain, then add to the asparagus mixture. Put in the remaining ingredients, then toss to coat. Enjoy immediately.

Nutrition Information

- Calories: 245 calories
- Total Carbohydrate: 36 g
- Cholesterol: 7 mg
- Total Fat: 7 g
- Fiber: 3 g
- Protein: 8 g
- Sodium: 217 mg

300. Asparagus With Fresh Basil Sauce

"This simple asparagus dip is a great addition to any appetizer plate. You can also use it as a sandwich spread."
Serving: 12 servings. | Prep: 10m | Ready in: 15m

Ingredients

- 3/4 cup reduced-fat mayonnaise
- 2 tbsps. prepared pesto
- 1 tbsp. grated Parmesan cheese
- 1 tbsp. minced fresh basil
- 1 tsp. lemon juice
- 1 garlic clove, minced
- 1-1/2 lbs. fresh asparagus, trimmed

Direction

- Combine the first 6 ingredients in a small bowl until incorporated. Chill until ready to serve.
- Boil 12 cups water in a Dutch oven; cook asparagus, in batches, for 2-3mins without cover until tender-crisp. Take the asparagus out then put in ice water right away; drain. Pat the asparagus dry then serve with sauce.

Nutrition Information

- Calories: 72 calories
- Total Carbohydrate: 3 g
- Cholesterol: 6 mg
- Total Fat: 6 g
- Fiber: 1 g
- Protein: 1 g
- Sodium: 149 mg

301. Baked Ziti With Cheese

"This recipe, made in individual serving pans, is a perfect weeknight dinner. It is ziti in a tomato sauce with cheese."
Serving: 8

Ingredients

- 1 (16 oz.) box Barilla® Ziti
- 5 tbsps. butter
- 4 tbsps. all-purpose flour
- 3 cups milk
- 1/2 tsp. ground nutmeg
- 2 tsps. kosher salt
- 2 tbsps. kosher salt (optional)
- 2 cups Barilla® Marinara Sauce
- 1 lb. buffalo mozzarella cheese, cut into 1/4-inch cubes
- 1/2 cup freshly grated Parmigiano-Reggiano cheese
- 1/2 cup fresh breadcrumbs

Direction

- To make bechamel sauce: Melt butter in a medium pot. Stir in flour until smooth. Cook until golden brown on medium heat, 6-7 minutes.
- In the meantime, in a different pan heat milk until it is just about to boil.
- One cup at a time, add milk to the butter mixture, stir constantly until mixture is very smooth and boiling. Cook it 30 seconds and then take away from heat. Season with 2 tsps. salt and nutmeg; set it aside.
- Start preheating oven to 425 degrees F.
- Boil 6 quarts of water in a large pot and, if desired, add 2 tbsps. of salt.
- Cook the ziti 30 seconds less than the package directions say.
- Add mozzarella, bechamel sauce, grated cheese, and marinara sauce to the ziti and stir well.
- Divide the mixture between six gratin individual pans. Sprinkle on bread crumbs.
- Bake until crusty and bubbly on top, 20 minutes. Enjoy immediately.

Nutrition Information

- Calories: 578 calories;
- Total Carbohydrate: 61.6 g
- Cholesterol: 75 mg
- Total Fat: 25.7 g
- Protein: 24.5 g
- Sodium: 2429 mg

302. Balsamic Arugula Salad

"You don't need expensive ingredients to make this tasty salad and making it will take you just a few minutes."
Serving: 4 servings. | Prep: 5m | Ready in: 5m

Ingredients

- 6 cups fresh arugula or baby spinach
- 1/2 cup cherry tomatoes, halved
- 1/4 cup grated Parmesan cheese
- 1/4 cup balsamic vinaigrette

Direction

- Mix cheese, tomatoes, and arugula in a big bowl. Use vinaigrette to sprinkle on and mix to coat. Eat immediately.

Nutrition Information

- Calories: 63 calories
- Total Carbohydrate: 4 g
- Cholesterol: 4 mg
- Total Fat: 4 g
- Fiber: 1 g
- Protein: 3 g
- Sodium: 211 mg

303. Basil Tomato Bread

"Serve spaghetti and sauce or a bowl of soup with this delicious bread. It will surely be gone in a flash."
Serving: 1 loaf (16 slices). | Prep: 15m | Ready in: 01h05m

Ingredients

- 1/2 cup shortening
- 3/4 cup sugar
- 1 large egg
- 2 cups all-purpose flour
- 2-1/2 tsps. baking powder
- 2 tsps. dried basil
- 1 tsp. salt
- 1 cup milk
- 1/2 cup shredded Swiss cheese
- 1/4 cup oil-packed sun-dried tomatoes, chopped

Direction

- Cream sugar and shortening in a big bowl until fluffy and light; stir in egg well. Mix salt, flour, basil, and baking powder; alternately stir with milk into the creamed mixture. Mix in tomatoes and cheese.
- Move to a greased 9-in by 5-in loaf pan. Bake for 50-60mins in a 325 degrees oven until an inserted toothpick in the middle comes out without residue. Cool in the pan for 10mins then move to a wire rack.

Nutrition Information

- Calories: 178 calories
- Total Carbohydrate: 23 g
- Cholesterol: 18 mg
- Total Fat: 8 g
- Fiber: 1 g
- Protein: 4 g
- Sodium: 234 mg

304. Broccoli Fettuccine Alfredo

"This recipe for a side dish is very versatile and is based on a recipe I have had for several years. You can replace the broccoli with carrots, beans, or whatever vegetable is your family's favorite. It can be made into an entrée by adding small chucks of cooked chicken."
Serving: 4 servings. | Prep: 30m | Ready in: 30m

Ingredients

- 1 package (12 oz.) fettuccine
- 1 cup chopped fresh or frozen broccoli
- 3 tbsps. butter
- 1 tbsp. all-purpose flour
- 2/3 cup milk
- 1/4 cup grated Parmesan cheese

Direction

- Follow directions on package to cook the fettuccine. Put about 1 in. of water and broccoli in bottom of a large pot and bring to a boil. Cover, decrease heat, and simmer until crisp and tender, 4-6 minutes. Drain the water off the broccoli. In separate pot, on medium heat melt butter. Mix in flour until smooth, then slowly stir in milk. Boil, stirring constantly until thick, 2 minutes. Remove the pot from the heat and mix in broccoli and Parmesan cheese. Drain the water off the fettuccine and pour broccoli mixture on top.

Nutrition Information

- Calories: 428 calories
- Total Carbohydrate: 64 g
- Cholesterol: 32 mg
- Total Fat: 13 g
- Fiber: 4 g
- Protein: 16 g
- Sodium: 233 mg

305. Broccoli N Tomato Pasta

"A beautiful addition to this filling spaghetti entrée both for the eyes and taste buds is fresh broccoli and tomatoes."
Serving: 4 servings. | Prep: 10m | Ready in: 20m

Ingredients

- 3 quarts water
- 8 oz. uncooked spaghetti
- 2 cups fresh broccoli florets
- 2 large tomatoes, peeled, seeded and coarsely chopped
- 2 garlic cloves, minced
- 1/4 to 1/2 tsp. crushed red pepper flakes
- 2 tbsps. olive oil
- 1/2 cup sliced ripe olives
- 1/2 cup minced fresh parsley
- 1/4 cup grated Romano cheese
- 3/4 tsp. salt
- 1/8 tsp. pepper

Direction

- Boil water in a large frying pan or Dutch oven. Place spaghetti in boiling water and simmer for 5 minutes, uncovered. Mix in broccoli and simmer until broccoli and spaghetti are tender 3-4 minutes. While waiting, sauté pepper flakes, garlic, and tomatoes in nonstick frying pan with oil for 2 minutes. Remove pasta and broccoli and add to the frying pan. Add the rest of the ingredients and mix until coated.

Nutrition Information

- Calories: 348 calories
- Total Carbohydrate: 51 g
- Cholesterol: 7 mg
- Total Fat: 12 g
- Fiber: 4 g
- Protein: 12 g
- Sodium: 688 mg

306. Bruschetta Polenta

"You can find prepared polenta in the Italian, refrigerated section or ethnic section of the grocery store."
Serving: 6 servings. | Prep: 5m | Ready in: 10m

Ingredients

- 1 tube (1 lb.) polenta, cut into 1/2-inch slices
- 1 tbsp. olive oil
- 1 cup bruschetta topping
- 3 tbsps. shredded Parmesan cheese

Direction

- In a large frying pan, cook polenta slices in oil over medium heat for 2 minutes per side or till golden.
- Place in a microwave-safe bowl the bruschetta topping; cook covered on high mode for 1 minute. On each slice of polenta, spoon 1 tbsp.; sprinkle with cheese.

Nutrition Information

- Calories: 116 calories

- Total Carbohydrate: 16 g
- Cholesterol: 2 mg
- Total Fat: 5 g
- Fiber: 1 g
- Protein: 2 g
- Sodium: 603 mg

307. Cannellini Spinach Pasta Salad

"This is a hearty spin of a spinach salad with the adding of pasta shells and white beans inside."
Serving: 10 servings. | Prep: 15m | Ready in: 15m

Ingredients

- 8 cups fresh spinach, coarsely chopped
- 3 cups small shell pasta, cooked and drained
- 1 can (15 oz.) cannellini or white kidney beans
- 3 tbsps. balsamic vinegar
- 2 tbsps. olive oil
- 2 tsps. sugar
- 2 garlic cloves, minced
- 1/2 tsp. salt
- 1/4 tsp. pepper
- 1/2 cup shredded Parmesan cheese

Direction

- Mix together beans, pasta and spinach in a big bowl. Mix together pepper, salt, garlic, sugar, oil and vinegar in a jar with a tight-fitting lid, then shake well together. Drizzle over salad and toss well to coat. Sprinkle with cheese on top and serve promptly.

Nutrition Information

- Calories: 157 calories
- Total Carbohydrate: 21 g
- Cholesterol: 3 mg
- Total Fat: 5 g
- Fiber: 3 g
- Protein: 7 g
- Sodium: 243 mg

308. Cheese & Pumpkin-filled Manicotti

"This soothing and warm recipe is best enjoyed on cold autumn nights. You can also use the filling in stuffed shells, tortellini, and ravioli."
Serving: 7 servings. | Prep: 30m | Ready in: 55m

Ingredients

- 1 package (8 oz.) manicotti shells
- 1 container (15 oz.) ricotta cheese
- 2 cups shredded part-skim mozzarella cheese, divided
- 1 cup canned pumpkin
- 1/4 cup grated Parmesan cheese
- 2 large egg yolks
- 1/4 tsp. ground nutmeg
- 1 jar (24 oz.) garlic pasta sauce, divided

Direction

- Preheat the oven to 350 degrees F. Cook the manicotti shells following the package instructions until al dente; drain.
- Combine nutmeg, ricotta cheese, egg yolks, a cup of mozzarella cheese, Parmesan cheese, and pumpkin in a big bowl; scoop into the manicotti.
- In a greased 13-in by 9-in baking dish, spread a cup of pasta sauce. Add stuffed manicotti on top. Transfer the rest of the pasta sauce on top; scatter the rest of the mozzarella cheese. Bake for 25-30mins while covering or until the cheese melts.

Nutrition Information

- Calories: 392 calories
- Total Carbohydrate: 41 g
- Cholesterol: 100 mg
- Total Fat: 16 g
- Fiber: 4 g
- Protein: 22 g
- Sodium: 704 mg

309. Colorful Grilled Veggies

"Everyone loves this side dish of well-seasoned veggie combination."
Serving: 6 servings. | Prep: 20m | Ready in: 30m

Ingredients

- 10 cherry tomatoes, halved
- 2 celery ribs, thinly sliced
- 1 medium green pepper, sliced
- 1 medium sweet red pepper, sliced
- 1 medium red onion, sliced and separated into rings
- 1 cup sliced fresh mushrooms
- 1 tbsp. red wine vinegar
- 1 tbsp. olive oil
- 1 tsp. lemon juice
- 1 garlic clove, minced
- 1 tsp. dried basil
- 1/2 tsp. salt
- 1/2 tsp. pepper

Direction

- Split the vegetables among two of 18-inch square heavy-duty foil piece. Mix the remaining ingredients in a small bowl; drizzle on top of the vegetables. Fold and seal the foil around the veggies tightly. On medium heat, grill for 10-15 mins while covering or until the veggies are tender-crisp.

Nutrition Information

- Calories: 51 calories
- Total Carbohydrate: 7 g
- Cholesterol: 0 mg
- Total Fat: 3 g
- Fiber: 2 g
- Protein: 1 g
- Sodium: 212 mg

310. Cool Cucumber Pasta

"This salad gets its amazing texture from crispy cucumbers and soft pasta. It's very refreshing and sweet."
Serving: 8-10 servings. | Prep: 20m | Ready in: 20m

Ingredients

- 8 oz. uncooked penne pasta
- 1 tbsp. canola oil
- 2 medium cucumbers, thinly sliced
- 1 medium onion, thinly sliced
- 1-1/2 cups sugar
- 1 cup water
- 3/4 cup white vinegar
- 1 tbsp. prepared mustard
- 1 tbsp. dried parsley flakes
- 1 tsp. salt
- 1 tsp. pepper
- 1/2 tsp. garlic salt

Direction

- Cook pasta as the package directs; strain and use cold water to rinse. In a big bowl, put the cooked pasta and mix in onion, cucumbers, and oil.
- Combine the rest of the ingredients in a small bowl. Put on the salad, mix to combine. Put a cover on and refrigerate for 4 hours, tossing sometimes. Use a slotted spoon to enjoy. Put the leftovers in the fridge.

Nutrition Information

- Calories: 226 calories
- Total Carbohydrate: 50 g
- Cholesterol: 0 mg
- Total Fat: 2 g
- Fiber: 2 g
- Protein: 4 g
- Sodium: 346 mg

311. Corn Relish Salad

"This salad is great for picnics as you grill trout or chicken in the campfire."
Serving: 10 servings. | Prep: 20m | Ready in: 20m

Ingredients

- 2 cups fresh or frozen corn
- 3 medium tomatoes, seeded and chopped
- 1 medium green pepper, diced
- 1/2 cup chopped red onion
- 1/2 cup sliced celery
- 1 can (2-1/4 oz.) sliced ripe olives, drained
- 1 jar (6-1/2 oz.) marinated artichoke hearts, undrained
- 1/4 cup reduced-fat Italian salad dressing
- 5 fresh basil leaves, finely chopped or 1 tsp. dried basil
- 1/2 tsp. garlic powder
- 1/2 tsp. dried oregano
- 1/4 tsp. lemon-pepper seasoning

Direction

- Mix the first 6 ingredients in a big bowl. Mix lemon-pepper, artichoke, oregano, salad dressing, garlic powder, and basil in a separate bowl; gently toss into the corn mixture. Cover then chill for at least 6 hrs then serve.

Nutrition Information

- Calories: 68 calories
- Total Carbohydrate: 13 g
- Cholesterol: 1 mg
- Total Fat: 2 g
- Fiber: 2 g
- Protein: 2 g
- Sodium: 193 mg

312. Cranberry Ricotta Gnocchi With Brown Butter Sauce

"A simple recipe to create light gnocchi."
Serving: 8 servings. | Prep: 30m | Ready in: 35m

Ingredients

- 3/4 cup dried cranberries, divided
- 2 cups ricotta cheese
- 1 cup all-purpose flour
- 1/2 cup grated Parmesan cheese
- 1 egg, lightly beaten
- 3/4 tsp. salt, divided
- 4 quarts water
- 3/4 cup butter, cubed
- 2 tbsps. minced fresh sage
- 1/2 cup chopped walnuts, toasted
- 1/8 tsp. white pepper

Direction

- Chop 1/4 cup of cranberries finely. Blend the chopped cranberries, 1/2 tsp. of salt, egg, Parmesan cheese, flour, and ricotta cheese in a large bowl; combine until mixed. Knead 10-12 times on a lightly floured surface until a soft dough forms. Rest, covered, for 10 minutes.
- Divide the dough into fourths. Roll each portion to a rope with 3/4-inch thickness on a floured surface; cut into 3/4-in. pieces. Using a lightly floured fork, press and roll each piece.
- Allow to boil water in a Dutch oven. Cook the gnocchi in batches until they float for 1/2-1 minute. Use a slotted spoon to remove gnocchi; keep them warm.
- Cook the butter in a large heavy saucepan on medium heat for 5 minutes. Add sage; cook and stir occasionally until the butter turns golden brown for 3-5 more minutes. Stir in the salt, the remaining cranberries, white pepper, and walnuts. Add gnocchi; gently stir to coat.

Nutrition Information

- Calories: 411 calories
- Total Carbohydrate: 26 g
- Cholesterol: 101 mg

- Total Fat: 30 g
- Fiber: 1 g
- Protein: 13 g
- Sodium: 503 mg

313. Crispy Eggplant Bruschetta

"Delicious eggplants topped with cheese. It can be served at room temperature or chilled."
Serving: 1 dozen. | Prep: 25m | Ready in: 45m

Ingredients

- 2 eggs, beaten
- 1/2 cup all-purpose flour
- 1/4 tsp. salt
- 1/4 tsp. pepper
- 1 cup seasoned bread crumbs
- 2 tbsps. grated Parmesan cheese
- 1 large eggplant, peeled and cut into 1/2-inch slices
- 1/3 cup olive oil
- 4 medium tomatoes, finely chopped
- 1/4 cup finely chopped red onion
- 1/2 cup minced fresh basil
- 8 oz. fresh mozzarella cheese, cut into 1/4-inch slices
- 1/2 cup balsamic vinaigrette

Direction

- Prepare 3 shallow bowls. Add eggs to the first bowl, and in the second bowl combine pepper, salt, and flour. In the third bowl, combine Parmesan cheese and breadcrumbs. Dip the eggplants in the bowls following this order: flour mixture, eggs, then bread crumb mixture.
- Cook the eggplants in a large skillet with oil until tender for 4 to 5 minutes on each side. Cook in batches. Transfer to a paper towel to drain excess oil.
- Combine basil, onion, and tomatoes in a small bowl. On each eggplant slice, add mozzarella cheese and the tomato mixture on top. Then drizzle some vinaigrette.

Nutrition Information

- Calories: 204 calories
- Total Carbohydrate: 15 g
- Cholesterol: 51 mg
- Total Fat: 13 g
- Fiber: 3 g
- Protein: 7 g
- Sodium: 267 mg

314. Cucumber-dill Pasta Salad

"This tasty salad takes no time to prepare. Combining with veggies, pasta, and cucumber salad dressing to have a fresh taste."
Serving: 4-6 servings. | Prep: 10m | Ready in: 10m

Ingredients

- 3 cups cooked pasta
- 1/2 cup thinly sliced carrot
- 1/2 cup thinly sliced celery
- 1 cup parboiled broccoli florets
- 1 green onion, thinly sliced
- 1/4 cup chopped onion
- 1/2 to 3/4 cup bottled cucumber salad dressing
- 1 tsp. dill weed
- Salt and pepper to taste

Dirzction

- In a big salad bowl, mix together all ingredients. Refrigerate until eating.

Nutrition Information

- Calories: 205 calories
- Total Carbohydrate: 24 g
- Cholesterol: 0 mg
- Total Fat: 11 g
- Fiber: 2 g
- Protein: 4 g
- Sodium: 164 mg

315. Dill Vinaigrette

"A delicious dip."
Serving: 2 | Prep: 15m | Ready in: 15m

Ingredients

- 1/4 cup vegetable oil
- 2 tbsps. red wine vinegar
- 1 1/2 tsps. white sugar
- 1/2 tsp. dried dill weed
- 1/8 tsp. salt
- 1/8 tsp. onion powder
- 1/8 tsp. garlic powder
- 1/8 tsp. dry mustard
- 1/8 tsp. ground black pepper

Direction

- Blend pepper, oil, dry mustard, vinegar, garlic powder, sugar, onion powder, salt, and dill weed in a blender until smooth. Cover then put in the fridge till chilled.

Nutrition Information

- Calories: 264 calories;
- Total Carbohydrate: 5.2 g
- Cholesterol: 0 mg
- Total Fat: 27.6 g
- Protein: 0.2 g
- Sodium: 147 mg

316. Four-cheese Spinach Pizza

"This is my version of a recipe from my aunt. The key to the flavor is fresh basil and spinach; therefore, this pizza is a good one to make in the summer."
Serving: 6 servings. | Prep: 15m | Ready in: 30m

Ingredients

- 2 packages (10 oz. each) fresh spinach
- 3/4 cup shredded part-skim mozzarella cheese, divided
- 1/2 cup fat-free cottage cheese
- 1/3 cup grated Parmesan cheese
- 1/4 tsp. salt
- 1/8 tsp. pepper
- 1 prebaked 12-inch thin pizza crust
- 1 medium tomato, chopped
- 1/4 cup chopped green onions
- 1/4 cup sliced ripe olives
- 1 tsp. minced fresh basil
- 1 tsp. olive oil
- 1 tsp. balsamic vinegar
- 1 garlic clove, minced
- 1/2 cup crumbled feta cheese

Direction

- Sauté spinach in a big greased frying pan until wilted, 2-3 minutes; remove from the pan. Let it cool a little; cut up.
- Mix Parmesan, 1/4 cup mozzarella, and cottage cheese in a big bowl. Mix in pepper, spinach, and salt. Spread on crust close to edge, within a 1/2 inch.
- Mix garlic, olives, tomato, vinegar, onions, oil, and basil in a big bowl; sprinkle on spinach mixture.
- Put the remaining mozzarella and feta cheese on top. Bake in a 400-degree oven until cheese is light brown and softens, 12-14 minutes.

Nutrition Information

- Calories: 270 calories
- Total Carbohydrate: 28 g
- Cholesterol: 24 mg
- Total Fat: 11 g
- Fiber: 1 g
- Protein: 17 g
- Sodium: 823 mg

317. Garlic Parmesan Orzo

"The Parmesan cheese and garlic does stand out in this dish."
Serving: 8 servings. | Prep: 5m | Ready in: 15m

Ingredients

- 2 cups uncooked orzo pasta
- 3 tsps. minced garlic
- 1/2 cup butter, cubed
- 1/2 cup grated Parmesan cheese
- 1/4 cup 2% milk
- 2 tbsps. minced fresh parsley
- 1 tsp. salt
- 1/4 tsp. pepper

Direction

- Cook orzo following the package directions; allow to drain. Sauté garlic in butter in a large skillet until softened. Add milk, Parmesan cheese, the orzo, pepper, salt, and parsley. Next, cook and stir until heated through.

Nutrition Information

- Calories: 321 calories
- Total Carbohydrate: 40 g
- Cholesterol: 36 mg
- Total Fat: 14 g
- Fiber: 2 g
- Protein: 9 g
- Sodium: 513 mg

318. Gnocchi Alfredo

"This comfort food is best prepared for potlucks and get-togethers in winter."
Serving: 5 servings. | Prep: 10m | Ready in: 25m

Ingredients

- 2 lbs. potato gnocchi
- 3 tbsps. butter, divided
- 1 tbsp. plus 1-1/2 tsps. all-purpose flour
- 1-1/2 cups whole milk
- 1/2 cup grated Parmesan cheese
- Dash ground nutmeg
- 1/2 lb. sliced baby portobello mushrooms
- Minced fresh parsley, optional

Direction

- Cook the gnocchi following the package instructions; drain. In the meantime, melt 1 tbsp. of butter in a small saucepan. Mix in flour until smooth then add milk while stirring gradually; boil while constantly mixing. Cook and stir for 1-2 mins or until thick. Take off the heat; mix in nutmeg and cheese until combined. Keep warm.
- On medium heat, melt the remaining butter in a big heavy skillet. Heat for 5-7 mins while constantly mixing or until golden brown. Add gnocchi and mushrooms immediately; cook and stir for 4-5 mins or until the gnocchi are slightly brown and the mushrooms are tender. Serve with sauce. Top with sprinkled parsley if desired.

Nutrition Information

- Calories: 529 calories
- Total Carbohydrate: 81 g
- Cholesterol: 46 mg
- Total Fat: 14 g
- Fiber: 5 g
- Protein: 19 g
- Sodium: 996 mg

319. Green Beans Provencale

"This dish is a perfect combination of garlic, tomatoes and olive oil with green beans."
Serving: 5 servings. | Prep: 20m | Ready in: 30m

Ingredients

- 1 lb. fresh green beans, trimmed and cut into 2-inch pieces
- 4 green onions, sliced
- 2 tbsps. minced shallot
- 4 garlic cloves, minced

- 2 tsps. minced fresh rosemary or 1/2 tsp. dried rosemary, crushed
- 1 tbsp. olive oil
- 1-1/2 cups grape tomatoes, halved
- 2 tbsps. minced fresh or 2 tsps. dried basil
- 1/2 tsp. salt
- 1/4 tsp. pepper

Direction

- In a steamer basket, add beans, then put over 1 inch of water in a big saucepan. Bring to a boil, cover and steam until tender-crisp, about 4 to 5 minutes.
- At the same time, sauté rosemary, garlic, shallot and onions in oil in a big skillet until vegetables are softened. Add pepper, salt, basil, tomatoes and green beans, then sauté until heated through, about 2 to 3 minutes more.

Nutrition Information

- Calories: 70 calories
- Total Carbohydrate: 10 g
- Cholesterol: 0 mg
- Total Fat: 3 g
- Fiber: 4 g
- Protein: 2 g
- Sodium: 248 mg

320. Herbed Cheesecake

"This savory cheesecake is perfect for the holidays."
Serving: 24 servings. | Prep: 15m | Ready in: 01h10m

Ingredients

- 3 packages (8 oz. each) cream cheese, softened
- 2 cups (16 oz.) sour cream, divided
- 1 can (10-3/4 oz.) condensed cream of celery soup, undiluted
- 3 eggs
- 1/2 cup grated Romano cheese
- 3 garlic cloves, minced
- 1 tbsp. cornstarch
- 2 tbsps. minced fresh basil or 2 tsps. dried basil
- 1 tbsp. minced fresh thyme or 1 tsp. dried thyme
- 1/2 tsp. Italian seasoning
- 1/2 tsp. coarsely ground pepper
- Assorted crackers

Direction

- Beat soup, a cup of sour cream, and cream cheese in a big bowl until smooth. Beat in pepper, eggs, Italian seasoning, Romano cheese, thyme, garlic, basil, and cornstarch until combined.
- Transfer to a greased nine-inch springform pan then put the pan on a baking sheet. Bake for 55-60mins in a 350 degrees oven until nearly set in the middle. Cool for 10mins on a wire rack. Slide a knife carefully around the edge of the pan to loosen the cheesecake. Cool for another hour.
- Chill for at least four hours to overnight; remove the pan sides. Slather the remaining sour cream on top. Serve the cheesecake with crackers. Chill any leftovers.

Nutrition Information

- Calories: 142 calories
- Total Carbohydrate: 3 g
- Cholesterol: 66 mg
- Total Fat: 12 g
- Fiber: 0 g
- Protein: 4 g
- Sodium: 183 mg

321. Herbed Pasta Sauce

"In my opinion, this garden-fresh pasta sauce is better than any variety carried in stores. It is definitely my go to throughout the summer."

Serving: about 3 servings (2-1/2 cups sauce). | Prep: 15m | Ready in: 15m

Ingredients

- 1 medium onion, chopped
- 3 to 4 celery ribs, chopped
- 2 tbsps. olive oil
- 2 cups chopped fresh tomatoes
- 2 garlic cloves, minced
- 2 tbsps. minced fresh parsley or 2 tsps. dried parsley flakes
- 1 tbsp. minced fresh oregano or 1 tsp. dried oregano
- 1 to 3 tsps. minced fresh cilantro
- 1 tsp. sugar
- Hot cooked pasta

Direction

- In oil, sauté celery and onion in a large pot until tender. Add oregano, sugar, tomatoes, cilantro, parsley, and garlic. Bring to a boil, and simmer for 5 minutes. Pour over pasta to eat.

Nutrition Information

- Calories: 142 calories
- Total Carbohydrate: 14 g
- Cholesterol: 0 mg
- Total Fat: 10 g
- Fiber: 3 g
- Protein: 2 g
- Sodium: 49 mg

322. Herbed Tomatoes

"This simple and delicious salad is very great for lunch when using with butter and French bread or use as a quick appetizer with double size."

Serving: 2 servings. | Prep: 15m | Ready in: 15m

Ingredients

- 2 medium tomatoes, cut into thin slices
- 2 slices sweet onion, separated into rings
- 4 tsps. olive oil
- 1-1/2 tsps. lemon juice
- 1/4 tsp. minced garlic
- 1 tsp. each minced fresh tarragon, basil and parsley
- Salt and pepper to taste

Direction

- Mix together onion and tomatoes in a bowl. Mix pepper, salt, herbs, garlic, lemon juice and oil together in a separate bowl. Drizzle over onion and tomatoes and gently stir to coat.

Nutrition Information

- Calories: 116 calories
- Total Carbohydrate: 8 g
- Cholesterol: 0 mg
- Total Fat: 10 g
- Fiber: 2 g
- Protein: 1 g
- Sodium: 14 mg

323. Honey-garlic Angel Hair

"One of my colleagues gave me this recipe. It's season beautifully with basil and garlic. It's also sweet with some honey."

Serving: 8 servings. | Prep: 5m | Ready in: 10m

Ingredients

- 1 package (16 oz.) angel hair pasta
- 2 to 3 garlic cloves, minced
- 1/2 cup butter, cubed

- 1/4 cup honey
- 1 tsp. dried basil
- 1 tsp. dried thyme
- 1/4 cup grated Parmesan cheese

Direction

- Cook pasta following the package instructions. In the meantime, sauté garlic with butter in a skillet, for 1 minute. Mix in thyme, basil, and honey.
- Strain the pasta, put into the garlic mixture and stir to coat. Use cheese to sprinkle.

Nutrition Information

- Calories: 356 calories
- Total Carbohydrate: 52 g
- Cholesterol: 33 mg
- Total Fat: 13 g
- Fiber: 2 g
- Protein: 9 g
- Sodium: 167 mg

324. Italian Cheese Twists

"These easy-to-make, elegant, and delicate breadsticks are made with bread dough. You'll surely love the taste of herbs in it."
Serving: 2 dozen. | Prep: 15m | Ready in: 25m

Ingredients

- 1 loaf (1 lb.) frozen bread dough, thawed
- 1/4 cup butter, softened
- 1/4 tsp. garlic powder
- 1/4 tsp. each dried basil, oregano and marjoram
- 3/4 cup shredded part-skim mozzarella cheese
- 1 egg
- 1 tbsp. water
- 2 tbsps. sesame seeds and/or grated Parmesan cheese

Direction

- Roll dough on a lightly floured surface to a 12-inch square. Mix seasonings and butter; slather over the dough then top with mozzarella cheese. Fold the dough into 1/3 then slice into 24 half-inch strips crosswise. Twist the strips two times then seal by pinching the ends; arrange on a greased baking sheet, two inches apart.
- Set aside in a warm area for half an hour while covered until it rises and doubles. Whisk water and eggs in a small bowl; slather on the twists. Scatter sesame seeds or/and Parmesan cheese all over. Bake for 10-12mins in a 375 degrees oven until pale golden.

Nutrition Information

- Calories: 173 calories
- Total Carbohydrate: 20 g
- Cholesterol: 33 mg
- Total Fat: 8 g
- Fiber: 1 g
- Protein: 7 g
- Sodium: 303 mg

325. Italian Herb Salad Dressing

"This delicious vinaigrette is a perfect topping for different salad greens."
Serving: 10 servings. | Prep: 5m | Ready in: 5m

Ingredients

- 3/4 cup olive oil
- 1/2 cup red wine vinegar
- 1 tbsp. grated Parmesan or Romano cheese
- 1 garlic clove, minced
- 1/2 tsp. salt
- 1/2 tsp. sugar
- 1/2 tsp. dried oregano
- Pinch pepper

Direction

- Combine all the ingredients in a jar with a tight-fitting lid; shake well. Chill in the refrigerator until ready to use. Shake the jar of dressing again just before serving.

Nutrition Information

- Calories: 150 calories
- Total Carbohydrate: 1 g
- Cholesterol: 0 mg
- Total Fat: 16 g
- Fiber: 0 g
- Protein: 0 g
- Sodium: 127 mg

326. Italian Side Salad

"You only need 4 simple ingredients to make this quick side salad that will liven up your chicken dishes."
Serving: 6 servings. | Prep: 5m | Ready in: 5m

Ingredients

- 1 package (5 oz.) spring mix salad greens
- 2 tbsps. sliced ripe olives, drained
- 1/4 cup Italian salad dressing or salad dressing of your choice
- 1/4 cup chopped walnuts

Direction

- Mix olives and salad greens in a big salad bowl; toss in dressing. Top with walnuts then serve right away.

Nutrition Information

- Calories: 75 calories
- Total Carbohydrate: 2 g
- Cholesterol: 0 mg
- Total Fat: 7 g
- Fiber: 1 g
- Protein: 1 g
- Sodium: 199 mg

327. Linguine With Artichoke-tomato Sauce

"This is the perfect choice when a toss-together pasta entrée is needed. The tomatoes are enhanced by the marinated artichokes. Since the sauce is tasty, the meat will not be missed."
Serving: 6 servings. | Prep: 15m | Ready in: 30m

Ingredients

- 12 oz. uncooked linguine
- 1 can (28 oz.) whole tomatoes with basil
- 1 jar (7-1/2 oz.) marinated quartered artichoke hearts
- 1 cup chopped sweet onion
- 2 garlic cloves, minced
- 3 tbsps. olive oil, divided
- 1/4 cup capers
- 1/4 cup tomato paste
- 8 fresh basil leaves, torn
- 2 tsps. sugar
- 1/2 tsp. salt
- 1/4 tsp. pepper
- Grated Parmesan cheese

Dirzection

- Follow directions on package to cook linguine.
- In the meantime, chop tomatoes coarsely, keep the liquid. Drain the artichokes, keep 1/4 cup of the marinade. Put 2 tbsps. oil in a big frying pan, sauté garlic and onion until tender. Add tomato paste, reserved artichoke marinade, basil, pepper, reserved tomato liquid, capers, tomatoes, sugar, artichokes, and salt.
- Heat to a boil. Do not cover, decrease heat, and simmer until slightly thick, 10 minutes. Drain water from linguine and move to a big bowl. Toss with remaining oil and tomato mixture. Sprinkle on cheese.

Nutrition Information

- Calories: 375 calories
- Total Carbohydrate: 56 g
- Cholesterol: 0 mg
- Total Fat: 14 g

- Fiber: 4 g
- Protein: 10 g
- Sodium: 740 mg

328. Makeover Penne With Vodka Cream Sauce

"A rich and creamy makeover Penne with Vodka Cream Sauce recipe with less cholesterol and fat."
Serving: 8 servings. | Prep: 15m | Ready in: 55m

Ingredients

- 1 large onion, chopped
- 1 tbsp. olive oil
- 4 garlic cloves, minced
- 2 cans (one 28 oz., one 14.5 oz.) diced tomatoes
- 1/4 cup vodka
- 1 package (12 oz.) whole wheat penne pasta
- 2 tsps. prepared pesto
- 1/4 tsp. salt
- 1/4 tsp. crushed red pepper flakes
- 2 tbsps. all-purpose flour
- 1/2 cup heavy whipping cream
- 1 cup whole milk
- 1/2 cup shredded Parmesan cheese

Direction

- Sauté the onion oil in a big saucepan until it becomes tender, then add garlic and let it cook for 1 minute more. Stir in vodka and tomatoes, then boil. Lower the heat and let it simmer for 30 to 35 minutes without cover or until it turns a bit thick, stirring from time to time.
- In the meantime, cook the penne following the package instructions.
- Stir the pepper flakes, salt and pesto into the tomato mixture. Mix together the cream and flour in a small bowl until it becomes smooth, then mix it into the pan. Add milk, then boil. Let it cook and stir for 2 minutes or until it becomes a bit thick. Drain the penne and serve it with the sauce. Sprinkle cheese on top.

Nutrition Information

- Calories: 324 calories
- Total Carbohydrate: 44 g
- Cholesterol: 27 mg
- Total Fat: 11 g
- Fiber: 7 g
- Protein: 12 g
- Sodium: 379 mg

329. Meatless Spinach Lasagna

"Impress the crowd with this cheesy and hearty dish. It can also be made as long as a week in advance. Serve with salad and crusty bread."
Serving: 12 servings. | Prep: 45m | Ready in: 01h50m

Ingredients

- 1/3 cup butter, cubed
- 1/3 cup all-purpose flour
- 3-3/4 cups half-and-half cream
- 1 cup heavy whipping cream
- 3/4 cup grated Parmesan cheese, divided
- 2 cartons (15 oz. each) ricotta cheese
- 1 package (10 oz.) frozen chopped spinach, thawed and squeezed dry
- 3/4 cup shredded carrot
- 12 no-cook lasagna noodles
- 2 cups shredded part-skim mozzarella cheese
- 1/2 cup seasoned bread crumbs
- 1 tbsp. butter, melted

Direction

- Melt butter in a big pot; mix in flour until it is smooth. Slowly pour in creams then boil. Cook and mix for 2 mins until the mixture is thick. Mix in half cup Parmesan cheese.
- Mix remaining Parmesan cheese, ricotta cheese, carrot, and spinach together in a big bowl.
- In a 13-inch by 9-inch greased baking dish, pour in 3/4 cup sauce mixture then add 4 noodles on top. Let the noodles overlap a little. Spread 1/2 of the ricotta mixture, a cup of

sauce, and 2/3 cup of mozzarella. Repeat process. Layer left noodles, sauce, and mozzarella. Mix butter and breadcrumbs together; spread the mixture on top of the lasagna until full.
- Bake in a 375 degrees F oven, covered, for 55 mins. Remove cover and bake for another 10-15 mins until the dish is bubbly. Set aside for 15 mins then cut.

Nutrition Information

- Calories: 503 calories
- Total Carbohydrate: 29 g
- Cholesterol: 124 mg
- Total Fat: 33 g
- Fiber: 2 g
- Protein: 22 g
- Sodium: 431 mg

330. Mini Italian Herb Bread

"This yummy bread is great paired with a delicious Italian meal! They are just so yummy that they're gone before you know it!"
Serving: 1 loaf (3/4 lb.). | Prep: 15m | Ready in: 60m

Ingredients

- 1/2 cup water (80° to 90°)
- 1 tbsp. canola oil
- 1-1/3 cups bread flour
- 1 tbsp. grated Parmesan cheese
- 2 tsps. sugar
- 1 tsp. dried minced onion
- 1 tsp. dried parsley flakes
- 1/2 tsp. dried basil
- 1/4 tsp. salt
- 1/4 tsp. garlic powder
- 2-1/4 tsps. bread machine or quick-rise yeast

Direction

- Put all the ingredients together into a small bread machine pan following the order recommended by the manufacturer. Choose the Basic Bread setting on the machine. Follow the instructions on the bread machine to bake the bread (after 5 minutes of the cycle, check on the dough and put 1-2 tbsps. of flour or water if necessary).

Nutrition Information

- Calories: 205 calories
- Total Carbohydrate: 35 g
- Cholesterol: 1 mg
- Total Fat: 4 g
- Fiber: 2 g
- Protein: 6 g
- Sodium: 173 mg

331. Mushroom Bread

"This baked crescent dough with cheese and mushrooms is the perfect party food, especially when served with hot sauce or garlic butter."
Serving: 12 servings. | Prep: 10m | Ready in: 25m

Ingredients

- 1 tube (8 oz.) refrigerated crescent rolls
- 2 cups thinly sliced fresh mushrooms
- 1 tbsp. butter, melted
- 1/2 cup grated Parmesan cheese
- 1/2 tsp. Italian seasoning
- 1/8 tsp. pepper

Direction

- Preheat the oven to 350 degrees F. Unroll the crescent dough on an ungreased baking sheet into a long rectangle; press and seal the perforations. Use a fork to prick the dough for a few times; bake for 5 mins
- In the meantime, mix melted butter and mushrooms in a bowl; put on the crust. Scatter with seasonings and cheese. Bake for another 12-14 mins or until the crust is golden brown. Slice into a dozen pieces.

Nutrition Information

- Calories: 100 calories

- Total Carbohydrate: 8 g
- Cholesterol: 5 mg
- Total Fat: 6 g
- Fiber: 0 g
- Protein: 3 g
- Sodium: 209 mg

332. One-pan Tuscan Ravioli

"Chickpeas can be used instead of cannellini beans, grated Asiago or Provolone instead of Parmesan. Very flexible."
Serving: 4 servings. | Prep: 10m | Ready in: 25m

Ingredients

- 1 tbsp. olive oil
- 2 cups cubed eggplant (1/2 inch)
- 1 can (14-1/2 oz.) Italian diced tomatoes, undrained
- 1 can (14-1/2 oz.) reduced-sodium chicken broth
- 1 medium zucchini, halved lengthwise and cut into 1/2-inch slices
- 1 package (9 oz.) refrigerated cheese ravioli
- 1 can (15 oz.) cannellini beans, rinsed and drained
- Shredded Parmesan cheese
- Thinly sliced fresh basil

Direction

- Heat oil in a big skillet over medium heat; sauté eggplant till browned lightly for 2 to 3 minutes.
- Mix in zucchini, broth and tomatoes; boil. Put the ravioli; allow to cook without cover over medium heat till ravioli are soft for 7 to 9 minutes, mixing from time to time. Mix in beans; heat through. Scatter basil and cheese over.

Nutrition Information

- Calories: 376 calories
- Total Carbohydrate: 56 g
- Cholesterol: 36 mg

- Total Fat: 10 g
- Fiber: 8 g
- Protein: 16 g
- Sodium: 1096 mg

333. Onion Tomato Soup

"This low-fat vegetarian soup tastes even better when it's cold out."
Serving: 6 servings. | Prep: 10m | Ready in: 50m

Ingredients

- 2 cups thinly sliced onions
- 4 tsps. olive oil
- 2-2/3 cups tomato juice
- 2 cups water
- 2 tbsps. minced fresh basil
- 2 tsps. minced fresh oregano
- 1 tsp. sugar
- 1 tsp. celery salt
- 2 cups diced seeded plum tomatoes

Direction

- Sauté onion in oil until softened in a large saucepan. Add celery salt, sugar, oregano, basil, water, and tomato juice. Boil, then reduce the heat; uncover, simmer for 20 minutes, stirring infrequently. Next, add tomatoes and cook for 10 minutes more.

Nutrition Information

- Calories: 82 calories
- Total Carbohydrate: 13 g
- Cholesterol: 0 mg
- Total Fat: 3 g
- Fiber: 3 g
- Protein: 2 g
- Sodium: 265 mg

334. Oregano Garlic Bread

"Use your leftover sub rolls in this simple recipe."
Serving: 2 servings. | Prep: 5m | Ready in: 30m

Ingredients

- 4-1/2 tsps. butter, softened
- 1/4 tsp. garlic powder
- 1/8 tsp. onion powder
- 1/8 tsp. dried oregano
- 1/8 tsp. paprika
- 1 submarine bun (about 6 inches), halved lengthwise

Direction

- Mix seasonings and butter in a small bowl; spread on the bun's cut sides. Arrange the bun on an ungreased baking sheet; bake for 10-15mins in a 350 degrees F oven or until toasted.

Nutrition Information

- Calories: 271 calories
- Total Carbohydrate: 34 g
- Cholesterol: 23 mg
- Total Fat: 12 g
- Fiber: 2 g
- Protein: 6 g
- Sodium: 465 mg

335. Parmesan Cloverleaf Rolls

"These gorgeous and flavorful brown rolls are made with a simple hot roll mix plus garlic powder, pizza seasoning and Parmesan on top."
Serving: 1 dozen. | Prep: 15m | Ready in: 30m

Ingredients

- 1 package (16 oz.) hot roll mix
- 2 tbsps. butter, melted
- 1/4 cup grated Parmesan cheese
- 2 tsps. pizza seasoning or Italian seasoning
- 1/4 tsp. garlic powder

Direction

- Prepare the roll mix following the package instructions. Split the dough to 12 parts then split each part into three portions; form each into a ball. Put 3 balls on each cup of a dozen well-greased muffin cups. Slather butter.
- Mix garlic powder, pizza seasoning, and cheese; scatter on top of the dough then cover. Set aside for 10-15mins in a warm area to rise.
- Bake for 15-20mins in a 375 degrees oven until golden brown. Take the rolls out of the pan then move to a wire rack. Serve rolls warm.

Nutrition Information

- Calories: 163 calories
- Total Carbohydrate: 27 g
- Cholesterol: 6 mg
- Total Fat: 4 g
- Fiber: 1 g
- Protein: 5 g
- Sodium: 302 mg

336. Parmesan Fondue

"A recipe that is easy to make and tasty like you use too much time making it. So delicious with little meatballs, vegetables or bread cubes. This is a perfect base to make your own version twist with seasonings or other cheese. Test with different cheese you desire; it's really great with a little sharp cheddar, or even Asiago, Romano cheese. Add a touch of hot sauce or cayenne pepper for an extra kick."
Serving: 14 | Prep: 5m | Ready in: 10m

Ingredients

- 1 (8 oz.) package Neufchatel cheese
- 1 cup milk
- 3/4 cup grated Parmesan cheese
- 1/2 tsp. garlic salt
- 1 small loaf French bread, cut into cubes

Direction

- Place a saucepan on the stove and turn on to medium-low heat and pour milk and neufchatel cream cheese together and stir for 2 to 3 minutes until melted. Add in garlic salt and parmesan cheese. Stir and cook for 2 to 3 minutes more until Parmesan melts. Pair with bread cubes when served.

Nutrition Information

- Calories: 116 calories;
- Total Carbohydrate: 10.6 g
- Cholesterol: 17 mg
- Total Fat: 5.6 g
- Protein: 5.7 g
- Sodium: 307 mg

337. Parmesan Herbed Noodles

"This tasty dish can taste even better when slightly add 1/4 cup of peas, cooked green and red pepper strips."
Serving: 2 servings. | Prep: 10m | Ready in: 20m

Ingredients

- 1-1/2 cups uncooked wide egg noodles
- 2 tbsps. shredded Parmesan cheese
- 1 tbsp. butter
- 1 tbsp. olive oil
- 2 tsps. minced fresh basil or 1/2 tsp. dried basil
- 1/2 tsp. minced fresh thyme or 1/8 tsp. dried thyme
- 1 garlic clove, minced
- 1/4 tsp. salt

Direction

- Following the package instructions, cook the noodles in a small saucepan; let drain. Add the remaining ingredients and toss to coat.

Nutrition Information

- Calories: 243 calories
- Total Carbohydrate: 21 g
- Cholesterol: 46 mg
- Total Fat: 15 g
- Fiber: 1 g

- Protein: 6 g
- Sodium: 444 mg

338. Pasta Salad With Poppy Seed Dressing

"This is a great pasta salad with the addition of poppy seed dressing that makes it even more delicious."
Serving: 16-18 servings. | Prep: 20m | Ready in: 20m

Ingredients

- 1 package (16 oz.) bow tie or small tube pasta
- 1 cup shredded cheddar cheese
- 2 cups broccoli florets
- 1 cup sliced carrots
- 1 cup diced cucumber
- 1 cup halved cherry tomatoes
- 1/2 cup chopped green onions
- DRESSING:
- 1/2 cup cider vinegar
- 1/2 cup sugar
- 1 garlic clove, minced
- 1 green onion, chopped
- 1/2 tsp. ground mustard
- 1/2 tsp. salt
- 1 cup vegetable oil
- 4 tsps. poppy seeds

Direction

- Follow the package directions to cook the pasta, then drain and rinse under cold water. Transfer into a big bowl, then put in onions, tomatoes, cucumber, carrots, broccoli and cheese. Mix together the salt, mustard, onion, garlic, sugar and vinegar in a blender, then pour the oil slowly and blend until smooth. Put poppy seeds, then pour over pasta mixture and toss. Cover and chill for a minimum of 1 hour.

Nutrition Information

- Calories: 255 calories
- Total Carbohydrate: 27 g

- Cholesterol: 7 mg
- Total Fat: 15 g
- Fiber: 2 g
- Protein: 5 g
- Sodium: 111 mg

339. Pasta With Marinara Sauce

"Simmer this marinara sauce that is full of vegetables in your slow cooker. You easily make a dish when you mix it with whole-grain pasta."
Serving: 8 | Prep: 20m | Ready in: 4h20m

Ingredients

- 1 (28 oz.) can whole Italian-style tomatoes, cut up and undrained
- 4 medium carrots, coarsely chopped (2 cups)
- 3 stalks celery, sliced (1½ cups)
- 1 large onion, chopped (1 cup)
- 2 small green bell peppers, chopped (1 cup)
- 1 (6 oz.) can no-salt-added tomato paste
- ½ cup water
- 2 tsps. sugar (optional)
- 2 tsps. dried Italian seasoning, crushed
- 3 cloves garlic, minced
- ½ tsp. salt
- ¼ tsp. black pepper
- 1 bay leaf
- 4 cups hot cooked whole-grain spaghetti (8 oz. dried)
- 1 oz. Parmesan cheese, shaved into shards
- Fresh herb sprigs (optional)

Direction

- Combine bay leaf, tomatoes, black pepper, carrots, salt, celery, garlic, onion, Italian seasoning, bell peppers, sugar if using, water, and tomato paste in a 3 1/2 or 4-qt slow cooker.
- Cook for 8-10hrs on low or 4-5hrs on high while covered.
- Remove the bay leaf. Serve sauce on top of hot cooked pasta with sprinkled Parmesan on top. Top with herb sprigs to garnish if desired.

Nutrition Information

- Calories: 188 calories;
- Total Carbohydrate: 35 g
- Cholesterol: 2 mg
- Total Fat: 2 g
- Fiber: 6 g
- Protein: 9 g
- Sodium: 401 mg
- Sugar: 10 g
- Saturated Fat: 1 g

340. Pinwheel Pizza Snacks

"Fantastic pizza snacks for appetizers."
Serving: 16 appetizers. | Prep: 15m | Ready in: 30m

Ingredients

- 1 tube (8 oz.) refrigerated crescent rolls
- 1/3 cup pizza sauce
- 1/4 cup grated Parmesan cheese
- 1/2 cup chopped seeded tomatoes
- 1/3 cup shredded part-skim mozzarella cheese
- Fresh basil leaves, thinly sliced

Direction

- Unroll crescent dough to one long rectangle. Seal perforations and seams. Within 1-in. of edges, spread with pizza sauce. Sprinkle on parmesan cheese. Roll up, beginning with a short side, like a jellyroll. Seal by pinching seams. Cut to 16 slices.
- Put pinwheels on a greased baking sheet, cut side down. Put mozzarella cheese and tomatoes on each top. Bake for 11-13 minutes or until cheese melts and golden brown at 375 degrees. Sprinkle basil on top.

Nutrition Information

- Calories: 67 calories
- Total Carbohydrate: 7 g
- Cholesterol: 3 mg
- Total Fat: 3 g
- Fiber: 0 g

- Protein: 2 g
- Sodium: 163 mg

341. Quick Fettuccini Alfredo

Serving: 4 servings. | Prep: 10m | Ready in: 20m

Ingredients

- 8 oz. uncooked fettuccine
- 6 tbsps. butter, cubed
- 2 cups heavy whipping cream
- 3/4 cup grated Parmesan cheese, divided
- 1/2 cup grated Romano cheese
- 2 egg yolks, lightly beaten
- 1/4 tsp. salt
- 1/8 tsp. each pepper and ground nutmeg

Direction

- Follow directions on package to cook fettuccine. In the meantime, melt butter in a pot on medium-low heat. Mix in Romano cheese, nutmeg, 1/2 cup Parmesan, pepper, egg yolks, cream, and salt. Stirring constantly, cook on medium-low heat until thermometer says 160 degrees. Be careful not to boil.
- Drain water from fettuccine; serve with remaining Parmesan and Alfredo sauce.

Nutrition Information

- Calories: 908 calories
- Total Carbohydrate: 44 g
- Cholesterol: 339 mg
- Total Fat: 73 g
- Fiber: 2 g
- Protein: 23 g
- Sodium: 821 mg

342. Quick Italian Salad Dressing

"I want to make a salad dressing that is different from the classic one. This tongue-tingling dressing recipe is perfect for the diabetics."
Serving: 2/3 cup. | Prep: 10m | Ready in: 10m

Ingredients

- 1/4 cup canola oil
- 1/4 cup red wine vinegar
- 1 garlic clove, minced
- 1 tsp. finely chopped onion
- 1/2 tsp. ground mustard
- 1/2 tsp. celery seed
- 1/2 tsp. paprika
- 1/4 tsp. Italian seasoning
- Sugar substitute equivalent to 2 to 4 tsps. sugar

Direction

- Put all the ingredients in a jar with a tight fitting lid. Shake until well-combined. Store the mixture inside the fridge overnight.

Nutrition Information

- Calories: 96 calories
- Total Carbohydrate: 1 g
- Cholesterol: 0 mg
- Total Fat: 10 g
- Fiber: 0 g
- Protein: 0 g
- Sodium: 1 mg

343. Ranch Garlic Bread

"I've filled in as a director of a drive-through joint for multi-year. At home, I like to make various things using regular ingredients. This is a rich portion of French bread rich of flavor basically with vegetable dressing blend and garlic powder."
Serving: 8 servings. | Prep: 5m | Ready in: 10m

Ingredients

- 1 cup butter, softened
- 2 to 3 tbsps. ranch salad dressing mix
- 2 tsps. garlic powder
- 1 loaf (1 lb.) French bread, halved lengthwise

Direction

- Stir garlic powder, dressing mix and butter together in a small bowl; beat until mixed. Distribute over cut bread sides. Put on a baking sheet. Broil for 3-4 minutes with 4-6-inch apart from the heat, or until golden.

344. Roasted Parmesan Potato Wedges

"A baked potato wedges with light cheese and herb taste and stunning golden color."
Serving: 6 servings. | Prep: 10m | Ready in: 55m

Ingredients

- 4 potatoes (2 lbs.)
- 2 tsps. canola oil
- 1/2 cup grated Parmesan cheese
- 1 tsp. dried basil
- 1 tsp. seasoned salt
- 1/4 tsp. onion powder
- 1/4 tsp. garlic powder
- 1/4 tsp. pepper

Direction

- Slice each potato into two halves lengthwise. Slice each half into 3 wedges. Drizzle oil over potatoes in a big bowl and mix to coat. Mix the rest ingredients together and mix the mixture into potatoes to coat.
- Use cooking spray to grease a 15x10x1-inch baking tray. Lay the potatoes in a single layer on the prepared tray. Dredge the rest of coating on potatoes. Set oven at 350°, bake until they turn tender and golden brown, about 45 to 55 minutes.

Nutrition Information

- Calories: 179 calories
- Total Carbohydrate: 31 g
- Cholesterol: 5 mg
- Total Fat: 4 g
- Fiber: 3 g
- Protein: 6 g
- Sodium: 387 mg

345. Roasted Red Pepper Sauce

"Get the flavors of summer by serving this bright and tangy red pepper sauce on top of fresh asparagus."
Serving: 8 | Ready in: 30m

Ingredients

- 2 small red bell peppers
- 1½ tbsps. tomato paste
- 1 tbsp. extra-virgin olive oil
- 2 tsps. cider vinegar
- Salt & freshly ground pepper to taste

Direction

- Roast peppers beneath a preheated broiler or directly on top of the flame in a gas burner for 8-10mins until black all over, turn regularly. Set the peppers aside to cool; slip the skins off then slice the stems away. Cut it open then discard the seeds.
- In a food processor, puree the peppers until you have half a cup of puree. Press the puree with a rubber spatula on a fine strainer placed on top of a small bowl; remove the solids. Stir in vinegar, oil, and tomato paste. Sprinkle pepper and salt.

Nutrition Information

- Calories: 24 calories;
- Total Carbohydrate: 2 g
- Cholesterol: 0 mg
- Total Fat: 2 g
- Fiber: 0 g
- Protein: 0 g
- Sodium: 61 mg
- Sugar: 1 g
- Saturated Fat: 0 g

346. Roasted Vegetable Lasagna

"It's a simple vegetarian lasagna recipe that would give you a blush whenever you taste its roasted vegetables and heavy pasta sauce."

Serving: 8 | Prep: 40m | Ready in: 1h40m

Ingredients

- 8 oz. carrots, halved lengthwise and cut into 2-inch pieces (2 cups)
- 1½ cups onion, cut in ½-inch thick slices
- 3 tbsps. olive oil
- 4 cloves garlic, minced
- ¼ tsp. crushed red pepper
- ¼ tsp. salt
- 4 cups chopped fresh broccoli
- 9 whole grain lasagna noodles
- 1½ cups part-skim ricotta cheese
- ¼ cup shredded part-skim mozzarella cheese (1 oz.)
- ½ tsp. Italian seasoning, crushed
- ½ tsp. freshly ground black pepper
- 1 Nonstick cooking spray
- 1 (24 oz.) jar tomato-basil pasta sauce, such as Classico®
- ¾ cup shredded part-skim mozzarella cheese (3 oz.)
- ¾ cup Parmesan cheese, shredded (1 oz.)
- ¼ cup small fresh basil leaves or torn fresh basil leaves (see Tip)

Direction

- Set your oven to 450°F for preheating. In a bowl, whisk the crushed red pepper, carrots, salt, garlic, onion, and olive oil and then coat by tossing. Pour it in a 15x10-in baking dish in one layer. Place it in the oven and bake for 25-30 minutes until the vegetables are just tender and brown in color. Be sure to stir it once during baking time. Let it cool and chop it into a bit large and irregular pieces. Add the broccoli.
- For the meantime, cook the lasagna noodles by following the directions on its package. Make sure not to add salt and fat while cooking it.
- Mix the ricotta cheese and Italian seasoning in a medium bowl together with the black pepper and 1/4 cup of mozzarella cheese.
- Change the oven's temperature into 375°F. Use a cooking spray to coat the 2-qt. rectangular baking sheet.
- In the prepared baking sheet, spread in half cup of pasta sauce and top it with 3 noodles. Pour 1/2 of vegetable mixture, 1/2 ricotta mixture, and half cup of the pasta sauce on the top of the noodles. Layer 3 noodles on its top again. Repeat layering the remaining vegetable mixture, ricotta mixture, half cup of the pasta sauce and remaining 3 noodles. Pour all the remaining sauce on the dish and drizzle some Parmesan cheese and 3/4 cup of mozzarella cheese on its top.
- Put a cover and then bake it for 45 minutes. Remove now the cover and bake again for another 10-15 minutes until it turns bubbly and golden in color. Set aside for 15-20 minutes and top it with fresh basil. Serve.

Nutrition Information

- Calories: 337 calories;
- Total Carbohydrate: 37 g
- Cholesterol: 26 mg
- Total Fat: 14 g
- Fiber: 7 g
- Protein: 18 g
- Sodium: 564 mg
- Sugar: 8 g

- Saturated Fat: 5 g

347. Rosemary Butternut Squash Lasagna

"I created this recipe when we had a bountiful harvest of butternut squash from our garden. Now, this is our preferred way of using it."
Serving: 8 servings. | Prep: 30m | Ready in: 01h20m

Ingredients

- 9 uncooked whole grain lasagna noodles
- 1 medium butternut squash (about 3 lbs.), peeled and cut crosswise into 1/4-inch slices
- 2 tbsps. olive oil
- 1 tsp. salt, divided
- 6 tbsps. all-purpose flour
- 4 cups fat-free milk
- 6 garlic cloves, minced
- 1 tbsp. minced fresh rosemary
- 1-1/3 cups shredded Parmesan cheese

Direction

- Set oven temperature to 425 degrees and leave aside to preheat. Follow the instructions on the package to cook noodles and strain. Add oil, 1/2 tsp. of salt, and squash in a large bowl and mix evenly with the noodles. Prepare a baking pan measuring 15x10x1-inch with cooking spray and add in mixture. Place dish inside oven and bake for 10 to 15 minutes or until appearance is tender, then remove tray from oven. Decrease temperature to 375 degrees. Add remaining salt and flour in a large saucepan, while slowly adding in milk. Keep stirring and increase temperature to a boil. Continue stirring for 1-2 minutes or until the mixture has a thick consistency. Add rosemary and garlic. Prepare a 13x9-inch baking tray with cooking spray and layer with 1 cup of sauce. Add in order, three noodles, 1/3 cup of cheese, a third of the squash mix, and a cup of sauce. Repeat layering two more times. Scatter remainder of the cheese on top. Cover the tray and leave to bake for 40 minutes. Then, remove the cover and bake for another 10 minutes, or until browning of the top occurs and bubbles appear. Leave the dish to cool for 10 minutes and serve.

Nutrition Information

- Calories: 275 calories
- Total Carbohydrate: 40 g
- Cholesterol: 12 mg
- Total Fat: 8 g
- Fiber: 6 g
- Protein: 14 g
- Sodium: 577 mg

348. Rosemary Olive Focaccia

"Instead of two, use 3-10 in rounds to make a crispier and thinner focaccia."
Serving: 2 loaves (8 slices each). | Prep: 35m | Ready in: 60m

Ingredients

- 3 cups all-purpose flour
- 1 package (1/4 oz.) active dry yeast
- 1 tsp. sugar
- 1 tsp. dried rosemary, crushed, divided
- 3/4 tsp. salt
- 1/8 tsp. coarsely ground pepper
- 1 cup warm water (120° to 130°)
- 4 tbsps. olive oil, divided
- 1/3 cup sliced ripe olives
- 2 tbsps. yellow cornmeal
- 2 tbsps. grated Parmesan cheese
- Additional coarsely ground black pepper and rosemary

Direction

- Mix pepper, flour, salt, yeast, half tsp. rosemary, and sugar in a big bowl. Mix in 2tbsp oil and warm water. Knead dough for 3mins on a lightly floured surface. Put the remaining rosemary and olives then knead for another minute. Put dough in a greased bowl

then flip to coat the top; cover. Set aside for 45mins until it doubles and rises.
- Press the dough down then split in half; cover. Let it sit for 5mins. Spread cornmeal on oiled baking sheets. Spread each dough pieces into a ten-inch round; arrange on baking sheets then cover. Set aside for half an hour until it rises and doubles. Form a few dimples over the dough with your fingertips.
- Slather the remaining oil on the dough. Top with cheese and more rosemary and pepper. Bake for 25-30mins in a 375 degrees oven until golden. Serve the focaccia warm.

Nutrition Information

- Calories: 128 calories
- Total Carbohydrate: 19 g
- Cholesterol: 0 mg
- Total Fat: 4 g
- Fiber: 1 g
- Protein: 3 g
- Sodium: 147 mg

349. Sicilian Salad

"This is more heavily dressed Sicilian-style salad that gives more vinegar and oil to soak up with bread than the others."
Serving: Makes 10 servings | Prep: 30m

Ingredients

- 3 bunches arugula (3/4 lb), coarse stems discarded and leaves torn into pieces
- 1/2 lb Bibb lettuce (2 small heads), leaves torn if large
- 1 celery heart (1/2 lb), thinly sliced on a sharp diagonal
- 1 small red onion, halved lengthwise and very thinly sliced crosswise
- 1/2 lb cherry tomatoes, halved
- 1/2 lb brine-cured black olives (1 cup), drained
- 2 tbsps. drained bottled capers, rinsed
- 1/3 cup extra-virgin olive oil
- 1 tsp. coarse sea salt (preferably Sicilian)
- 2 tbsps. red-wine vinegar

Direction

- To prepare: In a big bowl, mix together the capers, olives, tomatoes, onion, celery, lettuce and arugula. Drizzle the greens with oil and sprinkle sea salt on top, then give it a toss. Drizzle with vinegar and toss well again.
- Cooks' notes: If the sea salt you're using is pebblelike and very granular, crush it with the bottom of a heavy skillet or the flat side of a big heavy knife.
- (You can wash and tear the greens 1 day in advance and chilled in closed plastic bags lined with wet paper towels.)

Nutrition Information

- Calories: 101
- Total Carbohydrate: 5 g
- Total Fat: 9 g
- Fiber: 2 g
- Protein: 2 g
- Sodium: 313 mg
- Saturated Fat: 1 g

350. Spinach And Artichoke Pizza

"This pizza made from scratch featured beer-flavored whole wheat crust plus tomatoes, artichoke hearts, and spinach on top. If you want to add meat, you can use ham or chicken plus fresh basil."
Serving: 6 slices. | Prep: 25m | Ready in: 45m

Ingredients

- 1-1/2 to 1-3/4 cups white whole wheat flour
- 1-1/2 tsps. baking powder
- 1/4 tsp. salt
- 1/4 tsp. each dried basil, oregano and parsley flakes
- 3/4 cup beer or nonalcoholic beer
- TOPPINGS:
- 1-1/2 tsps. olive oil
- 1 garlic clove, minced

- 2 cups shredded Italian cheese blend
- 2 cups fresh baby spinach
- 1 can (14 oz.) water-packed quartered artichoke hearts, drained and coarsely chopped
- 2 medium tomatoes, seeded and coarsely chopped
- 2 tbsps. thinly sliced fresh basil

Direction

- Preheat the oven to 425 degrees F. Whisk dried herbs, 1 1/2 cups flour, salt, and baking powder until combined. Stir in beer until just moistened.
- On a well-floured surface, gently transfer then knead the dough 6 to 8 times, add more flour if necessary. Press the dough on a greased 12-inch pizza pan to fit. Pinch the sides to make a rim. Bake for 8 mins or until the edges are slightly brown.
- Combine garlic and oil; spread on the crust. Scatter half a cup of cheese then put tomatoes, artichoke hearts, and spinach in a layer; scatter the remaining cheese. Bake for 8-10 mins or until the cheese melts and the crust is golden. Garnish with fresh basil.

Nutrition Information

- Calories: 290 calories
- Total Carbohydrate: 32 g
- Cholesterol: 27 mg
- Total Fat: 10 g
- Fiber: 5 g
- Protein: 14 g
- Sodium: 654 mg

351. Spinach Cheese Swirls

"Using refrigerated pizza dough makes this super-fast! Great cold or warm."
Serving: 4 servings. | Prep: 10m | Ready in: 35m

Ingredients

- 1 tube (13.8 oz.) refrigerated pizza crust
- 1 package (10 oz.) frozen chopped spinach, thawed and drained
- 2 cups shredded part-skim mozzarella cheese
- 1 cup finely chopped onion
- 1 garlic clove, minced

Direction

- Roll pizza dough to a 14x10-in. rectangle on lightly floured surface. Mix garlic, onion, cheese and spinach in a big bowl. Spoon on dough within 1-in. of the edges. Roll up like a jellyroll, beginning with long side then tuck ends under. Seal by pinching seams.
- Put onto baking sheet that's coated with cooking spray, seam side down. Bake for 25-27 minutes till golden brown at 400°. Cut to slices.

Nutrition Information

- Calories: 379 calories
- Total Carbohydrate: 41 g
- Cholesterol: 44 mg
- Total Fat: 15 g
- Fiber: 4 g
- Protein: 20 g
- Sodium: 738 mg

352. Squash Provencal

"Serve this dish when there's a bounty of squash and other veggies in your house."
Serving: 8 servings. | Prep: 20m | Ready in: 01h05m

Ingredients

- 2 cans (14-1/2 oz. each) stewed tomatoes
- 1 medium zucchini, thinly sliced
- 1 medium onion, sliced
- 1/2 cup uncooked instant rice
- 3 tbsps. butter, divided
- 1 medium yellow summer squash, thinly sliced
- 3/4 tsp. garlic salt
- 1/2 tsp. pepper

- 1-1/2 cups shredded part-skim mozzarella cheese
- 2 tbsps. grated Parmesan cheese

Direction

- Drain the tomatoes and set a quarter cup of juice aside. Arrange the zucchini, rice, and onion in a layer in a greased 13-in by 9-in baking dish; spot with 1tbsp butter. Add squash and tomatoes on top.
- Mix the reserved juice, pepper, and garlic salt in a small bowl; pour all over the tomatoes. Spot with the rest of the butter.
- Bake for 40mins in a 350 degrees oven while covered until the rice is tender. Remove the cover then scatter the cheeses. Bake for another 5-10mins until the cheese melts. Serve using a slotted spoon.

Nutrition Information

- Calories: 165 calories
- Total Carbohydrate: 17 g
- Cholesterol: 25 mg
- Total Fat: 8 g
- Fiber: 2 g
- Protein: 8 g
- Sodium: 508 mg

353. Three-cheese Garlic Bread

"It's better to double this recipe since it will surely be gone in a flash."
Serving: Makes 12 slices

Ingredients

- 2 tbsps. mayonnaise
- 2 tbsps. (1/4 stick) butter, room temperature
- 1 garlic clove, pressed
- 1 1/3 cups crumbled feta cheese
- 1 1/4 cups (about) grated Parmesan cheese, divided (about 4 oz.)
- 1/2 cup (packed) grated Monterey Jack cheese
- 1/2 cup finely chopped green onions
- 12 3/4-inch-thick slices pain rustique or ciabatta bread

Direction

- Place rack in the middle of the oven then preheat to 475 degrees F. In a medium bowl, combine the first three ingredients. Stir in onions, feta, Jack cheese, and half cup Parmesan. Slather 2tbsp cheese mixture on each slice of bread. Add 1tbsp Parmesan on top of each then press to stick; arrange on a baking sheet. Lightly season with pepper and salt. Bake for 12mins until the cheese is bubbly and golden.
- Tip: The cheese mixture can be stored in the freezer for a month. You can have them on hand for get-togethers. Thaw the mixture then serve with veggies, crackers, or bread.

354. Tomato Basil Bruschetta

"Bruschetta with a mild spice to it."
Serving: 20 appetizers. | Prep: 15m | Ready in: 30m

Ingredients

- 3 tbsps. olive oil, divided
- 1 loaf (1 lb.) Italian bread, cut into 1/2-inch slices
- 1-1/2 cups chopped seeded plum tomatoes
- 1 jar (4 oz.) diced pimientos, rinsed and drained
- 2 tbsps. chopped fresh basil
- 1 tsp. red wine vinegar
- 1 tsp. minced fresh parsley
- 1 garlic clove, minced
- 1/4 tsp. salt
- 1/4 tsp. crushed red pepper flakes
- 1/8 tsp. pepper
- 1 tbsp. grated Romano cheese
- Fresh basil leaves

Direction

- Distribute 2 tbsps. of oil to brush one side of the bread slices. On an ungreased baking

sheet, arrange the slices with the oiled side facing up. Bake until lightly browned at 350°, about 15 minutes.
- Combine pepper, salt, pepper flakes, garlic, parsley, vinegar, chopped basil, pimientos, and tomatoes in a large bowl. Once combined stir in the cheese.
- On each toast, add a whole basil leaf and top it with the tomato mixture. Drizzle the rest of the olive oil, then serve.

Nutrition Information

- Calories: 85 calories
- Total Carbohydrate: 12 g
- Cholesterol: 1 mg
- Total Fat: 3 g
- Fiber: 1 g
- Protein: 2 g
- Sodium: 168 mg

355. Tomato N Cheese Pasta

"This pasta dish has a noticeable flavor from oregano, basil, and garlic. It goes really well with chicken or steaks."
Serving: 2 servings. | Prep: 25m | Ready in: 35m

Ingredients

- 1 cup uncooked small tube pasta
- 1 small onion, chopped
- 1 tbsp. olive oil
- 2 garlic cloves, minced
- 1 can (14-1/2 oz.) Italian diced tomatoes
- 1/2 tsp. dried basil
- 1/2 tsp. dried oregano
- 1/4 tsp. sugar
- 1/4 tsp. pepper
- 1/4 cup shredded part-skim mozzarella cheese
- 1/4 cup grated Parmesan cheese

Direction

- Cook pasta following the directions on the package. Sauté onion in oil in a small saucepan until softened. Add garlic; sauté for another minute. Mix in pepper, sugar, oregano, basil, and tomatoes. Bring to a boil. Lower the heat; simmer without covering for 15 minutes. Drain pasta well; mix into the saucepan.
- Pour pasta mixture into an oiled 1-quart baking dish. Sprinkle with cheeses. Bake, uncovered, for 10 to 15 minutes at 375° until cheese melts.

Nutrition Information

- Calories: 373 calories
- Total Carbohydrate: 50 g
- Cholesterol: 16 mg
- Total Fat: 13 g
- Fiber: 4 g
- Protein: 15 g
- Sodium: 1048 mg

356. Tomato-mushroom Bow Tie Pasta

"This dish is made with herbs, tomatoes, and mushrooms. It's flavorful just like the summer."
Serving: 4 servings. | Prep: 5m | Ready in: 25m

Ingredients

- 8 oz. uncooked bow tie pasta
- 1/2 lb. fresh mushrooms, sliced
- 1/2 cup sliced green onions
- 2 garlic cloves, minced
- 1 tbsp. butter
- 1 tbsp. olive oil
- 2 lb. plum tomatoes, peeled, seeded and chopped
- 1/4 cup minced fresh basil or 4 tsps. dried basil
- 2 tbsps. minced fresh parsley
- 1/2 tsp. salt
- 1/2 tsp. pepper
- 1/4 cup shredded Parmesan cheese

Direction

- Cook pasta following the package instructions.

- In the meantime, sauté garlic, onions, and mushrooms with oil and butter in a big nonstick skillet until soft, or for 5 minutes. Put in tomatoes, cook without a cover over medium heat until soft, or for 10 minutes, tossing from time to time. Mix in pepper, salt, parsley, and basil; cook for another 2-3 minutes. Strain the pasta, put Parmesan cheese and the tomato mixture on top.

Nutrition Information

- Calories: 358 calories
- Total Carbohydrate: 56 g
- Cholesterol: 13 mg
- Total Fat: 10 g
- Fiber: 6 g
- Protein: 14 g
- Sodium: 469 mg

357. Triple Tomato Flatbread

"The stars of this easy recipe are the cherry, sun-dried, and plum tomatoes."
Serving: 8 pieces. | Prep: 15m | Ready in: 20m

Ingredients

- 1 tube (13.8 oz.) refrigerated pizza crust
- Cooking spray
- 3 plum tomatoes, finely chopped (about 2 cups)
- 1/2 cup soft sun-dried tomato halves (not packed in oil), julienned
- 2 tbsps. olive oil
- 1 tbsp. dried basil
- 1/4 tsp. salt
- 1/4 tsp. pepper
- 1 cup shredded Asiago cheese
- 2 cups yellow and/or red cherry tomatoes, halved

Direction

- Unfurl the dough then press into a 15-in by 10-in rectangle. Move to an 18-in by 12-in heavy-duty foil piece that is covered in cooking spray; use the cooking spray to spritz the dough. Combine seasonings, plum tomatoes, oil, and sun-dried tomatoes in a big bowl.
- Invert the dough carefully on a grill rack then get rid of the foil. On medium heat, grill for 2-3mins while covered until golden brown at the bottom. Flip then grill for another 1-2mins until the other side starts to brown.
- Take the dough out of the grill then spread the plum tomato mixture all over. Add cherry tomatoes and cheese on top. Grill the flatbread again for 2-4mins while covered until the cheese melts and the crust is golden.

Nutrition Information

- Calories: 235 calories
- Total Carbohydrate: 29 g
- Cholesterol: 12 mg
- Total Fat: 9 g
- Fiber: 3 g
- Protein: 8 g
- Sodium: 476 mg

358. Vegetable & Cheese Focaccia

"One of my secret to make delicious bread to my family!"
Serving: 15 servings. | Prep: 20m | Ready in: 50m

Ingredients

- 1 cup water (70° to 80°)
- 4-1/2 tsps. olive oil
- 4-1/2 tsps. sugar
- 2 tsps. dried oregano
- 1-1/4 tsps. salt
- 3-1/4 cups bread flour
- 1-1/2 tsps. active dry yeast
- TOPPING:
- 1 tbsp. olive oil
- 1 tbsp. dried basil
- 2 medium tomatoes, thinly sliced
- 1 medium onion, thinly sliced
- 1 cup frozen chopped broccoli, thawed
- 1/4 tsp. salt
- 1/4 tsp. pepper

- 3/4 cup grated Parmesan cheese
- 1 cup shredded part-skim mozzarella cheese

Direction

- Measure the first seven ingredients in the pan of bread machine in order the manufacturer recommended. Choose dough setting (after 5 minutes of mixing, check dough; if needed add 1-2 tbsps. flour or water). Turn dough onto a lightly floured surface when completing the cycle. Punch down the dough. Shape into a 13x9-in. rectangle; and then move to sprayed baking dish in size of a 13x9-in. To make topping, spread olive oil; sprinkle the basil to the dough. Layer the onion, tomatoes and broccoli; sprinkle with Parmesan cheese, pepper and salt. Cover the dough and allow to rise in a warm environment for 30 minutes, until it has doubled in size. Bring to bake for 20 minutes at 350deg; Scatter mozzarella cheese; bring to bake until golden brown and cheese melted, about 10-15 minutes.

Nutrition Information

- Calories: 151 calories
- Total Carbohydrate: 22 g
- Cholesterol: 7 mg
- Total Fat: 4 g
- Fiber: 2 g
- Protein: 7 g
- Sodium: 315 mg

359. Vegetarian Cabbage Rolls

"A wonderful recipe yet a little time consuming."
Serving: 8 | Prep: 30m | Ready in: 1h35m

Ingredients

- 1/3 cup uncooked brown rice
- 2/3 cup water
- 2 cups textured vegetable protein
- 3/4 cup boiling water
- 2 (10.75 oz.) cans tomato soup
- 10 3/4 fluid oz. water
- 1 large head cabbage, cored
- 1 tbsp. vegetable oil
- 1 large onion, chopped
- 1/2 carrot, finely chopped
- 1/2 red bell pepper, diced
- 3 cloves garlic, minced
- 1 tbsp. white wine
- 1 (14.5 oz.) can whole peeled tomatoes, drained, juice reserved
- 1 egg, lightly beaten
- 1/2 cup frozen peas
- 2 pinches cayenne pepper
- 1/2 tsp. onion powder
- 1 tsp. garlic powder
- 1/2 tsp. dried basil
- 3 drops hot red pepper sauce
- toothpicks
- salt and pepper to taste

Direction

- In a pot, put 2/3 cup of water and the rice then set to a boil. Lower heat to low, simmer while covered for about 40 minutes until tender. In a medium bowl, blend 3/4 cup of boiling water and the textured vegetable protein together. Soak for 15 minutes until rehydrated. Stir in the cooked rice.
- Preheat oven to 350° F (175° C). Stir 10 and 3/4 fluid oz. of (1 soup can) water and tomato soup in a bowl.
- In a pot, put the cabbage and enough water to cover. Boil, then cook for 15 minutes till leaves can be removed with ease. Drain, cool, then separate the leaves.
- In a frying pan, heat the oil over medium heat. Mix in the garlic, red bell pepper, carrot, and onion. Cook until softened. Blend in wine, and keep cooking till most of the liquid has evaporated. Mix in textured vegetable protein and rice, reserved juice from tomatoes, peas, and egg. Flavor with hot pepper sauce, basil, garlic powder, onion powder, and cayenne pepper. Cook and whisk till heated through.
- On a cabbage leaf, position 1 tomato and 2 tbsps. of skillet mixture. Roll firmly, then secure using a toothpick. Do the same with the

leftover filling. Line in a casserole dish. Spread water and soup over cabbage rolls. Spice with pepper and salt.
- In the preheated oven, bake, covered, for 35 minutes while basting infrequently with the tomato sauce. Take off the cover, and go on baking for 10 minutes.

Nutrition Information

- Calories: 215 calories;
- Total Carbohydrate: 23.2 g
- Cholesterol: 23 mg
- Total Fat: 3.8 g
- Protein: 27.3 g
- Sodium: 435 mg

360. Vegetarian Pasta

"This quick and easy pasta dish is even more filling because of the can of beans."
Serving: 4 servings. | Prep: 5m | Ready in: 25m

Ingredients

- 2 cups uncooked angel hair pasta
- 1 can (15-1/2 oz.) great northern beans, rinsed and drained
- 3 tbsps. butter
- 1/4 tsp. garlic salt, optional
- 1/4 cup shredded Parmesan or Romano cheese
- Minced fresh parsley

Direction

- Cook the pasta following the package instructions. In the meantime, microwave beans for 1 1/4mins on High in a microwaveable dish until completely heated.
- Drain the pasta then move to a big serving bowl; toss in garlic salt if desired and butter until the butter melts. Toss in cheese and beans to coat. Top with parsley then serve right away.

Nutrition Information

- Calories: 311 calories
- Total Carbohydrate: 44 g
- Cholesterol: 1 mg
- Total Fat: 9 g
- Fiber: 0 g
- Protein: 14 g
- Sodium: 202 mg

361. Viva Panzanella

"This salad is a great way to use fresh tomatoes from the garden or farmer market"
Serving: 6 servings. | Prep: 30m | Ready in: 40m

Ingredients

- 3/4 lb. sourdough bread, cubed (about 8 cups)
- 2 tbsps. olive oil
- 2-1/2 lbs. tomatoes (about 8 medium), chopped
- 1 can (15 oz.) white kidney or cannellini beans, rinsed and drained
- 1 can (14 oz.) water-packed artichoke hearts, rinsed, drained and quartered
- 1 cup thinly sliced roasted sweet red peppers
- 1/2 cup fresh basil leaves, thinly sliced
- 1/3 cup thinly sliced red onion
- 1/4 cup Greek olives, quartered
- 3 tbsps. capers, drained
- DRESSING:
- 1/4 cup balsamic vinegar
- 3 tbsps. minced fresh parsley
- 3 tbsps. olive oil
- 3 tbsps. lemon juice
- 2 tbsps. white wine vinegar
- 3 tsps. minced fresh thyme or 1 tsp. dried thyme
- 1-1/2 tsps. minced fresh marjoram or 1/2 tsp. dried marjoram
- 1-1/2 tsps. minced fresh oregano or 1/2 tsp. dried oregano
- 1 garlic clove, minced

Direction

- Set the oven to preheat to 450°. Toss oil and bread together in a large bowl and place on a baking sheet. Bake for 8 to 10 minutes or until bread turns golden brown. Cool to room temperature.
- In a large bowl, combine bread, capers, olives, onion, basil, peppers, artichokes, beans and tomatoes.
- Whisk dressing ingredients in a small bowl. Add to salad and toss until well coated. Serve right away.

Nutrition Information

- Calories: 424 calories
- Total Carbohydrate: 59 g
- Cholesterol: 0 mg
- Total Fat: 15 g
- Fiber: 7 g
- Protein: 13 g
- Sodium: 1004 mg

362. Warm Goat Cheese In Marinara

"This spread is a fresh and alive finish with the cracked black pepper and chopped basil that is great for a family get-together."
Serving: 1-1/2 cups. | Prep: 20m | Ready in: 30m

Ingredients

- 1 log (4 oz.) goat cheese
- 1 cup marinara or spaghetti sauce
- 2 tbsps. minced fresh basil
- 1/4 tsp. cracked black pepper
- Toasted French bread baguette slices or assorted crackers

Direction

- Freeze cheese about 15 minutes, then unwrap and cut into 1/2-in. slices. Mix basil and marinara sauce in an ungreased small shallow baking dish. Place cheese slices on top and sprinkle with pepper.
- Bake at 350° without a cover, until heated through, for 8 to 10 minutes. Serve warm along with toasted baguette slices.

Nutrition Information

- Calories: 42 calories
- Total Carbohydrate: 4 g
- Cholesterol: 9 mg
- Total Fat: 2 g
- Fiber: 1 g
- Protein: 2 g
- Sodium: 112 mg

363. Warm Pesto Dip

"This pretty green dip is excellent for Christmas."
Serving: 2-1/2 cups. | Prep: 5m | Ready in: 20m

Ingredients

- 1/3 cup finely chopped onion
- 1 tsp. olive oil
- 1 cup prepared pesto
- 1 package (8 oz.) cream cheese, cubed
- 1/2 cup heavy whipping cream
- 1/4 cup grated Parmesan cheese
- Assorted fresh vegetables or bread cubes

Direction

- Sauté onion with oil in a small saucepan until softened. Stir in cream cheese and pesto, then cook and stir on low heat until smooth.
- Stir in Parmesan cheese and cream; cover and cook on low heat while stirring sometimes, about 10 minutes. Serve together with bread or vegetables.

Nutrition Information

- Calories: 259 calories
- Total Carbohydrate: 3 g
- Cholesterol: 51 mg
- Total Fat: 25 g

- Fiber: 1 g
- Protein: 7 g
- Sodium: 293 mg

364. Warm Tuscan Bean Salad

"Coat this white bean side dish with a tangy homemade vinaigrette."
Serving: 4 servings. | Prep: 10m | Ready in: 25m

Ingredients

- 1 small onion, thinly sliced
- 1 small green pepper, chopped
- 1 garlic clove, minced
- 3 tsps. olive oil
- 1 large tomato, coarsely chopped
- 1 tsp. dried basil
- 1 tsp. dried oregano
- 1/4 tsp. salt
- 1/4 tsp. pepper
- 1 can (15 oz.) white kidney or cannellini beans, rinsed and drained

Direction

- Coat a large nonstick skillet with cooking spray then place in garlic, green pepper and onion then sauté in oil till tender. Add seasonings and tomato, stir and cook for 3-4 minutes more. Add beans and cook while stirring to heat through.

Nutrition Information

- Calories: 136 calories
- Total Carbohydrate: 20 g
- Cholesterol: 0 mg
- Total Fat: 4 g
- Fiber: 6 g
- Protein: 5 g
- Sodium: 285 mg

365. White Bean Crostini

"A buttery bean puree with fresh flavors of garlic and thyme over slices of French bread."
Serving: 2 dozen. | Prep: 25m | Ready in: 30m

Ingredients

- 1 can (15 oz.) white kidney or cannellini beans, rinsed and drained
- 1/4 cup plus 2 tbsps. olive oil, divided
- 2 garlic cloves, peeled
- 1/4 tsp. salt
- 1/8 tsp. pepper
- 2 tbsps. chopped ripe olives
- 2 tbsps. minced fresh thyme or 2 tsps. dried thyme
- 24 slices French bread baguette (1/2 inch thick)
- Sliced ripe olives and additional fresh thyme, optional

Direction

- Put together the pepper, salt, garlic, 1/4 cup oil and beans in a food processor. Put cover and process till smooth. Put thyme and olives; process till blended.
- On an ungreased baking sheet, put the bread. Brush with leftover oil. Let broil 3 to 4 inches from the heat source for 1 to 2 minutes till golden brown. Slightly cool down. Scatter 1 tbsp. bean mixture on each slice. Jazz up with thyme and olives if wished.

Nutrition Information

- Calories: 76 calories
- Total Carbohydrate: 9 g
- Cholesterol: 0 mg
- Total Fat: 4 g
- Fiber: 1 g
- Protein: 2 g
- Sodium: 122 mg

Index

A

Almond, 30–31, 36, 62, 87–88, 141, 183

Anchovies, 11

Anise, 5, 127, 173

Apricot, 4, 87–88

Arborio rice, 15, 56, 121

Artichoke, 3, 5–7, 10, 92–93, 98, 119, 142, 165, 182, 189, 196, 207–208, 213–214

Asparagus, 5, 7, 65, 86, 103, 115–116, 179–180, 183–184, 204

B

Bacon, 5, 28, 45, 77, 84–86, 91, 104, 112–113, 115–116, 122–123, 133–134, 136, 146, 148,

151, 155–156, 173–174

Bagel, 117

Baguette, 16–17, 30, 58, 60, 88, 182, 214–215

Baking, 11–14, 17–18, 21–26, 29–33, 38–44, 46–48, 50–51, 53, 55, 57–60, 63–65, 67,

70–71, 73–74, 76, 79–80, 82–83, 85, 87–92, 94–96, 102, 105, 109–115, 117–121, 124,

131–132, 134–137, 139–141, 143, 146–154, 157–165, 167, 169, 171, 174–175, 179–182, 185,

187, 193, 195, 197–198, 200, 202, 204–210, 212–215

Baking powder, 74, 76, 185, 207

Balsamic vinegar, 16, 41, 46, 75, 150, 187, 191, 213

Banana, 127

Barbecue sauce, 14, 148

Basil, 4, 6–7, 10–14, 20–25, 29, 32, 36, 41–45, 47–49, 52–54, 57–59, 62–63, 66, 68–69, 73,

76, 81–83, 86, 88, 91–93, 95–98, 101–102, 105, 109–110, 112, 114, 116–117, 121–123,

125–126, 128–129, 133–140, 142–143, 145, 151–152, 154–157, 160, 163–164, 166, 168,

171–174, 177–178, 181–182, 184–185, 188–191, 193–196, 198–199, 201–202, 204–205,

207–215

Bay leaf, 142, 165–167, 202

Beans, 3–4, 6–7, 16–17, 35, 58, 65, 105, 143–145, 150, 157–158, 178–179, 185, 187,

192–193, 199, 213–215

Beef, 5–6, 28, 32–33, 37–38, 40, 43–44, 54, 60, 66, 80–81, 133–135, 143–144, 146–147,

149–151, 153–154, 156, 158, 161–162, 165–167, 173, 175, 179

Beer, 6, 145, 207–208

Berry, 3, 39–40

Biscuits, 3, 31, 40, 94, 161–162

Black beans, 6, 145, 157–158

Black pepper, 10–12, 21–22, 34, 38, 42–43, 49, 53, 58–59, 61–62, 65–69, 71–72, 81, 92,

96, 98, 168, 191, 202, 205–206, 214

Blackberry, 39–40

Blood orange, 3, 16

Blueberry, 39–40

Bread, 4–7, 14, 21, 24, 26, 28–31, 35, 41, 43–44, 46–47, 51–53, 55, 58, 60–64, 69–71, 80,

   87–89, 91–92, 95, 102–103, 105, 109, 111–112, 117, 119, 122, 124–125, 131–132, 135–136,

   139, 143, 146, 150–151, 154, 160, 162, 168, 174, 177, 179, 182, 184–185, 190, 194–195,

   197–198, 200–201, 204, 207, 209, 211–215

Breadcrumbs, 11, 15, 37–38, 41, 46, 66, 143, 168, 174, 184, 190, 198

Breadsticks, 195

Broccoli, 3, 7, 16, 34, 79–80, 83, 177–178, 185–186, 190, 201, 205, 211–212

Broth, 3, 16, 19, 23, 35–37, 54, 56, 69–70, 74, 105, 120–121, 130, 132–133, 138, 141–144,

   146, 151, 156, 160–161, 166, 169, 172–173, 175, 178–180, 183, 199

Brown rice, 212

Brown sugar, 154, 161, 169, 173

Brussels sprouts, 4, 59

Buns, 70–71

Burger, 6, 147

Butter, 7, 15–16, 19–20, 24–25, 28, 31, 34–36, 45–48, 50, 53–56, 61–62, 64–65, 70–71, 75,

   78–81, 83–89, 91–94, 102–103, 105, 109–111, 115–116, 120, 122, 124, 132–133, 138,

   141–142, 144, 147, 150, 153, 159–160, 164–169, 175–180, 183–186, 189, 192, 194–195,

   197–198, 200–201, 203–204, 208–211, 213

Buttermilk, 31, 35, 53, 82, 94, 161

Butternut squash, 7, 206

C

Cabbage, 5–7, 135, 151, 212–213

Cannellini beans, 144, 157, 199, 213, 215

Capers, 27, 30–31, 72, 145, 148–149, 196, 207, 213–214

Caraway seeds, 145

Carrot, 3, 18, 28, 32–33, 37, 39, 73, 133, 145, 149, 157–158, 173, 176–178, 185, 190, 197,

   201–202, 205, 212

Cauliflower, 101

Cayenne pepper, 18, 100, 102, 117, 146, 150, 153, 200, 212

Celery, 15, 27–28, 32–33, 37, 45–46, 141, 145, 149, 154–155, 165, 167, 176, 180, 188–190,

   193–194, 199, 202–203, 207

Champagne, 3, 34–35, 40

Chard, 3, 21–22

Cheddar, 4–5, 76–80, 83–86, 89, 95, 98, 100, 107, 112–113, 116, 118–120, 124, 127–131,

   134, 137, 147, 161–162, 171, 180, 200–201

Cheese, 3–7, 11–13, 16–19, 21–26, 28–32, 34–36, 38–42, 45–47, 50–52, 54–57, 59–66,

   68–71, 73–137, 139–149, 151–165, 167–168, 171–177, 179–187, 189–193, 195–214

Cheese sauce, 25, 160

Cherry, 3, 19, 27–28, 58, 62–63, 69, 92, 170, 185, 188, 201, 207, 211

Cherry tomatoes, 19, 27, 58, 62–63, 92, 170, 185, 188, 201, 207, 211

Chicken, 3–6, 14, 16, 19–20, 23–24, 37, 41–42, 46–47, 54, 56, 69, 74–75, 79, 82, 102, 105,

120, 130, 132–133, 136–142, 144, 146, 150–151, 159–161, 163–164, 166, 168–172, 174–175,

177–181, 183, 185, 189, 196, 199, 207, 210

Chicken breast, 6, 24, 41, 75, 79, 136, 138–139, 144, 150, 159, 163–164, 168, 174–175,

178, 181

Chicken stock, 133

Chicken thigh, 46, 102, 142, 169

Chickpea, 199

Chips, 141

Chives, 65, 83–84, 87, 91, 99, 102, 122, 126, 140

Chocolate, 115

Chopped tomatoes, 79–80, 133–134

Chorizo, 108

Ciabatta, 3, 21, 26, 51, 55, 209

Cider, 135, 201, 204

Cinnamon, 102, 137

Clams, 3, 35–36, 63

Cloves, 10, 13, 16, 19–20, 22, 24–26, 28–29, 32, 35–38, 41–43, 45–46, 56–64, 66–67, 69,

71, 73–74, 79, 81, 84, 89, 93, 97, 99–100, 102, 107–108, 117, 126, 129, 132–133, 137–138,

140, 142–143, 145–147, 150–152, 154–156, 163–166, 168–172, 174, 176–177, 179, 181, 183,

186–187, 192–194, 196–197, 202, 205–206, 210, 212, 215

Cocktail, 3, 34

Cod, 3, 15

Coffee, 35, 115

Coffee beans, 35

Coffee liqueur, 115

Cottage cheese, 60–61, 99, 137, 167, 191

Crab, 6, 82, 140, 167

Crackers, 193, 209, 214

Cranberry, 7, 189

Cream, 4, 6–7, 15, 35, 40, 49, 57, 69, 76–78, 81–82, 85, 87–88, 96–98, 100, 102, 105–106,

109–116, 119, 122, 128–129, 132, 134, 136–138, 141–144, 148, 152, 160–161, 167,

177–178, 185, 193, 197, 201, 203, 214

Cream cheese, 40, 81, 102, 114–115, 122, 136–137, 141, 143, 152, 193, 201, 214

Crostini, 4, 7, 51, 60, 69, 182, 215

Crumble, 11, 21, 26, 37, 56, 70, 102, 108, 134, 145, 150–151, 173, 176–178

Cucumber, 7, 39, 188, 190, 201

Cumin, 37, 98

Curd, 3, 39–40

Custard, 35, 122

D

Date, 91

Dijon mustard, 80, 85, 124, 140, 160, 165, 182

Dill, 7, 176, 190–191

E

Egg, 3–5, 11, 13–14, 21–22, 25–26, 29–30, 32–33, 35, 37–38, 42–44, 60–61, 64–66, 71,

73–132, 136–137, 139–140, 143, 150–151, 154, 159,

162–163, 167–168, 174, 185, 187,

   189–190, 193, 195, 201, 203, 212

Egg white, 60–61, 76, 82, 86, 91, 93, 96, 100, 107, 119, 123–124, 139, 150

Egg yolk, 35, 42, 91–92, 96, 187, 203

Evaporated milk, 76, 181

F

Farfalle, 3, 6, 23, 49, 65, 181

Fat, 10, 12–20, 23–28, 30–44, 47–57, 59–67, 69–87, 89–104, 106–151, 153–215

Fennel, 3–4, 15, 32, 43–45, 54, 58, 60, 69–70, 95, 105, 145, 151

Fennel seeds, 32, 43, 45, 69, 105

Feta, 26, 64, 83, 111, 139, 142, 157, 191, 209

Fettuccine, 6–7, 48, 145, 185–186, 203

Fig, 4, 51, 55

Fish, 15, 141, 147, 167

Flatbread, 3, 7, 21, 52, 211

Fleur de sel, 47

Flour, 11, 15, 18, 22–25, 46, 52–53, 64, 70, 74, 76, 85, 93, 102, 107, 111, 114–115, 117–118,

   121, 128, 130–132, 136, 138, 142, 144, 153, 160, 162, 164–165, 170–171, 175, 177–180,

   184–186, 189–190, 192, 197–198, 206–208, 211–212

Flour tortilla, 128

Focaccia, 7, 206–207, 211

Fontina cheese, 18, 64, 119, 156

French bread, 6, 88, 105, 117, 135, 146, 194, 200, 204, 214–215

Fruit, 5, 78, 101, 120, 127

Fusilli, 19

G

Garlic, 3–4, 6–7, 10–14, 16–17, 19–20, 22, 24–29, 32–33, 35–38, 40–47, 49, 53–54, 56–64,

   66–76, 78–81, 83–84, 86, 88–89, 91–93, 95–100, 102–103, 106–108, 112–113, 117, 119,

   121–123, 126, 129, 131–133, 135–140, 142–147, 149–152, 154–158, 160–166, 168–181,

   183–184, 186–189, 191–198, 200–213, 215

Garlic bread, 4, 7, 70–71, 146, 154, 179, 200, 204, 209

Ginger, 79

Gnocchi, 5, 7, 134, 189, 192

Gorgonzola, 3, 6, 17, 136–137, 160–161

Gouda, 105

Grain, 15, 69, 151, 202, 205–206

Grapefruit, 127

Grapes, 127

Grapeseed oil, 166

Gratin, 184

Green beans, 4, 7, 58, 143–144, 150, 192–193

H

Ham, 4–6, 28, 44–45, 49, 79–80, 82, 84–85, 89–90, 92, 100, 120, 126, 128–130, 148, 175,

   179–180, 207

Hazelnut, 4, 62–63

Heart, 3, 10, 39, 45, 92–93, 98, 119, 142, 149, 163,

165, 182, 189, 196, 207–208, 213

Herbs, 11, 30, 56, 97, 116, 121, 123, 126, 129, 152, 166, 170, 194–195, 208, 210

Hollandaise sauce, 92

Honey, 7, 30–31, 52–53, 68, 142, 194–195

Horseradish, 79

I

Ice cream, 35

Iceberg lettuce, 182

J

Jam, 55

Jelly, 113–114, 175

K

Kale, 3, 30–31

Ketchup, 134

Kidney, 143, 157, 179, 187, 213, 215

Kidney beans, 143, 187

L

Lamb, 26

lasagna, 3–7, 31–32, 38–40, 42–43, 45–46, 50, 64–65, 73, 120, 134–135, 149, 152–155,

    179, 197–198, 205–206

Lasagne, 3–4, 32–33, 40, 73

Leek, 15

Lemon, 3–4, 6, 15–17, 19–20, 30–31, 34–35, 37, 49, 59, 61, 64–65, 72, 92, 98, 127, 138,

140, 142, 146, 148–149, 163, 169–170, 176–178, 181, 183–184, 188–189, 194, 213

Lemon juice, 15–17, 30–31, 34–35, 37, 59, 61, 72, 92, 127, 138, 140, 146, 148–149,

    176–178, 181, 183–184, 188, 194, 213

Lettuce, 28, 39, 182, 207

Lime, 3, 39–40

Lime juice, 39–40

Linguine, 3, 6–7, 35–37, 62, 140–142, 148, 167–168, 172–173, 183, 196

Liqueur, 35, 115

M

Marjoram, 3, 19, 23, 30, 54, 152, 195, 213

Marsala wine, 144, 175

Mascarpone, 5, 18, 35, 40, 88, 97, 115

Mayonnaise, 28, 76–77, 79, 140, 184, 209

Meat, 4, 6, 28, 30–31, 33, 37, 40, 44, 51, 61, 68–69, 71, 81–82, 84, 86, 88–89, 95, 99–100,

    111, 114, 128, 131–135, 137, 144–147, 149, 151, 153–154, 158, 160, 162, 165, 174–180,

    196, 207

Melon, 124

Milk, 13, 15, 21, 24–25, 28, 32–33, 35, 43–44, 46, 57, 64, 66, 70–71, 76, 81–82, 85–87, 89,

    91–96, 98, 101–107, 109, 111–112, 114–115, 117–118, 120–121, 123–125, 127–129,

    131–132, 140, 153, 159, 161–165, 176, 180–181, 184–186, 192, 197, 200, 206

Mince, 73, 106

Mint, 3, 21–22, 34–35, 39

Mortadella, 30

Mozzarella, 4–5, 11, 13–14, 21–22, 24–25, 29–32, 38–45, 50, 53, 55, 57–61, 68–70, 73,

80–82, 85–89, 91–98, 100–103, 105, 108–110, 112–114, 116–117, 123, 125, 129, 131,

133–137, 139, 143, 145–146, 148–149, 152–156, 158–161, 167–168, 171, 173–174, 176,

179–180, 184, 187, 190–191, 195, 197–198, 202, 205, 208–210, 212

Muffins, 98, 120

Mushroom, 3–7, 38–39, 46–48, 60–62, 65, 68–69, 73–83, 85–90, 92, 94–97, 99, 105,

108–109, 112–119, 123–125, 128, 139, 141, 144–145, 147, 150, 154–159, 161–163, 166,

170–173, 175, 178, 180, 188, 192, 198, 210–211

Mussels, 4, 62

Mustard, 80, 84–85, 96–97, 107, 109, 116, 124, 131–132, 134, 140, 160, 165, 182, 188,

191, 201, 203

N

Nectarine, 127

Noodles, 4, 7, 24–25, 32–33, 38–43, 45–46, 50, 64–65, 120, 134–135, 149, 152–155,

179–180, 197–198, 201, 205–206

Nut, 4, 10, 17–18, 48–49, 57, 62, 102, 181

Nutmeg, 33, 46, 54, 86, 89, 100, 107–108, 111, 117, 124, 164, 167, 184, 187, 192, 203

O

Oil, 4, 10–14, 16–49, 51–64, 66–76, 78–84, 87, 89–91, 93–94, 96–103, 105–108, 110,

113–114, 117–119, 121–126, 129–132, 136, 138–140, 142–146, 148–149, 152–158, 160,

162–166, 168–175, 177–178, 180–183, 185–188, 190–199, 201, 203–215

Olive, 6–7, 10–14, 16–30, 32, 34–49, 51–54, 56–64, 66–75, 78, 82–83, 85–87, 90, 94, 97, 99,

102–103, 105–108, 117, 121–124, 126, 129–130, 132, 136, 138–140, 142–146, 148–149, 152,

154–160, 163–164, 168–169, 171–172, 174–175, 177, 180–183, 186–197, 199, 201, 204–207,

209–215

Olive oil, 10–14, 16–30, 32, 34–49, 51–54, 56–64, 66–75, 78, 82–83, 87, 90, 94, 97, 99,

102–103, 105–108, 117, 121–124, 126, 129–130, 132, 136, 138–140, 142–146, 148–149, 152,

155–158, 160, 163–164, 168–169, 171–172, 174–175, 177, 180–183, 186–188, 190–197, 199,

201, 204–207, 209–215

Onion, 3–5, 7, 10–20, 23–33, 35–37, 40, 42–43, 45–47, 51, 54–55, 58, 60–61, 66–68, 70–71,

73, 76–84, 86–89, 92–97, 99–101, 104–106, 108–121, 123–126, 128–135, 137–139, 141,

143–147, 149–158, 161–163, 165–167, 170–173, 175–176, 178–183, 188–194, 196–205,

207–215

Orange, 3, 16–17, 127, 140, 142

Orange juice, 17, 140, 142

Oregano, 7, 11, 19–21, 27–28, 32, 36, 40–45, 52–54, 64, 66–68, 71, 94–95, 97, 105, 108,

112, 116–119, 123, 125–126, 129–130, 137, 143–146, 149, 151–152, 154, 156–157, 160–161,

167–168, 171–174, 178–179, 189, 194–195, 199–200, 207, 210–211, 213, 215

Oyster, 3, 15

P

Pancakes, 6, 159

Pancetta, 3–4, 32–33, 45–46, 59, 87–88, 119

Pappardelle, 3, 28, 46–47

Paprika, 14, 75–76, 81, 99, 111, 140–141, 200, 203

Parmesan, 3, 5–7, 10–12, 16, 21–22, 24–25, 28–29, 32–34, 37–44, 46–49, 51, 53, 55–57,

60–61, 64–67, 69, 73, 78–79, 83, 85–88, 90–92, 95–99, 101–103, 110–111, 114–117,

120–121, 125–128, 130, 132–134, 137, 139–141, 143–144, 147–149, 151, 154–158, 162,

164–165, 168, 171–174, 179–187, 189–192, 195–206, 209–214

Parsley, 3, 11, 13, 15–17, 19–20, 26–27, 29–30, 36–40, 43–44, 47–49, 59–62, 66, 68, 71–73,

79–81, 87, 94, 98–100, 104–105, 107–108, 119, 123–126, 128, 137–138, 140, 144, 146,

150–152, 154, 156–158, 164–168, 170, 172–173, 175, 179–180, 186, 188, 192, 194, 198,

207, 209–211, 213

Pasta, 3–7, 10, 13–14, 19, 23, 25, 29, 31–32, 34–38, 42, 44, 46–51, 54, 57, 60–63, 65–67,

73, 88, 100, 132–133, 137–138, 141, 144–145, 147–148, 155–158, 162–164, 166–168,

172–173, 175, 177–181, 183, 186–188, 190, 192, 194–197, 201–202, 205, 210–211, 213

Pastry, 40, 76–77, 96–97, 100, 105–107, 110, 116

Pea shoots, 65

Pear, 5, 100

Peas, 49, 65, 166–168, 176, 201, 212

Pecan, 5, 100

Pecorino, 25, 30–31, 34, 36, 53–54, 71

Peel, 12, 15, 17, 22–23, 34–35, 39–40, 64–65, 68, 143, 146, 164, 169–170, 176, 181

Penne, 3–4, 6–7, 34, 51, 155–157, 177, 188, 197

Pepper, 3–7, 10–34, 36–38, 40–49, 51–100, 102–114, 117–147, 149–183, 186–198, 200–215

Peppercorn, 34

Pepperoni, 5–6, 68, 101, 103, 105, 109, 119–120, 122, 125, 158–159, 161

Pesto, 3–7, 36, 48–49, 54–55, 64–65, 69, 82, 91–92, 98, 102, 104–105, 141–142, 159, 181,

184, 197, 214

Pickle, 134

Pie, 4–5, 41, 60–61, 70, 76–77, 80–81, 86, 96–97, 100–101, 105–107, 110, 112–113, 116, 119,

128, 168

Pine nut, 4, 10, 48–49, 57, 102, 181

Pineapple, 44–45, 108, 127, 148, 170, 174–175

Pistachio, 4, 51

Pizza, 3–7, 17–18, 22–23, 26, 31, 44–45, 52–55, 63, 68, 70, 75–77, 85–86, 94, 103, 108, 110,

112–113, 117, 119–120, 127, 130–131, 146, 148, 158–161, 171, 174–175, 191, 200, 202,

207–208, 211

Plum, 13, 36, 41, 53, 65, 74, 76, 83, 95–96, 104, 114, 116, 122, 124–125, 133, 136, 159, 177,

199, 209–211

Polenta, 3–4, 7, 12, 45, 53–54, 59–60, 186

Poppy seeds, 107, 201

Pork, 6, 37, 43–44, 81, 85, 95, 104, 127–128, 133, 135, 151, 160–161, 169

Pork chop, 6, 169

Pork loin, 169

Port, 55

Portobello mushrooms, 75, 89, 117, 123, 144, 172, 192

Potato, 4–7, 15, 56, 71, 77, 81, 86, 104, 134, 141, 161, 192, 204

Potato wedges, 7, 204

Preserves, 88

Prosciutto, 3–5, 41, 44, 47–48, 55, 75, 91–93, 105, 136, 175

Pulse, 13, 17, 36

Pumpkin, 7, 187

R

Radicchio, 45

Raisins, 183

Raspberry, 39–40

Ratatouille, 5, 106

Red onion, 4, 10, 18, 23, 37, 55, 58, 60, 78, 108, 113, 117, 182, 188–190, 207, 213

Red wine, 19, 27–28, 30, 48, 51, 58, 142–143, 151, 156, 173, 182, 188, 191, 195, 203, 209

Red wine vinegar, 19, 27, 30, 51, 58, 151, 182, 188, 191, 195, 203, 209

Rice, 6, 15–16, 56, 69, 121, 138, 151, 170, 181, 208–209, 212

Rice vinegar, 69

Ricotta, 3, 5–7, 12–14, 21–22, 25, 32–33, 38, 40–43, 47–48, 62–65, 73–76, 88, 96–98, 107,

    125, 134–135, 149, 154, 167, 176–177, 179, 187, 189, 197, 205

Rigatoni, 3–4, 12–13, 57

Risotto, 3–6, 15–16, 56, 120–121, 147

Roast chicken, 41

Roast pork, 160

Roast turkey, 72

Roasted vegetables, 205

Rosemary, 4, 7, 19–20, 46–47, 52, 54–55, 72, 74, 83, 121, 142, 165, 170, 172, 175,

    178–179, 193, 206–207

S

Saffron, 16

Sage, 75, 86, 104, 124, 189

Salad, 3, 7, 16–17, 31, 39–41, 58–59, 63, 112, 117, 134, 142, 146, 150, 154, 169, 176–177,

    179, 182–183, 185, 187–190, 194–197, 201, 203–204, 207, 213–215

Salami, 5, 28, 30, 41, 52, 68, 87, 90, 92, 109, 132

Salmon, 4, 6, 58, 176

Salsa, 3, 27, 42, 77, 98, 104, 120, 128–131, 157, 175

Salt, 4, 10–34, 36–49, 52–89, 91–94, 96–98, 100, 102–115, 117–119, 121–131, 133–145, 147,

    149–154, 157, 160–179, 181–213, 215

Sauces, 168

Sausage, 3–6, 10, 15–16, 19, 26, 28, 30–32, 39, 42–43, 56, 58, 66–67, 69, 77, 81–82,

85–86, 88–89, 93–96, 99–100, 102, 104, 106–109, 111, 114, 121, 124, 127–128, 131–132,

135, 137, 143–145, 152–153, 156, 165, 171–173, 175–178

Savory, 5–6, 37, 55, 84, 87, 94, 109–110, 152, 166, 178, 193

Scallop, 6, 166–167

Sea salt, 36, 39, 52, 59, 69, 207

Seafood, 6, 26, 82, 140, 147, 166–167

Seasoning, 43, 60–61, 68–69, 76, 80, 85, 89–91, 96, 98, 100, 108–109, 112–115, 117, 126,

131, 134–135, 139, 145, 147, 152–153, 158–159, 161–162, 165–166, 172–173, 176, 178–179,

189, 193, 195, 198, 200, 202–203, 205, 211, 215

Seeds, 30, 32, 35, 43, 45, 69, 105, 107, 145, 195, 201, 204

Semolina, 52–53

Sesame oil, 69

Sesame seeds, 195

Shallot, 15, 25, 42, 47–49, 64, 68–69, 78, 93, 136–137, 144, 147–149, 166, 172–173,

192–193

Shellfish, 62

Sherry, 23

Shiitake mushroom, 144

Smoked trout, 4, 60

Soda, 115

Soup, 7, 63, 67, 139, 147, 150, 161, 168, 185, 193, 199, 212–213

Sourdough bread, 109, 213

Soy sauce, 170

Spaghetti, 3–4, 6, 10, 37, 43–44, 60–63, 66, 82, 89, 94, 118, 133–135, 139, 141, 145–146,

148–150, 154–156, 158, 162–163, 165–168, 171, 175, 178, 180, 185–186, 202, 214

Spices, 105

Spinach, 3–7, 23, 32–33, 38, 42–43, 50, 54, 64–65, 69, 75, 81–83, 87–90, 96–98, 108,

111–114, 121, 123, 125, 128, 130–132, 137–140, 142, 145, 152, 157, 164, 173–174, 185,

187, 191, 197, 207–208

Squash, 6–7, 79, 179, 206, 208–209

Squid, 3, 26–27

Steak, 3, 45, 162–163, 210

Stew, 6, 67, 143, 176

Stock, 8, 20, 133, 153

Strawberry, 39–40

Stuffing, 24, 137, 152–153

Sugar, 23, 29, 34–35, 39–40, 51–52, 56, 61, 63, 68, 71, 74, 81, 85, 94–95, 104, 115, 127,

130–131, 135, 137–138, 143, 146, 148–149, 151, 153–154, 160–161, 167–170, 172–173, 176,

179, 182, 185, 187–188, 191, 194–196, 198–199, 201–203, 205–206, 210–211

Swiss chard, 21

Syrup, 40, 115, 127

T

Taco, 84

Taleggio, 3, 45–46

Tapenade, 72

Tarragon, 5, 103, 194

Teriyaki, 157

Teriyaki sauce, 157

Thai basil, 4, 69

Thyme, 4, 15, 33, 45–46, 52, 54, 61, 97, 100, 116–117, 129, 142, 152, 157, 160, 175,

　177–178, 193, 195, 201, 213, 215

Tilapia, 6, 147

Tomato, 3–7, 10–14, 18–33, 35–37, 40–47, 53–71, 73–77, 79–80, 83–84, 86, 88, 91–93,

　95–98, 104–106, 109–110, 112, 114–118, 121–125, 128–131, 133–138, 143–159, 161,

　164–166, 168, 170–174, 176–179, 182, 184–186, 188–194, 196–197, 199, 201–202, 204–205,

　207–215

Tomato juice, 176, 199

Tomato purée, 53

Tongue, 203

Tortellini, 4, 6, 69, 163–164, 176–177, 187

Trout, 4, 60, 189

Turkey, 3–4, 6, 32, 51, 60–61, 70–72, 86, 93, 113, 121, 123, 163, 171, 177–180

Turkey breast, 6, 60, 72, 163, 177

V

Vanilla extract, 74, 115

Veal, 4, 18, 37, 43–44, 73–74

Vegetable oil, 24, 51–53, 55, 57–58, 74, 89, 100, 119, 191, 201, 212

Vegetables, 28, 31, 57, 60, 65, 79–80, 83, 86, 106, 108, 121, 125–126, 129, 145, 152, 155,

　157, 164, 173, 180, 188, 193, 200, 202, 205, 214

Vegetarian, 5, 7, 64, 117, 182, 199, 205, 212–213

Venison, 28

Vermouth, 37, 56

Vinegar, 16–17, 19–20, 23, 27–28, 30, 39, 41, 46–47, 51, 58, 69, 75–76, 92, 135, 150–151,

　170, 182, 187–188, 191, 195, 201, 203–204, 207, 209–210, 213

Vodka, 7, 197

W

Walnut, 17, 189, 196

Whipping cream, 15, 35, 40, 57, 69, 78, 85, 87, 97, 105, 132, 134, 136, 141, 144, 148,

　160–161, 197, 203, 214

White bread, 95, 117

White pepper, 13, 46, 59, 85, 93, 107, 110, 131, 189

White sugar, 68, 74, 172, 191

White wine, 10, 15–16, 18–19, 23, 25, 28, 32–33, 35–36, 54, 62, 64, 72, 74–75, 105, 130,

　132–133, 160–161, 166, 169, 183, 212–213

White wine vinegar, 213

Wine, 3, 5, 10–11, 15–16, 18–20, 23, 25, 27–28, 30, 32–36, 39, 48, 51, 54, 58, 62, 64, 72,

　74–75, 105, 130, 132–133, 142–144, 151, 156, 160–161, 166, 169, 173, 175, 182–183, 188,

　191, 195, 203, 207, 209, 212–213

Worcestershire sauce, 61, 80, 150

Y

Yeast, 52–53, 130–131, 160, 198, 206, 211

Z

Zest, 16, 34, 49, 61, 72, 140, 142

Conclusion

Thank you again for downloading this book!

I hope you enjoyed reading about my book!

If you enjoyed this book, please take the time to share your thoughts and post a review on Amazon. It'd be greatly appreciated!

Write me an honest review about the book – I truly value your opinion and thoughts and I will incorporate them into my next book, which is already underway.

Thank you!

If you have any questions, **feel free to contact at:** mrworld@mrandmscooking.com

Mr. World

www.MrandMsCooking.com

Manufactured by Amazon.ca
Bolton, ON